W9-CYC-988

AMERICAN HISTORY

Observations & Assessments from Early Settlement to Today

ST. LOUIS STAR-TIMES EXTRA

WAR DECLARED

3,000 Casualties In Attack On Hawaii

James P. Stobaugh

This book is dedicated to this new generation of young believers whose fervor and dedication to the purposes of the Lord shall yet bring a great revival. Stand tall, young people, and serve our Lord with alacrity and courage!

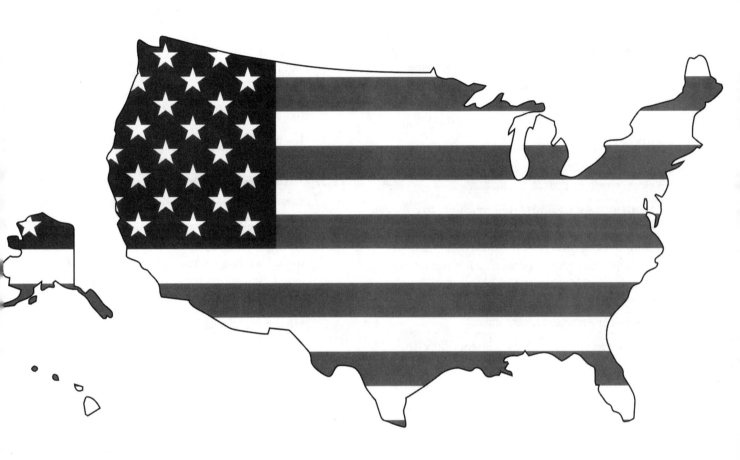

Using Your Student Textbook

How this course has been developed:

1. **Chapters:** This course has 34 chapters (representing 34 weeks of study).

2. **Lessons:** Each chapter has five lessons each, taking approximately 20 to 30 minutes each. There will be a short reading followed by critical thinking questions. Some questions require a specific answer from the text, while others are more open-ended, leading the student to think "outside the box."

3. **Weekly exams:** The final lesson of the week is the exam covering the week's chapter.

4. **Student responsibility:** Responsibility to complete this course is on the student. Students are to complete the readings every day, handing their responses to a parent or teacher for evaluation. Independence is strongly encouraged in this course, which was designed for the student to practice independent learning.

5. **Grading:** Turn in your assignments daily or weekly to your parent/teacher.

Thoughout this book you will find the following components:

1. **Narrative Background:** background on the period.

2. **Critical Thinking Questions:** questions based roughly on Bloom's Taxonomy.

3. **Concepts/Generalizations:** terms, concepts, and theories to be learned.

4. **History Maker:** a person(s) who clearly changed the course of history.

5. **Historiographies or Historical Debate:** an examination of historical theories surrounding a period or topic.

6. **World View Formation:** An overview of historical understandings of who God is. There is also a subsection where we examine important thinkers of the period/topic.

7. **History & World View Overview:** an overview of world views.

What the student will need each day:

1. **Notepad:** for writing assignments.
2. **Pen/pencil:** for the answers and essays.

About the Author

James P. Stobaugh and his wife, Karen, have homeschooled their four children since 1985. They have a growing ministry, For Such a Time As This Ministries, committed to challenging this generation to change its world for Christ.

Dr. Stobaugh is an ordained pastor, a certified secondary teacher, and an SAT coach. His academic credentials include: BA, cum laude Vanderbilt University; Teacher Certification, Peabody College for Teachers; MA, Rutgers University; MDiv, Princeton Theological Seminary; Merrill Fellow, Harvard University; DMin Gordon Conwell Seminary.

Dr. Stobaugh has written articles for magazines: *Leadership*, *Presbyterian Survey*, *Princeton Spire*, *Ministries Today*, and *Pulpit Digest*. Dr. Stobaugh's books include the *SAT Preparation Course for the Christian Student*, the *ACT Preparation Course for the Christian Student*, as well as *American History*, *British History*, and *World History* high school curriculum.

Contents

Preface

The writing of history is the selection of information and the synthesis of this information into a narrative that will stand the critical eye of time. History, though, is never static. One never creates the definitive theory of a historical event. History invites each generation to reexamine its own story and to reinterpret past events in light of present circumstances.

The creation of this story is more difficult than it seems. From the beginning the historian is forced to decide what sort of human motivation matters most: economic? political? religious? social?

For instance, what caused the American Revolution? The historian Bernard Bailyn argues that ideology or the history of thought caused the American Revolution. No, the historian Oscar Handlin argues, the Revolution was caused by social upheaval (i.e., the dislocation of groups and classes of people). Sydney Ahlstrom argues that religion was an important cause of the American Revolution. And so forth. Students will look at several theories of history, primary source material, and then decide for themselves what really happened.

In other words, *American History* invites students to be historians. Students look at the sources and scholarship available and make a decision. Students must know and accept that the past is constantly changing according to new scholarship discoveries. Therefore, as new sources are discovered, and old ones reexamined, students understand that theories of history may change. *American History* enables students to commit themselves to the task of examining these theories, primary source material, and ultimately to form their own theories of history. "Every true history is contemporary history," historians Gerald Grob and George Billias write. My students make the theories of historical events personal and contemporary.

While I know that my students can never be completely neutral about history, scholarly historical inquiry demands that they implement the following principles:

1. Historians must evaluate the veracity of sources. There must be a hierarchy of historical sources. Primary source material, for instance, usually is the best source of information.

2. Historians must be committed to telling both sides of the historical story. They may choose to lobby for one view over the other, but they must fairly examine all theories.

Statue of George Washington at the Indiana State Capitol. Photo by Rebecca White, 2011.

3. Historians must avoid stereotypes and archetypes. They must overcome personal prejudices and dispassionately view history in ruthlessly objective terms.

4. Historians must be committed to the truth no matter where their scholarship leads them. At times historians will discover unflattering information about their nation/state.

5. Finally, historians understand that real, abiding, and eternal history ultimately is made only by people who obey God at all costs.

After everything is said and done, historians are only studying the past. They cannot really change the past. Theories about the past come and go, and change with each generation. However, the past is past. It is over.

Historians will debate about history, but they can never change history. Only God can change history.

God alone can change history. When persons are reborn in Christ, their present, future, and, yes, even their past is changed. History is literarily rewritten. They are new creations. That bad choice, that sin, that catastrophe is placed under the blood of the Lamb, and everything starts fresh and new. A new history for new people.

Let me illustrate. 150 years ago my great-great-great-grandfather, whose passion was to kill Yankees, was a slave owner in Eastern Tennessee. With that inheritance, like most white Southerners who grew up in the 1960s, I grew up to mistrust African-Americans. Like so many people captured by their history and culture, present and future became my past. However, when I was a senior in high school, I was saved, Jesus Christ became my Lord and Savior. My attitudes changed. It took time but prejudices disappeared. Ultimately, I married my New Jersey wife, Karen, and we adopted three African-American children—whose ancestors, by the way, may have been owned by my great-great-great-uncle!

Three of my children are African-American. Imagine! Quite literally, my history was rewritten. It has been changed irrevocably by my decision to invite Jesus Christ to be Savior of my life. In a real sense, family prejudice and death existing for generations ended in my generation. The destructive, historical cycle that was part of my history has ended. No one, nothing can do that but the Lord. History has been rewritten!

My prayer is that if you do not know this God who can change history—even your history—this history text might encourage you to invite Jesus Christ into your heart as Savior.

South façade of the White House, the executive mansion of the president of the United States, located at 1600 Pennsylvania Avenue in Washington, D.C. By UpstateNYer, 2006 (CC BY-SA 3.0).

NATIVES OF THE NEW WORLD

First Thoughts . . .

Can you imagine what it was like to be living in North or South America in the early 16th century and suddenly seeing bearded white men landing on your shore carrying strange flags and metal instruments from huge ships? Or can you imagine how it felt to be cooped up in a scurvy-ridden, drafty ship for two and a half months and then, suddenly sighting a new land? This chapter will explore the developed civilizations of native peoples who greeted the new Europeans as they first explored and then settled in the Western Hemisphere.

Chapter Learning Objectives . . .

Chapter 1 presents the beginning of European America, for there were already Native American cultures when the Europeans arrived. We invite you to understand the complexity of the task of exploration, the difficulties of colonization, and the challenge of establishing relations with Native Americans. By not merely memorizing facts, but delving into controversial topics, you will understand, analyze, and then evaluate the triumphs and tragedies that comprised the European exploration and conquest of the Americas.

As a result of this chapter you should be able to:

1. Analyze the different world views extant in colonial society.
2. Describe what it was like to be indigenous Native Americans living in North and South America.
3. Describe in greater detail the Delaware, Lenape, Powhatan, Algonquin, Iroquois, Aztec, Mayan, and Incan people groups.
4. Discuss Columbus's legacy, describing the intricacies of his controversial effect on the Native American peoples.
5. Analyze primary sources and determine their credibility.

WAR OF THE WORLD VIEWS

The Vital Nature of World View

What is a **world view**? A world view is a way that a person understands, relates to, and responds from a philosophical position that he embraces as his own. World view is a framework that ties everything together, that allows us to understand society, the world, and our place in it.

If you are a committed Christian believer, you will be challenged to analyze the world views of individuals and institutions around you. You are inextricably tied to your culture; but that does not mean you can't be in this culture but not of this culture. Furthermore, you will be asked to explain your own world view and to defend it against all sorts of assaults. It is important that you pause and examine several world views that you will encounter. You also need to articulate your own world view.

A world view helps us make the critical decisions that will shape our future. A world view colors all our decisions and all our artistic creations. In the first *Star Wars* movie (1977), for instance, Luke Skywalker clearly values a Judeo-Christian code of ethics. That does not mean that he is a believing Christian—indeed he is not—but he does uphold and fight for a moral world. Darth Vader, on the other hand, represents chaos and amoral behavior. He does whatever it takes to advance the emperor's agenda, regardless of who he hurts or what rule he breaks. It is important that you articulate your world view now so that you will be ready to discern other world views later.

Contemporary World Views

"Life is what happens to you when you're busy making other plans."

—Yoko Ono

"I don't think any of us really know why we are here."

—Ray Charles

"Animal liberation will come!"

—Ingrid Newkirk

"Just chill out."

—Ice-T.

"If we had no other purpose in life, it would be good enough simply to goose people once in a while."

—Garrison Keillor

"The meaning of life is felt through relationship."
—Jonas Salk

"To fulfill the purpose of life is to ignite the spark of divinity in us and give meaning to our lives."
—Michael Jackson

SOPHOCLES · PLATO · ARISTOTLE · DEMOST

Seven Major World Views

Here is a short sketch of the seven major world views with examples:

1 **Theism:** God is personally involved with humankind. Theism argues that the universe is a purposive, divinely created entity. It argues that all human life is sacred and all persons are of equal dignity. They are, in other words, created in the image of God. History is linear and moves toward a final goal. Nature is controlled by God and is an orderly system. Humanity is neither the center of nature nor the universe, but is the steward of creation. Righteousness will triumph in a decisive conquest of evil. Earthly life does not exhaust human existence but looks ahead to the resurrection of the dead and to a final, comprehensive judgment of humanity (adapted from Carl F. H. Henry, *Toward a Recovery of Christian Belief*). This was the only viable world view until the Renaissance. Examples: Homer, Virgil, C. S. Lewis, A. J. Cronin, Tolkien.

2 **Deism:** God was present but is no longer present. The world is like a clock wound up by God many years ago, but He is now absent. The clock (i.e., the world) is present; God is absent. Still, though, Deism embraced a Judeo-Christian morality. God's absence, for instance, in no way mitigated His importance to original creation. He was also omnipotent but not omniscient. His absence was His decision. He was in no way forced to be absent from the world. He chose to assume that role so that Socratic empiricism and rationalism could reign as sovereign king. Speculative Theism replaced revelatory biblical Theism. Once the living God was abandoned, Jesus Christ and the Bible became cognitive orphans (Carl F. H. Henry). Examples: Ben Franklin, Thomas Jefferson.

3 **Romanticism:** Once Americans distanced themselves from the self-revealing God of the Old and New Testaments, they could not resist making further concessions to subjectivity. Romanticism, and its American version, Transcendentalism, posited that God was nature and "it" was good. The more natural things were, the better. Nature was inherently good. Nature alone was the ultimate reality. In other words, nature was the Romantic god. Man was essentially a complex animal, too complex to be controlled by absolute, codified truth (as one would find in the Bible). Human intuition replaced the Holy Spirit. Depending upon the demands on individual lives, truth and good were relative and changing. Romanticism, however, like Deism, had not completely abandoned Judeo-Christian morality. Truth and the good, although changing, were nonetheless relatively durable. Examples: James Fenimore Cooper, Goethe.

4 **Naturalism:** If God exists, He is pretty wimpish. Only the laws of nature have any force. God is either uninterested or downright mean. All reality was reducible to impersonal processes and energy events (Carl F. H. Henry). All life, including human life, was transient. Its final destination was death. Truth and good, therefore, were also transient. They were culture-conditioned distinctions that the human race projected upon the cosmos and upon history (Carl F. H. Henry). This maturation, as it were, of the human race, necessitated a deliberate rejection of all transcendentally final authority. Examples: Joseph Conrad, Stephen Crane.

5 **Realism:** Akin to Naturalism is Realism. Reality is, to a Realist, a world with no purpose, no meaning, no order. Realism insists that personality has no ultimate status in the universe, but is logically inconsistent when it affirms an ethically imperative social agenda congruent with universal human rights and dignity. Realism, then, throws around terms like "dignity" and "human rights" and "power." What Realists mean, however, is that these concepts are real when they fulfill a social agenda that enhances human dominance over the universal. Thus, Realism believes in a world where bad things happen all the time to good people. Why not? There is no God, no ontological controlling force for good. The world is a place where the only reality is that which we can experience, but it must be experience that we can measure or replicate. Certainly pain and misery fit that category. If an experience is a unique occurrence (e.g., a miracle) it is not real. Examples: Ernest Hemingway, F. Scott Fitzgerald.

6 **Absurdism:** A modern movement where there is neither a god nor any reason to have one. Everything is disorganized, anarchy rules. There is a compete abandonment of explaining the cosmos and therefore an abandonment of being in relationship with the deity. It is not that Absurdists are unsure about who creates everything, or is in control of everything. Absurdists simply do not care one way or the other. Examples: John Barth, Kurt Vonnegut, Jr.

7 **Existentialism:** The submergence of God in overwhelming data and in experience is the first step toward putting God out to die. Truth is open to debate. Everything is relative. A very pessimistic view. Examples: Albert Camus, Franz Kafka, and Jean-Paul Sartre.

World View Transitions

At the beginning of the 21st century there is truly an exciting phenomenon occurring in American society: Christian Theism is experiencing an unprecedented revival. As sociologist Peter Berger accurately observes, Evangelical Christians are growing in number and maturity.

We Christians generally subscribe to two strongly held propositions: that a return to Christian values is necessary if the moral confusion of our time is to be overcome, and that the Enlightenment is to be blamed for much of the confusion of our time.

In fact, I believe that Evangelicalism is one of the most potent anti-Enlightenment movements in world history. I most assuredly did not say "anti-intellectual." Excessives of Enlightenment rationalism have sabotaged the certitude of classicism and Christian theism that so strongly influenced Western culture long before the formidable onslaught of the likes of David Hume.

The good news is that things may be changing. Evangelical Christianity may be capturing the elite culture of America.

The Washington Post in 1993 coyly observed that evangelicals are "largely poor, uneducated, and easy to command." And, among our own, evangelical professor Mark Noll unkindly observed, "The scandal of the evangelical mind is that there is not much of an evangelical mind." Indeed. Not anymore. Today, more than ever, in the garb of Christian homeschooling and other sectors, Evangelicalism has gained new life.

By side-stepping the Enlightenment, Christian homeschooling has opened up a whole new arena for debate. So has the Christian school. While conceding that faith is not a makeshift bridge to overcome some Kierkegaardian gap between beliefs and evidence, Christian schooling, especially Christian homeschooling, posits that it still is important that we look beyond our experience for reality. Human needs and aspirations are greater than the world can satisfy, so it is reasonable to look elsewhere for that satisfaction. Worth is the highest and best reality (a decidedly anti-Enlightenment notion) and its genesis and maintenance come exclusively from relationship with God alone. Home schooling families, with their sacrificial love of one another and their extravagant gift of time to one another, offer a radical path into this new way of looking at reality.

Christian homeschooling and Evangelical Christian schooling, then, move backward in time, far back in time, when intellectualism was not separate from religion. This blows the claims of the Enlightenment to bits. Christian schooling has brought back stability into the lives of countless millions in America when the majority of Americans are living in a context of clashing activities where (as Kenneth J. Gergen explains) the very ground of meaning, the foundations and structures of thought, language, and social discourse are up for grabs; where the concepts of personhood, spirituality, truth, integrity, and objectivity are all being demolished, breaking up, giving way. And homeschoolers do it the old-fashioned way: Parents stay home and love the kids and in the process lay their lives down for all our futures.

Christian schooling. Millions strong. Unpretentious to a fault, this new cultural revolution is inviting Americans back to traditional truths that have been with us always and others that need to be rediscovered. Christian schooling has invited Americans to a comfortable marriage of intellectualism and transcendentalism that fares our culture and our nation well in the years ahead. In that sense, then, perhaps Christian schooling families, homeschooling and otherwise, are the new patriots, the hope for our weary nation and our dysfunctional culture. We shall see. . . .

Assignment

Oswald Chambers says, "The Bible does not say that God punished the human race for one man's sin, but that the nature of sin, namely, my claim to my right to myself, entered into the human race through one man. But it also says that another Man took upon Himself the sin of the human race and put it away—an infinitely more profound revelation (see Hebrews 9:26). The nature of sin is not immorality and wrongdoing, but the nature of self-realization, which leads us to say, 'I am my own god.' This nature may exhibit itself in proper morality or in improper immorality, but it always has a common basis—my claim to my right to myself. When our Lord faced either people with all the forces of evil in them, or people who were clean-living, moral, and upright, He paid no attention to the moral degradation of one, nor any attention to the moral attainment of the other. He looked at something we do not see, namely, the nature of man (see John 2:25)." Paraphrase Chambers' insight. Which world views manifest this problem?

NORTH AMERICAN INDIGENOUS PEOPLE GROUPS

It is instructive and tragic that the wildly popular Charles and Mary Beard's *History of the United States* (1921) begins the American story with a discussion of European immigration, without mention of Native Americans until page 56! Actually, between 10 million and 90 million Native Americans inhabited America at the time of the European arrivals, having traveled a land-bridge across the Bering Sound from Siberia, Russia, during the Ice Age into what is now Alaska. They had gradually migrated across the land and southward into Central America and beyond.

A stabilization in climate led to widespread migration, cultivation of crops, and subsequently a dramatic rise in population all over the Americas. One important group that emerged is the **Clovis people group**. The Clovis culture ranged over much of North America and also appeared in South America. The culture is identified by the distinctive Clovis point, a flaked flint spear-point with a notched flute, by which it was inserted into a shaft. They developed what we call "Indian head shafts" (above, by Bill Whittaker CC-BY-SA-3.0).

These were a people who owned no land, but owned all land. They worshiped no one god but worshiped all gods. Native Americans were people who belonged to no one but they belonged to everyone. They were not farmers, or doctors, or businessmen. They were hunters, warriors, and fishermen. I don't think they could have even conceived of what was heading their way.

The Native Americans of the East Coast met the new 16th- and 17th-century visitors from Europe with nonchalance. They regarded these bearded white men as strange but were delighted with the trade goods the colonists and explorers brought: copper pots, tools, and weapons. However, the Europeans also brought measles, **smallpox**, cholera, yellow fever, and many more devastating diseases that drastically diminished the Native American population and annihilated entire villages. But they also brought the gospel and, some argue (including this author) that the Jesuit, Anglican, and other missionaries brought new hope to these indigenous people groups.

Who were the Native American people groups whom the European immigrants met as they settled along the Eastern seaboard? While there were innumerable other tribes whose lives were affected by the coming European migration, we will examine the following: **Delaware, Powhatan, Iroquois Confederation, Aztec, and Mayan**.

Delaware Tribe

The name Delaware was given to the people who lived along the Delaware River, which had been named after Lord de la Warr, a later governor of the Jamestown colony. The name Delaware later came to be applied to almost all Lenape people. The Delaware were among the first Native people groups to come in contact with the Europeans (Dutch, English, and Swedish) in the early 1600s. These European settlers landed in New Jersey and Delaware. The Delaware were called the "Grandfather" tribe because they often served to settle disputes among rival tribes. At the same time, while they were fierce warriors, they preferred to choose a path of peace with the Europeans.

Many of the early treaties and land sales the Delaware signed with the Europeans were, in their minds, more like rental agreements. This is true of other Native American tribes. The notion of land ownership was entirely alien to this culture. The early Delaware had no idea that land was something that could be sold and owned.

The Delaware people signed the **first Indian treaty** with the newly formed United States government on September 17, 1778. Nevertheless, the Delaware continued to lose their land and ultimately moved westward, first to Ohio, then to Indiana, Missouri, Kansas, and, finally, Indian Territory, now Oklahoma (www.delawaretribeofindians.nsn.us).

Concentrated along the rivers, which provided both food and transportation, the folk who inhabited these rivers spoke a now-extinct form of **Algonquian**, a language that was common to many native peoples from present-day New York south to Florida.

Powhatan Tribe

The undisputed ruler of 1600 Tidewater Virginia was **Wahunsonacock**, usually referred to by the title "Powhatan." John Smith describes Powhatan as "a tall, well-proportioned man, with a sower look, his head somewhat gray, his beard so thinne, that it seemeth none at all, his age (as of 1608) neare sixtie, of a very able and hardy body to endure any labour."

Powhatan, by 1607, ruled over 30 tribes. Each tribe was governed by a chief who owed allegiance and tribute to Powhatan. Powhatan also had an extensive family—more than 100 wives and innumerable offspring—one of whom was **Pocahontas**.

Powhatan's people lived in villages, which could number as many as 100 homes. Some villages were protected by wooden palisades; each house boasted an extensive and carefully tended garden, in which was sown such staples as corn, beans, peas, squash, pumpkin, sunflowers, and maypops (passionflower). Tobacco, primarily used for ceremonial purposes, was grown apart from the rest of the crops. The waterways afforded a rich diet of fish, and shellfish and the woods yielded nuts, fruits, and berries. Since the dog was the only animal domesticated by the Powhatans, hunting was an important way to supplement the diet, and was a task relegated to the men of the tribe.

Although early interaction between the English and Powhatans was sometimes violent, leaders of both peoples realized the mutual benefit that could be derived from peaceful relations. The marriage of Powhatan's favorite daughter, Pocahontas, to settler John Rolfe in 1614 ensured a few peaceful years between the Powhatans and the English. This ended in 1617 with the death of Pocahontas during a trip to England and, the next year, of her father.

On March 22, 1622, the Powhatans made the first, and perhaps most successful, attack to end European colonization on the North American continent. About 400 English settlers died and the colony received a near-fatal blow.

The short-lived peace was over. For over a decade, the English killed men and women, captured children, and systematically razed villages, seizing or destroying crops. The precipitous decline of Powhatan dominance was well underway.

The Baptism of Pocahontas by John Gadsby Chapman, 1840.

Iroquois Confederation

Perhaps no Native American tribe was more influential in American history than the **Iroquois Confederation**. The six Iroquois nations, characterizing themselves as "the people of the longhouse," were the Mohawk, Oneida, Onondaga, Cayuga, Tuscarora, and Seneca.

As Encyclopedia Britannica explains, "The Iroquois Confederacy differed from other American Indian confederacies in the northeastern woodlands primarily in being better organized, more consciously defined, and more effective. The Iroquois used elaborately ritualized systems for choosing leaders and making important decisions. They persuaded colonial governments to use these rituals in their joint negotiations, and they fostered a tradition of political sagacity based on ceremonial sanction rather than on the occasional outstanding individual leader. Because the league lacked administrative control, the nations did not always act in unison; but spectacular successes in warfare compensated for this and were possible because of security at home" (www.britannica.com).

Pocahontas by Richard Norris Brooke (c1900).

Assignment

A. "The word annihilation, the word holocaust, the word atrocity come to mind when I think of 1607," said Adams, chief of the Upper Mattaponi tribe, in referring to the year a group of men and boys arrived in Jamestown and set up the first permanent English colony in the New World. Of the estimated 14,000 to 15,000 Native Americans who lived in the area around the Jamestown settlement in 1607, nearly 90 percent were wiped out within a century, mainly from smallpox, typhus, and other Old World diseases inadvertently brought by the colonists and to which the American Indians had never been exposed. Some also died in fighting with the settlers. For Adams and other Native Americans, these stark numbers gave little reason to celebrate as the country prepared to commemorate the quadricentennial of the settlement, with Britain's Queen Elizabeth and U.S. President George W. Bush in 2007. "We are certainly proud to be Americans but from our perspective we don't feel like the 400th anniversary of the Jamestown settlement is something to celebrate or commemorate," said Bill Miles, chief of Virginia's Pamunkey Indian tribe, one of some 40 tribes that lived in the area in the 17th century. What, if anything, can you suggest Native Americans might want to celebrate in the 400-year anniversary of the founding of the Jamestown Settlement?

B. Research your own community and describe what it was like circa 1500–1550. Discuss the Native Peoples who lived nearby.

SOUTH-CENTRAL AMERICAN INDIGENOUS PEOPLE GROUPS

Aztecs

While the Aztec Indians seem larger than life, in actuality, they were small in stature. Women were several inches shy of five feet tall, and the men barely topped that measurement. The society was Puritanical in its moral behavior. Drunkenness and promiscuity were often penalized by death in the Aztec culture.

One of the many rules of the Aztec Indian society was the dress code. The way **Aztecs** dressed had to reflect their social strata. For instance, commoners had to wear plain clothing, no adornments. Nobility could wear colorful clothing and jewelry. If they did not abide by the dress code, they could be put to death. Homes reflected the same idea. Commoners could only live in a one-story home, but noblemen were allowed multiple stories.

Aztecs believed that **human sacrifice** was necessary to appease the gods. Fighting was also a major aspect of their lives. Aztec warriors were fierce.

Unless they were in the noble class, the way of life for the Aztec Indians was tough. They lived in fear of breaking some moral or societal code and being put to death. They worried about being singled out for human sacrifice. It was a way of life for hundreds of years until **Hernando Cortez**, the Spanish explorer, discovered the Aztec civilization. After that, their lives were changed forever, as we will see later in this chapter (www.indians.org).

Aztec Pyramid at St. Cecilia Acatitlan, Mexico State by Maunus, 2008

Mayas

The earliest of the major Meso-American civilizations was the **Olmec culture**, which is often regarded as the fostering influence behind the Mayan, Aztec, and other later societies. The Olmec were prominent in eastern coastal Mexico between 1200 and 400 B.C. and are remembered for constructing massive earthen mounds, sculpting giant basalt heads, and building large and prosperous cities that existed for hundreds of years. As the Olmec declined, the Mayas rose to prominence.

Settlement was extensive in the Yucatán Peninsula and stretched southward into Central America. Unlike the later Aztecs, the **Mayas** did not exercise strong administrative control over an empire, but instead developed as a series of largely autonomous city-states, such as Palenque, Tikal, and Chichén Itzá. Fortified residential areas were often surrounded by meticulously cultivated farmlands.

Mayan contributions were many. They developed an advanced writing system. Their history, entrusted to cactus fiber parchment, fared poorly against the ravages of time, and Spanish censors saw to the destruction of much of the remainder. However, many Mayan carvings on stone have survived and provide much of what is known today about their civilization.

The Mayas were gifted mathematicians who independently developed the concept of zero, and astronomers who deduced that a solar year was slightly more than 365 days. Despite these achievements, the Mayas and other Meso-American cultures failed to discover the utility of the wheel.

The decline of Mayan civilization was well under way

by 1100 B.C., 2,000 years before Conquistadors arrived. The causes are uncertain, but speculation points to warfare, crop failures, and disease as leading possibilities. The society was also enervated by its religion, which emphasized that human blood was extremely pleasing to its gods. Nobles mutilated themselves and their blood flowed onto fabric, which was burned as an offering.

As time passed, those gifts were deemed insufficient, and human sacrifice became commonplace. Victims had their still-beating hearts cut from their chests and displayed to throngs gathered for these spectacles. Most of those so dispatched were captives from battles, but others were Mayan volunteers seeking to placate the gods.

By the time of the Spanish arrival around A.D. 1520, the Mayas were a starkly diminished civilization. Their great cities were abandoned, and the remnants of their population widely scattered (www.indians.org).

Incas

Elaborate, massive ancient Inca ruins at the foot of the peak of **Machu Picchu** in south-central Peru provide clear evidence that the Incas were a Native South American tribe who, at the time of the Spanish conquest in 1532, ruled an empire that extended along the Pacific coast and Andean highlands from the northern border of modern Ecuador to the Maule River in central Chile. The Incas established their capital at Cuzco (Peru) in the 12th century. They began their conquests in the early 15th century and within 100 years had gained control of an Andean population of about 12 million people.

The founder of the Incan dynasty, Manco Capac, led the tribe to settle in Cuzco, which remained thereafter their capital. Until the reign of the fourth emperor, Mayta Capac, in the 14th century, there was little to distinguish the Incas from the many other tribes inhabiting small domains throughout the Andes. Under Mayta Capac the Incas began to expand, attacking and looting the villages of neighboring peoples and probably assessing some sort of tribute. Under Capac Yupanqui, the next emperor, the Incas first extended their influence beyond the Cuzco valley, and under Viracocha Inca, the eighth, they began a program of permanent conquest by establishing garrisons among the settlements of the peoples whom they had conquered.

Incan technology and architecture were highly developed, although not strikingly original. Their irrigation systems, palaces, temples, and fortifications can still be seen throughout the Andes. The economy was based on agriculture, its staples being corn (maize), white and sweet potatoes, squash, tomatoes, peanuts (groundnuts), chili peppers, cocoa, cassava, and cotton. They raised guinea pigs, ducks, llamas, alpacas, and dogs. Clothing was made of llama wool and cotton. Houses were of stone or adobe mud. Practically every man was a farmer, producing his own food and clothing.

The Incas built a vast network of roads throughout this empire. It comprised two north–south roads, one running along the coast for about 2,250 miles (3,600 km), the other inland along the Andes for a comparable distance, with

Machu Picchu Panorama with Wyna Picchu to the left

many interconnecting links. Many short rock tunnels and vine-supported suspension bridges were constructed. Use of the system was strictly limited to government and military business; a well-organized relay service carried messages in the form of knotted cords (quipu) at a rate of 150 miles (240 km) a day. The network greatly facilitated the Spanish conquest of the Inca empire (www.archaeology.about.com).

Clay figurines are examples of Incan abstract traditions of sculpture.

Assignment

A. The debate over Christopher Columbus's character and legacy has continued into the 21st century. Though the United States celebrates a national holiday in his honor, much more attention has been paid in recent years to the various Spanish explorers' treatment of the Native Peoples. As a result, the word *discovery* has been replaced by *encounter* when used to describe Columbus's exploration of the Americas. Columbus died believing he had reached the shores of China, and that he was a divine missionary, ordained by God to spread Christianity into the New World. In modern society, many have made Columbus out to be a villain and a symbol for all that is evil about the colonization of the Americas by Europe. Read the following passage and argue whether Columbus was a devout Christian or a hypocrite using his faith to further his own selfish purposes.

"In order to win the friendship and affection of that people, and because I am convinced that their conversion to our Holy Faith would be better promoted through love than through force . . . they must be very good servants and very intelligent, because I see that they repeat very quickly what I told them, and it is my conviction that they would easily become Christians, for they seem not [to] have any sect. . . ."

—Christopher Columbus, Journals, October 12, 1492

B. If the Aztecs had conquered Spain, would they have treated the Spanish people differently? Why or why not?

COLUMBUS, CONQUISTADORS, AND COLONIZATION

The Age of Exploration

Around A.D. 1000, **Danish Vikings** sailed from Greenland to North America and set up a village on the tip of what is now Newfoundland. The real Vikings were nothing like the Minnesota Vikings! For one thing, they did not wear horned helmets!

The Vikings came from Denmark, Norway, and Sweden. From A.D. 800 to A.D. 1100 the Vikings raided Western Europe, from Ireland to Russia. The Vikings were a very warlike people who nonetheless had strong families and a well-developed culture. The Vikings were the first Europeans to settle in North America. No one knows why the settlement disappeared, but in less than 50 years the Vikings disappeared from North America.

If the Vikings were the first Europeans to explore North America, **Christopher Columbus** was the most famous. Born Cristoforo Colombo, between August and October 1451, in Genoa, Italy, Columbus was the eldest son of Domenico Colombo, a small-scale merchant. Columbus was largely schooled at home. Living in Renaissance Italy, Christopher Columbus saw the end of the Middle Ages and the beginning of the Age of Exploration.

The Age of Exploration grew out of largely economic impulses. For one thing, **Marco Polo** had introduced Europeans to exotic spices and teas from China and the East Indies. But Polo's access was a land route access from Venice, Italy, to Peking, China. However, toward the end of the 14th century, the vast empire of Kublai Kahn was breaking up; thus, merchants could no longer be assured of safe conduct along the land routes. Second, the growing power of Islamic Turkey blocked European attempts at trade. Still, in 1260, Marco Polo traveled east from Europe. In 1265, he arrived at Kaifeng, the capital of Kublai Khan's (also known as the Great Khan) Mongol Empire. In 1269, he returned to Europe with a request from Khan for the Pope to send 100 missionaries to the Mongol Empire, supposedly to help convert the Mongols to Christianity. The missionaries were not sent, but Marco Polo returned and set up a trade route to China.

Enormous profits could be made by traders who were able to bring even one caravan back from the Orient. At the same time, technological advances made exploration even more possible. For one thing, the Portuguese developed a new type of ship called the Caravel. The Caravel was a particularly seaworthy ship that was both fast and dependable. The development of the Caravel would be similar to the transformation of air flight from propeller-driven craft to jet airplanes. At the same time, with the further improvement of the mariner's compass, European traders were ready to leave the land behind and explore the unknown.

By the 15th century most educated Europeans believed that the world was round and that one could sail westward to reach China. Sailing there was another matter. Most scientists correctly postulated that the world was too big to sail westward to China. Christopher Columbus, on the other hand, was persuaded that the world was about 25 percent smaller than it really was. He thought that he would sail into Cathay a mere six weeks after he left Spain! Fifty years later, it actually took

Statue of Christopher Columbus located in Old San Juan, Puerto Rico.

another explorer, Magellan, almost a year!

In 1484, Columbus asked King John II of Portugal to back his voyage west, but King John calculated that it was too risky. The next year, Columbus went to Spain and asked **Queen Isabella** of Castile and her husband, **King Ferdinand** of Aragon. In January of 1492, after being twice rejected, Columbus finally obtained the support of Ferdinand and Isabella. With the fall of Granada, the last Moorish/Islamic stronghold in Spain, Spanish Christians believed they were close to eliminating the spread of Islam in southern Europe and beyond. Isabella and Ferdinand felt that they were ready now to support something more risky. Finally, in 1492, Spain sponsored Columbus's trip west to find a water route to the lucrative East Indies.

As the sun rose on August 3, 1492, three small ships left Palos de la Frontera, Spain, for the East Indies. At 2 a.m. on October 12, 1492, a member of Columbus's crew sighted land.

Colonization of the New World

Columbus traveled to the New World four times. He died without realizing that he had not reached the East Indies. It is difficult to exaggerate or understate the historical significance of Christopher Columbus. The world was never the same after his voyages. Although he failed to find a new route to China, Columbus made the lands and peoples of the western hemisphere known to Europeans, setting in motion a chain of events that altered human history on a global scale.

The Merriam-Webster Dictionary defines **colony** as a body of people living in a new territory but retaining ties with the parent state. During the 16th century Spain alone took seriously the colonization of her territories. While other nations of Europe were contenting themselves with occasional voyages of discovery, or with slave-carrying expeditions, the Spaniards extended their dominion in the New World. Colonies were established on the coasts of South and Central America, and the Caribbean.

Vasco Núñez de Balboa (above, 1475–1519) was a Spanish conquistador and explorer who, along with his dog, was the first European to see the eastern part of the Pacific Ocean (in 1513), while crossing the Isthmus of Panama.

Poor Balboa was charged with treason against Spain (although he was innocent and had been framed by a friend, Arias de Avila). Francisco Pizarro (who later conquered the Incas) arrested Balboa. Balboa was found guilty and was publicly beheaded in Acla in January, 1519.

Emanuel Leutze, Columbus Before the Queen (1843). Queen Isabella and King Ferdinand supported Columbus in 1492, in search of a water-route to the lucrative East Indies, after he had been rejected by King John II (PD-US).

Hernando Cortez fared much better. In 1519 Cortez landed in the area of Vera Cruz, Mexico. By November of that year, Cortez entered into Tenochtitlan (the capital of the Aztec Empire near Mexico City) and simply arrested the emperor of the Aztec, Montezuma. Within the span of two years, Cortez dismantled the Aztec monarchy and gained control of all of Tenochtitlan and many of its surrounding territories.

Why was the Aztec Empire taken so quickly by the Europeans led by Cortez? There are many factors to consider in answering such a question. Of the most important is the time in which Cortez entered into Tenochtitlan. Prior to his arrival, the Aztecs had seen many astrological phenomena that seemed to portend the collapse of the empire itself. These portents of doom ranged from a comet seen in the daytime to the destruction of two temples. In addition to these omens of doom, Cortez arrived at harvest time, when the Aztecs were generally not prepared for war, although there were battles. Also, the Tlaxcalans helped Cortez fight the Aztecs. Outbreaks of epidemics also helped to weaken the Aztecs (www.library.thinkquest.org).

Other explorers conquered nothing but swampland. As a reward for his service to Spain, Ponce de Leon was given the right to find Bimini, one of the islands in the Bahamas. The "Fountain of Youth" was supposed to be in Bimini. Legend has it that anyone who drank from the fountain would never grow old. Ponce de Leon organized an expedition to find the fountain in March of 1513. He landed near the site of what is now St. Augustine, Florida. He didn't realize he was in North America. He thought he had landed on an island. He named it Florida because he saw lots of flowers (*florida* in Spanish means "flowery").

In 1527, **Francisco Pizarro** (above), who had originally set off from Spain for the city of gold entered Peru, where, with his small band of 175 men armed with an ineffective cannon, he conquered the entire Incan Empire. On May 13, 1532, he began to advance toward the empire's capital. As Pizarro's group advanced, they were confronted by roughly 50,000 Incan warriors within the town square of the capital city, Cajamarca, who were bent on destroying Pizarro's band. However, the Incas did not attack. Rather, Pizarro asked the Inca leader, Atahualpa, to meet with him and his bodyguards unarmed, and both the Incas and Pizarro's men

stood at a standstill. Accepting Pizarro's offer was the Incas' worst mistake.

Pizarro knew that if he had the emperor, he would have the entire Incan Empire and all the gold that it held. Shortly after his meeting with Pizarro, Atahualpa's gold headband was torn from his head, and with the blast of a cannon, Pizarro's men slaughtered all of the Incas within the square of Cajamarca. Atahualpa attempted to bargain with Pizarro for his life, offering him a room filled with gold (roughly 17 feet by 22 feet by 9 feet), but shortly after Atahualpa showed Pizarro the room, he was murdered (www.library.thinkquest.org).

During the late 16th century, 200,000 Spaniards migrated to South America. Quickly South America began to change, with imported plants, large sugar plantations, vast estates, and imported animals overtaking the native landscape. Bureaucracy and government also took hold quickly in South America. The Spanish established the **encomiendas**, where the government granted conquerors the right to employ groups of Indians. The encomiendas, in truth, were a form of legalized slavery. Relegated to practical slave labor within sugar cane plantations and mining caves, the native population of Peru declined from 1.3 million in 1570, to 600,000 in 1620. In Meso-America the circumstances were no different. The population of Indians went from 25.3 million in 1519, to a scant 1 million in 1605. Though forced labor played the largest part in the decimation of the Incas and Aztecs, disease was by no means minor within this time frame. Widespread epidemics of smallpox and other diseases were not uncommon, and claimed the lives of millions. On the psychological front, historians and psychologists have offered another reason for the decimation of the Incan and Aztec populations, namely that the Indians had lost the will to survive. With the extreme and quick loss of culture, accompanied by the pressure of Christian missionaries and laws preventing the practice of any form of native religion (for which there were strong repercussions, even death), Native Americans were, in effect, slaves to the Spaniard immigrants (www.library. thinkquest.org).

Assignment

Primary Sources

I. During the early 1500s, men called conquistadors led expeditions into interior North and South America. Most expected to find great riches. These men were accustomed to achieving fame and fortune through assertive strategies—including violence. At the same time, many conquistadors felt it was their moral responsibility to convert people to Christianity. With the blessing of the Spanish king and church, therefore, conquistadors wandered through the new world claiming territory and souls for Spain and God.

One famous conquistador, Francisco Vásquez de Coronado, was born in Spain in 1510. Coronado set out in 1540, joined by a large expedition of 340 Spanish, 300 Indian allies, and 1,000 slaves, both native Americans and Africans. In the next two years Coronado explored most of the American West and Southwest. In 1542 he went back to Mexico by roughly the same route he had come. Only 100 of his men went back with him. Although the expedition was a complete failure, he remained governor of New Galicia until 1544, then retired to Mexico City, where he died in 1554.

The following excerpt was written by Pedro de Castaneda, one of Coronado's soldiers:

> To me it seems very certain, my very noble lord, that it is a worthy ambition for great men to desire to know and wish to preserve for posterity correct information concerning the things that have happened in distant parts. . . In truth, he who wishes to employ himself thus in writing out the things that happened on the expedition, and the things that were seen in those lands, and the ceremonies and customs of the natives, will have matter enough to test his judgment, and I believe that the result can not fail to be an account which, describing only the truth, will be so remarkable that it will seem incredible . . . The army rested here several days, because the inhabitants had gathered a good stock of provisions that year and each one shared his stock very gladly with his guests from our army. They not only had plenty to eat here, but they also had plenty to take away with them, so that when the departure came they started off with more than six hundred loaded animals, besides the friendly Indians and the servants—more than a thousand persons. After a fortnight had passed, the general started ahead with about fifty horsemen and a few foot soldiers and most of the Indian allies, leaving the army, which was to follow him a fortnight later.

A. How reliable is this primary source? When determining reliability ask yourself these questions: Did the speaker participate in the described event(s)? How long after the incident does he mention the incident? It is it a private journal or a public piece? Private journals are normally more reliable. Does he discuss his participation in the event? Does he appear objective? Does he have anything to gain if he tells a lie? Based on the preceding passage, defend your answers.

B. If this were the only resource you had available on Native Americans, how would you characterize them?

II. Cabeza de Vaca was, at first, part of but later became the leader of an expedition of about 300 men sent to conquer and colonize Florida. The expedition sailed into Tampa Bay about April 1528, and began an overland march to Mexico. During the next two years more than half the men died. He led a small band of survivors to an island, possibly Galveston Island, off the southwestern coast of what is now Texas, where the band was captured by Native Americans. Early in 1535, Cabeza de Vaca and the three other survivors of the expedition escaped and began a trek through what are now the southwestern United States and northern Mexico. In 1536 the four men finally reached Mexico.

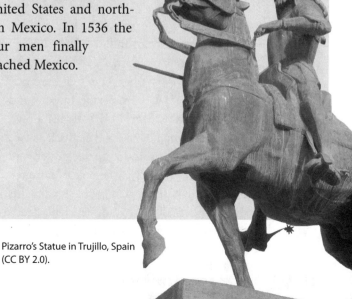

Pizarro's Statue in Trujillo, Spain
(CC BY 2.0).

The following is Vaca's reminiscences of what happened:

Passage I

It was Our Lord's pleasure, who many a time shows His favor in the hour of greatest distress, that at sunset we turned a point of land and found there shelter and much improvement. Many canoes came and the Indians in them spoke to us, but turned back without waiting. They were tall and well built, and carried neither bows nor arrows. We followed them to their lodges, which were nearly along the inlet, and landed, and in front of the lodges we saw many jars with water, and great quantities of cooked fish. The Chief of that land offered all to the Governor and led him to his abode. The dwellings were of matting and seemed to be permanent. When we entered the home of the chief he gave us plenty of fish, while we gave him of our maize, which they ate in our presence, asking for more. So we gave more to them, and the Governor presented him with some trinkets. While with the cacique at his lodge, half an hour after sunset, the Indians suddenly fell upon us and upon our sick people on the beach. They also attacked the house of the cacique, where the Governor was, wounding him in the face with a stone. Those who were with him seized the cacique, but as his people were so near he escaped, leaving in our hands a robe of marten-ermine skin, which, I believe, are the finest in the world and give out an odor like amber and musk. A single one can be smelt so far off that it seems as if there were a great many. We saw more of that kind, but none like these.

Passage II

To this island we gave the name of the Island of Ill-Fate. The people on it are tall and well formed; they have no other weapons than bows and arrows with which they are most dexterous. The men have one of their nipples perforated from side to side and sometimes both; through this hole is thrust a reed as long as two and a half hands and as thick as two fingers; they also have the under lip perforated and a piece of cane in it as thin as the half of a finger. The women do the hard work. People stay on this island from October till the end of February, feeding on the roots I have mentioned, taken from under the water in November and December. They have channels made of reeds and get fish only during that time; afterwards they subsist on roots. At the end of February they remove to other parts in search of food, because the roots begin to sprout and are not good any more. Of all the people in the world, they are those who most love their children and treat them best, and should the child of one of them happen to die, parents and relatives bewail it, and the whole settlement, the lament lasting a full year, day after day. Before sunrise the parents begin to weep, after them the tribe, and the same they do at noon and at dawn. At the end of the year of mourning they celebrate the anniversary and wash and cleanse themselves of all their paint. They mourn all their dead in this manner, old people excepted, to whom they do not pay any attention, saying that these have had their time and are no longer of any use, but only take space, and food from the children. Their custom is to bury the dead, except those who are medicine men among them, whom they burn, and while the fire is burning, all dance and make a big festival, grinding the bones to powder. At the end of the year, when they celebrate the anniversary, they scarify themselves and give to the relatives the pulverized bones to drink in water. Every man has a recognized wife, but the medicine men enjoy greater privileges, since they may have two or three, and among these wives there is great friendship and harmony.

C. Pretend that you are a public official in Spain in the early 1500s. Based on the three preceeding passages, speculate what the Native Americans are like and design a strategy to convert them to Christianity.

D. When two different cultures meet they have four choices: accommodation, amalgamation, assimilation, or extermination. State which process was employed in New Spain, and the result.

E. The technology of the Native Americans was simpler than that of the Europeans. Europeans, for instance, had more effective construction technology. Their health practices were also advanced. Did this give the Europeans the right to conquer the Native Americans? Why or why not?

Chapter 2

SLAVERY AND RELIGIOUS FREEDOM

First Thoughts . . .

"To express all our quarrels, trecheries and encounters amongst those Savages I should be too tedious: but in breefe, at all times we so incountred them, and curbed their insolencies, that they concluded with presents to purchase peace; at our first meeting our Captaine ever observed this order to demand their bowes and arrowes, swordes, mantells and furrs, with some childe or two for hostage, whereby we could quickly perceive, when they intended any villany" (John Smith). Even a cursory study of the early English Jamestown Colony in 1607 will persuade you that Native American/European relations were strained from the beginning. We will discuss historical debate surrounding the Jamestown settlement, and, finally, we will analyze the genesis of chattel slavery in North America.

Chapter Learning Objectives . . .

Chapter 2 presents the beginning of English colonization in North America. We begin with an overview and introduction of an important historical tool: world view. Later, we will analyze the genesis of chattel slavery in North America. Finally, we will look at Lord Baltimore's Roman Catholic colony in Maryland.

As a result of this chapter study you should be able to:

1. Evaluate European colonization in the early 16th century.

2. Make sense of the Virginia Company's attempt to found colonies in America.

3. Investigate the genesis of the most grievous of Western Hemisphere institutions: chattel slavery.

4. Unravel the 16th-century views of religious freedom and evaluate the effectiveness of Lord Baltimore's Roman Catholic experiment in the Chesapeake Bay area.

FRENCH EXPLORATION AND COLONIZATION

The only other people who showed any colonizing activity in the 16th century were the Portuguese. They slowly spread their settlements along the coast of Brazil, until by the end of the century the whole coast from the La Plata River to the Amazon River was full of Portuguese colonies.

France, on the other hand, lost interest in colonization of the New World because their initial attempts at colonization had failed. That is, they failed to find any gold or silver. They found plenty of furs, but not much else. More important, France itself was struggling with internal religious and political problems. France, as contrasted with England and Spain, contained few middle-class families, or yeoman farmers, who naturally sought to settle in a new agrarian colony.

Also, while there were Protestants and other aberrant Christian groups in France, as contrasted with the state church—Roman Catholic—their number and scope came nowhere near the British example. Thus, while New Spain promised instant wealth and New England promised religious freedom, New France promised a few beaver pelts.

Not until the 17th century—when it appeared that France would lose her North American colonies to the English—did France begin American colonization in earnest. In northeastern **Nova Scotia**, the permanent colony of New France was created in 1604.

In 1608 **Samuel de Champlain** ("Father" of New France) founded the first successful French settlement at Québec. He established friendly relations with the local Indians based on the fur trade. The French employed a technique called accommodation instead of annihilation (which the Spanish generally employed). All European powers subscribed to an economic theory called Mercantilism.

Mercantilism

Mercantilism posited a theory that in order for a nation to be great, it must have colonies to provide natural resources and markets for the home industries. This theory did not really catch hold until the next century, but it nonetheless had an influence on early French strategies of colonization.

France was a colonial power in North America from the early 16th century, the age of great European discoveries, fur trading, and fishing expeditions, to the early 19th century, when **Napoleon Bonaparte** sold Louisiana to the fledgling U.S.A. From the founding of Québec in 1608 to the ceding of Canada to Britain in 1763, France placed its stamp upon the history of the continent, much of whose lands, including the vast territory of Louisiana and the Mississippi Valley, lay under its control. The populations it established, especially in the St. Lawrence Valley, are still full of vitality today.

France became interested in the New World later than the other Western Christian powers. In 1524 Giovanni Verrazano followed the eastern shore of America from Florida to Newfoundland. Jacques Cartier then made three voyages of discovery for France. He took possession of the territory in the name of the king of France by planting a cross on the shores of the Gaspé in 1534. The next year he sailed up the St. Lawrence River and visited aboriginal settlements at Québec and Montréal.

In 1608 Champlain erected a habitation (building) at Québec. He continued Cartier's dream of finding an opening to the Indies, pursued the commercial interests of the businessmen, his sponsors, and followed the king's wishes. The settlement responded to economic demands: go out to the fur-rich areas, forge close contact with native suppliers, and try to obtain the

Statue of Samuel de Champlain, by Paul-Romain Chevré, Paris, c1896.

right of exploitation. The scale of the operation made it necessary to form private companies.

The colony's administration, 1608–63, was entrusted to these commercial companies, which were formed by merchants from various cities of France. Succeeding companies promised to settle and develop the French land in America in return for exclusive rights to its resources. They did not do a very good job.

In 1663 Québec was just a commercial branch operation: the fur trade was opposed to agriculture, cross-cultural contact meant war and disease for the natives, the French population was small, and the administration of the colony by commercial exploiters was a disaster. The company relinquished control of the colony to the king. Under Louis XIV New France flourished. He made the colony a province of France, giving it a similar hierarchical administrative organization. He watched over its settlement, extended its territory, and allowed its enterprises to multiply.

René-Robert Cavelier, Sieur de La Salle (1643–1687) was sent by King Louis XIV to travel south from Canada and sail down the Mississippi River to the Gulf of Mexico. He was the first European to travel the length of the Mississippi River (1682). His mission was to explore and establish fur-trade routes along the river. La Salle named the entire Mississippi basin Louisiana, in honor of the king, and claimed it for France on April 9, 1682. He also explored Lake Michigan (1679), Lake Huron, Lake Erie, and Lake Ontario.

History Maker

Inigo Lopez de Recalde, whom Roman Catholics later called **St. Ignatius de Loyola**, was born in 1491 in northern Spain. Ignatius had thousands of followers in Spain and France. In fact, most of the French and Spanish priests and monks who came to the New World were a part of Ignatius's order, the Jesuits or Society of Jesus, a religious order of men in the Roman Catholic Church. The motto of the order was "to the greater glory of God," and its object was the spread of Roman Catholicism. This included supporting almost any activity that advanced the gospel. As often happens, Ignatius's zealous followers took his admonitions too far, and committed many cruel acts in his name. Ignatius, though, was really a godly man who loved Christ with all his heart. Millions of Roman Catholics, and some Protestants, have found their lives transformed by Ignatius's words.

Napoleon Crossing the Alps by Jacques-Louis David, 1801.

The following is an excerpt from Ignatius's famous *Spiritual Exercises* (1522):

Man is created to praise, reverence, and serve God our Lord, and by this means to save his soul. And the other things on the face of the earth are created for man and that they may help him in prosecuting the end for which he is created. From this it follows that man is to use them as much as they help him on to his end, and ought to rid himself of them so far as they hinder him as to it. For this it is necessary to make ourselves indifferent to all created things in all that is allowed to the choice of our free will and is not prohibited to it; so that, on our part, we want not health rather than sickness, riches rather than poverty, honor rather than dishonor, long rather than short life, and so in all the rest; desiring and choosing only what is most conducive for us to the end for which we are created.

Assignment

A. The Shorter Westminster Catechism was perhaps the most famous Protestant Confession (or statement of faith) in 17th-century England. It was prepared primarily for instructing children in the Christian faith. It is composed of a brief introduction on the end, rule, and essence of religion and of 107 questions and answers. Give a paraphrase of the preceding statement from St. Ignatius's *Spiritual Exercises* and compare and contrast it with Questions 1, 2, 4, and 34 of the Westminster Shorter Catechism (below).

Q1: What is the chief end of man?

A1: Man's chief end is to glorify God, and to enjoy Him for ever.

Q2: What rule hath God given to direct us how we may glorify and enjoy Him?

A2: The Word of God, which is contained in the Scriptures of the Old and New Testaments, is the only rule to direct us how we may glorify and enjoy Him.

Q4: What is God?

A4: God is a Spirit, infinite, eternal, and unchangeable, in His being, wisdom, power, holiness, justice, goodness, and truth.

Q34: What is adoption?

A34: Adoption is an act of God's free grace, whereby we are received into the number, and have a right to all the privileges of the Sons of God.

B. Ignatius insisted that his followers practice spiritual disciplines (e.g., fasting, meditation, etc.). Dallas Willard in his book *The Spirit of the Disciplines: How God Changes Lives* (1991) argues that many modern Christians have de-emphasized spiritual disciplines to the detriment of us all.

Agree or disagree with Willard's concern and defend your answer.

Willard writes:

"When through spiritual disciplines I become able heartily to bless those who curse me, to pray without ceasing, to be at peace when not given credit for good deeds I've done, or to master the evil that comes my way, it is because my disciplinary activities have inwardly poised me for more and more interaction with the powers of the living God and His Kingdom. Such is the potential we tap into when we use the disciplines."

C. Many people consider Ignatius, and especially his followers, to be intolerant. S.D. Gaede, in his book *When Tolerance Is No Virtue* (1993) argues that in our culture, there is considerable confusion about how we ought to live with our differences and a cacophony of contradictory justifications for one approach as opposed to another. All appeal to the need for tolerance, but there is nothing like common argument on what that means. The question our culture raises by nature and development is what is truth and what can we believe? Our culture doesn't know the answers. In fact, we have lost confidence in truth and have come to the conclusion that truth is unattainable. Thus, tolerance moves to the forefront. G. K. Chesterton wrote: "Toleration is the virtue of the man without convictions." What would be a Christian response to so-called toleration?

D. John Jefferson Davis, PhD, Ethics Professor, Gordon-Conwell Seminary, argues that Christianity is credible as we demonstrate community that is "countercultural." In other words, Christianity must transcend culture, nationality, and/or race or it loses its meaning. Do you agree with that statement? Defend your answer.

E. On one hand, some scholars argue that the Spanish conquistadors and French explorers should have left Native American culture alone. They argue that these two cultures—European and Native American—should have learned to live side-by-side without changing each other. Other scholars argue that without some commonality—religious convictions for instance—two divergent cultures cannot have the moral cohesion necessary to maintain society. In other words, the Spanish would have to become Native American or the Native American become Spanish. Using historical research, defend one of these two arguments.

THE VIRGINIA COMPANY

Historians Charles and Mary Beard write:

The tide of migration that set in toward the shores of North America during the early years of the seventeenth century was but one phase in the restless and eternal movement of mankind upon the surface of the earth. The ancient Greeks flung out their colonies in every direction, westward as far as Gaul, across the Mediterranean, and eastward into Asia Minor, perhaps to the very confines of India. The Romans, supported by their armies and their government, spread their dominion beyond the narrow lands of Italy until it stretched from the heather of Scotland to the sands of Arabia. The Teutonic tribes, from their home beyond the Danube and the Rhine, poured into the empire of the Cæsars and made the beginnings of modern Europe. Of this great sweep of races and empires the settlement of America was merely a part. And it was, moreover, only one aspect of the expansion which finally carried the peoples, the institutions, and the trade of Europe to the very ends of the earth.

In one vital point, it must be noted, American colonization differed from that of the ancients. The Greeks usually carried with them affection for the government they left behind and sacred fire from the altar of the parent city; but thousands of the immigrants who came to America disliked the state and disowned the church of the mother country. They established compacts of government for themselves and set up altars of their own. They sought not only new soil to till but also political and religious liberty for themselves and their children.

Statue of Captain John Smith

One of the worst investments in the early 17th century was an investment in the Virginia Company. The **Virginia or London Company** was a stock-option company set up to raise funds for new colonizing enterprises. It was a bust for its investors.

Its first and only real undertaking was the Jamestown investment. The **Jamestown settlement** proved to be an extraordinarily bad investment because it lost vast amounts of money for its investors. Principally, this was due to the unwillingness of the early colonizers to do the necessary work of providing for themselves. At the same time, and in defense of the early settlers, the investors never really provided enough capital for adequate supply of the venture. Nevertheless, how extraordinary that the United States, whose business is business, President Calvin Coolidge once said, started as a bad business venture!

With very little prospect of profit, the English were much slower than the French, Spanish, Dutch, and even the Portuguese to explore and then to settle the New World. While Drake and others participated in exciting adventures, virtually no Englishman undertook a serious exploration of the New World (except John Cabot). Nonetheless, by 1607, 20 years after the ill-fated colony at Roanoke disappeared, England had a firm geopolitical claim to North America.

Jamestown, Virginia, was the object of this investment venture and the site of the first permanent British settlement in North America. It was founded on May 14, 1607, and was located on a peninsula (later an island) in the James River in Virginia. It was named in honor of King James. From the beginning, the colony was unsure about its reason for existence. Ostensibly, it was founded for the sole purpose of making profit for its investors.

One quick way to make money in the 17th century, of

course, was to find gold. This method was especially appealing to the yeoman (middle-class) farmers and second or third sons of aristocratic families (who had scant hope of inheriting any money in England) who made up the majority element of early British settlers. Gold was and still is hard to come by in southeastern tidewater Virginia. Finally, after starvation took over half the colony, the new colonists discovered that the cultivation of tobacco was about as good as gold. It was then grown everywhere—including the streets of Jamestown.

No one knows why the early profiteers chose such an unhealthy place as Jamestown for a settlement. No self-respecting Native American would have been caught dead near the place. Situated in an unhealthful marshy area, the colony always had a small population because of a high death rate from disease. What disease did not kill, fire often did.

In 1608 Jamestown was accidentally burned, and two years later it was about to be abandoned by its inhabitants when Thomas West, Lord De La Warr, arrived with new energy and new supplies. Other fires occurred in 1676 and 1698. Jamestown fell into decay when the seat of government of Virginia was moved in 1699 to the Middle Plantation (later Williamsburg). By this time quick profit had been abandoned for more long-term profit. However, from the beginning the Jamestown experiment was an experiment in profit making.

As stated in a previous history lesson, the main Native American tribe in the Virginia area in the early 17th century was the Lenape Powhatan Tribe. By the time the English colonists had arrived, the chief of the Powhatans, Chief Powhatan, ruled a formidable 30-tribe confederacy. He allegedly controlled 128 villages with about 9,000 inhabitants. Powhatan initially opposed the English settlement at Jamestown. According to legend, he changed his policy in 1607 when he released the captured Smith. In April 1614, Pocahontas, Powhatan's daughter, married the planter John Rolfe, and afterwards Powhatan negotiated a peace agreement with his son-in-law's people.

Peace reigned until after Powhatan died in 1618. In 1622 a great war broke out between the English settlers and the Powhatan Confederacy. Initially the Powhatan Confederation very nearly destroyed the Jamestown settlement. In the long term, however, the war destroyed the Confederacy as a viable entity. Considered from one side, colonization, whatever the motives of the emigrants, was an economic matter. It involved the use of capital to pay for

The First Thanksgiving at Plymouth by Jennie A. Brownscomb, 1914 (PD-US).

their passage, to sustain them on the voyage, and to start them on the way of production. Under this stern economic necessity, Puritans, Scotch-Irish, Germans, and all were alike laid.

The Process of Immigration

Most of the immigrants to America in colonial days paid their own passage. Historian Henry Cabot Lodge (left) argued:

> "The settlers of New England were drawn from the country gentlemen, small farmers, and yeomanry of the mother country . . . . Many of the emigrants were men of wealth, as the old lists show, and all of them, with few exceptions, were men of property and good standing. They did not belong to the classes from which emigration is usually supplied, for they all had a stake in the country they left behind."

That at least tens of thousands of immigrants were unable to pay for their passage is established beyond the shadow of a doubt by the shipping records that have come down to us. The great barrier in the way of the poor who wanted to go to America was the cost of the sea voyage. To overcome this difficulty a plan was worked out whereby shipowners and other persons of means furnished the passage money to immigrants in return for their promise to work for a term of years (usually seven) to repay debt. This system was called **indentured servitude**.

Indentured servants differed from the serfs of the feudal age in that they were not bound to the soil but to the master. They likewise differed from the chattel slaves in that their servitude had a time limit. Still they were subject to many special disabilities. It was, for instance, a common practice to impose on them penalties far heavier than were imposed upon freemen for the same offense. A free citizen of Pennsylvania who indulged in horse racing and gambling was let off with a fine; a white servant guilty of the same unlawful conduct was whipped at the post and fined as well.

The ordinary life of the white servant was also severely restricted. A bondman could not marry without his master's consent; nor engage in trade; nor refuse work assigned to him. For an attempt to escape or indeed for any infraction of the law, the term of service was extended. The condition of white bondmen in Virginia, according to Lodge, "was little better than that of slaves. Loose indentures and harsh laws put them at the mercy of their masters." It would not be unfair to add that such was their lot in all other colonies. Their fate depended upon the temper of their masters (Beard).

Rivaling in numbers, in the course of time, the indentured servants and whites carried to America against their will were the Africans brought to America and sold into slavery. When this form of bondage was first introduced into Virginia in 1619, it was looked upon as a temporary necessity to be discarded with the increase of the white population—although this is debated. This topic will be discussed at length in further lessons.

Assignment

A. Rate how Native Americans felt about a statement and then rate how Jamestown settlers felt. Finally, rate how you feel, 1 being not true at all, 5 being true all the time.

Statement	Native American	Jamestown Settler	Myself
A person should be brave all the time.			
A person can lie if it advances his purposes.			
A person should never lie under any circumstances.			
If one works hard enough, one will succeed.			
A person should not make hasty decisions.			
Be careful what you wish—it might come true.			
The good guys always win.			
Bad things happen to good people.			
Women and men are equal in all ways.			
Do what feels good.			
Do what is right, whether it feels good or not.			
Do unto others as you would have them do unto you.			
Obey your parents.			
Be faithful to your spouse.			
Keep your word.			

B. At first, Colonial settlers tried to own land together—in common tillage. However, this did not work. Without any research on the topic, why do you think that this did not work?

C. If you have seen the Disney movie *Pocahontas*, compare the Disney vision of Native Americans with the accurate historical version. Next, compare the Disney view of Europeans with the accurate historical version, then do the same concerning family relationships.

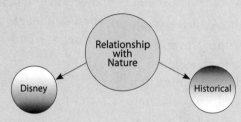

Native American	Europeans		Native American	Europeans

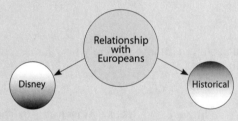

Native American	Europeans		Native American	Europeans

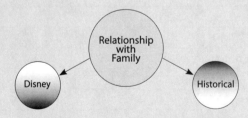

Native American	Europeans		Native American	Europeans

CHATTEL SLAVERY COMES TO THE NEW WORLD

The institution of slavery had existed in Western Civilization since biblical times, but the first slaves came to the Western Hemisphere in the early 1500s. However, not until 20 African slaves were brought to Jamestown, Virginia, in 1619, was slavery present in America. In fact, it is not altogether clear if the first African slaves were brought as indentured servants (to be released in seven years) or chattel slavery (never to be released). Nevertheless, it quickly became a moot point.

A series of complex colonial laws made sure that Africans and their descendants were to remain in perpetual slavery. What came first: racism or slavery? It is hard to say, but racism was not institutionalized in America until white Americans created a language to describe American people groups.

When the first African-American came to the Jamestown colony in 1619 that language was already present. Europeans from the 1200s to the early 1500s used terms such as "negro" to refer to persons with dark–colored skin. These terms, though, initially were not used to denigrate a "race" or caste, nor were they used in a genealogical sense. They were used to designate a different physical attribute. Later, "Negro" and "Mulatto" gained a negative connotation.

As white Americans learned to name minorities, a system of control arose. Racism was used as a justification for control. Racism with all its stereotyping components evolved into the deprecating form that exists today. The historian David R. Roediger argues, "The idea of race, then, emerges from the ways that social meaning becomes attached to physical differences. White Europeans gave such meaning an inherent, God-given origin, and [white] Americans kept up the tradition."

"Blackness" was considered to be a disease. The rhetoric of disease was a critical component in white American racism. White Americans loved to frame their racism in scientific terms. One favorite theory was that the skin color and physiognomy of the black were the result of congenital leprosy. Benjamin Rush, the Father of American Psychiatry, saw black people as the greatest threat to the public health in 18th-century America. Rush argued that the black skin of African-Americans was the result of a form of leprosy. Contemporary racist literature venerates these racist stereotypes and maintains them in the American language.

Slave Trade Routes

Most slaves were taken from the western part of Africa. The African-American historian Benjamin Quarles describes these West African people groups:

> Of the varied Old World people that entered America, none came with as wide a geographical area as the blacks. The vast majority came from the West Coast of Africa, a 3,000-mile stretch extending from the Senegal River . . . . to Angola. . . These groups shared no common language . . . . Indeed, there are more than 200 distinct languages in present-day Nigeria alone. There was no such thing as the 'African personality' since the varied groups differed as much in their way of life as in the physical characteristics they exhibited. . . . Whatever the type of society, the different groups of Africans all operated under well-organized social systems. . . . African societies before the coming of the Europeans were not backward and changeless. . . .

Quarles also described slave trading and the middle passage. Normally, European settlers established forts on the edge of the jungle. The Africans, wishing to obtain the trade goods, would capture young men and women and take them to the fort. The terror is unimaginable! African young people were stolen from their families and were never seen again. The slaves were kept in makeshift prisons or warehouses until their proprietor had enough to justify a shipment. That number was about 250.

One of the most awful parts of slavery was the middle passage. The United States outlawed the transatlantic slave trade in 1808, but the domestic slave trade and illegal importation continued for several decades.

The South Atlantic trade network involved several international routes. The best known of the triangular trades included the transportation of manufactured goods from Europe to Africa, where they were traded for slaves. Slaves were then transported across the Atlantic—the infamous **middle passage**—primarily to Brazil and the Caribbean, where they were sold.

It was not uncommon for up to one-eighth of the human cargo to die. Dead slaves were thrown overboard, and schools of sharks followed the slave ships. But profits were so vast that the loss was incidental. Often the slaves would stay in the West Indies for several weeks while they were acclimated to their new North American home.

The final leg of this triangular trade brought tropical products to Europe. In another variation, manufactured goods from colonial America were taken to West Africa; slaves were carried to the Caribbean and Southern colonies; and sugar, molasses, and other goods were returned to the home ports (www.memory.loc.gov).

Why did the English participate in slavery? After all, the Spanish and the Portuguese had a tradition of doing so. Normally English labor was fulfilled through indentured servants and apprenticeships. Both forms of labor were acceptable, but nothing was more profitable than chattel slavery. The profits were too great to ignore the benefits of chattel slavery.

Did the slaves resist their captors? Yes, indeed they did. In every conceivable way slaves resisted servitude. Never, ever did slaves passively, much less gratefully, accept their condition!

Therefore, slaves had to be controlled, to be managed. White masters created slave dependence upon their owners. The demon of white privilege lodged itself well into the institution of slavery.

A basic step toward successful slave management was to implant in the slaves an identity of personal inferiority. They had to keep their places, to understand that bondage was their natural status. Thus, from the beginning, African-Americans understood that their resistance to white domination was a question of identity survival. Indeed, resistance seemed to be the only way to survive in the face of profound white systemic racism. It was from this root that later separatism ideology sprang.

The Old Plantation, artist unknown, 1790 (PD-US).

More about Resistance

Slaves were resisting even before they were out of sight of Africa. Resistance became a way of life. Whether it was in the Stono Rebellion or in the Brer Rabbit stories, or everyday work in the cotton fields, African-Americans resisted. Slaves defiantly cut off the roots of the plants with their hoes, just under the ground so no one noticed. Slaves used work stoppages, self-injuries, and, especially in the first few weeks of bondage, suicide to resist white enslavement. African-Americans were resisting so vigorously that at times it seemed like a white minority was under siege. One of the most clever ways the African-Americans resisted the whites was by their maintenance of their own very rich culture.

This pattern of behavior continued into the 20th century. Numbers and size of African-American communities affected the degree and nature of resistance, but resistance existed. A chasm grew between whites and African-Americans that politics, religion, and economics would never bridge. This chasm, real or imagined, became an indelible part of the American ethos.

African-American slaves stayed aloof from the white world. This was especially true in their religious life. Many African-American church leaders resisted assimilation into church institutions in which whites participated. It was a fundamental way that African-Americans showed their defiance. In fact, to many observers, the early civil rights movement appeared to be a religious protest movement more than a political protest movement.

Brer Rabbit was constantly thrown into the briar patch but he always reminded his master that the briar patch, after all, was home. But what a price he had to pay! In Toni Morrison's book *The Bluest Eyes*, the young protagonist—an African-American girl—lamented that "she has no memories to be cherished." As slavery ended, most African-Americans had precious few good memories to cherish.

Robert William Fogel and Stanley L. Engerman skillfully argued that slaves did not resist their captivity. "Slaves are exploited in the sense that part of the income which they produced is expropriated by their owners . . . however . . . over his lifetime, the typical slave field hand has received about 90 percent of the income he produced" (Robert William Fogel and Stanley L. Engerman, *Time on the Cross: The Economics of American Negro Slavery* (New York: Lanham, 1974).

According to Engelman and Fogel, slaves had very little reason to resist. They were simply not treated very badly—for the masters to do so would have been unprofitable.

Crucial to Fogel's and Engerman's argument was the idea that slavery had to flourish in the capitalist's mecca: the city. "Slaves employed in industry compared favorably with free workers in diligence and efficiency."

But slavery did not thrive in the city and slaves in the city most assuredly resisted their masters. If anything, urban resistance was more blatant because slaves had free black support (Richard C. Wade). Furthermore, Barbara Fields in her study of slavery in the middle colonies, and especially in Baltimore, showed that urban slavery declined because slave resistance made it too much of a stress on Southern urban society (Barbara Jeanne Fields, *Slavery and Freedom on the Middle Ground*).

The most interesting evidence of slave resistance came from the generation of historians who studied the slaves themselves—including Genovese, Gutman, Levine, and Blassingame. Through history that seemed at times anecdotal, Blassingame painted a picture of a defiant and very complicated people. "Many of the Africans resisted enslavement at every step of their forced emigration" (John W. Blassingame). Even after the slaves discovered the "economic advantages" of slave life, "The plantation is a battlefield where slaves fought masters for physical and psychological survival. . . ." A former slave whose memoirs were recorded by Harvey Wish, Josiah Henson, when he was five, was separated permanently from his mother. She begged her master to keep Josiah. He refused. "This is one of my earliest observations of men; an experience which I only shared with thousands of my race, the bitterness of which to any individual who suffers it cannot be diminished by the frequency of its occurrence. . . ." (Harvey Wish).

Powerful evidence for slave resistance was the **Federal Writers' Project** of the Words Projects Administration in which more than 2,000 ex-slaves were interviewed. These interviews were compiled and analyzed by George P. Rawick in 18 volumes. Rawick concluded that slaves were constantly involved in resistance and subversion. They manifested a kind of anger that served as a protection against white domination. African suicides, runaway slaves, slowdowns in the field—all of these were examples of resistance.

Levine, Gutman, and Blassingame all agree that religion was the most productive form of African-American culture maintenance, and, therefore, I argue, the most important form of slave resistance. As historian Eugene Genovese argues, "For the slaves and for African-American people generally, religion does not constitute one feature of life or merely one element in an ideological complex; rather, it constituted the fundamental spiritual expression of their entire worldview, as manifested in attitudes toward time and work." In other words, as the slaves practiced their religion, they implicitly resisted slaveowner domination.

Religion was so intensely personal, so fundamentally part of their culture, that it was a form of slave resistance. No one could take this away from them.

Slave resistance is an important question because patterns of black-white relations established in antebellum history endure until today.

Though only 25 percent of the colonial population owned slaves, and most of those lived south of the Mason-Dixon Line, slavery factored heavily in the economy of all the British North American colonies, and not just in the plantation economy of the South. As one historian explained, while many Southerners found slavery morally repugnant, there was a clear business rationale: in the long run, it was cheaper to acquire Africans than to hire laborers. The North also profited immensely from the international trade in Africans.

Br'er Rabbit and the Tar-Baby, drawing by E.W. Kemble from *The Tar-Baby*, by Joel Chandler Harris, 1904 (PD-US).

The African slave-trade - slaves taken from a ship captured by H.M.S. *Undine*, artist unknown, 1884 (PD-US).

Its booming industries—shipbuilding, sail making, iron foundries, sawmills, and rum distilleries—were an integral part of the trading triangle between Europe, Africa, and North America.

Slavery did well even in isolated pockets in the North, especially in the farming regions of New York and New Jersey, Delaware, and Rhode Island. During the pre-Revolution days, 61 percent of all American slaves—nearly 145,000—lived in Virginia and Maryland, working the tobacco fields in small- to medium-sized gangs. This would change as Southern planters moved into Mississippi,

Alabama, and Tennessee. In any event, most slave owners owned no more than two or three slaves. The rule of thumb was this: If you were a slave you probably lived on a large plantation. If you were a white planter you owned fewer than 10 slaves.

The year 1750 was an important date. By 1750, both free and enslaved black people, despite the hardships of their lives, manifested a deepening attachment to America. By then, the majority of blacks had been born in America rather than in Africa.

Assignment

A. What came first, racism or slavery? By 1619 slaves were brought into Virginia on a regular basis. There were no slaves in the colonies before then—only indentured servants who were free in seven years. Some people believe that the slaves were also originally indentured servants, but that the colonists changed their minds and made them slaves forever. In any event, racism was common in America by 1619. But what came first, racism or slavery? Were the colonists prejudiced against African-Americans because they were slaves? Or did the colonists make African-Americans slaves because they were black Americans?

B. Pretend that you are an African warrior captured and held on a big ship. You are shackled in chains among hundreds of your fellow Africans. You don't know anyone. You are separated from your family; you are obviously held captive by some cruel people who hit you if you don't do what they say. You cannot do much but you can resist some. You can, for instance, refuse to eat. You might be able to escape. What do you do? Do you accept your situation? If you do, perhaps you will be rewarded and given things you need. Or should you fight with everything in you? If you do this you might die, but, as unlikely as it seems, you might escape. But escape where? You are on the open seas—too far to swim back to Africa. You'd better decide soon because each day that passes finds you weaker and weaker. Soon you will not be able to do anything. What do you do? Why?

OTHER EXPLORERS

There were, of course, other important explorers at this time. We will look at only two more.

Henry Hudson

In 1609 Henry Hudson, an English seacaptain, then sailing for the Dutch, discovered the river now called by his name.

Hudson was trying to discover a shortcut to China and the Indies. When he left England, he sailed to the Northwest, hoping that he could find a way open to the Pacific across the North Pole or not far below it. Hudson and other explorers called this the **Northwest Passage**. He knew that if he found such a passage, it would be much shorter than a voyage around the globe farther south, because, as anyone one can see, it is not nearly so far around the top of an apple, near the stem, as it is round the middle. Hudson could not find such a passage because it did not exist, but he went nearer to the North Pole than anyone had ever done before.

Holland had heard of Hudson's voyage, and a company of merchants of that country hired him to see if he could find a passage to Asia by sailing to the northwest.

He set out from the port of Amsterdam in 1609, in a vessel named the *Half Moon*. After he had gone quite a long distance, the sailors got so tired of seeing nothing but fog and ice that they refused to go any farther.

Then Captain Hudson turned his ship about and sailed for the coast of North America. He did that because his friend Captain Smith of Virginia had sent him a letter, with a map, that made him think that he could find the passage he wanted north of Chesapeake Bay.

Hudson got to Chesapeake Bay, but the

Henry Hudson and crew abondoned on Hudson's Bay in 1610, artist and date unknown.

weather was so stormy that he thought it would not be safe to enter it. He therefore sailed northward along the coast. In September 1609, he entered a beautiful bay, formed by the spreading out of a noble river. At that point the stream is more than a mile wide, and he called it the "Great River." On the eastern side of it, not far from its mouth, there is a long narrow island: the Indians of that day called it Manhattan Island (Montgomery).

One of the remarkable things about the river that Hudson had discovered is that it has hardly any current, and the tide from the ocean moves up for more than 150 miles. If no fresh water ran in from the hills, still the sea would fill the channel for a long distance, and so make a kind of salt-water river of it. Hudson noticed how salty it was, and that, perhaps, made him think that he had at last actually found a passage that would lead him through from the Atlantic to the Pacific. Of course he was on the Hudson River and he never reached anything but present-day Albany.

Henry Hudson Memorial Column, Bronx, New York City

Lord Baltimore

Lord Baltimore was a Catholic at a time when Roman Catholicism was illegal in England. Catholics were ordered by law to attend the Church of England, which some did, but they held their own private masses at home.

Lord Baltimore hoped to make a home for himself and for other English Catholics in the wilderness of Catholic New France in Newfoundland. But Baltimore did not like the French, and cold, inhospitable Newfoundland was an awful place to start a colony.

King Charles I of England, himself rumored to be a Roman Catholic, was a good friend to Lord Baltimore; and when the settlement in Newfoundland was given up, King Charles made Lord Baltimore a present of an immense three-cornered piece of land cut out of Virginia, north of the Potomac River.

The king's wife, Queen Mary, was a French Catholic. In her honor, Charles named the country he had given Lord Baltimore "Mary Land," or Maryland. Maryland was to be a shelter for many English people who believed in the same religion that the queen did.

All that Lord Baltimore was to pay for Maryland, with its 12,000 square miles of land and water, was two Indian arrows. These he agreed to send every spring to the royal palace of Windsor Castle, near London. The arrows showed that Lord Baltimore had the use of Maryland. . . . could do pretty much as he pleased with it. He had greater privileges than any other holder of land in America at that time.

Lord Baltimore died before he ever set foot in America. His eldest son sent over a number of emigrants; some were Catholics, some were Protestants; but all of them were to have equal religious rights in Maryland. In the spring of 1634, these people landed on a little island near the mouth

Replica of Henry Hudson's ship *Half Moon*, 1909 (PD-US).

of the Potomac River and named their settlement St. Mary's, because they had landed on a day kept sacred to Mary, the mother of Jesus. The Indians and the settlers lived and worked together side by side.

One final note: It was the Roman Catholic settlement in Maryland that truly offered religious freedom to its colonists for the first time. Maryland was the first settlement in America in which all Christian people had entire liberty to worship God in whatever way they thought right.

Assignment

Compare these three North American settlements.

Settlement	Founder	Religious Base	Purpose	Relations with Native Americans
Jamestown				
New Netherland				
Maryland				

Chapter 3

PILGRIMS AND PURITANS

FIRST THOUGHTS . . .

"And for the season, it was winter; and they that know the winters of that country know them to be sharp and violent, and subject to cruel and fierce storms, dangerous to travel to known places, much more to search an unknown coast. Besides what could they see but a hideous and desolate wilderness, full of wild beasts and wild men? And what multitudes there might be of them, they knew not."

—William Bradford

Can you imagine how it felt to arrive with women and children on the coast of one of the most inhospitable places on the face of the earth in the middle of winter? You will participate this week in the most important and personal of historical studies: you will visit a people in their private lives—in their journals, in their homes.

Chapter Learning Objectives . . .

Chapter 3 introduces the most abiding metaphors of American cultural history: the noble experiment and the founding of a City on a Hill. We will recite again the story of the tired Pilgrims and the pious Puritans. Next, you will immerse yourself in the idealism and wonder in joy at William Penn's refreshing, and unique, attempt to interact justly with the Native Peoples. William Oglethorpe, a contemporary of Penn, tried his own hand at justice by founding the Georgia Colony. Finally, we end the 17th century with a disturbing story of the Salem Witch Trials, an ominious movement for Puritan America.

As a result of this chapter study you should be able to:

1. Compare and contrast Pilgrim Separatism and Boston Puritanism.
2. Understand the Puritan views of religious freedom, judge its efficacy in its own context, and reframe the problem in contemporary America.
3. Describe Quakerism and analyze whether it was a realistic or naïve approach to Native American relations.
4. Differentiate between the Virginia Colony, founded for profit, and the Puritan colonies founded for the glory of God.
5. Debate the different theories of Puritanism and articulate your own theory.
6. Discuss the founding of Oglethorpe's Georgian Colony.

PILGRIMS

While colonies were forming in other parts of America, in New England, Englishmen were starting a holy experiment. The historian **Perry Miller** wrote, "Without some understanding of Puritanism . . . there is no understanding of America." Indeed. But who were the **Puritans**? What is the difference between a Boston Puritan and a Plymouth Pilgrim? Were Puritans bigots? Saints? Puritanism, a movement arising within the Church of England in the latter part of the 16th century, sought to carry the reformation of that church beyond the point the early Anglican Church (Church of England) had gone. The Church of England was attempting to establish a middle course between Roman Catholicism and the ideas of the Protestant reformers. This was unacceptable to a growing number of reformers, called Puritans, who wanted the Church of England to reject Anglicanism and embrace Calvinism. The term *Puritanism* was also used in a broader sense to refer to attitudes and values characteristic of these radical reformers. Thus, the Separatists (i.e., Pilgrims) in the 16th century, the Quakers in the 17th century, and Nonconformists after the Restoration were called Puritans, although they were no longer part of the established church. For our purposes, though, we will refer to the Puritans in two ways: Puritans and Pilgrims.

Pilgrim by Gheorghe Tattarescu, date unknown.

The **Pilgrims**, or founders of Plymouth in Massachusetts, were, like their countrymen in Virginia, initially dependent upon private investments from profit-minded backers to finance their colony. In other ways, however, these intensely religious people were nothing like the Jamestown settlers. "The Pilgrims: a simple people, inspired by an ardent faith in God, a dauntless courage in danger, a boundless resourcefulness in the face of difficulties, an impregnable fortitude in adversity: thus they have in some measure become the spiritual ancestors of all Americans" (Miller).

The stated purpose of the Pilgrim expedition was to worship God in a place and in a fashion that was more conducive to their world view. This world view was decidedly Theistic/Calvinistic. These religious Separatists believed that the true church was a voluntary company of the faithful under the spiritual direction of a pastor. In all Puritanism, including Separatism, there was not a clear distinction between what was secular and what was sacred. The church

Puritans going to church, artist unknown, 1884.

Mayflower by Charles Austin Needham, c1900.

This bas-relief depicting the signing of the Mayflower Compact is on Bradford Street in Provincetown below the Pilgrim Monument. Photo by Peter Whitlock (CC BY-SA

and the state were one, and the notion that they were separate was a ludicrous thought indeed to the Puritans. The Pilgrims, unlike the Puritans who settled in Boston, wanted to separate from the Church of England—not merely "purify" the church—but they did not wish to separate the church from the state.

The Pilgrims, then, were committed Christians but they were also loyal Englishmen. They came to the New World as English patriots with a strong faith in Jesus Christ.

In 1620 the Pilgrims, whose legal destination really lay 300 miles south in Virginia, mistakenly landed on Cape Cod. They called their new settlement Plimouth Plantation. In the first year of settlement, nearly half the settlers died of disease. Thanks to help from the local natives, a few survived. Although none of their principal economic pursuits—farming, hunting, fishing, and trading—promised instant wealth, the Pilgrims were, nonetheless, after only five years, self-sufficient. They were free to focus on more eternal issues—like advancing the kingdom of God in a wilderness.

Before disembarking from the *Mayflower* in 1620, **William Bradford** demanded that all the adult males sign a compact promising obedience to a legal covenant promoting a very narrow theistic legal plan. The Compact placed biblical law above British common law. The **Mayflower Compact**—which was more of an Old Testament religious covenant than it was a constitution—was an important step in the evolution of American democracy.

On the first Monday after they had reached the Cape, all the women went on shore to perform domestic duties. No doubt everyone was delighted to be ashore! Shortly after that, Captain Myles Standish, with a number of men, explored the surrounding country. They stole Native American corn buried in the sand.

On clear days the people on board the Mayflower, anchored in Cape Cod Harbor, could see a blue hill, on the mainland in the west, about forty miles away. Later, the Pilgrims would establish their colony on that hill.

Myles Standish, with the others, went back to the Mayflower with a good report. They had found just what they wanted—an excellent harbor; drinking water; and last of all, a piece of land that was nearly free from trees, so that nothing would hinder their planting corn early in the spring. Captain John Smith of Virginia had been there before them, and had named the place Plimouth on his map of New England. The *Mayflower* soon sailed across the Bay to what they called Plimouth Plantation. Next, they landed literally on a shoreline, with a rock (i.e., Plymouth Rock), on which the early settlers first stepped.

During that winter nearly half the Pilgrims died. When these graves were filled, they were smoothed down flat so that Native Americans wouldn't count them and see how few Europeans were left. It was a terrible time in the life of this young colony.

One day in the spring the Pilgrims were shocked at seeing a Native American walk boldly into their little settlement. He spoke in clear English, "Welcome! Welcome!" This visitor was named **Samoset**; he had met some sailors years before, and had learned a few English words from them.

The next time Samoset came he brought with him another Native American whose name was Squanto. **Squanto** was the only one left of the tribe that had once lived at Plimouth. All the rest had died of a plague. He had been stolen by some sailors and carried to England; there he had learned the language. After his return he had joined an Indian tribe that lived about thirty miles farther west. The chief of that tribe was named Massasoit, and Squanto said that he was coming directly to visit the Pilgrims.

Soon Massasoit, the chief of the Wampanoag Tribe, with sixty warriors, appeared on a hill just outside the settlement. Captain Standish, attended by a guard of honor, went out and brought the chief to Governor Carver. Then Massasoit and the governor made a solemn promise or treaty. When the Pilgrims had their first Thanksgiving, they invited Massasoit and his men to come and share it. The Native Americans brought venison and other good things; there were plenty of wild turkeys roasted; and so they all sat down together to a great dinner, and had a merry time in the wilderness (Montgomery).

Assignment

The following is the Mayflower Compact. In spite of its brevity it remains one of the most important early documents in American history. Why?

In The Name of God, Amen. We, whose names are underwritten, the Loyal Subjects of our dread Sovereign Lord King James, by the Grace of God, of Great Britain, France, and Ireland, King, Defender of the Faith. Having undertaken for the Glory of God, and Advancement of the Christian Faith, and the Honor of our King and Country, a Voyage to plant the first colony in the northern Parts of Virginia; Do by these Presents, solemnly and mutually in the Presence of God and one another, covenant and combine ourselves together into a civil Body Politick, for our better Ordering and Preservation, and Furtherance of the Ends aforesaid; And by Virtue hereof do enact, constitute, and frame, such just and equal Laws, Ordinances, Acts, Constitutions, and Offices, from time to time, as shall be thought most meet and convenient for the general Good of the Colony; unto which we promise all due Submission and Obedience. In WITNESS whereof we have hereunto subscribed our names at Cape Cod the eleventh of November, in the Reign of our Sovereign Lord King James of England, France, and Ireland, the eighteenth and of Scotland, the fifty-fourth. Anno Domini, 1620.

Massasoit and His Warriors, a wood engraving by Alfred Bobbett, c1857.

THE PURITANS: A HOLY EXPERIMENT

The Puritans of Boston, Massachusetts Bay, arriving in 1630, like the Pilgrims, sailed to America to worship God freely. As mentioned, unlike the Pilgrims, the Puritans did not desire to separate themselves from the Church of England but, rather, hoped to reform it. Nonetheless, the later notions of freedom and equality, so precious to later New England patriots, were completely foreign to Puritan leaders. The leaders of the Massachusetts Bay enterprise never intended their colony to be a bastion of freedom and toleration in the New World; rather, they intended it to be a "City on a Hill," a model of Christian felicity and fervency.

Massachusetts Bay was not a democracy; it was an autocracy under the law of the land and the perceived laws of the Bible. This was one of the first efforts to create a new society entirely on the Word of God. The first governor, John Winthrop, believed that it was not the duty of the public officials of the commonwealth to act as the direct representatives of their constituents but rather to act entirely according to the laws of the land and the laws of the Word of God. The will of the people was suspect and even spurious when stacked against the Bible.

Nonetheless, in 1634 the General Court, the ruling body of Massachusetts Bay, under the stated authority of Scripture, adopted a new plan of representation that became a prototype for American representative democracy. Each town was allowed to send representatives to a sort of legislature. This was a new phenomenon, even in British political history.

However, Puritan society was certainly not egalitarian, and several disenchanted Puritans founded other colonies, notably

A puritan hearthstone, photographer unknown, c1906.

Connecticut and Rhode Island. In fact, Roger Williams ironically founded Rhode Island as a religious sanctuary from orthodox Massachusetts Bay Colony!

One final note: Most of us think of Puritans as colorless, unhappy, stuffy, white-collared, black-coated, frowning saints. Nothing could be further from the truth. They were fun-loving, active people whose love of life was surpassed only by their love of God. We will discover that the Puritan civilization was a successful marriage between cultural sonority and Christian devotion.

John Eliot

John Eliot was born in England in 1604. In 1631 he went to New England and was ordained to preach at Roxbury, which was then the frontier. Eliot had a burden for the Native Americans in the area and first began to preach to the Indians in 1646. He published a Bible for them in their native language and also wrote the Bay Psalm Book, the first book to be published in North America. Eliot gave up on any attempts at assimilation with Europeans, and planned towns (14 in all) for Native American converts. Before Eliot died in 1690 he brought many to a saving relationship with Jesus Christ. Eliot's commitment to indigenous missions changed missionary strategies for a generation.

The following is a missionary report that John Eliot sent home to his missionary board:

John Eliot preaching to the Indians, artist unknown, 1856.

To the Right Worshipful the Commissioners under his Majestie's Great-Seal, for Propagation of the Gospel amongst the poor blind Indians in New-England Right Worshipful and Christian Gentlemen:

That brief Tract of the present state of the Indian-Work in my hand, which I did the last year on the sudden present you with when you call'd for such a thing; That falling short of its end, and you calling for a renewal thereof, with opportunity of more time, I shall begin with our last great motion in that Work done this Summer, because that will lead me to begin with the state of the Indians under the hands of my Brethren Mr. Mahew and Mr. Bourn. 1 Upon the 17th day of the 6th month, 1670, there was a Meeting at Maktapog near Sandwich in Plimouth-Pattent, to gather a Church among the Indians: There were present six of the Magistrates, and many Elders, (all of them Messengers of the Churches within that Jurisdiction) in whose presence, in a day of Fasting and Prayer, they making confession of the Truth and Grace of Jesus Christ, did in that solemn Assembly enter into Covenant, to walk together in the Faith and Order of the Gospel; and were accepted and declared to be a Church of Jesus Christ. These Indians being of kin to our Massachuset-Indians who first prayed unto God, conversed with them, and received amongst them the light and love of the Truth; they desired me to write to Mr. Leveredge to teach them: He accepted the Motion: and performed the Work with good success; but afterwards he left that place, and went to Long-Island, and there a godly Brother, named Richard Bourne (who purposed to remove with Mr. Leveredge, but hindered by Divine Providence) undertook the teaching of those Indians, and hath continued in the work with good success to this day; him we ordained Pastor: and one of the Indians, named Jude, should have been ordained Ruling-Elder, but being sick at that time, advice was given that he should be ordained with the first opportunity, as also a Deacon to manage the present Sabbath-Day Collections, and other parts of that Office in their season. The same day

also were they, and such of their Children as were present, baptized. From them we passed over to the Vineyard, where many were added to the Church both men and women, and were baptized all of them, and their Children also with them; we had the Sacrament of the Lords Supper celebrated in the Indian-Church, and many of the English-Church gladly joyned with them; for which cause it was celebrated in both languages. . . . The Ruler [or chief] hath made his Preparatory Confession of Christ, and is approved of, and at the next opportunity is to be received and baptized. I obtained of the General-Court a Grant of a Tract of Land, for the settlement and encouragement of this People; which though as yet it be by some obstructed, yet I hope we shall find some way to accomplish the same. Quanatusset is the last of our Praying-Towns, whose beginnings have received too much discouragement; but yet the Seed is alive: they are frequently with me; the work is at the birth, there doth only want strength to bring forth. The care of this People is committed joyntly to Monatunkanit, and Tuppunkkoowillin, the Teachers of Hassunemeesut, as is abovesaid; and I hope if the Lord continue my life, I shall have a good account to give of that People. Thus, I have briefly touched some of the chiefest of our present Affairs, and commit them to your Prudence, to do with them what you please; committing your Selves, and all your weighty Affairs unto the Guidance and Blessing of the Lord, I rest, Your Worships to serve you in the Service of our Lord Jesus.

— John Eliot
Roxbury, this 20th of the 7th month, 1670

The Landing of William Penn by Jean Leon Gerome Ferris, 1932.

Roger Williams

Another Puritan who was not welcome in Boston was Roger Williams. In fact, lawyer Roger Williams was a Puritan when he came to Plymouth 1630. Nonconformist leanings lured him across the Atlantic to Plymouth in 1631. However, as so often happens, nonconformity breeds its own intolerance, and, to the Massachusetts Bay Colony officials, Williams was too much to bear.

His views on religion and government quickly embroiled him in disputes with the Massachusetts authorities in Salem and Boston. For one thing, he upset the elders by denouncing the Massachusetts Bay charter, which allowed the confiscation of Native American lands without compensation and the punishment of purely religious transgressions by the civil officials. Both of those practices offended Williams' sensibilities.

In 1635 he was expelled from the church and placed under an order of expulsion from the colony. He was granted time to tidy up his affairs, but continued his agitation. Exasperated officials decided to send him back to England, but Williams departed from Massachusetts on his own accord and spent three months living with local Native Americans. In 1636 he and a number of followers established the settlement of Providence on Narragansett Bay, a colony notable for the fact that Native Americans were paid for the title to their lands. Williams founded the first Baptist church in America, but soon withdrew and thereafter referred to himself as a

Roger Williams statue, Providence, R.I.

"seeker," meaning basically a nondenominational Christian in search of spiritual truth.

One of Williams' beliefs had caused particular grief among the authorities. He argued that an individual Christian would know when he was saved, but could not know about the salvation of others. Therefore, it was senseless to require a religious qualification for voting. In essence, Williams was calling for the complete separation of church and state, a position that undercut the authority of the church and civic leaders. Under Williams' influence, Rhode Island became a haven for those who suffered from religious persecution, including Jews and Quakers (www.u-s-history.com).

Assignment

A. In the 17th century the best histories were written by Puritan ministers who saw history as the working out of God's will. Based on the concept of the chosen people of God, America was presented as a Promised Land for God's faithful people. Later historians ridiculed this view of history. However, in a real sense, at least in Puritan New England, this was a fairly accurate appraisal of the motivations of an entire generation of early settlers. Why was it so difficult for later historians to believe that people can be motivated strictly by their faith?

B. By their own admission, New England Puritans saw themselves as intolerant. They felt no obligation to tolerate world views that they perceived as heretical. Was this a correct way to establish an English colony?

OTHER COLONIES

William Penn

King Charles II of England owed a large sum of money to a young Englishman named **William Penn**. The king was not careful with his funds and he spent so much money on himself and his friends that he had none left to pay his just debts. Penn knew this; so he told His Majesty that if he would give him a piece of land in America, he would ask nothing more. Charles was very glad to settle the account so easily. He therefore gave Penn a great territory that is approximately close to what became the state of Pennsylvania.

Penn belonged to a religious society called the Society of Friends; today they are generally spoken of as Quakers. They are a people who try to find out what is right by asking their own hearts. They believe in showing no more signs of respect to one man than to another, and at that time they would not take off their hats even to the king himself.

Penn wanted the land that had been given him here as a place where the Friends, or Quakers, might go and settle. A little later the whole of what is now the state of New Jersey was bought by Penn and other Quakers for the same purpose.

Penn accordingly sent out a number of people who were anxious to settle in Pennsylvania. When William Penn reached America in 1682, he sailed up the broad and beautiful Delaware River for nearly twenty miles. There he stopped and resolved to build a city on its banks. He gave the place the Bible name of Philadelphia, or the City of Brotherly Love, because he hoped that all of its citizens would live together like brothers (Montgomery).

James Oglethorpe

In 1733 James Oglethorpe founded a colony named Georgia in honor of King George II, who gave a piece of land for it, on the seacoast below South Carolina. Georgia was originally known as a haven for English criminals; however, most of them were debtors and that was the worst crime that they had committed.

The Birth of Pennsylvania by Jean Leon Gerome Ferris, 1932 (PD-US).

13 Colonies

It is beyond the scope of this unit to discuss in great depth the founding of all 13 original colonies; however, the following chart gives an overview (from Fenton, New American History).

The Establishment of American Colonies

Colony	Founder	Date	Reasons for Settlement
Virginia	London Company	1607	Profit
Plimouth Plantation	Pilgrims	1620	Religious Freedom
New Hampshire and Maine	John Mason and Ferdinando Gorges	1622	Religious Freedom (from Massachusetts)
Massachusetts	Puritans	1630	Religious Freedom
Connecticut	Massachusetts Colonists	1636	Economic Opportunity
Rhode Island	Roger Williams	1636	Religious Freedom (from Massachusetts)
Maryland	Lord Baltimore	1634	Religious Freedom for Catholics
Delaware	Swedish	1638	Profit
North Carolina	Virginians	1653	Profit
New York	Dutch	1624	Profit
New Jersey	John Berkeley	1664	Profit
South Carolina	Eight Proprietors	1670	Profit
Pennsylvania	William Penn	1681	Religious Freedom for Quakers
Georgia	James Oglethorpe	1733	Refuge for Criminals

One of the most remarkable and bizarre—depending on the reader's perspective—events in early colonial history occurred during May through October 1692. Around Salem Village, Massachusetts, north of Boston, 19 convicted "witches" were hanged and many other suspects were imprisoned in the town of Salem in the Massachusetts Bay Colony. Alarmed by tales told by West Indian slave Tituba, local officials, encouraged by Pastor **Samuel Parris** (my great-great-great-great-grandfather—my middle name is Parris), set up a special court in Salem to try those accused of practicing witchcraft. The list of the accused increased until over 100 people were put in jail. While there could well have been witches among the accused, this whole affair was reflective of the growing concern that the hold of Puritanism was being replaced rapidly by a growing Yankee spirit of commercialism and secularism.

Assignment

Some historians have argued that the Salem Witch Trials were merely a way for threatened orthodox officials to control recalcitrant church members. Others saw it as an internal dispute among economic interests. Still others believed that while there were some excesses, no doubt there truly were witches in Salem. Take a position and argue your case well. You may need to research the event further.

Regardless of the reason the 13 colonies were founded, by the late 17th century most towns along the Atlantic Ocean had become fairly stable and sedentary. As immigration increased, the American character took root and eventually propelled America to a war of independence in 1776.

The witch no. 1. Fanciful representation of the Salem witch trials, lithograph by Joseph E. Baker, 1892 (PD-US).

HISTORICAL DEBATE AND WORLD VIEW

Historiography or historical debate, briefly, is the study of the way that history is written. Believe it or not, history is actually written differently by each generation! For instance, American military history was written much differently by post–Vietnam War era historians than by early 20th-century historians. Another example: One can imagine that Southern historians would have a vastly different view of Reconstruction than Northern historians. Puritanism, as the reader can well imagine, was a particularly controversial topic (this discussion is informed by Gerald N. Grob and George Athan Billias, *Interpretations of American History: Patterns and Perspectives*).

To one group of historians the Puritans were reactionary, religious fanatics. The Puritans were opposed to basic freedoms. Massachusetts was an autocratic theocracy, not a democracy. Therefore, these bigots banished independent-thinking people like Anne Hutchinson and Roger Williams (Grob, p. 27). The net result of this draconian attitude was a stagnation of intellectual thought until the American Revolution (Grob, p. 28). H. L. Mencken wrote in the 1920s that Puritanism was "the haunting fear that someone, somewhere, may be happy." Mencken compared the age of Puritanism to the narrow nativism of the 1920s. Likewise, James Truslow Adams argued that the Puritans were entirely undemocratic. Puritanism suppressed individuality and freedom. No detail of the Puritans' personal conduct was too small to escape influence. "The cut of clothes, the names he bore, the most ordinary social usages, could all be regulated in accordance with the will of God," argued Adams (Grobs, p. 31). Historian Vernon Parrington argued that orthodox Puritanism was a reactionary theology. It "conceived of human nature as inherently evil . . . postulated a divine sovereignty absolute and arbitrary, and projected caste divisions into eternity." To Parrington, Williams and Hutch-inson were heroes whose clear, liberal thinking was anathema to the cold, selfish Puritans.

A second group of historians, however, had a much more sympathetic view of the Puritans. The strict discipline was necessary and entirely appropriate in light of the obstacles that they faced on the "edge of the wilderness." Also, the Puritans were no opponents of progress, education, or science. After all, they founded Harvard College. From this environment of discipline, frugality, and hard work grew the seeds of individual freedom and rights that became the bedrock of the American Revolution. Leading the charge in this direction was the brilliant Perry Miller. Miller evaluated Puritan ideas on their own merit and came to the conclusion that Puritanism was both intellectually stimulating and nurturing of the democratic vision. Miller argued that the first generation of Puritans was imbued with a deep sense of mission. During the second and especially the third generations much of this zeal was lost. Nonetheless, Puritanism deposited a rich and laudable inheritance into American history. A colleague of Perry Miller, Samuel Eliot Morison, argued that the Puritans were intellectual heirs of the Renaissance (which to Morison was good). Morison wrote that Puritanism was "an intellectualized form of Christianity that steered a middle course between a passive acceptance of ecclesiastical authority on the one hand and ignorant emotionalism on the other, [and] stimulated mental activity on the part of those who professed it."

Philosophers and World views

Thomas Hobbes (1588–1679)

Thomas Hobbs by John Michael Wright, c17th century.

Thomas Hobbes was a very important political thinker of the 17th century. His most famous work, *The Leviathan*, provided a view of the state that was far beyond its age. Hobbes began his political theory with an argument that nature is neutral (presaging the Naturalist world view expressed 200 years later). Truth, justice, even reason, are inventions of human civilization for the sake of social convention (Martyn Oliver, *History of Philosophy*). This is the opposite of prevalent 17th-century philosophy, which argued that the absolutes of God's will ensure that there is inherent good possible for every man to obtain. Hobbes argued that there is nothing natural about faith at all—man, left in his "natural" state, is brutish and evil. Religion is, therefore, a sort of tonic that keeps human selfishness under control. Hobbes, as one will see, became a popular philosopher of Hegel and later Marx. The implications of this pessimistic view are obvious: Humans can live under the threat of violent chaos or accept the safety of an autocratic state. There is no middle ground: Humans cannot govern themselves; they are incapable of doing so because they are so selfish and violent.

A passage from *The Leviathan* (of Religion):

Seeing there are no signs nor fruit of religion but in man only, there is no cause to doubt but that the seed of religion is also only in man; and consisteth in some peculiar quality, or at least in some eminent degree thereof, not to be found in other living creatures. And first, it is peculiar to the nature of man to be inquisitive into the causes of the events they see, some more, some less, but all men so much as to be curious in the search of the causes of their own good and evil fortune. Secondly, upon the sight of anything that hath a beginning, to think also it had a cause which determined the same to begin then when it did, rather than sooner or later.

Thirdly, whereas there is no other felicity of beasts but the enjoying of their quotidian food, ease, and lusts; as having little or no foresight of the time to come for want of observation and memory of the order, consequence, and dependence of the things they see; man observeth how one event hath been produced by another, and remembereth in them antecedence and consequence; and when he cannot assure himself of the true causes of things (for the causes of good and evil fortune for the most part are invisible), he supposes causes of them, either such as his own fancy suggesteth, or trusteth to the authority of other men such as he thinks to be his friends and wiser than himself. The two first make anxiety. For being assured that there be causes of all things that have arrived hitherto, or shall arrive hereafter, it is impossible for a man, who continually endeavoureth to secure himself against the evil he fears, and procure the good he desireth, not to be in a perpetual solicitude of the time to come; so that every man, especially those that are overprovident, are in an estate like to that of Prometheus. For as Prometheus (which, interpreted, is the prudent man) was bound to the hill Caucasus, a place of large prospect, where an eagle, feeding on his liver, devoured in the day as much as was repaired in the night: so that man, which looks too far before him in the care of future time, hath his heart all the day long gnawed on by fear of death, poverty, or other calamity; and has no repose, nor pause of his anxiety, but in sleep.

This perpetual fear, always accompanying mankind in the ignorance of causes, as it were in the dark, must needs have for object something.

The frontispiece of the book *Leviathan* by Thomas Hobbes, 1651 (PD-US).

And therefore when there is nothing to be seen, there is nothing to accuse either of their good or evil fortune but some power or agent invisible: in which sense perhaps it was that some of the old poets said that the gods were at first created by human fear: which, spoken of the gods (that is to say, of the many gods of the Gentiles), is very true. But the acknowledging of one God eternal, infinite, and omnipotent may more easily be derived from the desire men have to know the causes of natural bodies, and their several virtues and operations, than from the fear of what was to befall them in time to come. For he that, from any effect he seeth come to pass, should reason to the next and immediate cause thereof, and from thence to the cause of that cause, and plunge himself profoundly in the pursuit of causes, shall at last come to this, that there must be (as even the heathen philosophers confessed) one First Mover; that is, a first and an eternal cause of all things; which is that which men mean by the name of God: and all this without thought of their fortune, the solicitude whereof

both inclines to fear and hinders them from the search of the causes of other things; and thereby gives occasion of feigning of as many gods as there be men that feign them.

And for the matter, or substance, of the invisible agents, so fancied, they could not by natural cogitation fall upon any other concept but that it was the same with that of the soul of man; and that the soul of man was of the same substance with that which appeareth in a dream to one that sleepeth; or in a looking-glass to one that is awake; which, men not knowing that such apparitions are nothing else but creatures of the fancy, think to be real and external substances, and therefore call them ghosts; as the Latins called them imagines and umbrae and thought them spirits (that is, thin aerial bodies), and those invisible agents, which they feared, to be like them, save that they appear and vanish when they please. But the opinion that such spirits were incorporeal, or immaterial, could never enter into the mind of any man by nature; because, though men may put together words of contradictory signification, as spirit and incorporeal, yet they can never have the imagination of anything answering to them: and therefore, men that by their own meditation arrive to the acknowledgment of one infinite, omnipotent, and eternal God choose rather to confess He is incomprehensible and above their understanding than to define His nature by spirit incorporeal, and then confess their definition to be unintelligible: or if they give him such a title, it is not dogmatically, with intention to make the Divine Nature understood, but piously, to honour Him with attributes of significations as remote as they can from the grossness of bodies visible.

Then, for the way by which they think these invisible agents wrought their effects; that is to say, what immediate causes they used in bringing things to pass, men that know not what it is that we call causing (that is, almost all men) have no other rule to guess by but by observing and remembering what they have seen to precede the like effect at some other time, or times before, without seeing between the antecedent and subsequent event any dependence or connexion at all: and therefore from the like things past, they expect the like things to come; and hope for good or evil luck, superstitiously, from things that have no part at all in the causing of it: as the Athenians did for their war at Lepanto demand another Phormio; the Pompeian faction for their war in Africa, another Scipio; and others have done in diverse other occasions since. In like manner they attribute their fortune to a stander by, to a lucky or unlucky place, to words spoken, especially if the name of God be amongst them, as charming, and conjuring (the liturgy of witches); insomuch as to believe they have power to turn a stone into bread, bread into a man, or anything into anything. Thirdly, for the worship which naturally men exhibit to powers invisible, it can be no other but such expressions of their reverence as they would use towards men; gifts, petitions, thanks, submission of body, considerate addresses, sober behaviour, premeditated words, swearing (that is, assuring one another of their promises), by invoking them. Beyond that, reason suggesteth nothing, but leaves them either to rest there, or for further ceremonies to rely on those they believe to be wiser than themselves. Lastly, concerning how these invisible powers declare to men the things which shall hereafter come to pass, especially concerning their good or evil fortune in general, or good or ill success in any particular undertaking, men are naturally at a stand; save that using to conjecture of the time to come by the time past, they are very apt, not only to take casual things, after one or two encounters, for prognostics of the like encounter ever after, but also to believe the like prognostics from other men of whom they have once conceived a good opinion.

Portrait of René Descartes by Frans Hal, c1964 (PD-US).

René Descartes (1596–1650)

Some scholars argue that Descartes is the founding father of modern philosophy. His ideas are the first and most organized arguments in favor of a world view which postulates that human beings are autonomous that rational beings rather than beings whose fate is in the hands of an absolute being (i.e., God). Descartes is most famous for his dictum "I think, therefore I am." As Martyn Oliver states, "For Descartes, human rationality is founded upon a distinction between mind and body (often referred to in philosophy as mind-body dualism or Cartesian dualism). The mind, or the realm of the intellect, must contain innate ideas which are prior to experience, because it is experience which causes the demons of doubt." The whole dialogue of experience vs. rationalism vs. theism was joined at this point and has not ended even today.

A passage from *Discourse on the Method of Rightly Conducting the Reason and Seeking for Truth in the Sciences* (1637):

> I formed for myself a code of morals for the time being which did not consist of more than three or four maxims, which maxims I should like to enumerate to you. The first was to obey the laws and customs of my country, adhering constantly to the religion in which by God's grace I had been instructed since my childhood, and in all other things directing my conduct by opinions the most moderate in nature, and the farthest removed from excess in all those which are commonly received and acted on by the most judicious of those with whom I might come in contact. For since I began to count my own opinions as naught, because I desired to place all under examination, I was convinced that I could not do better than follow those held by people on whose judgment reliance could be placed. And although such persons may possibly exist amongst the Persians and Chinese as well as amongst ourselves, it seemed to me that it was most expedient to bring my conduct into harmony with the ideas of those with whom I should have to live; and that, in order to ascertain that these were their real opinions, I should observe what they did rather than what they said, not only because in the corrupt state of our manners there are few people who desire to say all that they believe, but also because many are themselves ignorant of their beliefs. For since the act of thought by which we believe a thing

is different from that by which we know that we believe it, the one often exists without the other. And amongst many opinions all equally received, I chose only the most moderate, both because these are always most suited for putting into practice, and probably the best (for all excess has a tendency to be bad), and also because I should have in a less degree turned aside from the right path, supposing that I was wrong, than if, having chosen an extreme course, I found that I had chosen amiss. I also made a point of counting as excess all the engagements by means of which we limit in some degree our liberty. Not that I hold in low esteem those laws which, in order to remedy the inconstancy of feeble souls, permit, when we have a good object in our view, that certain vows be taken, or contracts made, which oblige us to carry out that object. This sanction is even given for security in commerce where designs are wholly indifferent. But because I saw nothing in all the world remaining constant, and because for my own part I promised myself gradually to get my judgments to grow better and never to grow worse, I should have thought that I had committed a serious sin against commonsense if, because I approved of something at one time, I was obliged to regard it similarly at a later time, after it had possibly ceased to meet my approval, or after I had ceased to regard it in a favorable light. My second maxim was that of being as firm and resolute in my actions as I could be, and not to follow less faithfully opinions the most dubious, when my mind was once made up regarding them, than if these had been beyond doubt. In this I should be following the example of travelers, who, finding themselves lost in a forest, know that they ought not to wander first to one side and then to the other, nor, still less, to stop in one place, but understand that they should continue to walk as straight as they can in one direction, not diverging for any slight reason, even though it was possibly chance alone that first determined them in their choice. By this means if they do not go exactly where they wish, they will at least arrive somewhere at the end, where probably they will be better off than in the middle of a forest. And thus since often enough in the actions of life no delay is permissible, it is very certain that, when it is beyond our power to discern the opinions which carry most truth, we should follow the most probable; and even although we notice no greater probability in the one opinion than in the other, we at least should make up our minds to follow a particular one and afterwards consider it as no longer doubtful in its relationship to practice, but as very true and very certain, inasmuch as the reason, which caused us to determine upon it is known to be so. And henceforward this principle was sufficient to deliver me from all the penitence and remorse which usually affect the mind and agitate the conscience of those weak and vacillating creatures who allow themselves to keep changing their procedure, and practice as good, things which they afterwards judge to be evil.

John Locke (1632–1704)

John Locke, artist and date unknown (PD-US).

John Locke developed theories of human rationalism that emphasized the role of human experience in the pursuit of knowledge and truth. Many of Locke's political theories influenced American Revolutionary thinkers. Descartes argued that knowledge, as opposed to mere opinion, stems from a set of distinct ideas contained innately in the psyche. Locke, on the other hand, argued that knowledge is not developed prior to experience. To Locke, the mind is a blank sheet of paper upon which experience is written. Insight and understanding are not based on anything inherent in the human soul or spirit. Rather, understanding occurs naturally and systematically through experience. The senses, then, were critical to Locke. Locke (right) also took issue with Hobbes: Mankind is not inherently bad; he is naturally good. Only bad experiences make bad people. Locke believed that the best government is the one that rules the least. The best government is a contract between the people and its rulers. There are, finally, certain unalienable rights that cannot be taken away from people.

Did the Puritans and Virginia settlers really read Locke, Descartes, and Hobbes? Absolutely! If we examine, the library of early Puritan leader Cotton Mather, we will find books from all three authors. Contrary to popular opinion, the Puritans were intellectuals who read and believed the Bible, but they also read significant philosophical works. They were not trying to escape the world: they were trying to change the world for Christ.

A passage from *Of Human Reason* (1689):

Or not contrary to reason, if revealed, are matters of faith; and must carry it against probable conjectures of reason. But since God, in giving us the light of reason, has not thereby tied up his own hands from affording us, when he thinks fit, the light of revelation in any of those matters wherein our natural faculties are able to give a probable determination; revelation, where God has been pleased to give it, must carry it against the probable conjectures of reason. Because the mind not being certain of the truth of that it does not evidently know, but only yielding to the probability that appears in it, is bound to give up its assent to such a testimony which, it is satisfied, comes from one who cannot err, and will not deceive. But yet, it still belongs to reason to judge of the truth of its being a revelation, and of the signification of the words wherein it is delivered. Indeed, if anything shall be thought revelation which is contrary to the plain principles of reason, and the evident knowledge the mind has of its own clear and distinct ideas; there reason must be hearkened to, as to a matter within its province. Since a man can never have so certain a knowledge that a proposition which contradicts the clear principles and evidence of his own knowledge was

divinely revealed, or that he understands the words rightly wherein it is delivered, as he has that the contrary is true, and so is bound to consider and judge of it as a matter of reason, and not swallow it, without examination, as a matter of faith. Revelation in matters where reason cannot judge, or but probably, ought to be hearkened to. First, whatever proposition is revealed, of whose truth our mind, by its natural faculties and notions, cannot judge, that is purely matter of faith, and above reason. Secondly, all propositions whereof the mind, by the use of its natural faculties, can come to determine and judge, from naturally acquired ideas, are matter of reason; with this difference still, that, in those concerning which it has but an uncertain evidence, and so is persuaded of their truth only upon probable grounds, which still admit a possibility of the contrary to be true, without doing violence to the certain evidence of its own knowledge, and overturning the principles of all reason; in such probable propositions, I say, an evident revelation ought to determine our assent, even against probability. For where the principles of reason have not evidenced a proposition to be certainly true or false, there clear revelation, as another principle of truth and ground of assent, may determine; and so it may be matter of faith, and be also above reason. Because reason, in that particular matter, being able to reach no higher than probability, faith gave the determination where reason came short; and revelation discovered on which side the truth lay.

Assignment

A. Review the historical debate about Puritanism and discuss which theory you prefer and why.

B. Contrast Hobbes' view of power with biblical views of power.

C. Decartes and Locke completely disagreed about human reasoning. Explain.

Photo shows the children's colonial costume pageant at the dedication of the William J. Gaynor Park in New York City, Bain Collection, 1913.

Chapter 4

COLONIAL LIFE

First Thoughts . . .

You will learn what it meant to be a colonial woman. You will understand how the Harvard University of today evolved from the Harvard University of 1636, and you will predict how evangelical education will change in the next century. Next, can you imagine being in one of the great Jonathan Edwards revivals? On the edge of the dark wilderness, with unfriendly Native Americans lurking in the forest, you are sitting on an uncomfortable church bench listening to Edwards' interminably long sermon being read in a monotone. Suddenly, in that instance, the Holy Spirit descends and all of world history changes, in the First Great Awakening. Now, too, for the first time, you will analyze 17th-century philosophers whose pens created most of the world views that battled in this important period of American colonial history.

Chapter Learning Objectives . . .

Chapter 4 will explore a more general topic, American colonial women who worked hard and had no rights whatsoever, but in no way felt gender conflict. We want you to meet Jonathan Edwards, who would begin one of the great revivals of history, and, as some historians argue, the American Revolution. Next, we want to introduce three more seminal philosophers whose influences transformed world history through the pens of Jefferson and Adams. Finally, using Harvard as a case study, we will invite you to analyze the beginning of the American university, and to speculate upon its future.

As a result of this chapter study you should be able to:

1. Imagine what it was like to be a colonial woman.

2. Categorize colonial evangelical families and reframe the same categories in contemporary American families.

3. Evaluate a contemporary religious problem that was quite evident in the First Great Awakening too.

4. Outline five events that moved the evangelical university that was Harvard University in 1636 to Harvard University in 2010.

5. Analyze the world views of influential philosophers Paine, Descartes, and Burke.

6. Reconstruct the life of an American colonist living in the early 18th century.

COLONIAL WOMEN

Roles evolved in colonial America from necessity more than convention. There was too much work to do so no one really talked about who did what.

Nonetheless, there were some major differences. Women sewed, cooked, cared for domestic animals, and made many houshold necessities such as soap and candles. But women also helped in the planting and sowing during stressful growing seasons. The demarcation between roles was rarely, if ever, crossed by men—so women regularly helped men with their work and men almost never helped women with theirs!

Women were considered to be the "weaker vessels," but clearly that was an oxymoron! They could not vote, hold public office, or participate in legal matters on their own behalf, and opportunities for them outside the home were frequently limited. Women were expected to defer to their husbands and be obedient to them without question. Husbands, in turn, were expected to protect their wives against all threats, even at the cost of their own lives if necessary.

Since women were in short supply in the colonies, as indeed was all labor, they tended to be more highly valued than in Europe. The wife was an essential component of the nuclear family, and without a strong and productive wife a family would struggle to survive. A total of 147 women came to Virginia between 1620 and 1622. By 1624, fewer than 18 percent, 230 of the 1,240, Europeans were adult women (Brown 1996, page 82). The year 1691 still found a 3:2 ratio, and the gap between the numbers of men and women didn't close until the early 18th century.

The leadership in the family practice of religion in New England was often taken by the wife. It was the mother who brought up the children to be good Christians, and the mother who often homeschooled them to read so they could study the Bible.

Despite the traditional restrictions on colonial women, many examples can be found indicating that women were often granted legal and economic rights and were allowed to pursue businesses. Many women were more than mere housewives, and their responsibilities were important and often highly valued in colonial society. Although women in colonial America were by no means considered "equal" to men, they were as a rule probably as well off as women anywhere in the world, and in general probably better off (Henry J. Sage).

Shenandoah Valley, William Louis Sonntag, Sr., 1860 (PD-US).

Colonial houses - fireside fancier by Wallace Nutting, 1913.

Assignment

A. Historian Philip Greven studies in depth the American colonial family. He identifies three distinct Protestant temperaments prevailing among Americans at the time: the Evangelical (the Christian believer), the Moderate (somewhat religious but with no open conversion experience), and the General (secular). Now your job is to identify today's American families. What three categories would you offer?

1. _____

2. _____

3. _____

B. My favorite American poet, Anne Bradstreet, was a colonial homeschooling mom with eight children who lived very close to the bridge I took across from Harvard Yard to visit my brother at Harvard Business School (on the Charles River). One insightful poem by Anne Bradstreet reminds us of how precarious life was then. She left it in a drawer to be found after her death should she not survive childbirth. The last stanza leaves this request:

And if by chance to thine eyes shall bring this verse,
With some sad sighs honor my absent hearse;
And kiss this paper for thy love's dear sake,
Who with salt tears this last farewell did take.

Even after colonial settlers became established in America, a woman's daily life was still difficult. Typically she would be expected to spin, sew, preserve food, cook, clean, and perhaps raise chickens and geese while caring for her children. Families tended to be large; Anne Bradstreet bore eight children, but many women had more.

Life was fragile and childbearing dangerous. The term "now-wife" came to refer to a man's present wife as compared to those whom he had previously lost. Many children didn't survive to adulthood. An early gravestone in Vermont displays symbolic faces of 13 infants and one older child whom one woman lost before her own death at age 40. As I think about these women, I find myself first wondering how a woman could carry such a load of work and at the same time bear so much loss. Perhaps the hard daily labor necessary to survive helped these women bear their grief. The truth is, many women died before their 30th birthday. Many men were married two or three times (www.historyofquilts.com).

Imagine that you are a mother living on the edge of the colonial American wilderness. Write a letter to your family in England explaining to them what life is like.

THE FIRST GREAT AWAKENING

The **First Great Awakening** was a watershed event in the life of the American people. Before it was over, it had swept the colonies of the eastern seaboard, transforming the social and religious life of the land. Although the name is slightly misleading—the Great Awakening was not one continuous revival, but several revivals in a variety of locations—it says a great deal about the state of religion in the colonies.

Neither the Anglicans who came to dominate religious life in Virginia after royal control was established over Jamestown, nor the Puritans in Massachusetts Bay, were terribly successful in maintaining, much less increasing, religious fervency among their converts. The small farms were spread out into the wilderness, making both communication and church discipline difficult. Because people often lived great distances from a parish church, membership and participation suffered. In addition, on the frontier concern for theological issues was overshadowed by the concern for survival and wresting a living from a hard and difficult land. Because the individual was largely on his own, and depended on himself for survival, authoritarian structures of any sort—be they governmental or ecclesiastical—met with great resistance. As a result, by the second and third generations, the vast majority of the population was outside the membership of the church. Indeed, many saw themselves outside the authority of the Lord!

Revival began in New England. One of the principal figures in the Great Awakening was Jonathan Edwards. Edwards preached his effective "Sinners in the Hands of an

Engraving showing the enthusiasm displayed by evangelical Methodist minister George Whitefield, 1739.

Angry God" sermon in which he used the image of a spider dangling by a web over a hot fire to describe the human predicament. In spite of the fact that he showed virtually no emotion, his audience broke out in repentant tears. There was no altar call, per se, but there were nonetheless many conversions.

Another principal figure in the Awakening was **George Whitefield**. Known as the "Great Itinerant," Whitefield was an associate of John Wesley in England. He had a loud voice, and it is said one conversion occurred three miles from where he was preaching. He was a dramatic man who, it was said, could pronounce the word "Mesopotamia" in such a way that it could melt an audience. He would always say it at least once in a sermon, no matter the topic.

Whitefield traveled up and down the eastern seaboard carrying the Awakening with him, and he offered a new quality to the prevailing view of how one obtains citizenship in the kingdom of God. The key test of one's election, Whitefield asserted, was whether one had had an emotional experience of conversion.

One historian explains, "In the North, where the Awakening began, revival tended to be an urban phenomenon where flamboyant and highly emotional preaching appeared in Puritan churches. The compromises of the **Half-Way covenant** were swept aside, and the notion of the church as a body of saints was reclaimed. Standards of membership were increased, and yet, membership still grew. In the South, the Great Awakening was more of a frontier phenomenon than was the case in the Middle Colonies or New England. In areas that were nominally Anglican (the Tide-water) it had little impact. In part this was because the residents of the Tidewater had just enough religion to inoculate them from catching the real thing, and also because authorities were better able to enforce the established church and protect it from the itinerant evangelists. But in the Piedmont and mountains of Virginia and North Carolina the revival had a wide open field. These areas were populated by less prosperous settlers from the Tidewater moving beyond the fall line, and by Scotch-Irish and Germans coming down the Shenandoah Valley. The result was a population that had few ties to the Anglican establishment" (Beard).

Assignment

A. Many Christians in the Great Awakening, as in other periods, felt threatened by science. With the publication of Isaac Newton's *Principia Mathematica* in the 17th century, traditional religious formulations had been under pressure. That is because implicit in the work of Newton and others was the assumption that human beings have the ability to discover the secrets of the universe and thereby exert some control over their own destiny. If human beings could in fact think the thoughts of God—if they could discover and read the blueprints whereby God had made and ordered the world—there would be a lessening of the gulf between God and man. The result was a growing emphasis on man and his morality, with religion becoming more rational and less emotional. Discuss contemporary problems that religion has with science (e.g., stem cell research).

B. One concern of Jonathan Edwards and others was that American Christianity would become existential and not confessional. In other words, faith would be centered on emotion and not on the Word of God. In light of the modern "seeker" movement, state your views of this phenomenon.

THE AMERICAN UNIVERSITY: AN ESSAY

BY DR. STOBAUGH

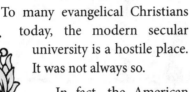

To many evangelical Christians today, the modern secular university is a hostile place. It was not always so.

In fact, the American university was built solidly on evangelical principles. An early brochure, published in 1643, stated that the purpose of Harvard University (the oldest American university) was "To advance Learning and perpetuate it to Posterity; dreading to leave an illiterate Ministry to the Churches." In fact, most of the U.S. universities founded before the 20th century had a strongly religious, usually Protestant Evangelical Christian character. Yale, Princeton, Chicago, Stanford, Duke, William and Mary, Boston University, Michigan, and the University of California had a decidedly evangelical Christian character in the early years of their existence and abandoned it in the 20th century. By the 1920s, the American university had stepped completely back from its evangelical roots. This was true of every American university founded in the first 200 years of our existence.

Readers would be surprised to see how evangelical early universities were. They had pastors as presidents. These men closely tied the identity of their university to a strong Christian world view. The core curriculum included Bible courses and Christian theology. These were mandatory Bible courses. All American universities insisted on a doctrinally sound content for sensitive courses and often required that faculty be born-again Christians! Imagine this:

the famous historian Frederick Jackson Turner was refused a professorship at Princeton because he was a Unitarian! Chapel attendance was required at Harvard and Yale! It is more than coincidental that the architects who designed early universities designed them to look like churches. At the University of Pittsburgh, for instance, the most prominent building on campus is the Cathedral of Learning (J. A. Appleyard, SJ, www.bc.edu).

Universities were founded because early Americans earnestly believed that American society should be governed by evangelical Christian people. They believed that American industry should be run by evangelical Christian entrepreneurs. They believed that American culture should be created by evangelical Christians. The desire to assure that America would be ruled by an evangelical elite was no doubt the primary reason that American universities were founded from 1636 to 1800.

The marriage of spiritual maturity and elite education is a potent combination and to a large degree assured the success of the American experiment. Its divorce may presage its demise.

As early as 1800 evangelicals began to lose the American university. Religious commitment was perceived as psychological phenomenon, and moved to the fringes of university life. In fact, religious commitment was perceived as a voluntary activity, an aberration rather than an expressed purpose of the institution. Christianity was taught along with other religious expressions in religious departments. Christian ministry was relegated to insignificant graduate schools or dropped altogether.

By the 1920s the university was not even loosely a Christian institution. Religion in the university and in public life was to be relegated to the private experience. So-called academic freedom became a sacrosanct concept and precluded anything that smacked of religiosity—especially old-time religion that evangelicals so enthusiastically

Statue at Harvard University. Photo by Alain Edouard (CC BY-SA 3.0).

embraced. Religion was represented on campus in sanitary denominational ministries and token chapel ministries (that were hardly more than counseling centers). The separation has been so thorough that when the *New York Times'* reporter Ari Goldman spent a year at Harvard Divinity School he was pleased to find, after all, God at Harvard! (Ari L. Goldman, *The Search for God at Harvard*. NY: Random House, 1991).

At the same time, with growing persecution, evangelicals abandoned the secular university in earnest and founded their own universities. This whole process accelerated after the Scopes Trial in the 1920s.

To a large degree, then, the American university abandoned the evangelical and the evangelical abandoned the American university.

This created a crisis in the American university and in the evangelical community. The secular American university compromised its "soul" for naturalistic positivism (to use George Marsden's terminology); evangelicalism compromised its epistemological hegemony for ontological supremacy. In other words, the secular university became a sort of academic hothouse for rationalism. Evangelicals abandoned the secular university and, until recently, more or less compromised their academic base. Evangelicals even founded their own universities, but they were poor academic substitutes for secular offerings. That is changing in our present-day culture.

The true crisis of the university lies not in financial exigencies, political assaults from the left or right, or the myopia of modern life; it lies in the crisis of confidence within the university itself about its abiding nature/purpose (Alven Neiman, *Review of Politics*, Winter 1994). The university, as it were, is having an Ericksonian self-identity crisis. It is a modern crisis fairly gained by embracing the spirits of the age. The university has lost something, but like the main character in Camus's *The Stranger*, it (he) has lost its way, lost its identity, but he does not quite know where he has come, how he got where he is, or where he is to go from here. In any event, it is a quest for an existential goal—not a Judeo-Christian one.

Evangelicals are wandering in the wilderness—but they have a goal. The secular university is wandering in the wilderness with no goal. The difference is that evangelicals are on a journey; the secular university is just plain lost with no destination.

This author resonates with John Henry Newman's *The Idea of a University Defined and Illustrated* (1852). Newman's

Engraving of Harvard College by Paul Revere, 1767 (PD-US).

Idea of a University grew out of his own struggle with the rise of scientific learning—a struggle that continues today. Newman, it seems to me, was a 19th-century evangelical trying to make sense of his culture. Most American universities are full of intellectuals coming to grips with their Christianity.

In the modern secular university there is only one viewpoint that is deemed legitimate: the conviction of uniform toleration! The net result is that people are forced to choose between their beliefs (epistemology) and their education (cosmology). People are forced to give up convictions regarding what they believe to be true and right if their views appear remotely intolerant. Thus, if an evangelical believes that homosexuality is a sinful lifestyle because his world-view framework, based on the truth of the Word of God, demands that he believe it, his belief cannot be militated or compromised by circumstances or exigencies.

The problem, according to S. D. Gaede, author of *When Tolerance Is No Virtue* (Downers Grove, IL: Inter Varsity Press, 1993) is that the university asks a question it has no right to ask and then offers no satisfactory answer: What is truth? The American secular university does not have a clue. Many secular scholars know it and they conclude that there is no truth. They have lost confidence in truth searching and have come to the conclusion that truth is unattainable. Universities conclude that holding to a plurality of truths and tolerating them is virtuous. This author, however, agrees with G. K. Chesterton, who argued, "Tolerance is the virtue of a man without conviction."

Assignment

Outline five events that moved the evangelical Harvard University of 1636 to secular Harvard University of 2010.

PHILOSOPHERS AND WORLD VIEWS

Thomas Paine (1737–1809)

It is remarkable that such a mediocre, morally reprehensible, and uneducated man like Thomas Paine could have such an impact on world history. He was a loser most of his life, but during the beginning stages of the American Revolution he profoundly affected the cause of liberty. A staunch Locke adherent, Paine enthusiastically advanced the notion that mankind had certain natural rights that could not be abrogated by any civil authority. Son of a Quaker, Paine was intensely anti-slavery. Unfortunately, though, he did not accept his parents' faith and was one of the earliest outspoken agnostics (in an age when that was unheard of). Paine openly advocated revolution (as opposed to the arguments of Edmund Burke) as a necessary and desirable way to bring down unjust governments. "It is impossible that such governments as have hitherto existed in the world could have commenced by any other means than a total violation of every principle sacred and moral." The state is a necessary evil whose only function was to protect the rights of the individual. In summary, what strikes the reader immediately is the superficiality of Paine's arguments. Nonetheless, it is difficult to find a more influential 18th-century philosopher. The following is a discussion of the virtues of self-government from Paine's most influential pamphlet "Common Sense."

Mankind being originally equals in the order of creation, the equality could only be destroyed by some subsequent circumstance; the distinctions of rich, and poor, may in a great measure be accounted for, and that without having recourse to the harsh, ill-sounding names of oppression and avarice. Oppression is often the consequence, but seldom or never the means of riches; and though avarice will preserve a man from being necessitously poor, it generally makes him too timorous to be wealthy.

But there is another and greater distinction for

Thomas Paine by Auguste Millière, 1880.

which no truly natural or religious reason can be assigned, and that is, the distinction of men into KINGS and SUBJECTS. Male and female are the distinctions of nature, good and bad the distinctions of heaven; but how a race of men came into the world so exalted above the rest, and distinguished like some new species, is worth enquiring into, and whether they are the means of happiness or of misery to mankind.

In the early ages of the world, according to the scripture chronology, there were no kings; the consequence of which was there were no wars; it is the pride of kings which throw mankind into confusion. Holland without a king hath enjoyed more

peace for this last century than any of the monarchial governments in Europe. Antiquity favors the same remark; for the quiet and rural lives of the first patriarchs hath a happy something in them, which vanishes away when we come to the history of Jewish royalty.

Government by kings was first introduced into the world by the Heathens, from whom the children of Israel copied the custom. It was the most prosperous invention the Devil ever set on foot for the promotion of idolatry. The Heathens paid divine honors to their deceased kings, and the Christian world hath improved on the plan by doing the same to their living ones. How impious is the title of sacred majesty applied to a worm, who in the midst of his splendor is crumbling into dust. As the exalting one man so greatly above the rest cannot be justified on the equal rights of nature, so neither can it be defended on the authority of scripture; for the will of the Almighty, as declared by Gideon and the prophet Samuel, expressly disapproves of government by kings. All anti-monarchial parts of scripture have been very smoothly glossed over in monarchial governments, but they undoubtedly merit the attention of countries which have their governments yet to form. "Render unto Caesar the things which are Caesar's" is the scriptural doctrine of courts, yet it is no support of monarchial government, for the Jews at that time were without a king, and in a state of vassalage to the Romans.

Near three thousand years passed away from the Mosaic account of the creation, till the Jews under a national delusion requested a king. Till then their form of government (except in extraordinary cases, where the Almighty interposed) was a kind of republic administered by a judge and the elders of the tribes. Kings they had none, and it was held sinful to acknowledge any being under that title but the Lord of Hosts. And when a man seriously reflects on the idolatrous homage which is paid to the persons of Kings, he need not wonder, that the Almighty, ever jealous of his honor, should disapprove of a form of government which so impiously invades the prerogative of heaven.

Jean-Jacques Rousseau (1712–1778)

Rousseau (below, PD-US), for my money, was the Friedrich Nietzsche of his day. Like Nietzsche, Rousseau wrote in a radical vein. He explored the darker side of the Age of Reason or Enlightenment (like Sartre, et al., did 200 years later). He was the first philosopher to do so without evoking Christian faith as a criticism. More than this impulse, however, was Rousseau's strong Romanticism (advanced in later years by Emerson and Thoreau). "Man was born free, and he is everywhere in chains" was the way Rousseau's most famous book, *Social Contract*, began. People did not have freedom merely by giving in to force or control, as Hobbes implied. Freedom came by reverting to what Rousseau called "a state of nature." This state of nature would be mankind in nature before he embraced civil society. It would be safe to say that Jean-Jacques Rousseau's position was the opposite of that taken by Edmund Burke.

A passage from *Social Contract*:

The passage from the state of nature to the civil state produces a very remarkable change in man, by substituting justice for instinct in his conduct, and giving his actions the morality they had formerly lacked. Then only, when the voice of duty takes the place of physical impulses and right of appetite, does man, who so far had considered only himself, find that he is forced to act on different principles, and to consult his reason before listening to his inclinations. Although, in this state, he deprives himself of some advantages which he got from nature, he gains in return others so great, his faculties are so stimulated and developed, his ideas so extended, his feelings so ennobled, and his whole soul so uplifted, that, did not the abuses of this new condition often degrade him below that which he left, he would be bound to

Statue of Rousseau in Geneva.

bless continually the happy moment which took him from it forever, and, instead of a stupid and unimaginative animal, made him an intelligent being and a man.

Let us draw up the whole account in terms easily commensurable. What man loses by the social contract is his natural liberty and an unlimited right to everything he tries to get and succeeds in getting; what he gains is civil liberty and the proprietorship of all he possesses. If we are to avoid mistake in weighing one against the other, we must clearly distinguish natural liberty, which is bounded only by the strength of the individual, from civil liberty, which is limited by the general will; and possession, which is merely the effect of force or the right of the first occupier, from property, which can be founded only on a positive title. We might, over and above all this, add, to what man acquires in the civil state, moral liberty, which alone makes him truly master of himself; for the mere impulse of appetite is slavery, while obedience to a law which we prescribe to ourselves is liberty. But I have already said too much on this head, and the philosophical meaning of the word liberty does not now concern us.

Professor Martyn Oliver echoes the concerns of a generation of philosophical critics:

Rousseau's philosophy is filled with paradoxes, but any inconsistency or apparent contradiction is no oversight. Throughout his works Rousseau juggles concepts of "the particular" and "the universal." For Rousseau these paradoxes are necessary ingredients of modern thought and progress requires us to reconcile them. Critics have been keen to point out the dangers of this philosophy. In particular, commentators have noted the danger of arbitrary definitions of the general will, for instance, those leaders who claim to express the general will and believe themselves justified in enforcing it with coercion. Nonetheless, the problem of reconciling liberty and equality continues to overwhelm political philosophy.

Edmund Burke (1729–1797)

Most of us will, ironically, find the writings of Edmund Burke (below, PD-Art) to be far more appealing than those of some of our early Founding Fathers; however, Burke was an Englishman intensely opposed to the American efforts at revolution. Burke criticized revolutions as being too abstract and idealistic. He was a strong advocate of "real politics." Burke argued that relations between people were purely artificial and political contracts were established on tradition (e.g., the Word of God) and custom—not on humanistic notions of human rights. "Government is not made in virtue of natural rights," he was fond of saying, "which may exist in total independence of it; and exist in much greater clearness, and in a much greater degree of abstract perfection: but their abstract perfection is their practical defeat" (Oliver, *History of Philosophy*, p. 98). Burke was far more comfortable with pragmatism than he was with idealism. Better to trust in British common law, for instance, than the tyranny of man-made natural laws that invited a form of nihilism that infamously shadowed the later French Revolution.

The following are several quotes from Burke:

Parliament is not a congress of ambassadors from different and hostile interests; which interests each must maintain, as an agent and advocate, against other agents and advocates; but parliament is a deliberative assembly of one nation, with one interest, that of the whole; where, not local purposes, not local prejudices ought to guide, but the general good, resulting from the general reason of the whole. You choose a member indeed; but when you have chosen him, he is not a member of Bristol, but he is a member of

Statue of Edmund Burke in Washington, DC (CC BY-SA 3.0).

'A literary party at Sir Joshua Reynolds'. Burke is in the center with his back toward the artist (D. GeorgeThompson, 1851 (PD-US).

All government, indeed every human benefit and enjoyment, every virtue, and every prudent act, is founded on compromise and barter we give and take; we remit some rights, that we may enjoy others (speech, "Conciliation with America," 1775).

The government is a juggling confederacy of a few to cheat the prince and enslave the people (*A Vindication of Natural Society*, 1756).

It is one of the finest problems in legislation, what the state ought to take upon itself to direct and what it ought to leave, with as little interference as possible, to individual discretion (1795).

Popular remedies must be quick and sharp, or they are very ineffectual (1774).

parliament . . . Your representative owes you, not his industry only, but his judgment; and he betrays instead of serving you if he sacrifices it to your opinion (speech to the Electors of Bristol, November 3, 1774).

The objects of society are of the greatest possible complexity (*Reflections on the Revolution in France*, 1790).

Assignment

A. Restate Professor Oliver's concern in your own words. In what ways does the quoted passage from *Social Contract* manifest the same inconsistencies that concern Professor Oliver?

B. While Paine was not a professing Christian, he nonetheless used images from Scripture. Why, and what are they?

C. Compare and contrast Paine and Burke. At what points do they agree? Disagree?

A ballroom scene depicting colonial days—our great-grand-parents were young once too, photographic print on stereo card—stereograph. Photograph shows couples dressed in historical costumes posing as if at a ball, Underwood & Underwood, c1900.

CAUSES OF THE AMERICAN REVOLUTION

First Thoughts . . .

This week you will examine colonial America as it emerges in the middle 1700s. Gone are the Cotton Mathers and George Whitefields. They are replaced by men like Samuel Adams and Patrick Henry. The Puritans, most assuredly, are now Yankees. Then, the first world war(s) occur: a series of conflicts between England and France over world domination. England wins an empire but may be in danger of losing its colonies.

Chapter Learning Objectives . . .

Chapter 5 will explore the genesis of the American Revolution. You will analyze the causes of this complicated filial conflict. You will examine the French and Indian War and its aftermath. You will examine a secondary historical source and determine its effectiveness. Finally, you will read a short biography of George Washington and discern its prejudices and its controversial agenda.

As a result of this chapter study you should be able to:

1. Analyze secondary historical sources.
2. Delineate different causes of the American Revolution.
3. Memorize facts about and reconstruct theories about the French and Indian War.
4. Read a juvenile biography of George Washington and identify several moral points that the author is advancing.

COLONIAL PERIOD

A Summary of the Colonial Period by Mary and Charles Beard (1927)

In the period between the landing of the English at Jamestown, Virginia, in 1607, and the close of the French and Indian war in 1763—a period of a century and a half—a new nation was being prepared on this continent to take its place among the powers of the earth. It was an epoch of migration. Western Europe contributed emigrants of many races and nationalities. The English led the way. Next to them in numerical importance were the Scotch-Irish and the Germans. Into the melting pot were also cast Dutch, Swedes, French, Jews, Welsh, and Irish. Thousands of slaves were brought from Africa to till Southern fields or labor as domestic servants in the North.

Why did they come? The reasons are various. Some of them, the Pilgrims and Puritans of New England, the French Huguenots, Scotch-Irish and Irish, and the Catholics of Maryland, fled from intolerant governments that denied them the right to worship God according to the dictates of their consciences. Thousands came to escape the bondage of poverty in the Old World and to find free homes in America. Thousands, like the Negroes from Africa, were dragged here against their will. The lure of adventure appealed to the restless and the lure of profits to the enterprising merchants.

How did they come? In some cases religious brotherhoods banded together and borrowed or furnished the funds necessary to pay the way. In other cases great trading companies were organized to found colonies. Again it was the wealthy proprietor, like Lord Baltimore or William Penn, who undertook to plant settlements. Many immigrants were able to pay their own way across the sea. Others bound themselves out for a term of years in exchange for the cost of the passage. Negroes were brought on account of the profits derived from their sale as slaves.

Whatever the motive for their coming, however, they managed to get across the sea. The immigrants set to work with a will. They cut down forests, built houses, and laid out fields. They founded churches, schools, and colleges. They set up forges and workshops. They spun and wove. They fashioned ships and sailed the seas. They bartered and traded. Here and there on favorable harbors they established centers of commerce—Boston, Providence, New York, Philadelphia, Baltimore, and Charleston. As soon as a firm foothold was secured on the shore line they pressed westward until, by the close of the colonial period, they were already on the crest of the Alleghenies.

Though they were widely scattered along a thousand miles of seacoast, the colonists were united in spirit by many common ties. The major portions of them were Protestants. The language, the law, and the literature of England furnished the basis of national unity. Most of the colonists were engaged in the same hard task; that of conquering a wilderness. To ties of kinship and language were added ties created by necessity. They had to unite in defense; first, against the Indians and later against the French. They were all subjects of the same sovereign—the king of England. The English Parliament made laws for them and the English government supervised their local affairs, their trade, and their manufactures. Common forces assailed them. Common grievances vexed them. Common hopes inspired them.

J. A. Krohn (a.k.a. "Colonial Jack") in colonial outfit, Bain Collection, date unknown.

Many of the things which tended to unite them likewise tended to throw them into opposition to the British Crown and Parliament. Most of them were freeholders; that is, farmers who owned their own land and tilled it with their own hands. A free soil nourished the spirit of freedom. The majority of them were Dissenters, critics, not friends, of the Church of England, that staunch defender of the British monarchy. Each colony in time developed its own legislature elected by the voters; it grew accustomed to making laws and paying taxes for itself. Here were a people learning self-reliance and self-government. The attempts to strengthen the Church of England in America and the transformation of colonies into royal provinces only fanned the spirit of independence which they were designed to quench.

Nevertheless, the Americans owed much of their prosperity to the assistance of the government that irritated them. It was the protection of the British navy that prevented Holland, Spain, and France from wiping out their settlements. Though their manufacture and trade were controlled in the interests of the mother country, they also enjoyed great advantages in her markets. Free trade existed nowhere upon the earth; but the broad empire of Britain was open to American ships and merchandise. It could be said, with good reason, that the disadvantages which the colonists suffered through British regulation of their industry and trade were more than offset by the privileges they enjoyed. Still that is somewhat beside the point, for mere economic advantage is not necessarily the determining factor in the fate of peoples. A thousand circumstances had helped to develop on this continent a nation, to inspire it

Samuel Adams by Charles Goodman, c1810.

with a passion for independence, and to prepare it for a destiny greater than that of a prosperous dominion of the British Empire. The economists, who tried to prove by logic unassailable that America would be richer under the British flag, could not change the spirit of Patrick Henry, Samuel Adams, Benjamin Franklin, or George Washington.

Assignment

A. Benjamin Franklin wrote the following note to a young friend contemplating marriage.

Pray make my compliments and best wishes acceptable to your bride. I am old and heavy, or I should ere this have presented them in person. I shall but make small use of the old man's privilege, that of giving advice to younger friends. Treat your wife always with respect; it will procure respect to you, not from her only, but from all that observe it. Never use a slighting expression to her, even in jest; for slight in jest, after frequent bandyings are apt to end in angry earnest. Be studious in your profession, and you will be learned. Be industrious and frugal, and you will be rich. Be sober and temperate, and you will be healthy. Be in general virtuous,

and you will be happy! At least you will by such conduct, stand the best chance for such consequences. I pray God to bless you both! Being ever your affectionate friend.

This note reflects a commonly held view in colonial society that if one worked hard enough, and long enough, one would be rich. Is this view necessarily true? Why or why not?

B. Some critics argue that historians Charles and Mary Beard were too pro-English in their discussion. They also argue that the Beards put too much emphasis on economic forces. What do you think? Why?

LESSON 2

THE ROAD TO REVOLUTION

In the beginning of the 18th century, the American Colonies clearly felt isolated from England. While England was experiencing the beginning of an industrial revolution and was also dealing with the problems of being an empire, America was trying to survive on the frontier. Besides, Boston and New York were nothing like London and Birmingham. New York was located approximately 3,400 miles from England's center of power, London. It seemed to be all right, though. It was the British way to administrate the colonies in a hands-off way that would allow the colonists to have all the rights of Englishmen. Initially at least, it also seemed fiscally advantageous to the mother county. Happy colonies were prosperous colonies and everyone made a lot of money.

Colonial legislatures were spoiled! They had a great deal of power, including the ability to muster troops, levy taxes, and pass laws—more power than any English county. They became accustomed to these rights and were unwilling to relinquish them when England finally decided to involve itself in colonial affairs.

By 1700, the predominating economic theory was called **mercantilism**. Mercantilism was an economic theory stating that colonies existed solely for the benefit of the mother country. After all, England had founded and nurtured the colonies and still provided military protection. At the very least the colonies should pay for these privileges. Mercantilism also argued that there was a limited amount of wealth and that it must be controlled by limited entities (e.g., countries). Therefore, it was important for countries like England to preserve their wealth. The most important thing, then, for Britain to do was keep its wealth in the Empire and not trade with other countries to get necessary items. Naturally, some outside trade was necessary—no one thought America could provide tea and spices, but the colonies were expected to provide agricultural items.

Meanwhile, several philosophers offered the American colonists an alternative view of government altogether. **Thomas Hobbes** wrote an influential book titled *Leviathan* where in, he detailed the idea of the social contract, which stated that men originally formed governments because of their need for protection. Hobbes had no problem with British-type, representative monarchies (although personally he preferred a good old dictatorship). The payback for all this safety was that folks gave up their rights to control the state and the right to revolt. While American colonists did not particularly want to give up natural rights to obtain the privilege of social safety, they nonetheless liked the idea of a "social contract." Social contracts could be made and broken.

John Locke argued, there were certainly inalienable rights that even states could not take away. Thus, free people had rights that no government should tamper with. **Jean-Jacques Rousseau's** *Social Contract* (1762) stated that government existed only by consent of the governed. Social contracts combined with inalienable rights and consent government made a potent combination.

In any event, these views contradicted mercantilism. Eighteenth-century Western social philosophy and political theory were in conflict. These three political theories conspired to cause many Americans to question British dominance over a place so distant and different from the British Isles. These ideals gave the colonists permission to question openly British right to rule in the American colonies. Very few really questioned British right to rule, even after the beginning of the Revolutionary War. Most Americans, however, felt that they had a right, even an obligation, to determine what form that rule would take. This obviously did not sit well with the British monarchy or Parliament.

That was only the start. There were many other unresolved problems and issues. By 1700, the trans-Appalachian region of North America remained basically uninhabited by Europeans. As the British colonies became more populated, colonists began to look to the West for new opportunities. This was, however, inhabited land. Native Americans liked the land, thank you very much, and so did French trappers. While neither group really wished to build barns on it, they still considered it their land. The mercantilist British saw raw material opportunities that could not be overlooked. Thus, an epic world contest ensued among the British and their Native American allies and the French and their Native American allies. This contest eventually led to the French and Indian War.

However, as Charles and Mary Beard explain, it was neither the Indian wars nor the French wars that finally brought forth the American nation. The character of the English crown, the course of events in English politics, and English measures of control over the colonies—executive, legislative, and judicial—must all be taken into account. The American revolution began in the courts of England.

The struggle between Charles I (1625–1649) and Parliament and the turmoil of the Puritan reign (1649–1660) so absorbed English attention that there was little time to think of colonial policies or to interfere with colonial affairs. The restoration of the monarchy in 1660 changed all that. During the reign of Charles II (1660–1685), an easygoing person, the policy of regulating trade by act of Parliament was greatly enhanced. In fact, one could argue that the colonial turmoil that emerged was partially due to the increased power of Parliament. At the same time, a system of stricter control over the dominions was ushered in by the annulment of charters (Beard).

Charles's successor, James II, a grumpy, moody man, continued the policy thus inaugurated and enlarged upon it. He was removed by a quiet, peaceful revolution in 1688. Nonetheless, in his short reign, he attempted to unite the Northern colonies. He made a lackey, Sir Edmund Andros, governor of all New England, New York, and New Jersey. For several months, Andros gave the Northern colonies a taste of ill-tempered despotism.

The overthrow of James, followed by the accession of William and Mary and by assured parliamentary supremacy, had an immediate effect in the colonies. The new order was greeted with thanksgiving. Massachusetts was given another charter that restored the spirit of self-government. In the other colonies the old course of affairs was resumed.

On the death in 1714 of Queen Anne, the successor of King William, the throne passed to a Hanoverian (German) prince who, though grateful for English honors and revenues, was more interested in Hanover than in England. Thus, George I and George II, whose combined reigns extended from 1714 to 1760, never even learned to speak the English language, at least without an accent. During a large part of this period, the direction of affairs was in the

Her Highness the Lady Anne, the future Queen of Great Britain and Ireland by Willem Wissing and Jan van der Vaardt, c1685 (PD-US).

hands of an astute leader, Sir Robert Walpole, who took a benign, passive role toward the colonies. He coined the phrase "let sleeping dogs lie."

While no English ruler from James II to George III ventured to interfere with colonial matters personally, constant control over the colonies was exercised by royal officers acting under the authority of the crown. Systematic supervision began in 1660, when there was created by royal order a committee of the king's council to meet on Mondays and Thursdays of each week to consider petitions, memorials, and addresses respecting the plantations. In 1696 a regular board was established, known as the "Lords of Trade and Plantations," which continued, until the American Revolution, to scrutinize closely colonial business. The chief duties of the board were to examine acts of colonial legislatures, to recommend measures to those assemblies for adoption, and to hear memorials and petitions from the colonies relative to their affairs (Charles and Mary Beard).

Supplementing this administrative control over the colonies was a constant supervision by the English courts. They enacted an immense body of legislation regulating the shipping, trade, and manufactures of America, all of it based on the aforementioned "mercantile" theory where the colonies of the British empire should be confined to agriculture and the production of raw materials, and forced to buy their manufactured goods of England.

First created, for example, were the navigation laws. **The Navigation Acts**, in effect, gave a monopoly of colonial commerce to British ships. No trade could be carried on between Great Britain and her dominions save in vessels built and manned by British subjects. No European goods could be brought to America save in the ships of the country that produced them or in English ships. But, in the long run, these measures profited the American colonies. These measures stimulated shipbuilding in the colonies, where the abundance of raw materials gave the master builders of

America an advantage over those of the mother country. Thus the colonists in the end profited from the restrictive policy written into the Navigation Acts.

The second group of laws was deliberately aimed to prevent colonial industries from competing too sharply with those of England. Among the earliest of these measures may be counted the Woolen Act of 1699, forbidding the exportation of woolen goods from the colonies. However, things really heated up after the French and Indian War.

Three of the major events commonly regarded as preludes to the American Revolution occurred immediately after the end of the French and Indian War: the Proclamation of 1763, the enactment of the Sugar Act (1764), and the Stamp Act (1765). The latter two were designed to increase British tax revenues to pay for the costly French and Indian War. Parliament and Grenville, the prime minister, increasingly felt the colonies should at least pay a part of their debt and future protection. The American colonies did not see it that way. They saw these acts to be governmental intrusions without the consent of the governed. The fact is, Americans were growing increasingly uneasy with British representative democracy that they felt did not give them enough self-government.

The greatest irritant, however, was the **Proclamation of 1763,** which mandated that no further settlements would occur west of the Appalachian Mountains. To the British, this seemed to be a just way to placate the desires and needs of their Indian allies. No argument there, and besides, it made costly forts in Ohio unnecessary. To the American colonies, though, who constantly needed more land, this arbitrary limit on expansion was not merely illegal, it was immoral. The British parliament had no right to make such a law.

This was an important turning point in the American attitude because from then on, opposition was based not only on practical politics, but it became increasingly grounded on fundamental political and philosophical objections.

Another phenomenon arose in the American colonies: organized opposition. With written protests and nonviolent civil disobedience, colonial legislatures challenged the right of the British to tax the territories. This was an entirely new strategy. Never had a governed people systematically opposed the governmental actions of a higher authority. The commotion surrounding the Sugar Act and the Stamp Act was only the beginning. Within a year, the issue was raised again with the implementation of the **Townshend Duties.**

In 1767 the English Parliament cut its own unpopular property taxes, and, to balance the budget, Prime Minister Townshend promised that he would tax the Americans to make up the difference. Townshend placed import duties at American ports on paper, lead, glass, and tea shipped from England. The money that was collected was used to pay the salaries of British colonial officials. By doing this, the British tried to make these officials independent of colonial legislatures and better able to enforce British orders and laws. The use of writs of assistance was authorized, and British federal courts were established. The British, in other words, asked the Americans to pay for their own bureaucracy.

Colonial opposition to the Townshend Revenue Act was swift and powerful. Colonial nonimportation agreements sharply cut British exports to America. British political leaders soon realized that the Act was foolish, for what it really did was establish protective tariffs against the shipment of British manufactures to the colonies. Furthermore, very little money was collected because of the nonimportation agreements. In 1770, Parliament, led by a new ministry headed by Lord North, repealed all the Townshend Revenue Act except for the tax on tea, which was kept in order to maintain the principle of the right of parliament to tax the colonies.

Americans were still angry and continued protesting. In Massachusetts in 1768, the assembly was dissolved because they didn't want to collect the Townshend Duties. In the same year in Boston a mob attacked customs officers responsible for collecting the hated tea tax. This led to the infamous Boston Massacre. The British soldiers, ably defended by John Adams, were acquitted.

On December 16, 1773, Samuel Adams led three groups of 50 men dressed like Mohawk Indians and broke into 342 chests and threw all the tea overboard. They destroyed about a million dollars' worth of tea in today's money! This was called the Boston Tea Party.

The **Intolerable Acts** were passed in 1774 to punish the colonists for the Boston Tea Party. The first was the Boston Port Bill, and it closed the Boston Harbor until the people of Boston paid for the tea that they threw into the harbor. It went into effect on June 1, 1774. The Administration of Justice Act became effective May 20, and it did not allow British soldiers to be tried in the colonies for any crimes

Boston Tea Party by Robert Reid, 1912.

they might commit. This meant the soldiers could do anything they wanted since they would probably not be punished for their crimes. The Massachusetts Government Act, which also took effect on May 20, 1774, restricted town meetings to one a year unless the governor approved any more. The Massachusetts Assembly could still not meet. The governor would appoint all the officials, juries, and sheriffs.

The Quebec Act was established May 20, 1774. This act extended the Canadian borders to cut some of Massachusetts, Connecticut, and Virginia. There was also the Quartering Act that was established on March 24. It required the colonial authorities to provide housing and supplies for the British troops. These laws added fuel to the fire, and by April 1775, Britain and her colonists were very close to war.

Assignment

A. Enumerate five important measures of the English government affecting the colonies between 1763 and 1765. Explain each in detail.

B. For the first time in history, pre-Revolution American colonists were talking about "natural" rights vs. "constitutional" rights. Why? What are some of the differences between these rights?

THE FRENCH AND INDIAN WAR

The French and Indian War was part of a world war called the "seven years' war." France, England, and Spain were all belligerents. However, for our purposes, we will concentrate on the North American phase.

Professor Seymour I. Schwartz reminds us that the French and Indian War took more lives than the American Revolution. In fact, this war was the bloodiest 18th-century war on North American soil. "It erased France's political influence from the continent and established English dominance east of the Mississippi and in Canada. And it set the stage for the American Revolution and the establishment of the United States of America" (Schwartz, *French and Indian War: The Imperial Struggle for North America*).

The conflict between England and France in North America centered on the fur trade and control of inland waterways.

When European people began settling on the coast of North America in the early 17th century, the French occupied the most convenient route to the interior—the St. Lawrence River. From their posts at Québec and Montréal they rapidly moved up the St. Lawrence River to explore the continent and trade for furs with the native peoples. But this movement westward was blocked by the pro-British Iroquois.

Louis-Joseph de Montcalm trying to stop Native Americans from attacking British soldiers and civilians as they leave Fort William Henry at the Battle of Fort William Henry. Engraved by Alfred Bobbett, c1870 (PD-US).

Bank note illustration showing colonists praying for deliverance from imminent Indian attack, artist unknown, 1856.

The Iroquois, perhaps the most politically powerful group of native people in the history of North America, had early confrontations with the French. Their hostility lasted until the French had been driven from North America.

To restore the balance of power in favor of their allies, the French began selling firearms and ammunition in limited numbers to the Huron and Algonquin. These weapons, as well as steel hatchets and knives, soon spread to other tribes, and the Dutch responded by providing guns to the Iroquois. Meanwhile, the Swedes along the Delaware River and the British in New England were arming other tribes. An arms race developed, in which tribes providing the most fur had a military advantage over those that did not. The initial confrontations during the 1630s took place in the eastern Great Lakes region, mainly between the Iroquois and Huron (Wyandot), but as the trading tribes exhausted the beaver in their homelands, they began seizing hunting territory from others, and the Beaver Wars spread west (www.centuryinter.net/tjs11/hist/fiwar.htm).

The turn of the 18th century was marked by open colonial warfare between France and England. King William's War (1689–1697) and Queen Anne's War (1702–1713) also involved the Iroquois and other Indian nations. France moved to consolidate her position on the Great Lakes. A post constructed at Detroit in 1701 blocked the British from the three northwestern lakes. In 1715 a new fort at Michilimackinac assured their influence in the north. Niagara and its portage was the linchpin, however. Control of it would assure the exclusion of the English from the Great Lakes and the safe movement of goods and furs to and from New France.

By 1667 repeated attacks by French soldiers on their homeland had forced the Iroquois to make peace. Their agreement with the French was significant in that it also extended to French native allies and trading partners, including those in the Great Lakes. Meanwhile, through a treaty signed at a grand council at Sault Ste. Marie in 1671, the Great Lakes tribes consented to Simon Daumont's formal annexation of the region for France. The French had annexed territory they had never seen, so there was immediate interest in exploring it. Hearing of the "Great River" to the west, the Jesuit priest Jacques Marquette and fur trader Louis Joliet, accompanied by five Miami guides and canoe paddlers, set off in 1673 from St. Ignace (Mackinac) to find it. They did, and established French hegemony from the Great Lakes to New Orleans.

In 1749 France made claim to the Ohio Valley and in particular noticed that the confluence of three rivers at present-day Pittsburgh was a particularly valuable location. The French built a fort there and named it Fort Duquesne.

Two other minor wars occurred before the decisive conflict opened in 1754. General Braddock led an army of British regulars and colonial irregulars (including George Washington) to attack Fort Duquesne. Braddock was annihilated.

It took the English several years, but eventually they won this war. In 1758 British General Forbes captured Fort Duquesne and renamed it Fort Pitt. In 1759 General James Wolfe took Québec but he lost his own life. Finally, General William Johnson captured Montréal and New France fell.

Assignment

In a short essay, speculate what would have happened if France had won the French and Indian War.

GEORGE WASHINGTON

Historical Biography: George Washington, by D. H. Montgomery (1893)

In 1732, when Franklin was at work on his newspaper, a boy was born on a plantation in Virginia who was one day to stand higher even than the Philadelphia printer.

That boy when he grew up was to be chosen leader of the armies of the Revolution; he was to be elected the first president of the United States; and before he died he was to be known and honored all over the world. The name of that boy was George Washington.

Washington's father died when George was only eleven years old, leaving him, with his brothers and sisters, to the care of a most excellent and sensible mother. It was that mother's influence more than anything else which made George the man he became.

Washington went to a little country school, where he learned to read, write, and cipher. By the time he was twelve, he could write a clear, bold hand. In one of his writing-books he copied many good rules or sayings. But young Washington was not always copying good sayings; for he was a tall, strong boy, fond of all outdoor sports and games. He was a well-meaning boy, but he had a hot temper, and at times his blue eyes flashed fire. In all trials of strength and in all deeds of daring, George took the lead; he could run faster, jump further, and throw a stone higher than anyone in the school.

When the boys played "soldier," they liked to have "Captain George" as commander. When he drew his wooden sword, and shouted "Come on!" they would all rush into battle with a wild hurrah. Years afterward, when the real war came, and George Washington drew his sword in earnest, some of his school companions may have fought under their old leader.

Once, however, Washington had a battle of a different kind. It was with a high-spirited colt which belonged to his

George Washington by Gilbert Stuart, 1800 (PD-US).

mother. Nobody had ever been able to do anything with that colt, and most people were afraid of him. Early one morning, George and some of his brothers were out in the pasture. George looked at the colt prancing about and kicking up his heels. Then he said: "Boys, if you'll help me put a bridle on him, I'll ride him." The boys managed to get the colt into a corner and to slip on the bridle. With a leap, George seated himself firmly on his back. Then the fun began. The colt, wild with rage, ran, jumped, plunged, and reared straight up on his hind legs, hoping to throw his rider off. It was all useless; he might as well have tried to throw off his own skin, for the boy stuck to his back as though he had grown there. Then, making a last desperate bound into the air, the animal burst a blood-vessel and fell dead. The battle was over, George was victor, but it had cost the life of Mrs. Washington's favorite colt.

Statue of George Washington at the Indiana State Capitol.
Photo by Rebecca White., 2011.

When the boys went in to breakfast, their mother, knowing that they had just come from the pasture, asked how the colt was getting on. "He is dead, madam," said George; "I killed him." "Dead!" exclaimed his mother. "Yes, madam, dead," replied her son. Then he told her just how it happened. When Mrs. Washington heard the story, her face flushed with anger. Then, waiting a moment, she looked steadily at George, and said quietly, "While I regret the loss of my favorite, I rejoice in my son, who always speaks the truth."

George's eldest brother, Lawrence Washington, had married the daughter of a gentleman named Fairfax, who lived on the banks of the Potomac. Lawrence had a fine estate a few miles above, on the same river; he called his place Mount Vernon. When he was fourteen, George went to Mount Vernon to visit his brother.

Lawrence Washington took George down the river to call on the Fairfaxes. There the lad made the acquaintance of Lord Fairfax, an English nobleman who had come over from London. He owned an immense piece of land in Virginia. Lord Fairfax and George soon became great friends. He was a gray-haired man nearly sixty, but he enjoyed having this boy of fourteen as a companion. They spent weeks together on horseback in the fields and woods, hunting deer and foxes.

Lord Fairfax's land extended westward more than a hundred miles. It had never been very carefully surveyed; and he was told that settlers were moving in beyond the Blue Ridge Mountains, and were building log-cabins on his property without asking leave. By the time Washington was sixteen, he had learned surveying; and so Lord Fairfax hired him to measure his land for him. Washington was glad to undertake the work; for he needed the money, and he could earn in this way from five to ten dollars a day.

Early in the spring, Washington, in company with another young man, started off on foot to do this business. They crossed the Blue Ridge Mountains, and entered the Valley of Virginia, one of the most beautiful valleys in America.

The two young men would work all day in the woods with a long chain, measuring the land. When evening came, Washington would make a map of what they had measured. Then they would wrap themselves up in their blankets, stretch themselves on the ground at the foot of a tree, and go to sleep under the stars.

Every day they shot some game—squirrels or wild turkeys, or perhaps a deer. They kindled a fire with flint and steel, and roasted the meat on sticks held over the coals. For plates they had clean chips; and as clean chips could always be got by a few blows with an axe, they never washed any dishes, but just threw them away, and had a new set for each meal.

While in the Valley they met a band of Indians, who stopped and danced a war-dance for them. The music was not remarkable—for most of it was made by drumming on a deer-skin stretched across the top of an old iron pot—but the dancing itself could not be beat. The savages leaped into the air, swung their hatchets, gashed the trees, and yelled till the woods rang.

When Washington returned from his surveying trip, Lord Fairfax was greatly pleased with his work; and the governor of Virginia made him one of the public surveyors. By this means he was able to get work which paid him handsomely.

By the time Washington was twenty-one he had grown to be over six feet in height. He was straight as an arrow and tough as a whip-lash. He had keen blue eyes that seemed to look into the very heart of things, and his fist was like a blacksmith's sledgehammer. He knew all about the woods, all about Indians, and he could take care of himself anywhere.

At this time the English settlers held the country along the seashore as far back as the Allegheny Mountains. West of those mountains the French from Canada were trying to get possession of the land. They had made friends with many of the Indians, and they hoped, with their help, to be able to drive out the English and get the whole country for themselves.

Statue of General George Washington on public display at the Boston Public Garden.

In order to hold this land in the west, the French had built several forts south of Lake Erie, and they were getting ready to build some on the Ohio River. The governor of Virginia was determined to put a stop to this. He had given young Washington the military title of major; he now sent Major Washington to see the French commander at one of the forts near Lake Erie. Washington was to tell the Frenchman that he had built his forts on land belonging to the English, and that he and his men must either leave or fight.

Major Washington dressed himself like an Indian, and attended by several friendly Indians and by a white man named Gist, who knew the country well, he set out on his journey through what was called the Great Woods.

The entire distance to the farthest fort and back was about a thousand miles. Washington could go on horseback part of the way, but there were no regular roads, and he had to climb mountains and swim rivers. After several weeks' travel he reached the fort, but the French commander refused to give up the land. He said that he and his men had come to stay, and that if the English did not like it, they must fight.

On the way back, Washington had to leave his horses and come on foot with Gist and an Indian guide sent from the fort. This Indian guide was in the pay of the French, and he intended to murder Washington in the woods. One day he shot at him from behind a tree, but luckily did not hit him. Then Washington and Gist managed to get away from him, and set out to go back to Virginia by themselves. There were no paths through the thick forest; but Washington had his compass with him, and with that he could find his way just as the captain of a ship finds his at sea. When they reached the Allegheny River they found it full of floating ice. They worked all day and made a raft of logs. As they were pushing their way across with poles, Washington's pole was struck by a big piece of ice which he says jerked him out into water ten feet deep. At length the two men managed to get to a little island, but as there was no wood on it, they could not make a fire. The weather was bitterly cold, and Washington, who was soaked to the skin, had to take his choice between walking about all night, or trying to sleep on the frozen ground in his wet clothes.

When Major Washington got back to Virginia, the governor made him colonel. With a hundred and fifty men, Colonel Washington was ordered to set out for the west. He was to "make prisoners, kill or destroy," all Frenchmen who should try to get possession of land on the Ohio River. He built a small log fort, which he named Fort Necessity. Here the French attacked him. They had five men to his one. Colonel Washington fought like a man who liked to hear the bullets whistle past his ears—as he said he did—but in the end he had to give up the fort.

Defeat of General Braddock, in the French and Indian War, in Virginia in 1755 by John Andrew.

Then General Braddock, a noted English soldier, was sent over to Virginia by the king to drive the French out of the country. He started with a fine army, and Washington went with him. He told General Braddock that the French and the Indians would hide in the woods and fire at his men from behind trees. But Braddock paid no attention to the warning. On his way through the forest, the brave English general was suddenly struck down by the enemy, half of his army were killed or wounded, and the rest put to flight. Washington had two horses shot under him, and four bullets went through his coat. It was a narrow escape for the young man. One of those who fought in the battle said, "I expected every moment to see him fall"—but he was to live for greater work.

The war with the French lasted a number of years. It ended by the English getting possession of the whole of America from the Atlantic Ocean to the Mississippi River. All this part of America was ruled by George the Third, king of England. The king now determined to send over more soldiers, and keep them here to prevent the French in Canada from trying to get back the country they had lost. He wanted the people here in the 13 colonies to pay the cost of keeping these soldiers. But this the people were not willing to do, because they felt that they were able to protect themselves without help of any kind. Then the king said, "If the Americans will not give the money, I will take it from them by force—for pay it they must and shall." This was more than the king would have dared say about England; for there, if he wanted money to spend on his army, he had to ask the people for it, and they could give it or not as they thought best. The Americans said, "We have the same rights as our brothers in England, and the king cannot force us to give a single copper against our will. If he tries to take it from us, we will fight. Some of the greatest men in England agreed with us, and said that they would fight, too, if they were in our place."

Washington Crossing the Delaware by Emanuel Leutze, 1851 (PD-US).

Assignment

A. Read another short biography of George Washington (from an encyclopedia or the Internet) and compare it with Montgomery's biography on the three preceding pages. Find three similarities and three differences:

Similarities	Differences

B. Montgomery wrote the preceding biographical sketch for a young audience. What character qualities of George Washington did he extol?

Chapter 6

PATRIOTS AND REVOLUTION

First Thoughts . . .

"Gentlemen may cry, Peace, Peace—but there is no peace. The war is actually begun! The next gale that sweeps from the north will bring to our ears the clash of resounding arms! Our brethren are already in that field! Why stand we here idle? What is it that gentlemen wish? What would they have? Is life so dear, or peace so sweet, as to be purchased at the price of chains and slavery? Forbid it, Almighty God! I know not what course others may take; but as for me give me liberty or give me death!"

—Patrick Henry, March 23, 1775

In this chapter you will see America starting and then finishing its Revolution. You will be amazed at the incompetence of gentleman Johnny Burgoyne, the treachery of Benedict Arnold, and the providential leadership of George Washington. You will read the journals of Abigail Adams, the brilliant spouse of patriot and second president John Adams.

Chapter Learning Objectives . . .

Chapter 6 takes you from the first shots fired on Lexington Green to the final drumbeat at Yorktown, Virginia. You will analyze the war from both an American and a British perspective. You will critique decisions made by friend and foe alike. At the end of the chapter you will be amazed at how God birthed this new nation.

As a result of this chapter study you should be able to:

1. Compare America's view of terrorism at the beginning of the 21st century, with subversive groups like the Sons of Liberty.

2. Evaluate whether acts of civil disobedience, like the Boston Tea Party, are ever justified.

3. Assess the debated value of Thomas Paine to the Revolutionary cause.

4. Formulate a logical reason why America won her revolution.

5. Explore the life of colonial women and discuss why Abigail Adams would be concerned about their station in life.

6. Analyze historical debate surrounding causes of the American Revolution.

THE COMING CONFLICT

The news of the tea riot in Boston confirmed King George in his conviction that there should be no soft policy in dealing with his American subjects. "The die is cast," he stated with evident satisfaction. "The colonies must either triumph or submit. . . . If we take the resolute part, they will undoubtedly be very meek."

Parliament, concurring with King George (left), passed five harsh measures, known as the five Intolerable Acts. The first of them was a bill absolutely shutting the port of Boston to commerce with the outside world. The second, following closely, revoked the Massachusetts charter of 1691 and provided that the government should be appointed by the king. A third measure, after denouncing the "utter subversion of all lawful government" in the provinces, authorized royal agents to transfer to Great Britain or to other colonies the trials of officers or other persons accused of murder in connection with the enforcement of the law—in other words, dissolving the authority of colonial courts. The fourth act legalized the quartering of troops in Massachusetts towns. The fifth of the measures was the Québec Act, which granted religious toleration to the Catholics in Canada, extended the boundaries of Québec southward to the Ohio River, land which by that time was perceived by most Americans as being American.

To enforce these intolerable acts the military arm of the British government was brought into play. The commander-in-chief of the armed forces in America, General Gage, was appointed governor of Massachusetts. Reinforcements were brought to the colonies.

When the news of the Intolerable Acts reached America, to local committees and provincial conventions was added a Continental Congress, appropriately called by Massachusetts on June 17, 1774, at the instigation of Samuel Adams. The response to the summons was electric. By hurried and irregular methods delegates were elected during the summer, and on September 5 the Congress duly assembled in Carpenter's Hall in Philadelphia. Many of the greatest men in America were there—George Washington and Patrick Henry from Virginia and John and Samuel Adams from Massachusetts.

The Congress agreed to stop the importation of British goods into America, and it placed the enforcement of this agreement in the hands of local "committees of safety and inspection," to be elected by the qualified voters. The significance of this action is obvious. Congress went on record in violation of British law.

When the news of the action of the American Congress reached England, Pitt and Burke warmly urged a repeal of the obnoxious laws, but in vain. All they could wring from the prime minister, Lord North, was a set of "conciliatory resolutions" proposing to relieve from taxation any colony that would assume its share of imperial defense and make provision for supporting the local officers of the crown. This "olive branch" was accompanied by a resolution assuring the king of support at all hazards in suppressing the rebellion and by the restraining act of March 30, 1775, which in effect destroyed the commerce of New England (Beard).

Meanwhile, the British authorities in Massachusetts relaxed none of their efforts in upholding British sovereignty. General Gage, hearing that military stores had been collected at Concord, dispatched a small force to seize them. By this act he precipitated the conflict he had sought to avoid. At Lexington, on the road to Concord, occurred "the little thing" that produced "the great event." An unexpected collision beyond the thought or purpose of any man had transferred the contest from the forum to the battlefield.

Though blood had been shed and war was actually at hand, the second Continental Congress, which met at Philadelphia in May 1775, was not yet convinced that conciliation was beyond human power. It petitioned the king to interpose on behalf of the colonists in order that the empire might avoid the calamities of civil war. On the last day of July, it made a temperate but firm answer to Lord North's offer of conciliation, stating that the proposal was unsatisfactory because it did not renounce the right to tax or repeal the offensive acts of Parliament.

Just as the representatives of America were about to present the last petition of Congress to the king on August 23, 1775, George III issued a proclamation of rebellion. This announcement declared that the colonists, "misled by dangerous and ill-designing men," were in a state of insurrection; it called on the civil and military powers to bring "the traitors to justice"; and it threatened with "condign punishment the authors, perpetrators, and abettors of such traitorous designs." It closed with the usual prayer: "God, save the king." Later in the year, Parliament passed a sweeping act destroying all trade and intercourse with America. Congress was silent at last. Force was also America's answer.

Although the Congress had not given up all hope of reconciliation in the spring and summer of 1775, it had firmly resolved to defend American rights by arms if necessary. It transformed the militiamen who had assembled near Boston, after the battle of Lexington, into a Continental army and selected Washington as commander-in-chief. It assumed the powers of a government and prepared to raise money, wage war, and carry on diplomatic relations with foreign countries.

Things moved quickly. On June 17, the American militia, by the stubborn defense of Bunker Hill (or Breed's Hill), showed that war in earnest had begun. On July 3, Washington took command of the army at Cambridge, Massachusetts.

The Death of General Warren at the Battle of Bunker Hill
by John Trumbull, 1786.

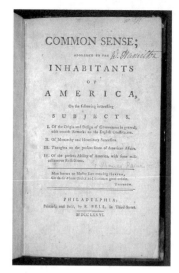

Britain meanwhile, had to go to Germany to hire recruits called **Hessians**. These infuriated the Americans, who, by that time, had driven Lord Howe from Boston.

America was drifting toward independence in sentiment and in fact. "American independence," as the historian George Bancroft said, "was not an act of sudden passion nor the work of one man or one assembly. It had been discussed in every part of the country by farmers and merchants, by mechanics and planters, by the fishermen along the coast and the backwoodsmen of the West; in town meetings and from the pulpit; at social gatherings and around the camp fires; in county conventions and conferences or committees; in colonial congresses and assemblies."

In the midst of this ferment of American opinion, a bold and eloquent pamphleteer broke in upon the hesitating public with a program for absolute independence, without fears and without apologies. In the early days of 1776, Thomas Paine issued the first of his famous tracts, "**Common Sense**," a passionate attack upon the British monarchy and an equally passionate plea for American liberty. Some levelheaded Americans thought the atheistic, opportunistic Paine may have gone too far.

Meanwhile, the Continental Congress was alive to the course of events outside. The subject of independence was constantly being raised. "Are we rebels?" exclaimed Wyeth of Virginia during a debate in February. "No: we must declare ourselves a free people."

The way was fully prepared, therefore, when, on June 7, the Virginia delegation in the Congress moved that "these united colonies are and of right ought to be free and independent states." A committee was immediately appointed to draft a formal document setting forth the reasons for the act, and on July 2 all the states save New York went on record in favor of severing their political connection with Great Britain. Two days later, July 4, Jefferson's draft of the Declaration of Independence, changed in some slight particulars, was adopted. The Liberty Bell in Independence Hall announced this portentous event! A new nation took its place among the nations of the world. However, before that was to become a reality, a war needed to be fought and won!

Assignment

A. Social historian Robert Gross, in his book *The Minutemen and Their World*, studies 1775 Concord, Massachusetts. He argues that it was a town struggling to hold on to its past even as current events and other more local and personal changes threatened individual and family stability. Overcrowding, religious tensions, social tensions, and new political tensions threatened over a hundred years of stability and prosperity (pp. 105–107). Concord was facing the loss of many of its young people to the frontier due to land shortages and declining crop yields (pp. 84–87). In fact, in summary, to Concord folk, the world was changing too rapidly and too radically to suit most desires. Faced with the loss of control in so many areas, Concord determined not to lose control of their political freedom (p. 105). This motivated them, therefore, to join the American cause and fight a war. (Taken from an unpublished book review by Andrew Funka; used by permission.) Do you agree with this hypothesis?

B. In light of America's problems with terrorism at the beginning of the 21st century, should we rethink the secret, subversive organization called the Sons of Liberty? Were they patriots or terrorists?

C. To a Christian, revolution is a very knotty issue. At what point, if ever, should a Christian rebel against authority? Looking at the events leading to the Revolutionary War, why do you think America was or was not justified in its rebellion?

D. The Boston Tea Party was an act of civil disobedience. In your opinion, was it justified? At what point is it right to commit civil disobedience?

E. Christine Leigh Heyrman, Department of History, University of Delaware, argues that Thomas Paine's book *Common Sense* is an example of how religion caused the Revolutionary War.

This celebrated (and admirably brief and accessible) treatise was the eighteenth-century equivalent of a runaway bestseller. Published in January of 1776, it became an overnight sensation—a pamphlet pored over by people in the privacy of their homes and read aloud in taverns and other public gathering places everywhere in British North America. In short, a wide range of colonials, literate as well as illiterate, felt the force of Paine's arguments for breaking with Britain, and what he wrote persuaded enough undecided men and women to embolden the Continental Congress to endorse the Declaration of Independence by July of 1776.

Why did *Common Sense* succeed so brilliantly as a piece of political propaganda? Among other reasons, because it is a kind of secular sermon, an extraordinarily adroit mingling of religion and politics. Look at the opening paragraphs ("Time makes more converts than reason") in which Paine casts the decision to support the cause of rebellion as a matter of feeling rather than thought, as a process akin to that of evangelical conversion. Review his assault on monarchy, which boils down to the proposition that all kings are blasphemous usurpers who claim a sovereign authority over other human beings that rightfully belongs only to God. Notice, too, how vehemently Paine insists that the Jews of the Old Testament rejected monarchical government—the obvious conclusion being that God's new "chosen people" in America should follow that example. Consider his assertion that the colonies are an asylum of religious liberty, implying that Americans must pass from argument to arms to protect freedom of conscience for religious dissenters. And, finally, don't miss how often the cadences of *Common Sense* echo and even reiterate the language of the Bible.

Other historians feel that putting Thomas Paine in the same category as Jonathan Edwards is improbable. What do you think?

THE WAR

The war that opened with the battle of Lexington on April 19, 1775, and closed with the surrender of Cornwallis at Yorktown on October 19, 1781, passed through two phases—the northern phase until 1778 and the southern phase until the end. Memorable aspects of the contest were the evacuation of Boston by the British, the defeat of American forces in New York and their retreat through New Jersey, the battle of Trenton, the seizure of Philadelphia by the British (September 1777), the invasion of New York by Burgoyne, and his collapse at Saratoga in October 1777. Along the way are memorable stories of the encampment of American forces at Valley Forge for the terrible winter of 1777–1778 and the infamous betrayal by Benedict Arnold.

In 1775 the 13 colonies—it would be inaccurate to call them a nation—were ill-prepared to wage war against the most powerful nation on the face of the earth. The American colonies had no army. The first military force consisted of colonial militia (untrained volunteers) headed by local leaders with virtually no military training and unaccustomed to taking orders from a commander. There was no central system for housing, paying, or feeding the troops, and supplies of gunpowder and clothing were inadequate. When a national army was formed, enlistments were short and often soldiers were mustered out about the time they were most effective! The American Army—called the Continental army—never contained more than one-tenth of military-age Americans. Even worse, states—particularly southern states–were full of **Tories** or Loyalists. Perhaps a third of Americans remained faithful to the king. As one historian stated, "All

The Tory's day of judgment by Elkanah Tisdale, 1795.

in all, it was a stupendous task that faced the patriots. They had to improvise an army and a new government at the same time, to meet unusual situations arising daily, to find trusted leaders, and to get 13 proud states to work for the common cause. And all this had to be done with little preparation, at a time when the menace of defeat and reprisals for rebellion and treason cast dark shadows over the land."

On the other hand, the American colonies had substantial advantages. For one thing, they were defending their homeland; the British were enforcing their national will. The American nation was huge and a long way from England. Essentially, all America had to do was hold out until Great Britain grew too tired to fight. For the British the theater of the war offered many problems. From first to last it extended from Massachusetts to Georgia, a distance of almost a thousand miles. It was nearly 3,000 miles from the main base of supplies, and though the British navy kept the channel open, transports were constantly falling prey to daring privateers and fleet American war vessels. The sea, on the other hand, offered an easy means of transportation between points along the coast and gave ready access to the American centers of wealth and population. Of this the British made good use. Though early forced to give up Boston, they seized New York and kept it until the end of the war; they took Philadelphia and retained it until threatened by the approach of the French fleet; and they captured and held both Savannah and Charleston. Wars, however, are seldom won by the conquest of cities. America was a land of rural farms and small towns—it was not dependent upon its urban centers (Beard).

Finally, if disorganized, the Americans were natural soldiers and showed ingenuity and poise in the face of adversity. Given time, the Americans would win. General George Washington knew it. A mediocre general at best, George Washington managed to lose virtually every battle he fought, but he won the war! Washington knew that eventually the British would grow tired and abandon their efforts to subjugate the colonists. The British were in fact battered and worn down by a guerrilla war and outdone on two important occasions by superior forces—at Saratoga and at Yorktown. As America learned in Vietnam and Iraq, the British understood that an immense army, which could be raised only by a supreme effort, would be necessary to subdue the colonies, and there was doubt anything would work. To the British, the American colonies just were not worth it. Cornwallis surrendered at Yorktown, Virginia, in 1781, and the military phase of the war was over.

American Revolutionary Summary

This time line is drawn largely from the work of Richard B. Morris, in particular his *Encyclopedia of American History*.

1776

- "Common Sense." Thomas Paine moved many to the cause of independence with his pamphlet titled "Common Sense." In a direct, simple style, he cried out against King George III and the monarchical form of government.

- The British evacuate Boston. American General Henry Knox arrived in Boston with cannons he had moved with great difficulty from Fort Ticonderoga, New York. Americans began to entrench themselves around Boston, planning to attack the British. British General William Howe planned an attack but eventually retreated from Boston.

- Congress authorizes the colonies to write constitutions. In May, the Second Continental Congress adopted a resolution authorizing the colonies to adopt new constitutions; the former colonial governments had dissolved with the outbreak of war.

- Congress declares independence. When North Carolina and Virginia empowered their delegates to vote for American independence, Virginian Richard Henry Lee offered a resolution stating that the colonies "are, and of right ought to be, free and independent States." A committee was appointed to draft a declaration of independence, and Thomas Jefferson was chosen to write it. On July 2, Congress voted in favor of independence, and on July 4, the Declaration of Independence was approved. Copies were sent throughout the colonies to be read publicly.

- Battle of Long Island. After leaving Boston, British General Howe planned to use New York as a base. The British captured Staten Island and began a military build-up on Long Island in preparation for an advance on Brooklyn. Washington succeeded in saving his army by secretly retreating onto Manhattan Island. Washington eventually retreated from Manhattan, fearing the prospect of being trapped on the island, and the British occupied New York City.

- Congress names commissioners to negotiate with foreign nations. Congress sent a delegation of three men to Europe—Silas Deane, Benjamin Franklin, and Arthur Lee—to prepare treaties of commerce and friendship, and to attempt to secure loans from foreign nations.

- The Battle of White Plains. British and American forces met at White Plains, New York, where the British captured an important fortification. Washington once again retreated, still attempting to save his army from the full force of the British army.

- Retreat through New Jersey. Washington and his army retreated across New Jersey, crossing the Delaware River into Pennsylvania. Congress, fearing a British attack on Philadelphia, fled to Baltimore.

- Battle of Trenton. On December 26, Washington launched a surprise attack against a British fortification at Trenton, New Jersey, that was staffed by Hessian soldiers. After one hour of confused fighting, the Hessians surrendered. Only five American soldiers were killed.

1777

- Battle of Princeton. British General Howe reacted to the Battle of Trenton by sending a large force of men to New Jersey. At Princeton, Washington once again launched a surprise attack, and succeeded in defeating the British. His efforts cleared most of New Jersey of enemy forces, and greatly boosted American morale.

- America has a flag. On June 14, Congress declared that the flag of the United States would consist of 13 alternating red and white stripes, and a blue field with 13 white stars.

- The British attack Philadelphia. British and Americans met at Brandywine Creek, Pennsylvania. The Americans retreated, and the British soon occupied Philadelphia, forcing Congress once again to flee the city. After retreating further during the Battle of Germantown, Washington settled his army for the winter in Valley Forge—a winter of extreme cold and great hunger.

- Saratoga. On October 7, British and American troops

engaged in New York. Fatigued from battle and short of supplies, British General John Burgoyne's troops were repulsed by American forces under General Horatio Gates. On October 8, Burgoyne retreated to Saratoga; by October 13, he asked for terms of surrender. The "Convention of Saratoga" called for Burgoyne's army to be sent back to England, and for each soldier to pledge not to serve again in the war against the colonies.

- The "Conway Cabal." Many in Congress were unhappy with Washington's leadership; some murmured the name of General Horatio Gates as a possible replacement. Thomas Conway, the army's inspector general, wrote a critical letter to Gates about Washington, leading many to believe there was an organized effort to replace Washington. Conway resigned from the army, and eventually apologized to Washington.

- Articles of Confederation. When Richard Henry Lee made a motion for independence (1776), he also proposed a formal plan of union among the states. After a discussion lasting more than a year, the Articles of Confederation were adopted by Congress, although the states did not ratify the Articles until 1781.

1778

- France and America become allies. France and America formed an alliance, negotiated by Benjamin Franklin, stating that each would consider the other a "most favored nation" for trade and friendship; France would be obligated to fight for American independence; and America would be obligated to stand by France if war should occur between France and Great Britain. Within four months, France and Great Britain were at war.

- The British attempt to make peace. Threatened by the alliance between France and America, Parliament proposed the repeal of the Tea Act (1773) and Coercive Acts (1774), pledged not to tax the colonies, and sent peace commissioners to America. However, most Americans were interested only in British recognition of American independence. When a British commissioner tried to bribe congressmen Joseph Reed, Robert Morris, and

This painting depicts the forces of British Major General Charles Cornwallis, 1st Marquess Cornwallis (1738–1805) (who was not himself present at the surrender), surrendering to French and American forces after the Siege of Yorktown (September 28–October 19, 1781) during the American Revolutionary War. The United States government commissioned Trumbull to paint patriotic paintings, including this piece, for them in 1817, paying for the piece in 1820 (PD-US).

Francis Dana, Americans became even less interested in reconciliation. Competing for support from the American people, both Congress and the desperate commissioners appealed directly to them with broadsides, but the British commissioners soon returned to Great Britain, their mission a failure.

- John Paul Jones wins victories. Although Esek Hopkins was never very successful with the American navy, Captain John Paul Jones won several victories against the British with his ship, the *Ranger*.

- The Battle of Monmouth. When the British headed for New York, Washington left Valley Forge to follow. At the Battle of Monmouth, American General Charles Lee gave several confused orders, and then ordered a sudden retreat. Washington's arrival on the scene saved the battle, although the British escaped to New York during the night. Lee was later court-martialed.

1779

- The British attack in North and South. Fighting continued in both the northern and southern states. In the frontier settlements of Pennsylvania, Loyalists and Indians led by Mohawk Joseph Brant attacked American settlers. The Loyalists soon were defeated, and Americans went on to destroy many Native American villages whose residents were fighting on the side of the British.

- Spain joins the war. Spain asked Britain for Gibraltar as a reward for joining the war on the British side. When Britain refused, Spain joined with France in its war against Britain, although refusing to recognize American independence.

1780

- The British take Charleston, South Carolina. After a brief fight, the British took Charleston, capturing 5,400 men and four American ships in the harbor. It was the worst American defeat of the war.

- A mutiny in the Continental Army. When the value of Continental currency sank to a new low, Congress had problems supplying the American army. Great shortages of food led to a short-lived mutiny among some Connecticut soldiers at Washington's camp in New Jersey.

- The treason of Benedict Arnold. American General Benedict Arnold, frustrated and ambitious, began dealing with British General Sir Henry Clinton. After he was promised the command at West Point by General Washington, Arnold told Clinton that he would give the strategic American fortification to the British. But when

Benedict Arnold, by H.B. Hall after John Trumbull, 1879.

British Major John André, acting as messenger, was captured, Arnold fled to a British ship, revealing his involvement in the treasonous plan. André was executed as a spy, and Arnold was made a brigadier general in the British army.

1781

- Congress creates a Department of Finance. American finances were in such dire straits that Congress saw the need for a separate department of finance. Robert Morris was appointed superintendent of finance.

- The Articles of Confederation are ratified. With the ratification of the Articles of Confederation, under discussion since 1777, Congress assumed a new title, "The United States in Congress Assembled."

- The Battle of Yorktown. French and American forces joined at Yorktown, on land and at sea, and attacked British fortifications. Key British points were soon held by the Americans and French, and British General Cornwallis soon surrendered, giving up almost 8,000 men. With this defeat, Britain lost hope of winning the war in America.

Assignment

Why did the American colonists win the American Revolution?

ABIGAIL ADAMS

John Adams, second president of the United States by Asher B. Durand, c1800 (PD-US).

Abigail Adams, later in life, by Gilbert Stuart, c1830 (PD-US).

As a girl growing up, Abigail Adams was obviously bright. Women at that time normally did not participate in formal education but that did not stop Adams from being a successful homeschooler. Basically self-taught, Adams loved books and read everything she could. Because of her intelligence and strong character, she was a threat to some 18th-century young men. But not to young John Adams. He always admired her acumen and outspokenness. When they were wed in 1764, they were very much in love. John at first wished to be a pastor but gave that up to become a lawyer. Abigail supported John's decision. She gave birth to three sons and two daughters. Abigail home schooled the children. Abigail Adams was no feminist by today's standards, but she openly expressed her opinion, especially to her influential husband. As a strong supporter of human rights, she thought a broad education for children, especially her daughters, was necessary. She made sure that this happened. By her words and her actions she was a Deborah (Judges 5)—a mother who shared her godly faith with her family and brought them up to be notable citizens.

This was at times hard for Abigail because she and John were separated for quite a while due to his long absences while in public service.

As the wife of the first vice president who became the second U.S. president, the First Lady had a great influence on the many people of the nation, especially her husband John and son John Quincy, both of whom served as presidents. She courageously objected to laws that did not allow equal rights and privileges for women—for example, the law that stated married women could not own property. She also was fervently opposed to slavery.

Later in 1801, the Adamses retired to Quincy. They spent 17 memorable years together in retirement. Throughout her life, Abigail stood for justice and equality. She took care of one president and homeschooled another. Abigail was truly a history maker (www.greatwomen.org).

The following is a quote from a letter Abigail wrote her husband John:

Do not put such unlimited power into the hands of the husbands. Remember all men would be tyrants if they could. If particular care and attention is not paid to the ladies we are determined to foment a rebellion, and will not hold ourselves bound by any laws in which we have no voice, or representation.

Assignment

Explore the life of colonial women and discuss why Abigail Adams would be concerned about their station in life.

HISTORICAL DEBATE: AMERICAN REVOLUTION

Historians agree that the American Revolution was the single most important event in this nation's history. Within 20 years—1763 to 1783—Americans declared their independence, waged a successful war, and became a Republic (Grob and Billias, p. 109). The historical controversies surrounding this important event include the following:

- Was the Revolution a colonial rebellion aimed at achieving independence from England?

- Was the Revolution a violent social upheaval, a class war, so to speak?

- What caused the Revolution? A struggle over ideology? Social conflict? Was religion a cause?

The first leading proponent of the theory that the American Revolution was merely a struggle of liberty vs. tyranny whose sole aim was to gain independence was George Bancroft. Bancroft saw the Revolution as a great epic struggle between good and evil. This view held until the early 21st century when historians like Arthur Schlesinger argued that the revolution was a struggle between classes, as evidenced by the very large loyalist group.

One particularly knotty issue surrounding the American Revolution was whether or not religion caused the War. Professor Christine Leigh Heyrman has explored this issue and offers several helpful insights.

She writes, "There are two notable trends in recent scholarship on this subject. The first is represented by those historians who argue that the revivals became a means by which humbler colonials challenged the prerogatives of their social 'betters'—both by criticizing their materialistic values and undermining their claims to deference and respect." The strongest case for this interpretation in the North has been advanced by Gary Nash in *The Urban Crucible*, a wide-ranging study of major seaports in the eighteenth century. A similar view of the Awakening in the upper South appears in Rhys Isaac, *The Transformation of Virginia, 1740–1790*. Indeed, some scholars like Harry Stout (*The New England Soul*) have argued that the first Great Awakening radically transformed and democratized modes of mass communication, thereby setting the stage for the emergence of a new, popular politics in the revolutionary decades that followed.

But this interpretation has been sharply criticized by Professor Christine Leigh Heyrman, who views the first Great Awakening, at least in the North, as an essentially conservative movement, a continuation of earlier religious traditions. As for the South, even those scholars who credit the potentially radical implications of early evangelical teachings in that region argue that challenges to slavery and class privilege faded quickly in the wake of the War (www.nhc.rtp.nc.us).

Assignment

In light of the above discussion, what do you think caused the American Revolution?

John Trumbull's famous painting is often identified as a depiction of the signing of the Declaration, but it actually shows the drafting committee presenting its work to the Congress, 1819.

The Spirit of "76", artist unknown, 1926.

Chapter 7

U.S. CONSTITUTION

First Thoughts . . .

"We have staked the whole future of American civilization, not upon the power of government, far from it. We've staked the future of all our political institutions upon our capacity…to sustain ourselves according to the Ten Commandments of God." —James Madison.

This week you will experience the euphoria of victory mitigated by the fact that Americans also had to form a new nation. You will read with concern the words of Hume and Voltaire—who had so much influence on Western thought—and you will refute their words. Next, you will examine the historical debate surrounding the creation of the U.S. Constitution, and you will form your own conclusion. Finally, you will look at the first internal crisis of this new nation: the problem of staying neutral in Franco-English European conflicts.

Chapter Learning Objectives . . .

Chapter 7 will analyze why the Articles of Confederation failed and how the U.S. Constitution was created and ratified. We will discuss the emerging nation and its first international crisis.

As a result of this chapter study you should be able to:

1. Discern and analyze the Confederation period of American history.
2. Evaluate why the Articles of Confederation did not work.
3. Compare and contrast the Articles of Confederation and the United States Constitution.
4. Reframe some contemporary legal issues in terms of original intent of the framers of the U.S. Constitution.
5. Debate the world views of Hume and Voltaire.
6. Analyze present historical debate surrounding the creation of the U.S. Constitution and propose your own theory.

THE CONSTITUTION : PART ONE

The War was won, but there was no American nation. There were now 13 autonomous free countries in place of the 13 colonies. Most of the jealousies of colonial times continued. America was more like the German states in Europe than a unified nation. They were tentatively held together by a document known as the **Articles of Confederation**. It was not a constitution; it was a sort of "gentleman's agreement."

Drafted in 1777 by the same Continental Congress that passed the Declaration of Independence, the articles established a covenant among the 13 states. The fact is, though, there was not much love lost among states, and the Confederation could do little to ameliorate petty state rivalry.

In the Continental Congress, which consisted of a single legislative chamber, each state had one equal vote. When a federal decision was necessary, each state delegation would struggle for consensus. If there was no unanimous affirmation for the proposal, the state delegation would abstain. To make things worse, the affirmative vote of nine states was required to pass any measure. The Continental Congress had no power to make laws binding individuals.

As anticipated, many disputes among the states arose, and there was no federal judicial or legislative branch to solve them. Not that it really mattered, because Congress had no way to mediate disagreements. Nor did it have the right to punish offenders. Congress had very little power under the Confederation. For example, it could not tax anyone so it had no funds. Therefore, there was no army or federal police force to enforce laws.

Things went from bad to worse. Some people were calling for a return to a monarchy—much like the British system from which they had departed. However, Washington strongly opposed this idea.

If the Confederation was a failure, the economy was nonetheless booming. Industry and agriculture were benefitting from the expanded markets generated by post-war peace, immigration, and western expansion. Without a

Alexander Hamilton by John Trumbull, 1806.

strong federal government, however, there was no way to consolidate and to preserve this new prosperity.

This was bad enough, but even worse things were coming. In 1786 an armed rebellion called **Shays Rebellion** broke out in western Massachusetts. Farmers, some of whom were former continental soldiers, could not produce enough to pay the interest on mortgages. They were in danger of losing their land. They were commanded by a former army officer, Daniel Shays. The rebellion was put down, but

Monument for The Last Battle of Shays Rebellion, southwest Massachusetts. Photo taken by John Bessa, 2007.

it was a wake-up call to everyone. The Confederation had to be abolished.

Eventually the opportunity came. Disputes between Maryland and Virginia led to a conference of representatives of five states at Annapolis, Maryland, in 1786. One of the delegates, **Alexander Hamilton**, advocated calling upon all the states to appoint representatives for a meeting to be held the following spring in Philadelphia.

It was a gathering of colonial scions of that time. Washington, Franklin, Madison, Hamilton—the best America had to offer were at this gathering. They assembled at the Federal Convention in the Philadelphia State House in May 1787. George Washington was chosen as the convener of the meeting.

Prominent among the more active members were two Pennsylvanians: Gouverneur Morris, who clearly saw the need for a strong federal government. Joining him was the sagacious and now ancient Benjamin Franklin. From

Virginia came James Madison, the "Father of the Constitution."

Massachusetts sent Rufus King and Elbridge Gerry, young men of ability and experience. Roger Sherman, shoemaker turned judge, was one of the representatives from Connecticut. From New York came Alexander Hamilton, who had proposed the meeting. Absent from the Convention were Thomas Jefferson, who was serving in France as minister, and John Adams, serving in the same capacity in Great Britain. Youth predominated among the 55 delegates—the average age was 42. (The last three paragraphs are quotes from an article written in the U.S. Archives.)

Assignment

Why did the Articles of Confederation fail?

THE CONSTITUTION: PART TWO

Most of the participants in the Constitutional Convention had no intentions of creating a new government, much less a constitution. Most had come to revise the Articles of Confederation. It was evident immediately, however, to all the delegates that a revision of the Articles would not work. Quickly, then, the delegates abandoned all efforts to revise the Articles and set out to write an entirely new constitution.

From the beginning, there were two competing interests: large, populated states and sparsely populated states. However, both agreed that the paramount need was to reconcile two different powers—the power of local control, which was already being exercised by the 13 states, and the power of a strong central government. They adopted the principle that the powers of the national government, being new, general, and inclusive, had to be carefully defined and stated, while all other unwritten powers were to be understood as belonging to the states (Archives).

Generally the delegates were proponents of the philosopher John Locke, who argued that the government that governed the least, governed the best. They also firmly believed that there were certain rights that were given to man by God Himself and could be neither modified nor abrogated by man. The best government was a balanced government. This view led to the conviction that three equal and separate branches of government should be established: legislative, executive, and judicial. The delegates agreed that the legislative branch, like the colonial legislatures and the British Parliament, should consist of two houses. Finally, they also agreed that all the proceedings of the Constitutional Convention would be highly confidential and would not be shared with the public until the proceedings were over (Archives).

On Tuesday morning, May 29, 1787, Edmund Randolph, governor of Virginia, opened the debate with a long speech decrying the evils that had befallen the country under the Articles of Confederation and stressing the need for

Portrait of James Madison author of the Bill of Rights by John Vanderlyn, 1816 (PD-US).

creating a strong national government. He set forward the **Virginia Plan**. Highly centralized, the government would have veto power over laws enacted by state legislatures.

Many smaller, less-populated states naturally opposed the Virginia Plan and set forth an alternative plan. On June 13 delegates from smaller states rallied around proposals offered by New Jersey delegate William Paterson. The "New Jersey Resolutions" proposed to keep more power in the local states.

The **New Jersey plan** was ultimately rejected.

A compromise was reached. The compromise created a House of Representatives and a Senate. The House of Representatives was composed of delegates whose number was determined by state population. The Senate, on the other hand, was to be composed of an equal number of representatives from all the states. All fiduciary responsibilities lay with the House; foreign policy and treaty making lay in the Senate.

Another knotty issue concerned how to count slaves. A compromise was reached whereby slaves were counted as three-fifths of all persons.

On Monday, August 6, 1787, the convention accepted the first draft of the Constitution. George Washington ordered 500 copies printed and distributed. On September 17 the members met for the last time. The debate for the ratification of the Constitution among the states had just begun.

The Convention had decided that the Constitution would take effect upon ratification by conventions in nine of the 13 states. In New York, Alexander Hamilton, John Jay, and James Madison pushed for the ratification of the Constitution in a series of essays known as the **Federalist Papers**. Ultimately the efforts of these, and other American leaders, assured ratification of the Constitution, and the same was accomplished in 1789. As one historian explains, "When the first Congress convened in New York City in September 1789, the calls for amendments protecting individual rights were virtually unanimous. Congress quickly adopted 12 such amendments; by December 1791, enough states had ratified 10 amendments to make them part of the Constitution. Collectively, they are known as the **Bill of Rights**. George Washington was unanimously chosen president on April 30, 1789. Congress quickly created the departments of State and Treasury, with Thomas Jefferson and Alexander Hamilton as their respective secretaries. Simultaneously, the Congress established the federal judiciary, establishing not only a Supreme Court, with one chief justice and five associate justices, but also three circuit courts and 13 district courts. Both a secretary of war and an attorney general were also appointed. And since Washington generally preferred to make decisions only after consulting those men whose judgment he valued, the American Presidential Cabinet came into existence, consisting of the heads of all the departments that Congress might create" (Archives, www.barefootsworld.net).

In the autumn of 1788, elections were held to fill the places in the new government. Washington was more or less appointed by acclamation, because he did not seek the office. Yielding to the pleas of friends, he accepted the post in the spirit of public service. On April 30, 1789, he took the oath of office at Federal Hall in New York City. Although one of the first tasks of the new government was to strengthen the domestic economy and make the nation financially secure, the United States could not ignore foreign affairs. Seeking to give the new nation time to mature, Washington sought to keep America out of foreign intrigues as long as possible. The French Revolution and later Napoleonic ambition made this impossible. This problem was brought into focus with the Citizen Genet incident.

Engraving of Edmond-Charles Genêt Harper's Encyclopædia of United States History, Vol. IV, p. 42, Harper & Brothers, 1905.

After the execution of King Louis XVI in January 1793, Britain, Spain, and Holland had become involved in war with France. According to the French Alliance of 1778, the United States and France were perpetual allies, and America was obliged to help France when she was attacked. However, the United States, militarily and economically a very weak country, was in no position to become involved in another war. On April 22, 1793, Washington effectively abrogated the terms of the 1778 treaty that made American independence possible by proclaiming the United States to be "friendly and impartial toward the belligerent powers." This set a pattern for generations of American policy makers.

The French ignored the American policy and sent a very undiplomatic diplomat named **Citizen Genêt.** Genêt so aggravated the Washington Administration that the United States requested his recall by the French government. The French and some Americans were outraged.

The Genêt incident strained American relations with France at a time when relations with Great Britain were not much better. In spite of the 1783 Peace of Paris, British troops still occupied forts in the West, and, even worse, the British navy was seizing American ships bound for French ports. To settle these matters, Washington sent John Jay, first chief justice of the Supreme Court, to London as a special envoy, where he negotiated a very pro-British treaty securing withdrawal of British soldiers from western forts and London's promise to pay damages for Britain's seizure of ships and cargoes in 1793 and 1794 but said nothing about "impressment"—the forcing of American sailors into British naval service. The whole treaty was a blow to the pride of every patriotic American.

Nonetheless, no sane American was willing to go to war with one, much less two, European powers. After long and acrimonious debate, the Senate ratified the treaty and Washington signed it into law.

The concept of two political parties was frightening to most Americans, and there was no such thing in America until the middle of the 19th century. There were two caucus groups. They were the Republicans and the Federalists. The Republicans generally supported minimum federal government intervention; the Federalists supported a strong federal government. While the Republicans and Federalists organized against each other along approximately ideological lines, in fact there was really not much difference between them. They had no national headquarters, no campaign finance funds, and no slate of candidates. They were more like two groups of polite lobbyists for their positions, which were nothing like a party platform.

Washington retired in 1797, firmly declining to serve for more than eight years as the nation's head. He had no constitutional reason to do so. However, he set a precedence that served us well until Franklin D. Roosevelt broke rank and was elected for four terms. Soon after that, the Constitution was amended to limit presidential terms to two.

Washington's vice president, John Adams of Massachusetts, was elected the new president. He had served as vice president under Washington for eight years. The office, which was intended to provide a head of government in case of the president's death, did not suit the spirited and ambitious Adams. He regarded the vice presidency "the most insignificant office that ever the invention of man contrived" (library.thinkquest.org).

Now problems arose internationally again. France, angered by Jay's recent treaty with Britain, used the British argument that food supplies, naval stores, and war material bound for enemy ports were subject to seizure by the French navy. By 1797 France had seized 300 American ships and had broken off diplomatic relations with the United States. When Adams sent three other commissioners to Paris to negotiate, agents of Foreign Minister Charles Maurice de Talleyrand (whom Adams labeled X, Y, and Z in his report to Congress) informed the Americans that negotiations could begin only if the United States loaned France $12 million and bribed officials of the French government. The so-called XYZ Affair almost led to war between the two nations.

In this crisis, Adams sent three new commissioners to France. Napoleon, who had just come to power, received them cordially, and the danger of conflict subsided with the negotiation of the Treaty of 1800, which formally released the United States from its 1778 defense alliance with France. Nothing, however, was done about the 300 hijacked American ships.

Hostility to France led Congress to pass the controversial **Alien and Sedition Acts**. The Alien Act, operative for two years only, gave the president the power to expel or imprison aliens in time of war. The Sedition Act proscribed writing, speaking, or publishing anything of "a false, scandalous, and malicious" nature against the president or Congress.

The acts met with resistance. Jefferson and Madison sponsored the passage of the Kentucky and Virginia Resolutions by the legislatures of the two states in 1798. According to the resolutions, states could "nullify" federal laws if they contradicted the will of the state. The student will hear this argument voiced again during the pre–Civil War Years.

By 1800 the American people were ready for a change. The Federalists had established a strong government but had followed policies that alienated large groups. In the election of 1800 Thomas Jefferson soundly defeated John Adams. In his inaugural address, the first such speech in the new capital of Washington, DC, Jefferson promised "a wise and frugal government" to

Portrait of Charles-Maurice de Talleyrand-Périgord by Pierre-Paul Prud'hon, 1817 (PD-US).

preserve order among the inhabitants but would "leave them otherwise free to regulate their own pursuits of industry, and improvement." (Note: Most of the above material can be found online. Source: Online Outline of American history 1994.)

Assignment

A. How did the Constitution distribute power among the three branches of the federal government?

B. If you could rewrite the Constitution today, what changes would you make?

C. The Constitution defines treason in Article 3, Section 3, as making war against the United States, or supporting the enemy by giving them "aid and comfort." Given this definition, would you agree with the federal government that the U.S. citizen who joined Bin Laden's group in Afghanistan was guilty of treason?

PHILOSOPHERS AND WORLD VIEWS

Immanuel Kant (1724–1804)

Immanuel Kant invited philosophy to take an entirely new direction: he brought philosophy away from the other academic disciplines and placed it squarely on its own. He argued that, although our knowledge cannot completely transcend our experience, there is an essential structure to our knowledge that cannot be directly gained from experience (Martyn Oliver, *History of Philosophy*, p. 88). The greatest damage, however, that he did to Christian thought was his argument that morality began with rational thought (as contrasted with a basis in the authoritative, inspired Word of God). This viewpoint, developed by later philosophers, ushered in the modern age.

Excerpts from *The Fundamental Principles of the Metaphysics of Ethics*:

To be beneficent when we can is a duty; and besides this, there are many minds so sympathetically constituted that, without any other motive of vanity or self-interest, they find a pleasure in spreading joy around them, and can take delight in the satisfaction of others so far as it is their own work. But I maintain that in such a case an action of this kind, however proper, however amiable it may be, has nevertheless no true moral worth, but is on a level with other inclinations. . . . For the maxim lacks the moral import, namely, that such actions be done from duty, not from inclination.

Immanuel Kant, artist and date unknown.

. . . as to moral feeling, this supposed special sense, the appeal to it is indeed superficial when those who cannot think believe that feeling will help them out, even in what concerns general laws: and besides, feelings which naturally differ infinitely in degree cannot furnish a uniform standard of good and evil, nor has any one a right to form judgments for others by his own feelings. . .

Act as if the maxim of your action were to become through your will a general natural law.

Statue of Ilmmanuel Kant in Kaliningrad, Russia (CC BY-SA 2.5).

Voltaire (1694–1778)

Voltaire was both a great philosopher and a prolific writer—a dangerous combination. Voltaire argued persuasively that all knowledge comes from experience. "If God did not exist," he was fond of saying, "He would have to be invented." Along with Rousseau, he was the father of both the Enlightenment and the French Revolution.

Excerpts from a letter written by Voltaire:

I always reduce, so far as I can, my metaphysics to morality. I have honestly sought, with all the attention of which I am capable, to gain some definite idea of the human soul, and I own that the result of all my researches is ignorance. I find a principle—thinking, free, active—almost like God Himself: my reason tells me that God exists: but it also tells me that I cannot know what He is.

Is it indeed likely that we should know what our soul is, when we can form no idea of light if we have had the misfortune to be born blind? I see then, with regret, that all that has been written about the soul teaches us nothing at all.

After my vain groping to discover its nature, my chief aim has been to try at least to regulate it: it is the mainspring of our clock. All Descartes' fine ideas on its elasticity tell me nothing of the nature of the spring: I am ignorant even of the cause of that flexibility: however, I wind up my timepiece, and it goes passably well.

I examine man. We must see if, of whatsoever materials he is composed, there is vice and virtue in them. That is the important point with regard to him—I do not say merely with regard to a certain society living under certain laws: but for the whole human race; for you, sir, who will one day sit on a throne, for the wood-cutter in your forest, for the Chinese doctor, and for the savage of America. Locke, the wisest metaphysician I know, while he very rightly attacks the theory of innate ideas, seems to think that there is no universel moral principle. I venture to doubt, or rather, to elucidate the great man's theory on this point. I agree with him that there is really no such thing as innate thought: whence it obviously follows that there is no principle of morality innate in our souls: but because we are not born with beards, is it just to say that we are not born (we, the inhabitants of this continent) to have beards at a certain age?

Voltaire at 24, by Catherine Lusurier after Nicolas de Largillière's painting, 1778 (copy); 1718 (original) (PD-US).

We are not born able to walk: but everyone, born with two feet, will walk one day. Thus, no one is born with the idea he must be just: but God has so made us that, at a certain age, we all agree to this truth. Animals have these advantages over man: they never hear the clock strike, they die without any idea of death, they have no theologians to instruct them, their last moments are not disturbed by unwelcome and unpleasant ceremonies, their funerals cost them nothing, and no one starts lawsuits over their wills.

It seems clear to me that God designed us to live in society—just as He has given the bees the instincts and the powers to make honey: and as our social system could not subsist without the sense of justice and injustice, He has given us the power to acquire that sense. It is true that varying customs make us attach the idea of justice to different things. What is a crime in Europe will be a virtue in Asia, just as German dishes do not please French palates: but God has so made Germans and French that they both like good living. All societies, then, will not have the same laws, but no society will be without laws. Therefore, the good of the greatest number is the immutable law of virtue, as established by all men from Peking to Ireland: what is useful to society will be good for every country. This idea reconciles the contradictions which appear in morality. Robbery was permitted in Lacedaemonia: why? because all goods were held in common, and the man who stole from the greedy who kept for himself what the law gave to the public was a social benefactor.

There are savages who eat men, and believe they do well. I say those savages have the same idea of right and wrong as ourselves. As we do, they make war from anger and passion: the same crimes are committed everywhere: to eat your enemies is but an extra ceremonial. The wrong does not consist in roasting, but in killing them: and I dare swear there is no cannibal who believes that he is doing right when he cuts his enemy's throat. I saw four savages from Louisiana who were brought to France in 1723. There was a woman among them of a very gentle disposition. I asked her, through an interpreter, if she had ever eaten the flesh of her enemies and if she liked it; she answered, Yes. I asked her if she would be willing to kill, or to have killed, any one of her fellow-countrymen in order to eat him: she answered, shuddering, visibly horrified by such a crime. I defy the most determined liar among travellers to dare to tell me that there is a community or a family where to break one's word is laudable. I am deeply rooted in the belief that, God having made certain animals to graze in common, others to meet occasionally two and two, rarely, and spiders to spin webs, each species has the tools necessary for the work it has to do.

Put two men on the globe, and they will only call good, right, just, what will be good for them both. Put four, and they will only consider virtuous what suits them all: and if one of the four eats his neighbour's supper, or fights or kills him, he will certainly raise the others against him. And what is true of these four men is true of the universe.

Assignment

A. As a Christian believer, take Voltaire to task for what he says. What does the Bible have to say about his world view?

B. Based on the quotes of Kant (pg. 104), and other evidence, in what ways does Kant violate the basic principles of Christianity?

Voltaire at 70. Engraving from 1843 edition of his *Philosophical Dictionary* (PD-US).

HISTORICAL DEBATE: THE CONSTITUTION

Among historians, the Constitution remains one of the most controversial documents in American history. Generations of Supreme Court Justices have interpreted the document according to their prejudices and the times in which they lived (Grob and Billias, p. 159). Controversy, however, is not tied only to interpretations of the document. Greater controversy is tied to the purpose of the original framers of the Constitution. This is not only a historiography question, it is a legal question. Lawyers have argued for two centuries what the framers intended, for it is within this context that court cases are won and lost.

From the end of the Constitutional Convention to the American Civil War, most arguments were conceptualized in discussions about states' rights and slavery. Politicians in the North and in the South were fond of citing the Constitution to support their positions. Historians followed this line of interpretation: states' rights vs. national sovereignty, loose construction of the Constitution vs. strict interpretation of the Constitution.

That particular issue was settled by the Civil War. After the Civil War, five distinct theories arose concerning the Constitution.

The first school, the Nationalist school, 1870–1880, subscribed to the idea that the orderly progress of civilization was due largely to the ability of America to provide leadership to the entire world. Preeminent in this leadership was the creation of what is essentially an "inspired" document: the United States Constitution. James Madison, George Washington, et al., were more than statesmen: they were prophets who led mankind into the Promised Land.

The next generation of historians, called Progressives, 1880–1920, took this view to task. The Constitution to them was a reactionary document—one written by the conservatives at the convention to abrogate the radical ideas promulgated during the Revolution. The Nationalists saw the Constitution as the capstone of the American Revolution. The Progressives saw it as a radical break from the Revolution (Grob and Billias, pp. 162–163).

The third group, called the Neoconservatives, 1920–1950, argued that the Constitution was more of a consensus than a break from the past. They saw the Constitution as a very natural, even basic document, reflective of the unanimity reflected in American society. It was neither, then, a radical break from the Revolution nor a glorious culmination of Revolutionary ideas, it was merely a conservative document created by conservative leaders seeking to express the world view of their age and nation.

The fourth view grew from this view. These historians, called the New Intellectuals, 1950–1960, argued that the Constitution was not an American document at all. To understand the Constitution fully, one will have to look at European ideology and precedence. It was, quintessentially, an 18th-century European statement of reality that could very clearly be tied to the Reformation.

Finally, the most recent interpretation of the Constitution has come from New Left historians. These historians argue that the Constitution was a radical departure from European history. They argue it was a veiled attempt to control Americans and to bring a form of tyranny. They openly prefer a more socialistic government.

Assignment

Which historical view(s) seem most plausible to you? Why?

Scene at the Signing of the Constitution of the United States by Howard Chandler Christy. Date unknown (PD-US).

Chapter 8

NATIONALISM

First Thoughts . . .

You will experience the first peaceful revolution in American history. In 1800, for the first time in history, a democratically elected government peacefully replaced an entirely different standing ideological government. Next, you will decide whether President Jefferson did the right thing when he ignored the Constitution and bought the Louisiana Purchase. With a new president came the War of 1812—the first useless war that no one expected and no one wanted. James Monroe, the next president, ushered in a new Era of Good Feeling. This period—the Middle Period of American history—saw more cultural revolutions than any other in American history. Finally, in the back of every American mind was the issue of slavery, which was already becoming a national problem.

Chapter Learning Objectives . . .

Chapter 8 will describe the first peaceful revolution in American history and the resulting Era of Good Feeling that extended into the middle decades of the 19th century.

As a result of this chapter study you should be able to:

1. Analyze why the Federalists lost power in 1800.
2. Evaluate what were the causes and results of the War of 1812.
3. Discuss the impact of the transportation revolution on American lives.
4. Review the election of 1824 and decide whether Adams was fairly elected.
5. Analyze the impact of the Missouri Compromise of 1820.

A PEACEFUL REVOLUTION

In 1800, for the first time in history, a democratically elected government peacefully replaced an entirely different ideological government. The major political parties we know today did not exist in 1800. That contest was **Democratic Republicans** vs. Federalists. Nonetheless, it is remarkable and a credit to the American civilization that two candidates could vigorously debate issues and remain friends and colleagues after one was elected. Though Federalists lost and the Democratic Republicans won, the whole world won when the young nation transferred its power without bloodshed. Contrast this with what was happening in France! France decapitated its deposed king; the U.S. honorably retired its losing president.

Nation building invites dissension, discord, and violence. These elements were remarkably absent from the young American nation, 1800–1828. Let's look more closely at the 1800 election.

The Federalist John Adams had been elected in 1796 without much opposition. But, in 1800, the Republicans left no stone unturned in their efforts to discredit the Federalist candidate. President Adams, blamed for the unpopular Alien and Sedition laws, made a poor campaign. Federalists tried to discredit Thomas Jefferson with epithets of "Jacobin" and "Anarchist." When the vote was counted, it was found that Adams had been defeated; the Republicans had carried the entire South and New York and secured 8 of the 15 electoral votes cast by Pennsylvania.

Jefferson's election, however, was still uncertain. By a strange provision in the Constitution, presidential electors were required to vote for two persons without indicating which office each was to fill, the one receiving the highest number of votes to be president and the candidate standing next to be vice president. Remember, there were no political parties. Aaron Burr, the Republican candidate for vice president, had received the same number of votes as Jefferson; as neither had a majority, the election was thrown into the House of Representatives, where the Federalists held the balance of power. Although it was well known that Burr was not even a candidate for president, his friends and many Federalists promoted his election to that high office. Had it not been for vigorous opposition by Alexander Hamilton, Aaron Burr (later convicted of treason) would have been the third president of the United States. Not until the 36th ballot on February 17, 1801, was Jefferson officially president.

Thomas Jefferson, the author of the Declaration of Independence and a clear proponent of "the government that governs the least governs the best" was elected. Jefferson's mere presence in the White House encouraged democracy. Jefferson insisted that his staff regard themselves as servants of the people. He saw the unsettled, pristine West as the key to America's future. He encouraged agriculture and westward expansion. Believing America to be a haven for the oppressed, he urged a liberal naturalization law.

Jefferson also showed particularly inspired fiduciary leadership. By the end of his second term, his farsighted secretary of the treasury, Albert Gallatin, had reduced the national debt to less than $560 million. As a wave of Jeffersonian fervor swept the nation, state after state abolished property qualifications for the ballot and passed more humane laws for debtors and criminals. (Note: Most of the above material can be found online. Source: Outline of American history 1994.)

Jefferson began his presidency like most successful politicians: calling for

Statue of Jefferson at Jefferson Memorial by Rudulph Evans, 1943 (CC BY-SA 3.0).

unity. "We are all Republicans, we are all Federalists."

Jefferson pursued a policy of expansion. He seized the opportunity when Napoleon Bonaparte offered to sell the Louisiana Territory for pennies an acre. This is called the **Louisiana Purchase**. Even though Jefferson had no constitutional sanction for such an exercise of executive power, he nevertheless doubled the territory of the United States. The nation was young with a new Constitution, and the president, more than at any other time in history, could do all sorts of things that today would be considered unconstitutional. Jefferson really did not know what he had, so he sent **Meriwether Lewis** and **William Clark** on an expedition of exploration across the continent. All this territorial expansion was not without problems—some aberrant, even seditious, movements arose. The first secession arose in the Northeast: a Confederacy formulated by New England Federalists. Aaron Burr, who had been elected Jefferson's vice president in 1800 but was replaced in 1804, led several western conspiracies. He also killed Alexander Hamilton in a duel.

LEWIS AND CLARK TRAIL

President Jefferson argued with members of the judiciary, many of whom had been late appointments by the Federalist Adams. Jefferson's main nemesis was Chief Justice John Marshall. In the case of **Marbury v. Madison** (1803), the Supreme Court first exercised the power of judicial review. The courts used judicial review to stop legislation that it considered unconstitutional.

By the start of Jefferson's second term in office, Europe was consumed with the Napoleonic Wars. The United States remained neutral, but both Britain and France imposed decrees severely restricting American trade with Europe and they confiscated American ships for violating the new rules. Britain also conducted impressment raids in which U.S. citizens were sometimes seized. Jefferson tried to coerce both Britain and France into ceasing to violate "neutral rights" with a total embargo on American exports. The results destroyed American commerce and ignited a fire storm in New England. The embargo was not abolished until 1809 when James Madison was elected president.

Madison's presidency was dominated by foreign affairs. Both Britain and France violated American rights, but Britain was more resented because it had the larger navy. Also, some Americans saw a chance to expand into Florida and Canada. War was declared in June 1812 on a vote of 79–49 in the House and 19–13 in the Senate. There was almost no support for war in the Northern states. The war began and ended in irony. The British had already removed the offending laws, but the news had not reached the United States at the time of the declaration of war! The only big victory for America was the **Battle of New Orleans**. Nonetheless, there were no long-term victors—the **Treaty of Ghent** in 1814 was a draw. Individuals like Andrew Jackson, though, launched careers from this war.

Assignment

A. Why did the Federalists lose power in 1800?

B. It is doubtful that Jefferson could have obtained the Louisiana Purchase if he had had to wait for congressional approval. When should the president ignore the rule of law to accomplish altruistic goals?

C. What were the causes and results of the War of 1812?

AN ERA OF GOOD FEELING

The years between the election to the presidency of James Monroe (right) in 1816 and of John Quincy Adams in 1824 have long been known in American history as the Era of Good Feelings.

The **Monroe Doctrine** (1823) declared that the United States would not become involved in European affairs and would not accept European interference in the Americas.

Internally, the decisions of the Supreme Court under Chief Justice John Marshall in such cases as **McCulloch v. Maryland** (1819) and **Gibbons v. Ogden** (1824) promoted nationalism by strengthening Congress and national power at the expense of the states. The congressional decision to charter the second Bank of the United States (1816) was explained in part by the nation's financial weaknesses, exposed by the War of 1812 and a strong feeling of national unity. In fact, Monroe was almost unanimously elected in 1820. The Federalist "Party" was officially dead.

If unity prevailed nationally, disunity grew among the states. Namely, there was the growing struggle over slavery expansion. As long as the United States was confined to the eastern seaboard and southern and northern states had approximately the same representation in Congress, slavery was only a moral issue. With the acquisition of the Louisiana Purchase that all changed. The **Missouri Compromise of 1820** tried to answer the problem of slavery expansion by stating that slavery was to be confined to the area south of the Missouri border (which was a slave state). Of course, the problem was not solved, only postponed.

The real changes in America, however, from 1800 to 1828 (and beyond) were in the social realm. The advent of steam travel and railroad transportation profoundly changed American life. A trip from Philadelphia, Pennsylvania, to Pittsburgh, Pennsylvania, for instance, could take two months in 1820. By 1835 it would take two days!

At the same time, steamboats replaced rafts on the Mississippi and sharply reduced the price of Mississippi commerce. The Erie Canal, the most successful private project constructed during the era, enabled efficient western grain producers to ship their produce east and therefore encouraged western expansion.

Keep off! Monroe doctrine by Thomas E. Powers, 1912

All of this expansion stimulated a critical question: Would the federal government pay for public projects? This question was answered tentatively by the federal government's support of the **National Road** (Route 40 across Ohio).

Efficient transportation naturally had a positive effect on industrialization. Products could be quickly and efficiently transported to market. At the same time that industry was booming in the North, cotton remained king of the South. Ironically, then, while the country grew closer together by more efficient transportation, it grew further apart ideologically and politically.

It comes as no surprise that the Era of Good Feeling ended. As President Monroe's second term drew to a close in 1824, there was a lack of good feeling among his official advisers, three of whom—Secretary of State John Quincy Adams (son of second U.S. president John Adams) Secretary of War John C. Calhoun, and Secretary of the Treasury William H. Crawford—sought to be president. Henry Clay (left), speaker of the House, and General Andrew Jackson were also candidates. Calhoun was nominated for the vice presidency. Of the other four, Jackson received 99 electoral votes, Adams 84, Crawford 41, and Clay 37. Because no one had a majority the House of Representatives had to make its choice. Clay despised Jackson so he made sure that Adams won. A few days later Adams offered Clay the office of secretary of state. Jackson was naturally outraged and was sure that the presidency had been stolen from him. As a result, John Quincy Adams, an intelligent, principled man, saw his presidency sabotaged by Jacksonian Democrats. By the time Jackson was elected in 1828, the line had been drawn in the sand and a democratic revolution was dawning.

Assignment

A. What caused the American nation to experience an Era of Good Feeling from 1816-1824?

B. How did the development of the cotton culture in the South early in the 19th century affect the American civilization?

C. What impact did the transportation revolution have on American lives?

D. Discuss the historical events surrounding the Missouri Compromise and speculate on why it set a dangerous precedence for later history.

E. How did Adams win the election of 1824? Was his election fair?

HISTORY MAKER: JOHN QUINCY ADAMS

John Quincy Adams was a history maker because he refused to give up, even when the nation and some friends rejected him. He was not only defeated in 1828, he was also humiliated. Other men would have retired from public life; not John Quincy Adams. He committed his life to worthy causes—like ending slavery.

In 1830 his home state of Massachusetts sent him to the House of Representatives, and there for the remainder of his life he served as a powerful leader. He was a tireless supporter of civil rights.

For instance, in 1836 southern Congressmen passed a "gag rule" providing that the House automatically table petitions against slavery. Adams tirelessly fought the rule for eight years until finally he obtained its repeal.

In 1848 he collapsed on the floor of the House from a stroke and was carried to the Speaker's Room, where two days later he died. Adams always fought for what was right, no matter what it cost him personally or politically.

A copy of a lost daguerreotype of John Quincy Adams taken by Philip Haas in 1843 (PD-US).

John Quincy Adams a few hours prior to his death. A sketch by Arthur J. Stansbury Esqr., 1848.

Assignment

Adams was a man of principle and did what he knew was right, even when it was politically unpopular. What biblical character(s) can you recall who exhibited this character quality?

HISTORICAL DEBATE: NATIONAL PERIOD

Historians have long been impressed by the formative influences that the National Period brought on American history. It was a period of good feeling and struggle: aristocracy versus democracy, industrialism versus agrarianism, federal rule versus states' rights (Grob, p. 203). These roots of conflict, though, would flower later. The earliest historians viewed this Era of Good Feeling as the last time of basic unanimity before the nation embarked on the long road to civil war.

Throughout most of the 19th century the majority of American historians who wrote about the National Period more or less summed it up as an amicable conflict between Jeffersonian Democrats and Hamiltonian Federalists. These same historians argued that the Jeffersonian Democrats were even responsible for the Civil War—if the Hamiltonian Federalists had prevailed earlier and formed a strong central government there would not have even been a hint of rebellion in 1860. Hamilton, then, grew in esteem among historians, and Jefferson took a lot of hits.

Historical opinions changed considerably in 1900. Early 19th-century historians flip-flopped the whole story and now claimed that the progressive, democratic Jefferson was the real hero of the National Period. He was the innovative thinker who invited America to a place of freedom and of democracy. Jefferson did this in the face of substantial opposition from virulent, anti-democratic Federalists.

With the coming of the New Deal, the Jeffersonian

DEMOCRACY'S OPPORTUNITY.

REPUBLICAN :—"Hey, what can I do without them?"   DEMOCRACY :—"What have you done with them—only cast them off!"

tradition had even more appeal to American historians. With the rise of totalitarian regimes in Europe, Jeffersonian Democracy was a cause for which one could fight and die. (Grob and Billias, Vol. 1, pp. 210–211).

Later historians finally were to draw a consensus opinion that argued that Hamilton and Jefferson were really not that different after all.

Assignment

Which theory (Hamiltonian or Jeffersonian) do you find most convincing? Why?

Twenty Years After, illustration shows a man labeled "Republican Party" picking up the clothing of a man labeled "Democratic Party" swimming in the "Democratic Issue Pond" which is labeled "Socialism, Bryanism, Populism, Free Silver, Anti-Expansion, [and] Jeffersonian Simplicity", by J.S. Pughe, printed in Puck, (1902 November 19). In the upper right corner is an insert that shows a scene twenty years earlier, only this time it is a man labeled "Democrat" picking up the clothing of a "Republican" swimming in the "Republican Corruption Water", by J. Keppler, printed in Puck, (1882 August 2).

General Andrew Jackson stands on the parapet of his makeshift defenses as his troops repulse attacking Highlanders by painter Edward Percy Moran, 1910 (PD-U

NATIONALISM

Chapter 9

DEMOCRACY AND NEW GOVERNMENTS

First Thoughts . . .

In the election of 1824, the representatives of the "aristocracy" made their last successful stand. Until then the leadership by men of "wealth and talents" had been undisputed. There had been five presidents—Washington, John Adams, Jefferson, Madison, and Monroe—all East Coast men brought up in prosperous families. None of them had ever worked a day in their lives! They were "old money" aristocrats. Then came Andrew Jackson—who never finished high school and was a rough, self-made Westerner. Some Americans loved Andrew Jackson, the hero of the Battle of New Orleans. Others hated him—Andrew Jackson, the cause of the destruction of thousands of Native American Cherokees on the Trail of Tears. Democracy, everyone agrees, is the best form of government, but in the Middle Period of American history, limitations of egalitarianism emerged that have yet to be addressed. Finally, we understand again that history is always open to interpretation.

Chapter Learning Objectives . . .

We will explore different aspects of Jacksonian democracy and determine for ourselves whether it was a good thing for America. We will walk again the Trail of Tears and experience the horror that was inflicted on a Native American people.

As a result of this chapter study you should be able to:

1. Discuss why a Christian theist would find Ralph Waldo Emerson's philosophy to be objectionable, and analyze present manifestations (e.g., Unitarianism) of the same world view.

2. Discuss the distinctives of a democratic society and the limits of democracy.

3. Understand that public education was one fruit of American democracy and evaluate whether its development was a positive thing for America.

4. Assess whether the Jacksonian democratic revolution moved America toward mediocrity.

5. Measure the limits of Jacksonian democracy, especially as it affected minorities and women.

6. Evaluate the historical debate surrounding Jacksonian democracy and determine which arguments you find most persuasive.

7. Discuss the impact of Daniel Webster on American History.

PHILOSOPHERS AND WORLD VIEWS

Ralph Waldo Emerson (1803–1882)

Emerson was a frustrated pastor who gave up his faith, embraced **Transcendentalism**, and wrote excellent (if flawed in world view) literature and philosophy.

Emerson was part of the Transcendentalist movement, which was the American version of Romanticism. Romanticism questioned the power and virtue of reason. To Emerson and all Transcendentalists/Romantics the subjective, the emotional, the feelings were the epicenter of human existence. Emerson was, therefore, suspicious of reason and empiricism. As philosopher Martyn Oliver remarked, "To the Romantic the unthinkable was a common and enduring characteristic." This provided a stark contrast with Enlightenment philosophy, which was concerned to start, at least, with that which could be known with certainty. The Enlightenment epitomized the values of logic, certainty, and consistency, and the Romantic reveled in contradiction and uncertainty. For the first time since the Classical/Christian era, that which was abstract, that which could not be quantified was celebrated and extolled.

Ralph Waldo Emerson engraved and published by S. A. Schoff ... from an original drawing by Sam W. Rowse, 1878 (PD-US).

The following is a portion of Emerson's essay "Conduct of Man" (1860):

We are born believing. A man bears beliefs, as a tree bears apples. A self-poise belongs to every particle; and a rectitude to every mind, and is the Nemesis and protector of every society. I and my neighbors have been bred in the notion, that, unless we came soon to some good church—Calvinism, or Behmenism, or Romanism, or Mormonism—there would be a universal thaw and dissolution. No Isaiah or Jeremy has arrived. Nothing can exceed the anarchy that has followed in our skies. The stern old faiths have all pulverized. 'Tis a whole population of gentlemen and ladies out in search of religions. 'Tis as flat anarchy in our ecclesiastic realms, as that which existed in Massachusetts, in the Revolution, or which prevails now on the slope of the Rocky Mountains or Pike's Peak. Yet we make shift to live. Men are loyal. Nature has self-poise in all her works; certain proportions in which oxygen and azote combine, and, not less a harmony in faculties, a fitness in the spring and the regulator.

The decline of the influence of Calvin, or Fenelon, or Wesley, or Channing, need give us no uneasiness. The builder of heaven has not so ill constructed his creature as that the religion, that is, the public nature, should fall out: the public and the private element, like north and south, like inside and outside, like centrifugal and centripetal, adhere to every soul, and cannot be subdued, except the soul is dissipated. God builds his temple in the heart on the ruins of churches and religions.

Henry David Thoreau (1817–1862)

When I entered Harvard Divinity School in 1976, Divinity Hall where I lived was already rich with stories—some of which were apocalyptic—about Emerson, Channing, and Thoreau, all three champions of the early Transcendental movement. Writer, philosopher, and naturalist Henry David Thoreau was a bona fide eccentric who has been the champion of advocates of nonviolence for at least three generations. "Eccentric" is a polite way to describe Thoreau–less generous individuals, in modern vernacular, would call him a certifiable "nut." To his friends Melville, Emerson, Hawthorne, and the Alcotts, Thoreau was always a lot of fun, for one never knew what Thoreau would do. But Thoreau was not harmless: he advanced the heresy called Transcendentalism. The problem with Emerson and Thoreau was that they were not merely writers—they were preachers, philosophers. People read their poems and essays. People were influenced by them. The same could be said for the Alcott sisters (one of whom wrote *Little Women*), Melville (*Moby Dick*), and Cooper (*Deerslayer*, et al.), but these three were primarily literary authors, not theologians.

A portion of Thoreau's "Civil Disobedience:"

The authority of government, even such as I am willing to submit to—for I will cheerfully obey those who know and can do better than I, and in many things even those who neither know nor can do so well—is still an impure one: to be strictly just, it must have the sanction and consent of the governed. It can have no pure right over my person and property but what I concede to it. The progress from an absolute to a limited monarchy, from a limited monarchy to a democracy, is a progress toward a true respect for the individual. Even the Chinese philosopher was wise enough to regard the individual as the basis of the empire. Is a democracy, such as we know it, the last improvement possible in government? Is it not possible to take a step further towards recognizing and organizing the rights of man? There will never be a really free and enlightened State until the State comes to recognize the individual as a higher and independent power, from which all its

Henry David thoreau portrait by Benjamin D. Maxham (daguerreotype), 1856 (PD-US).

own power and authority are derived, and treats him accordingly. I please myself with imagining a State at last which can afford to be just to all men, and to treat the individual with respect as a neighbor; which even would not think it inconsistent with its own repose if a few were to live aloof from it, not meddling with it, nor embraced by it, who fulfilled all the duties of neighbors and fellow men. A State which bore this kind of fruit, and suffered it to drop off as fast as it ripened, would prepare the way for a still more perfect and glorious State, which I have also imagined, but not yet anywhere seen.

Assignment

A. Why would a Christian theist find Emerson's quote to be objectionable?

B. Transcendentalism, represented in the declining Unitarian Church, is still very much alive in American culture. For instance, familiar songs and advertising slogans proclaiming "I did it my way," "Have it your way," and "You're worth it!" exhibits a great deal of Emersonian subjectivity. Explain.

THE RISE OF THE AMERICAN POLITICAL TRADITION

The presidency of James Monroe (1817–1825) was termed the Era of Good Feelings, but in many ways it was just the opposite. While consensus appeared on the surface, it was a period of vigorous political and regional disagreement. Political opponents quietly built coalitions and advanced agendas. All of this posturing burst onto the political arena in the controversial 1824 election (described below).

Nonetheless, the administrations of Madison and especially Monroe clearly marked the end of the Federalist Party, and the appearance of a consensus—of some sorts—under the Jeffersonian Democratic banner. However, within a very few years the Federalist Party agenda would reappear in the Whig Party, and political hegemony by Jeffersonian Democrats was again challenged.

I use the word "party" with some trepidation. With political parties indelibly a part of contemporary American political life, it is difficult for Americans to understand that until the middle of the 19th century most Americans were not comfortable with the concept of "political parties," which were perceived as divisive, even seditious. The fact is, most Americans were suspicious of "factionalism." Also, in the case of the presidential election, the president was elected by the **electoral college** chosen by state legislatures, not by direct voters. Most people, therefore, really did not vote. This changed slowly over the course of the early 19th century.

Of course, the Founding Fathers knew there would be "factions" and special interest groups, but they never planned for or expected to see permanent political parties emerge. Early Federalist leaders, schooled in the British constitutional system, hoped that factions would remain fluid and temporary rather than crystallize into firm organizational structures of established political parties. By 1800, however, the factions of Federalists and anti-Federalists had structured themselves into the beginnings of political parties.

Ironically, in his Farewell Address, President Washington expressed great anxiety about the development of political parties.

The following is a portion of President Washington's Farewell Address:

All combinations and associations under whatever plausible character, with the real design to direct, control, counteract, or awe the regular deliberations and actions of the constituted authorities, are destructive. . . . They serve to organize faction, to give an artificial and extraordinary force, to put in the place of the delegated will of the nation the will of the party, often a small but artful and enterprising minority of the community; and, according to the alternate triumphs of different parties, to make the public administration the mirror of the ill-concerted and incongruous projects of faction, rather than the organ of consistent and wholesome plans di-gested by common councils, and modified by mutual interests."

Caption: *An Available Candidate. The One Qualification for a Whig President.* used at Whig party convention in Philadelphia, 1948.

By 1828, Americans were growing more comfortable with political parties (see chart on following page). But these early political "parties" were more like caucuses than organized entities. There was no party chairperson, or organized fundraising. Political parties were groups of people crystallized around political issues, but they did not permanently advance a particular platform or agenda. This all changed with the election of Andrew Jackson.

No candidate gained a majority in the Electoral College, so, according to the provisions of the Constitution, the election was thrown into the House of Representatives, where Henry Clay was the most influential politician. Clay, though, knew that he would never win enough votes to carry the election. So, feeling great animosity toward Jackson and satisfied merely to be Secretary of State, Clay cut a deal with Adams, who ultimately gained the presidency. Jackson immediately cried foul-play, but Adams had won fair and square. Jackson correctly argued that Adams had not won the popular vote—Jackson had—and Jackson returned in 1828 to make his point by winning the presidency hands down.

During Adams's administration, for the first time really, extant, permanent political parties appeared. Adams's followers took the name of "National Republicans," later to be changed to "Whigs." As one historian explained, "Though he governed honestly and efficiently, Adams was not a popular president, and his administration was marked with frustrations. Adams failed in his effort to institute a national system of roads and canals. His years in office appeared to be one long campaign for reelection, and his coldly intellectual temperament did not win friends. Jackson, by contrast, had enormous popular appeal, especially among his followers in the newly named Democratic Party that emerged from the Republican Party, with its roots dating back to presidents Jefferson, Madison, and Monroe. In the election of 1828, Jackson defeated Adams by an overwhelming electoral majority."

In 1824 Tennessee and Pennsylvania chose Andrew Jackson with South Carolina Senator John C. Calhoun (left) as his running mate. Kentucky selected Speaker of the House Henry Clay; Massachusetts, Secretary of State John Quincy Adams; and a congressional caucus, Treasury Secretary William Crawford. Personality sectional allegiance played important roles in determining the outcome of the election. Without a majority of the popular vote. Adams nevertheless won the election.

Date	Hamiltonians	Jeffersonians
1791	Federalists	Democratic-Republicans
1829	Republicans "Era of Good Feelings"	
1824	National Republicans	Democratic-Republicans
1834	Whigs	Jackson Democrats
1840	Nothern Whigs Anti-slavery Democrats	Southern Democrats
1854	Republicans	Democrats
Present	Republicans	Democrats

Assignment

A. What is distinctive of a democratic society?

B. The rise of a democratic spirit encouraged the creation of public schools. The Workingman's Advocate (1830) stated, " There can be no real liberty without education. The members of a republic should all be taught the nature and character of their equal rights and duties as human beings and citizens. Education should develop a just disposition, virtuous habits, and a rational, self-governing character" (Fenton, et al.). Agree or disagree with this statement.

JACKSONIAN DEMOCRACY

Probably no candidate for the presidency ever had such passionate popular support as Andrew Jackson had in 1828. He was truly a man of the people. On the march and in camp, he endeared himself to his men by sharing their hardships, sleeping on the ground with them, and eating parched corn when nothing better could be found for the privates. From local prominence he sprang into national fame by his exploit at the Battle of New Orleans. His reputation as a military hero was enhanced by the feeling that he had been a victim of political treachery in 1824. The farmers of the West and South claimed him as their own. The mechanics of the Eastern cities, newly enfranchised, also looked upon him as their friend. Though his views on the tariff, internal improvements, and other issues before the country were either vague or unknown, he was readily elected president.

The returns of the electoral vote in 1828 revealed the sources of Jackson's power. In New England, he received but one ballot, from Maine; he had a majority of the electors in New York and all of them in Pennsylvania; and he carried every state south of Maryland and beyond the Appalachians. Adams did not get a single electoral vote in the South and West.

When Jackson took the oath of office on March 4, 1829, the government of the United States entered into a new era. Until this time the inauguration of a president—even that of Jefferson, the apostle of simplicity—had brought no rude shock to the course of affairs at the capital. When he was inaugurated, men and women journeyed hundreds of miles to witness the ceremony. Masses of people pressed into the White House, "upset the bowls of punch, broke the glasses, and stood with their muddy boots on the satin-covered chairs to see the people's President." If Jefferson's inauguration was, as he called it, the "great revolution," Jackson's inauguration was a cataclysm (Beard).

Andrew Jackson—Tennessee politician, Indian fighter, and hero of the Battle of New Orleans during the War of 1812—drew his support from the small farmers of the West,

Andrew Jackson, Ralph Eleaser Whiteside Earl, date unknown (PD-US).

and the workers, artisans, and small merchants of the East, who sought to use their vote to resist the rising commercial and manufacturing interests associated with the industrial revolution. For the first time, an American politician consciously built a coalition to advance his cause.

The election of 1828 was a significant benchmark in the trend toward broader voter participation. By 1828 presidential electors were chosen by popular vote in every state but Delaware and South Carolina. Nothing dramatized this democratic sentiment more than the election of "Old Hickory" Andrew Jackson. He, however, ruled more like a federal despot than a popularly elected man of the people.

Toward the end of his first term in office, Jackson was forced to confront the state of South Carolina on the issue of the protective **tariff**. In their view, all the benefits of protection were going to Northern manufacturers, and while the country as a whole grew richer, South Carolina grew poorer, with its planters bearing the burden of higher prices. South Carolina planters, Southern planters in general, sold their products to British industrials who sold manufactured products to Southerners. As a result, when Northern tariffs raised the price of industrial goods, the price of cotton likewise fell. If one British table was worth 30 pounds of cotton, after tariffs increased British prices, the same table would then be worth 50 pounds of cotton.

Ironically, it was the Southern planter president, Jackson, who insisted that tariffs be increased. The protective tariff passed by Congress and signed into law by Jackson in 1832 was milder than that of 1828, but it further embittered many in the state. In response, a number of South Carolina citizens endorsed the states' rights principle of "nullification," which was enunciated by John C. Calhoun, Jackson's vice president until 1832, in his South Carolina Exposition and Protest (1828). South Carolina dealt with the tariff by adopting the **Ordinance of Nullification**, which declared both the tariffs of 1828 and 1832 null and void within state borders. The legislature also passed laws to enforce the

ordinance, including authorization for raising a military force and appropriations for arms.

This was only the most recent in a series of state challenges to the federal government. For instance, the Hartford Convention in New England had voiced its opposition to President Madison and the war against the British. Ironically, Northerners first suggested splitting the Union.

In response to South Carolina's threat, Jackson sent the navy to Charleston, South Carolina, in November 1832. On December 10, he issued a harsh warning to the confederates. Old Hickory refused to negotiate. Congress judiciously worked out a compromise. The South would try again in April 1861.

Even before the nullification issue had been settled, another more controversial issue challenged Jackson's leadership. It concerned the re-chartering of the **Second Bank of the United States.** Hamilton had created the first bank in 1791. It had been chartered for a 20-year period. The national bank functioned as the caretaker of federal assets, much as our Federal Reserve System today. Though the government held some of its stock, it was not a government bank; rather, the bank was a private corporation with profits passing to its stockholders. It had been designed to stabilize

Battle of New Orleans by Henry Bryan Hall after W. Momberger.

the currency and stimulate trade; but it was resented by Westerners and working people who believed that it used nepotism to benefit a few urban Northerners. Besides, their land speculation required a fluid money supply. Thus, when its charter expired in 1811, it was not renewed.

With the expanding economy, this could not remain forever. For the next few years, the banking business was in the hands of state-chartered banks, which issued currency in excessive amounts, creating great confusion and runaway inflation. It became increasingly clear to everyone that state banks run by Uncle Roy or other local interests could not provide the country with a uniform currency and economic stability. In 1816 a second Bank of the United States, similar to the first, was again chartered for 20 years.

From its inception, the second bank was unpopular in frontier territories, and with working class people everywhere. In other words, it was anathema among Jackson's supporters. Opponents claimed the bank possessed a virtual monopoly over the country's credit and currency, and that it represented the interests of the wealthy few. On the whole, the bank was well-managed, though, and fulfilled its charter. Jackson, elected as a popular champion against it, vetoed a bill to re-charter the bank. Jackson was involved in the greatest battle of his life. The effort to override the veto, however, failed.

In the election campaign that followed, America experienced division that seemed to confirm the Founding Fathers' worst nightmare. Division was shamelessly divided along special interests. Statesmanship seemed to have disappeared.

The bank question caused a fundamental division between the merchant, manufacturing and bankers, and the laboring and farming communities, who were often in debt to banks and therefore favored an increased money supply and lower interest rates. The outcome was an enthusiastic endorsement of "Jacksonism." Jackson saw his reelection in 1832 as a popular mandate to crush the bank irrevocably—and found a ready-made weapon in a provision of the bank's charter authorizing removal of public funds. The second National Bank charter did not expire until 1836, but Jackson intended to kill it prematurely. One historian explains, "In September 1833 he ordered that no more government money be deposited in the bank, and that the money already in its custody be gradually withdrawn in the ordinary course of meeting the expenses of government. Carefully selected

state banks, stringently restricted, were provided as a substitute. For the next generation the United States would get by on a relatively unregulated state banking system, which helped fuel westward expansion through cheap credit but kept the nation vulnerable to periodic panics. It wasn't until the Civil War that the United States chartered a national banking system."

One final tragic footnote to the Jacksonian legacy: the Cherokee relocation, the "Trail of Tears." In 1819 Georgia appealed to the U.S. government to remove the Cherokee from Georgia lands, and when the appeal failed, attempts were made to purchase the territory. In retaliation, the Cherokee Nation enacted a law forbidding any such sale on punishment of death.

Since the presidency of Thomas Jefferson, America's policy had been to allow Native Americans to remain east of the Mississippi as long as they settled in one place, farmed the land, divided communal land into private property, and adopted democratic government. Nonetheless, in 1828 the Georgia legislature outlawed the Cherokee government and confiscated tribal lands. Cherokee appeals were rejected by President Andrew Jackson.

In fact, President Andrew Jackson signed into law the Indian Removal Act in 1830. The Removal Act provided for the government to negotiate removal treaties with the various tribes. Some Cherokees sold the tribal land, but the majority of Cherokees refused to accept the deal. However, most of the tribe were driven west some 800 miles in a forced march that became known as the Trail of Tears. About 4,000 perished during the journey or in stockades awaiting removal.

Because Jackson's political opponents had no hope of success so long as they remained divided, they attempted to bring all the dissatisfied elements together into a common party called the Whigs. Although they organized soon after the election campaign of 1832, it was more than a decade before they reconciled their differences and were able to draw up a platform. Largely through the magnetism of Henry Clay and the charismatic Daniel Webster, the party solidified its membership. However, even in the 1836 election, the Whigs were still too divided to unite behind a single man or upon a common platform. New York Jacksonian Martin Van Buren (above), Jackson's vice president, won the contest hands down.

An economic depression and Jackson's larger-than-life

shadow weakened Van Buren's merits. His leadership aroused no enthusiasm, and his foibles offered the Whigs a great opportunity in the 1840 election.

"Tippecanoe and Tyler too," the 1840 Whig campaign jingo went. The Whig candidate for president was William Henry Harrison of Ohio, vastly popular as a hero of Indian conflicts as well as the War of 1812. He was regarded, like Jackson, as a representative of the democratic West. Electing Harrison, then, was perceived as electing Jackson all over again, even though Harrison was a Whig. His vice presidential candidate was John Tyler—a Virginian whose views on states' rights and protectionism were applauded in the South. Harrison won a sweeping victory.

Within a month of his inauguration, however, the feeble 68-year-old Harrison died, and Tyler became president. Tyler was not a typical Whig. In fact, his beliefs differed sharply from those of Clay and Webster, still the most influential men in Congress and the Whig Party. These differences led to an open break between the president and the party that had elected him and put Tyler in an uncomfortable place of being rejected by country and party.

Americans, however, found themselves divided in more complex ways than simple partisan conflicts between Whigs and Democrats. For example, the large number of Catholic immigrants in the first half of the 19th century, primarily Irish and German, triggered a backlash among native-born Protestant Americans (*An Outline of American History*).

Immigrants brought more than strange new customs and religious practices to American shores. They competed with the native-born for jobs in cities along the Eastern seaboard. Moreover, political changes in the 1820s and 1830s increased the political clout of the foreign-born. During those two decades, state constitutions were revised to permit universal white-male suffrage. This led to the end of rule by patrician politicians, who blamed the immigrants for their fall from power. Finally, the Catholic church's failure to support the temperance movement gave rise to charges that Rome was trying to subvert the United States

Uncle Sam's youngest son, Citizen Know Nothing., Sarony & Co., 1854

through alcohol (*An Outline of American History*).

The most important of the **Nativist** organizations that sprang up in this period was a secret society, the Order of the Star-Spangled Banner, founded in 1849. When its members refused to identify themselves, they were swiftly labeled the "Know-Nothings." In 1855 the organization managed to win control of legislatures in New York and Massachusetts; by 1855, about 90 U.S. congressmen were linked to the party.

However, like so many antebellum political movements, disagreements over the slavery issue prevented the party from playing a role in national politics. The "Know-Nothings" of the South supported slavery while Northern members opposed it. At a convention in 1856 to nominate candidates for president and vice president, 42 Northern delegates walked out when a motion to support the Missouri Compromise was ignored, and the party died as a national force.

Assignment

A. Some historians argued that the movement toward democratic rule doomed America to mediocrity. They argued that after Andrew Jackson's presidency, American politicians had to hold wide appeal to many different interest groups or they would not be elected. This invited politicians to be manipulative rather than principled, to be people-pleasers rather than statesmen. Agree or disagree and offer evidence from American political history.

B. No doubt Jackson had an aggressive policy toward equality for all—except minorities and women. In fact, Jackson himself was a slave owner. Also, he disenfranchised the Cherokee Native Americans and moved them away from their land. Discuss how Jackson could exhibit so blatant a contradictory policy.

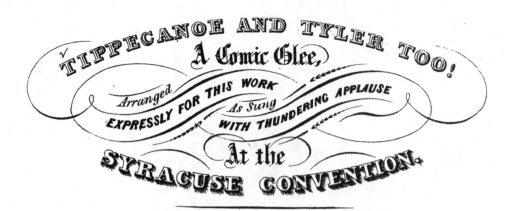

TIPPECANOE AND TYLER TOO!

A Comic Glee,

Arranged EXPRESSLY FOR THIS WORK

As Sung WITH THUNDERING APPLAUSE

At the SYRACUSE CONVENTION.

Some of the Loco Foco party have prepared and paraded a Log Cabin Trap, representing a Log Cabin set on a figure 4; and baited with a barrel of hard Cider. By the above it will be seen that the Trap has been sprung, and a sly nibbler from 'Hook is looking out through the gratings. An elderly gentleman with an hickory pole is intent on prying him out; but it is manifestly no go'. — The logs are too heavy, and growing more so daily.

Log Cabin.

Philadelphia, G.E.Blake, 13 So Fifth Street.

Blake's Log Cabin Music — Copyright secured 1840.

A score of the song as published by G. E. Blake of Philadelphia, Pennsylvania.

HISTORY MAKER: DANIEL WEBSTER

Daniel Webster—statesman, lawyer, and orator—was his era's foremost advocate of American **nationalism**. A farmer's son, he graduated from Dartmouth College in 1801. After a legal apprenticeship, Webster opened a legal practice in Portsmouth, New Hampshire, in 1807. His life represented the paradox that was the Middle Period of American history.

Webster was elected (1812) to the U.S. House of Representatives. Being a man of principle, Webster vigorously opposed the War of 1812. In 1816 he left Congress.

Over the next six years, he established himself as the nation's leading lawyer and an outstanding orator. In 1823 Webster was returned to Congress from Boston, and in 1827 he was elected senator from Massachusetts. Webster joined the National Republican Party, allying himself with Westerner Henry Clay and endorsing federal aid for roads in the West. In 1828, the dominant economic interests of Massachusetts having shifted from shipping to manufacturing, Webster backed the high-tariff bill of that year. Angry Southern leaders condemned the tariff, and South Carolina's John C. Calhoun argued that his state had the right to nullify the law. Webster defended the Union.

Webster became a champion of American nationalism. His words "Liberty and Union, now and forever, one and inseparable!" won wide acclaim. Webster and President Andrew Jackson, both ideological opposites, joined forces in 1833 to suppress South Carolina's attempt to nullify the tariff.

The annexation of Texas in 1845 and the resulting popular war with Mexico, both opposed by Webster, forced the country to face the issue of the expansion of slavery. Webster opposed such expansion but feared even more a dissolution of the Union. In that vein, Webster supported the Compromise of 1850.

Jacksonian Democracy

To many historians, the election of Andrew Jackson as

Daniel Webster, photographer unknown, c1847 (PD-US).

president in 1828 represents a pivotal point in American history. Before Jackson, the presidents had all come from established Eastern elite constituents. Jackson, however, appeared to be anything but an aristocrat. A Southerner/Westerner, Jackson represented the ultimate triumph of American democracy. Billias and Grob write, "Americans traditionally had attempted to define the unique characteristics that separated them from the rest of the world—a quest that inevitably led to an extended discussion of democracy and its meaning." The Jacksonian era appeared to be this watershed event.

In fact, though, early historians like James Parton were very ungenerous with Jackson. He argued that Jackson was a despot who introduced awful things such as the **spoils system** to the American political system.

All this changed with the rise of the **Progressive movement** in the beginning of the 20th century. Now Jackson was seen as a champion of the people, a courageous reformer.

Later historians argued that Jackson was merely an instrument of another elite: Southern slave interests. Finally, Richard McCormick, a professor under whom I studied at Rutgers University, argued that there was really nothing distinctive about Jackson. This view was echoed by Lee Benson, who argued that Americans voted according to ethnicity and national origin, not according to income or education. Thus, there was no democratic revolution after all.

Cartoon showing statue of Andrew Jackson on a pig, which is over "fraud," "bribery," and "spoils," eating "plunder." By Thomas Nast. Illus. in: Harper's weekly, 1877 April 28, p. 325.

Chapter 10

AGE OF REFORM

First Thoughts . . .

While the statesmen were nation building, American pioneers were rapidly expanding the new nation and, in the process, instigating new problems beyond the Alleghenies. The West was rising in population and wealth. Between 1783 and 1829, 11 states were added to the original 13. All but two were in the West. And they were optimistic! This optimism infected the whole nation. After all, a nation that could build a railroad between Baltimore and Harrisburg could surely solve the problem of prison reform. A nation that beat the mighty British twice surely could solve the slavery problem.

In short, the Middle Period of American history is a time of unlimited hopes and vast expectations. Americans dared to dream that society could be perfect. They reached for utopia. Women's rights, abolition of slavery, public education, and temperance were all part of this great surge of civil faith in the American experiment. Much like the 1960s, though, human sin thwarted many of the laudable goals. Nonetheless, join us now as we explore together the Age of Reform!

Chapter Learning Objectives . . .

Chapter 10 will analyze the reform movements that were so much a part of the Middle Period of American History.

As a result of this chapter study you will be able to:

1. Analyze 19th-century prison reformers and contrast these efforts with 21st-century prison reforms.

2. Compare and contrast the reform movements of antebellum America with the reform movements of the 1960s.

3. Discuss when it is and is not appropriate for the federal government to intervene in affairs that are usually within local or private domain. One example is caring for the mentally challenged.

4. Evaluate how far, or if at all, Christians can support human rights that violate the Word of God (e.g., homosexuality).

5. Describe a 21st-century virtuous woman and contrast that with a biblical view of a virtuous woman, based on contemporary and secular understandings.

6. Evaluate the impact of Fournier and Kierkegaard on American history.

PRISON REFORM

The election of Andrew Jackson heralded a new phase of American optimism that argued strenuously for **Lockian basic rights** extending much farther than propertied white American voting males: these rights also belonged to minorities, to women, to the poor, to criminals, and to organized labor. In short, Americans now demanded that all individuals should be afforded the same rights and privileges. That, combined with a growing romantic world view that argued that mankind was basically good if society would only leave him alone, ushered in an age of optimistic reform unparalleled in American history until the 1960s.

The clearest manifestation of this unbridled optimism was the clamor for more voting rights and, as a result, more participation in the political process. If Americans were to vote in ever-increasing numbers, then they should know how to read and write. Thus, public education grew considerably. The public school system became common throughout the northern part of the country. In other parts of the country, however, the battle for public education continued for years, only to be finally resolved in the 1920s.

This was only the beginning. Americans dared to dream that society could be perfect. They reached for **utopia**. Women's rights, abolition, public education, and temperance all were part of this great surge of civil faith in the American experiment.

An influential social movement that emerged during this period was the **temperance** movement, which consisted of opposing the sale and use of alcohol. It stemmed from a variety of concerns and motives: biblical beliefs, the cost of alcohol abuse in the work place, and the suffering families experienced at the hands of heavy drinkers. In 1826 Boston ministers organized the Society for the Promotion of Temperance. Seven years later, in Philadelphia, the Society convened a national convention, which formed the American Temperance Union. The Union called for the renunciation of all alcoholic beverages, and pressed state legislatures to ban their production and sale. Thirteen states

Woman's holy war. Grand charge on the enemy's works, Currier & Ives, 1874.

had done so by 1855, although the laws were subsequently challenged in court. They survived only in northern New England, but between 1830 and 1860 the temperance movement reduced Americans' per capita consumption of alcohol (American Archives of Public Address).

Other reformers addressed the problems of prisons and care for the mentally challenged. Efforts were made to turn mentally challenged asylums and prisons, which stressed punishment, into penitentiaries, where the guilty and infirmed would undergo rehabilitation.

Lips That Touch Liquor Shall Not Touch Ours, nps.gov (www.ixplora.com/wtf-photos-times/).

What has been called "the first American penitentiary, if not the first one in the world," was established in Philadelphia, in 1790, in the Walnut Street Jail, a building formerly operated as a city jail. The cell blocks constructed in the Walnut Street Jail, pursuant to the law of 1790, introduced in permanent fashion the structural pattern of outside cells, with a central corridor, the chief architectural feature of the Pennsylvania system of prison construction. Here, for the first time in prison history, the use of imprisonment through solitary confinement as the usual method of stopping crime was permanently established. The basic principles of the new system, so it appears from contemporary accounts, were the effort to reform those in the prison, and to segregate them according to age, sex, and the type of offenses charged against them (from the *Handbook of Correctional Institution Design and Construction*, United States Bureau of Prisons, 1949). The idea was that a person, if isolated from others, would ultimately choose the right course of action.

A new type of prison reform arose in the early part of the 19th century. Notably, **Auburn Prison** was built. It was the first of two prisons authorized by the New York law of 1816. The second prison was Sing-Sing. The emphasis was on individual cell-block architecture to create an environment to rehabilitate and reform, to separate the criminal from all contact with corruption and then teach him moral habits of order and regularity by means of severe discipline.

Inmates worked as contract convict labor ten hours per day, six days per week. The Auburn model influenced the emergence of reform schools and workhouses in the 1820s, such as the New York House of Refuge in 1825 that separated juveniles from the adult prisoners, and the workhouse on Blackwell's Island for vagrants and drunks. This was the first systematic attempt to reform criminals (from the *Handbook of Correctional Institution Design and Construction*, United States Bureau of Prisons, 1949).

The final attempts at prison reform occurred through the **Eastern State Model**. This was a huge fortress with thick walls at Cherry Hill near Philadelphia. The philosophy emphasized a complete solitary confinement (the "Pennsylvania system") rather than contract labor (the "Auburn system"). New inmates wore hoods when marched to their cells to avoid seeing other prisoners. Regimentation included use of the lockstep into the 1930s, marching in close order single file with head turned right. There were no visitors or mail or newspapers allowed (from the *Handbook of Correctional Institution Design and Construction*, United States Bureau of Prisons, 1949).

Leon F. Czolgosz, the assassin of President William McKinley, in Auburn State Prison. Copyrighted by Judge Company, 1901 (PD-US).

Assignment

A. At the heart of this age of reform was a world view called Transcendentalism. Identify conflicts that this world view had with Christian Theism from one historian's description:

Transcendentalism was a philosophical and literary movement during the 19th century (1836–1860). Ultimately, the philosophical ideas can be traced back to Plato and his affirmation of ultimate goodness, knowable only by intuition. Religious philosophers applied the concepts Plato brought forth to God. The idea of God's transcendence, or existence outside the realm of nature, became a core belief in many religions. In the Middle Ages, the term *transcendent* narrowed in scope, focusing on concepts such as: unity, essence, goodness, and truth. It was Immanuel Kant, a German philosopher, who made a distinction between transcendent, ideas like God and the soul that are unknowable, and transcendental, which are ideas considered a priori, or unlearned knowledge. Eventually transcendentalism became synonymous with metaphysical idealism.

It was from the influences of Immanuel Kant, Samuel Coleridge, and William Wordsworth that jump-started the interest in transcendentalism in New England, originating in small groups reacting against Calvinism and the Unitarian Church. This group of intellects held the idea that God was eminent in man and nature and the individual intuition is the highest source of knowledge. These beliefs eventually led to ideas of self-reliance and individualism, resulting in a rejection of traditional ideas and authority.

B. To what extent were the 19th-century reformers nave or on target in their attempts to rehabilitate 19th-century criminals?

C. One of the most innovative prison ministries today is Prison Fellowship. Prison Fellowship founder Chuck Colson has long argued that crime is fundamentally a moral and spiritual problem that requires a moral and spiritual solution. For example, offenders do not simply need rehabilitation; they require regeneration of

a sinful heart. Crime victims long for more than just surviving after a trauma; they crave new life filled with hope and joy. Prisoners' families need more than a sprinkling of social services to help them get by; they need to be washed clean of shame and despair, and infused with new confidence to move forward. Communities need more than an absence of criminal activity; they need the presence of shalom, a unifying peace and harmony that far surpasses anything the world has to offer (from prison fellowship.org). Respond to these comments. How much is crime an individual act and how much is it a weakness of society?

D. Many of the early social reformers lived close to Boston. Why?

THE RIGHTS OF WOMEN AND THE MENTALLY CHALLENGED

Frances Wright, History of Woman Suffrage, Vol. 1, 1848–1861 (New York: Fowler & Wells, 1881).

be present in the home in the same way that they once were. Middle-class marriages became partnerships. Women lived longer and had more leisure time. This conspired to give women more rights (McPherson, *Battle Cry of Freedom*).

Organized women's liberation movements began with the visit to America of **Frances Wright**, a Scottish lecturer and journalist, who publicly promoted women's rights throughout the United States during the 1820s. At a time when women were often forbidden to speak in public places, Wright not only spoke out but shocked audiences by her views advocating the rights of women to seek information on birth control and divorce (from American Archives of Public Address).

Reforms continued. In Massachusetts, Dorothea Dix led a struggle to improve conditions for mentally challenged persons who were confined in deplorable conditions. The southern United States escaped many of these reforms. But they could not escape Dorothea Dix. After winning improvements in Massachusetts, she took her campaign to the South, where nine states established hospitals for the mentally challenged between 1845 and 1852.

Perhaps the most radical changes occurred, however, in women's rights. Other social reforms brought many women to a realization of their own unjust position in society. Women were not permitted to vote, and their education in the 17th and 18th centuries was limited largely to reading, writing, and sewing.

As the Princeton historian James McPherson explains, the economic transformation of Northern society from exclusively agrarian interests to a growing industrial base took men away from the home and elevated women to leadership in the home. For better or for worse, fathers ceased to

19th Amendment, Woman Suffrage. Relief by Alan LeQuire, state capitol in Nashville, Tennessee, 1997. Photo by Rebecca White, 2011.

By the 1840s a group of American women emerged who would forge the first women's rights movement. Foremost in this distinguished group was Elizabeth Cady Stanton. In 1848 Cady Stanton and Lucretia Mott, another women's rights advocate, organized a women's rights convention—the first in the history of the world—at Seneca Falls, New York. Delegates drew up a declaration demanding equality with men before the law, the right to vote, and equal opportunities in education and employment (American Archives of Public Address).

Another reform movement whose impact far surpassed its small membership was the slavery abolition movement. William Lloyd Garrison was one of the main leaders. Abolitionism was of two main types. One group argued for the radical and the immediate abolition of slavery. Other groups argued for a more gradual abolition policy. In any event, this group influenced politicians and policy makers and in many ways hastened the coming of the Civil War.

Finally, this early 19th-century generation that so closely resembled the generation of the 1960s dabbled in utopia, or a perfect society. In 1516 an Englishman named Sir Thomas More had coined the word *utopia* when he wrote his book by the same name. Between 1840 and 1850 Americans founded 40 utopian communities. These early attempts at perfection were founded on the notion that mankind could be perfect if it lived in a cooperative—not competitive—community.

One notable attempt to live this life was **Brook Farm**. This experiment in communal living was both scandalous and revolutionary. The founder, George Ripley (above left, PD-US), described it this way:

Our objectives, as you know, are to insure a more natural union between intellectual and manual labor than now exists; to combine the thinker and the worker, as far as possible, in the same individual; to guarantee the highest mental freedom, by providing all with labor, adapted to their tastes and talents, and securing to them the fruits of their

The Print Shop, constructed in about 1890, is the last remaining historic building at Brook Farm, Midnightdreary, 2008 (CC BY-SA 3.0).

industry; to do away with the necessity of menial services, by opening the benefits of education and the profits of labor to all; and thus to prepare a society of liberal, intelligent, and cultivated persons, whose relations with each other would permit a more simple and wholesome life than can be led amidst the pressure of our competitive institutions.

The Song of the Shirt (mid-19th century) by Frank Holl, c1863 (PD-US).

Founded in 1841, Brook Farm existed for only a few years, but more than anything else, it represented the hope and optimism of this age of reform.

Assignment

A. At what point is it appropriate for the federal government to intervene in affairs that are usually a local or private affair? In particular, consider the problem of caring for the mentally challenged.

B. Human rights is a knotty issue. On one hand, a person should applaud women's suffrage; however, when human rights are extended to homosexual rights, the issue is far more complicated. Why?

C. Describe a 21st-century virtuous woman and contrast that with a biblical view of a virtuous woman, based on contemporary and secular understandings.

D. *The Young Housekeeper's Friend* (1850) warns a mid-century wife to avoid providing "bad bread" for her husband. Paraphrase this passage:

Women's suffragists demonstrate in February 1913. The triangular pennants read "VOTES FOR WOMEN". The negative is labeled "ROSE SANDERSON", the woman holding the trumpet.

A symmetrical education is extremely rare in this country. Nothing is more common than to see young ladies, whose intellectual attainments are of a high order, profoundly ignorant of the duties which all acknowledge to belong peculiarly to women. Consequently, many have to learn, after marriage, how to take care of a family; and thus their housekeeping is, frequently, little else than a series of experiments; often unsuccessful, resulting in mortification and discomfort in the parlor, and waste and ill temper in the kitchen. How often do we see the happiness of a husband abridged by the absence of skill, neatness, and economy in the wife! Perhaps he is not able to fix upon the cause, for he does not understand minutely enough the processes upon which domestic order depends, to analyze the difficulty; but he is conscious of discomfort. However improbable it may seem, the health of many a professional man is undermined, and his usefulness curtailed, if not sacrificed, because he habitually eats Bad Bread. If this subject has a direct bearing upon the health of families, so also does it exert an immediate influence upon their virtue. There are numerous instances of worthy merchants and mechanics, whose efforts are paralyzed, and their hopes chilled by the total failure of the wife in her sphere of duty; and who seek solace under their disappointment in the wine party, or the late convivial supper. Many a day laborer, on his return at evening from his hard toil, is repelled by the sight of a disorderly house, and a comfortless supper; and perhaps is met by a cold eye instead of the "thrifty wife's smile"; and he makes his escape to the grog shop, or the underground gambling room. Can any human agency hinder the series of calamities entailed by these things? No! the most active philanthropy, the best schemes of organized benevolence, cannot furnish a remedy, unless the springs of society are rectified. The domestic influence of women is certainly one of these. Every woman is invested with a great degree of power over the happiness and virtue of others. She cannot escape using it, and she cannot innocently pervert it. There is no avenue or channel of society through which it may not send a salutary influence; and when rightly directed, it is unsurpassed by any human instrumentality in its purifying and restoring efficacy.

HISTORY MAKER: DOROTHEA DIX

Dorothea Dix (right) was a teacher in Boston when she observed the mistreatment of a group of mentally challenged people in an 1841 jail. After that revelation, Dix devoted herself to a ministry to the mentally challenged throughout the United States. Dix was truly a history maker.

The following is a report by Dorthea Dix to the Massachusetts legislature:

I come to present the strong claims of suffering humanity. I come to place before the legislature of Massachusetts the condition of the miserable, the desolate, the outcast. I come as the advocate of helpless, forgotten, mentally challenged, and idiotic men and women: of beings sunk to a condition from which the most unconcerned would start with real horror. . . . I proceed, gentlemen, briefly to call your attention to the present state of mentally challenged persons . . . a woman in a cage . . . one subject chained and in a close stall for seventeen years. . . . One losing the use of his limbs because of inactivity. . . . I commit to you this sacred cause. . . . May you exercise that "wisdom which is the breath of the power of God" (Francis Tiffany, *Life of Dorothea L. Dix*).

Morristown insane asylum of the state of New Jersey

Assignment

In the 1850s, an intense debate over what role the federal government should play in providing services and support to the mentally disabled was carried out in Congress. The issue pitted Dorothea Dix against President Franklin Pierce, an outspoken critic of federal involvement in local issues. Dix had petitioned Congress to sell federal lands to states who in turn would sell the lands again and hold the proceeds in a trust that would pay for the building and administration of several state mentally challenged asylums. Despite broad support for the spirit of the plan, Pierce ultimately vetoed it, sympathetically explaining that the bill would set an untenable precedent and draw the federal government into an inappropriate and unconstitutional relationship with the mentally challenged. "Despite this stance, Dix had reason to hope that Pierce would look with favor upon her efforts. In his first State of the Union Address, he had described the erection of the asylum for the mentally challenged of the District of Columbia and the Army and Navy—a product of her agitations—in highly complimentary terms. Motivated by a 'liberal spirit' and its arrangements informed 'with the large experience furnished within the last few years in relation to the nature and treatment of the disease,' the asylum, Pierce declared, 'will prove an asylum indeed to this most helpless and afflicted class of sufferers and stand as a noble monument of wisdom and mercy' " (Hall, 217).

The following commentary on and text of Pierce's veto were edited and written by Peter Dobkin Hall, in *The Documentary History of Philanthropy and Voluntarism Project, Program on Non-Profit Organizations*, Yale University:

> The bill Dorothea Dix was urging on Congress proposed that 10,000,000 acres of land be distributed to each of the states as endowments for the care of the mentally challenged. Under this plan each state would receive 100,000 acres, with the remainder to be distributed on a ratio determined by its geographical area and representation in Congress. Having campaigned extensively through the states in the decade previous to her federal crusade (by the mid-1840s, she had traveled some 60,000 miles and personally visited over 9,000 mentally challenged, epileptic, and idiotic persons throughout the country), she had a wide and warm acquaintance among the nation's politicians. Her influence with congressional leaders led the body to give her an office in the Capitol from which she could lobby for her bill. President Pierce had personally assured

Franklin Pierce, by George Peter Alexander Healy, 1853.

her of his interest in the legislation.

> The bill completed its passage through Congress on March 9, 1854. "I have lifted up my eyes," wrote Dix to her friend Ann Heath. "My cup runneth over" [Marshall, 149]. Congratulatory messages poured in from friends and supporters around the country. But the President did not sign the legislation. And soon, distressing rumors began to circulate that he would not do so. After months of delay, President Pierce vetoed the bill, justifying his action with an extended argument about the nature and extent of federal power. While most reformers—including Dix herself—condemned Pierce's action as typical of "a Northerner with Southern principles" (some, indeed, believed that the message had been written by Jefferson Davis), a disinterested reading of the document suggests that there was far more thought and reflection behind it than the kind of reflexive yahooism that so typified the debate over the Smithsonian Institution. The message was an important statement of public policy—and set forth guidelines for the federal role as a philanthropic agent until well into the twentieth century.

Paraphrase this article. In your paraphrase, discuss Dix's arguments and Pierce's arguments.

PHILOSOPHERS AND WORLD VIEWS

Charles Fourier (1772–1837)

Because of the French Revolution, Fourier, a French Romantic writer, had adverse feelings about violent revolutions and sought a better way of life. He spent a lot of time developing social theory; i.e., the way people live and work together in an efficacious way. But he was interested in other subjects too. He offered opinions on the creation and destruction of our solar system, the psychological makeup of people, and the course of human and animal history, along with many other ideas, one being the concept of a freelove utopian community. It was the ideas of these utopian communities that began to interest people like Ralph Waldo Emerson. As one historian concluded: "Fourier believed people could live together in a state of nature, free from government intervention, and thrive. He believed by taking 1,620 men, women and children, twice the number of distinct human personalities he recognized, and gathering them into a large enclosed structure called a phalanx, and providing them with a verity of work, these communities would eventually develop across the county and bring about an economic stability. The phalanges were designed to be large buildings, similar to apartment complexes or dormitories, in the country with plenty of land for farming and shops for making items they would need. Charles Fourier claimed the concept of the phalanges and communities were deduced from rational planning, and were destined to succeed." They didn't.

Statue of Søren Kirkegaard in the Royal Library Garden of Slotsholmen in Copenhagen, Denmark. Photo by Jean-Pierre Dalbéra, 2002 (CC BY 2.0).

Sketch of Charles Fourier, artist and date unknown.

Søren Kirkegaard(1813–1855)

Kierkegaard's religious Existentialism has piqued theologian's interests for at least two generations. Nonetheless, Kierkegaard was raised in a Christian family and confessed Christ as his Savior. His most famous theological contribution was the "leap in the dark" in which the new convert steps out in bold faith into his new life. Kierkegaard invited Christians to what many believers consider to be intuitive subjectivity instead of confessional orthodoxy. What do you think?

The following is a portion of *That Single Individual* by Søren Kirkegaard (1846):

"The crowd is untruth. Therefore was Christ crucified, because he, even though he addressed himself to all, would not have to do with the crowd, because he would not in any way let a crowd help him, because he in this respect absolutely pushed away, would not found a party, or allow balloting, but would be what he was, the truth, which relates itself to the single individual. And therefore everyone who in truth will serve the truth, is *eo ipso* in some way or other a martyr; if it were possible that a human being in his mother's womb could make a decision to will to serve "the truth" in truth, so he also is *eo ipso* a martyr, however his martyrdom comes about, even while in his mother's womb. For to win a crowd is not so great a trick; one only needs some talent, a certain dose of untruth and a little acquaintance with the human passions. But no witness for the truth—alas, and every human being, you and I, should be one—dares have dealings with a crowd. The witness for the truth—who naturally will have nothing to do with politics, and to the utmost of his ability is careful not to be confused with a politician—the godfearing work of the witness to the truth is to have dealings with all, if possible, but always individually, to talk with each privately, on the streets and lanes—to split up the crowd, or to talk to it, not to form a crowd, but so that one or another individual might go home from the assembly and become a single individual. "A crowd," on the other hand, when it is treated as the court of last resort in relation to "the truth," its judgment as the judgment, is detested by the witness to the truth, more than a virtuous young woman detests the dance hall. And they who address the "crowd" as the court of last resort, he considers to be instruments of untruth. For to repeat: that which in politics and similar domains has its validity, sometimes wholly, sometimes in part, becomes untruth, when it is transferred to the intellectual, spiritual, and religious domains. And at the risk of a possibly exaggerated caution, I add just this: by "truth" I always understand "eternal truth." But politics and the like has nothing to do with "eternal truth." A politics, which in the real sense of "eternal truth" made a serious effort to bring "eternal truth" into real life, would in the same second show itself to be in the highest degree

Kierkegaard in a coffee-house, an oil sketch by Christian Olavius, 1843 (PD-US).

the most "impolitic" thing imaginable.

The crowd is untruth. And I could weep, in every case I can learn to long for the eternal, whenever I think about our age's misery, even compared with the ancient world's greatest misery, in that the daily press and anonymity make our age even more mentally challenged with help from "the public," which is really an abstraction, which makes a claim to be the court of last resort in relation to "the truth"; for assemblies which make this claim surely do not take place. That an anonymous person, with help from the press, day in and day out can speak however he pleases (even with respect to the intellectual, the ethical, the religious), things which he perhaps did not in the least have the courage to say personally in a particular situation; every time he opens up his gullet—one cannot call it a mouth—he can all at once address himself to thousands upon thousands; he can get ten thousand times ten thousand to repeat after him—and no one has to answer for it; in ancient times the relatively unrepentant crowd was the almighty, but now there is the absolutely unrepentant thing: No One, an anonymous person: the Author, an anonymous person: the Public, sometimes even anonymous subscribers, therefore: No One. No One! God in heaven, such states even call themselves Christian states. One cannot say that, again with the help of the press, "the truth" can overcome the lie and the error. O, you who say this, ask yourself: Do you dare to claim that human beings, in a crowd, are just as quick to reach for truth, which is not always palatable, as for untruth, which is always deliciously prepared, when in addition this must be combined with an admission that one has let oneself be deceived! Or do you dare to claim that "the truth" is just as quick to let itself be understood as is untruth, which requires no previous knowledge, no schooling, no discipline, no abstinence, no self-denial, no honest self-concern, no patient labor! No, "the truth," which detests this untruth, the only goal of which is to desire its increase, is not so quick on its feet. Firstly, it cannot work through the fantastical, which is the untruth; its communicator is only a single individual. And its communication relates itself once again to the single individual; for in this view of life the single individual is precisely the truth. The truth can neither be communicated nor be received without being as it were before the eyes of God, nor without God's help, nor without God being involved as the middle term, since he is the truth. It can therefore only be communicated by and received by "the single individual," which, for that matter, every single human being who lives could be: this is the determination of the truth in contrast to the abstract, the fantastical, impersonal, "the crowd"—"the public," which excludes God as the middle term (for the personal God cannot be the middle term in an impersonal relation), and also thereby the truth, for God is the truth and its middle term.

And to honor every individual human being, unconditionally every human being, that is the truth and fear of God and love of "the neighbor";

but ethico-religiously viewed, to recognize "the crowd" as the court of last resort in relation to "the truth," that is to deny God and cannot possibly be to love "the neighbor." And "the neighbor" is the absolutely true expression for human equality; if everyone in truth loved the neighbor as himself, then would perfect human equality be unconditionally attained; every one who in truth loves the neighbor, expresses unconditional human equality; every one who is really aware (even if he admits, like I, that his effort is weak and imperfect) that the task is to love the neighbor, he is also aware of what human equality is. But never have I read in the Holy Scriptures this command: You shall love the crowd; even less: You shall, ethico-religiously, recognize in the crowd the court of last resort in relation to "the truth." It is clear that to love the neighbor is self-denial, that to love the crowd or to act as if one loved it, to make it the court of last resort for "the truth," that is the way to truly gain power, the way to all sorts of temporal and worldly advantage—yet it is untruth; for the crowd is untruth.

Assignment

A. Summarize in a few sentences what Kierkegaard was saying. How do you think his theory supports or contradicts Scripture?

B. Why are Fourier's perfect communities doomed to fail?

ANTEBELLUM SLAVERY

First Thoughts . . .

At the time of the adoption of the Constitution, slavery was lawful in all the Northern states except Massachusetts. In fact, in 1789 there were almost as many slaves in New York as in Georgia, and New Jersey had more slaves than Delaware and Tennessee combined! Of course that changed. This chapter will show how that change doomed America to fight a bloody civil war.

Ultimately, though, this chapter is not about white Americans, it is about the many important contributions that African-Americans have made to American cultural life.

Chapter Learning Objectives . . .

Chapter 11 will analyze antebellum slavery in America. The slave system in America was unique in human history. Sometimes slaves were treated cruelly; at other times with kindness. Previously, slavery had existed in hierarchical societies in which the slave was at the bottom of a social ladder, the most inferior in a society of unequal people. American society, however, was largely egalitarian. While a society normally preferred to choose its slaves from alien people, it did not limit its selection exclusively to the members of any one race. In contrast to this, slavery in America was set apart by three characteristics: capitalism, individualism, and racism (Norman Coombs).

As a result of this chapter study you will be able to:

1. Assess the way cotton was vital to both the Southern and Northern economies.
2. Discuss three arguments offered in support of slavery.
3. Interpret why the framers of the U.S. Constitution refused to abolish slavery.
4. Discuss why free blacks were treated as poorly as some slaves.
5. Analyze the relationship between masters and slaves.
6. Reframe the slavery issue in the context of a Christian working for an organization that is unjust or sinful (e.g., movie industry or a cigarette factory). You will debate whether the Christian is sinful and unjust to participate in these behaviors.
7. Read about Harriet Tubman and decide when/if Christians are free to disobey laws.

SLAVERY

At the time of the adoption of the Constitution, slavery was lawful in all the Northern states except Massachusetts. There were almost as many slaves in New York as in Georgia. New Jersey had more than Delaware or Tennessee, indeed nearly as many as both combined. However, there were only about 40,000 in the North and nearly 700,000 in the South. Moreover, most of the Northern slaves were domestic servants, not laborers necessary to keep mills going or fields under cultivation. Nonetheless, in 1789 slavery was legal and practiced almost everywhere in the United States. However, in the next few years all the states north of the Mason-Dixon Line outlawed slavery.

There were a few free blacks. By 1810 the free black population had swelled to 186,446, but slavery too continued to flourish and spread westward with the growing new nation. As one historian explained, "During its first 50 years the United States transformed itself from a small republic into an expansive democracy for white Americans. The nation tripled its population, doubled in size, and extended slavery to parts of the Western frontier." For African-Americans, this same period was a contradictory mix of advancement for free blacks and increased enslavement for those not yet emancipated. Slavery grew stronger as the invention of the cotton gin and a booming Southern economy made slavery very profitable.

At the same time, slavery abolition became a powerful force in America. William Lloyd Garrison founded in Boston his anti-slavery paper, *The Liberator*. He promised his readers that he would be "harsh as truth and uncompromising as justice"; that he would not "think or speak or write with moderation." Then he flung out his defiant call: "I am in earnest—I will not equivocate—I will not excuse—I will not retreat a single inch—and I will be heard. . . .'Such is the vow I take, so help me God'" (Beard).

What about the Church and slavery?

By 1810 the slave trade to the United States had come to an end and the slave population began to increase naturally, giving rise to an increasingly large native-born population of African-Americans. With fewer migrants who had experienced Africa personally, these transformations allowed the myriad cultures and language groups of enslaved Africans to blend together, making way for the preservation and transmission of religious practices that were increasingly "African-American." This transition coincided with the Second Great Awakening. In the Southern states beginning in the 1770s, increasing numbers of slaves converted to evangelical faiths. Many pastors within these denominations actively promoted the idea that all Christians were equal in the eyes of God. They also encouraged worship in ways that many Africans found to be similar, or at least adaptable, to African worship patterns, with enthusiastic singing, clapping, dancing, and even spirit deliverance. Still, many white owners and clergy insisted on slave attendance at white-controlled churches, since they were fearful that if slaves were allowed to worship independently they would ultimately desire freedom.

In the slave quarters, however, African-Americans organized their own "invisible institution." Through signals, passwords, and messages not discernible to whites, they called believers to "hush harbors" where they freely mixed African

A portrait of an older William Lloyd Garrison, artist and date unknown.

rhythms, singing, and beliefs with evangelical Christianity. Spirituals, with their double meanings of religious salvation and freedom from slavery, flourished as a subversive activity. The African-American slave, in other words, learned to survive and to endure in a marginalized condition. Church meetings provided one of the few ways for enslaved African-Americans to express and rehearse their hopes for a better future.

Although there was some hope immediately after the Revolution that the ideals of independence and equality would extend to African-Americans, this hope died with the invention of the cotton gin by Eli Whitney in 1793. With the gin (short for engine), seeds from raw cotton could be quickly removed. Suddenly cotton became a hugely profitable crop. It was the growth industry of antebellum America. This transformed the Southern economy and changed the dynamics of slavery. The first federal census of 1790 counted 697,897 slaves; by 1810, there were 1.2 million slaves, a 70 percent increase. Within ten years after the cotton gin was put into use, the value of the total United States crop leaped from $150,000 to more than $8 million (Africans in America, www.pbs.org). Cotton became the foundation for the developing textile industry in New England, spurring the industrial revolution that transformed America in the 19th century. Cotton was truly king!

Assignment

A. In what way was cotton vital to both the Southern and Northern economies?

B. What were three arguments offered in support of slavery?

C. Why did the framers of the U.S. Constitution refuse to abolish slavery?

D. If a Christian works for an organization that is unjust or sinful (e.g., movie industry or a cigarette factory), is the Christian sinful and unjust?

E. Unfortunately, life for free blacks was far from idyllic, due to Northern racism. As one historian explained, "Most free blacks lived in racial enclaves in the major cities of the North: New York, Boston, Philadelphia, and Cincinnati. There, poor living conditions led to disease and death. In a Philadelphia study in 1846, practically all poor black infants died shortly after birth. Even wealthy blacks were prohibited from living in white neighborhoods due to whites' fear of declining property values. African-Americans were either refused admission to, or segregated in, hotels, restaurants, and theaters. Blacks had limited work and educational opportunities. They were often denied access to public transportation in cities, and allowed on trains only in 'Jim Crow' segregated cars. They were also denied civil rights, such as the right to vote and the right to testify in court in many states, thus leaving them open to attack by thieves and mobs, and to being captured and sold by slave catchers. Black men and women were routinely attacked in the streets, and from 1820 to 1850, black churches, schools, and homes were looted and burned in riots in major cities throughout the North, forcing many blacks to flee to Canada. Northern blacks were forced to live in a white man's democracy, and while not legally enslaved, subject to definition by their race. In their all-black communities, they continued to build their own churches and schools and to develop vigilance committees to protect members of the black community from hostility and violence (www.pbs.org).

Why were freed slaves treated so poorly?

F. The relationship between masters and slaves was complex. Many slaveowners justified their exploitation of slaves by assuming that they were unintelligent and incapable of deep feeling, or by proclaiming that they were like members of the family, fed, clothed, and sheltered. The institution of slavery had negative effects on slaveowners, as well as on slaves (www.pbs. org). Explain.

HISTORY MAKER: HARRIET TUBMAN

Harriet Tubman was an African-American who fled slavery and then guided runaway slaves to freedom in the North for more than a decade before the Civil War. Harriet Tubman was one of 11 children born to slaves on a plantation in Maryland. In 1844 she married John Tubman, a free black man. For the next five years Harriet Tubman lived in a very awkward place—not really free but not really a slave either—until she finally fled to the North and freedom. Her husband remained in Maryland. In 1849 Harriet Tubman moved North, but returned hoping to persuade her husband to come North with her. By this time John Tubman had remarried. Harriet, a pious Christian, did not marry again until after her former husband died. While Mrs. Tubman did not condemn believers who did otherwise, she refused to violate what she felt was a charge by Scripture against divorce.

Ultimately, Harriet Tubman joined the militant abolitionist cause and worked hard to end slavery. She returned to the South and brought all her family to freedom. Over a period of 10 years Tubman made an estimated 19 expeditions into the South and personally escorted about 300 slaves to the North. Naturally most Southerners hated her, and many tried to kill her. The godly Tubman came to be known as "Moses."

Harriet Tubman by H. Seymour Squyer, c1885.

Slave Story, National Photo Company Collection (Library of Congress) date unknown.

Assignment

Harriet Tubman, a committed Christian, nonetheless violated the laws of the land. She could have been put in jail for her actions. Why do you think her actions were appropriate or inappropriate?

HISTORICAL DEBATE

The existence of slavery in American culture had a profound and indelible impact on American history. From the genesis of the American nation, it was not lost on Americans that there was an inherent contradiction and hypocrisy in the American experiment. "Paradoxically," a historian wrote, "a people who prided themselves on having created one of the freest societies in the world also sanctioned slavery—an institution that many other nations less free had long abolished."

What were some of the issues surrounding historical discussions of slavery? Scholars disagreed on most everything. They disagreed on the origins of slavery. They disagreed on whether or not racism preceded slavery. They disagreed on whether or not slavery was profitable.

The parameters of the debate were established even before slavery was abolished (Grobs and Billias, p. 347). Given the emotional impact of the American Civil War, the first serious discussion of slavery did not happen until the 1880s. Historians, most of whom were Northerners, argued that slavery was a brutal, evil institution, victimizing planters and slaves alike. It was not long, however, until there was an effective Southern response. These historians agreed that slavery was a bad thing for the South. It was a burden, though, that white planters reluctantly accepted. They regretted slavery's genesis, but once it was a permanent institution in their culture, they felt it was their Christian duty to take care of the docile, inferior Africans. Slavery was the best thing for American blacks. Slavery was a safe place for these obviously inferior persons. It provided safety and structure for these childlike people. Rarely, if ever, were slave families separated from each other. Slavery was a bad institution, no doubt. But it was the best system for the circumstances in which Americans found themselves. Marshaling massive anecdotal evidence for their arguments, these historians persuaded most Americans—North and South—that slaves gratefully accepted their station in life and whites reluctantly accepted their Christian duty, a paternalistic role.

Three African-American Boys, part of the Du Bois collection 1899.

Partly as a reaction to the racist views of Nazi Germany, 1940 historians vigorously contradicted these views. These historians refused to accept the notion that African slaves were inherently inferior, and that white planters were inherently superior. They argued that slavery was a brutal, evil, destructive system of control. They argued that slavery had a devastating effect on the slave family. They saw slavery as an evil system that benefited no one, and harmed everyone.

Furthermore, these historians argued that slaves resisted slavery at all times, in every way, that they never willingly accepted, much less liked, their subservient role, and that slavery was a very profitable industry for white people.

Assignment

Was slavery a bad institution for America, or was it a necessary way to handle a bad situation, and, in that way, good for America? Give evidence for your argument.

PHILOSOPHERS AND WORLD VIEWS

Frederick Douglass (1817?—1895)

Frederick Douglass was born in slavery as Frederick Augustus Washington Bailey near Easton in Maryland. He was not sure of the exact year of his birth, but he knew that it was 1817 or 1818. As a young boy he was sent to Baltimore to be a house servant, where he learned to read and write, with the assistance of his master's wife. In 1838 he escaped from slavery and went to New York City, where he married Anna Murray, a free black woman whom he had met in Baltimore. He changed his name to Frederick Douglass. In 1841 he addressed a convention of the Massachusetts Anti-Slavery Society in Nantucket and so greatly impressed the group that they immediately employed him as an agent. He was such an impressive orator that numerous persons doubted if he had ever been a slave, so he wrote *Narrative of the Life of Frederick Douglass* (Aaron Ezis, Americanlit. com).

The following is the way Douglass finishes his narrative:

Frederick Douglass, photograph by George K. Warren, c1879 (PD-US).

The Christianity of America is a Christianity, of whose votaries it may be as truly said, as it was of the ancient scribes and Pharisees, "They bind heavy burdens, and grievous to be borne, and lay them on men's shoulders, but they themselves will not move them with one of their fingers. All their works they do for to be seen of men.—They love the upper most rooms at feasts, and the chief seats in the synagogues . . . . and to be called of men, Rabbi, Rabbi.—But woe unto you, scribes and Pharisees, hypocrites! For ye shut up the kingdom of heaven against men; for ye neither go in yourselves, neither suffer ye them that are entering to go in. Ye devour widows' houses, and for pretence make long prayers; therefore ye shall receive the greater damnation. Ye compass sea and land to make one proselyte, and when he is made, ye make him twofold more the child of hell than yourselves.—Woe unto you, scribes and Pharisees, hypocrites! for ye pay tithe of mint, and anise, and cumin, and have omitted the weightier matters of the law, judgment, mercy, and faith; these ought ye to have done, and not to leave the other undone. Ye blind guides! Which strain at a gnat, and swallow a camel. Woe unto you, scribes and Pharisees, hypocrites! for ye make clean the outside of the cup and of the platter; but within, they are full of extortion and excess—Woe unto you, scribes and Pharisees, hypocrites! for ye are like unto whited sepulchres, which indeed appear beautiful outwardly, but are within full of dead men's bones, and of all uncleanness. Even so ye also outwardly appear righteous unto men, but within ye are full of hypocrisy and iniquity."

Dark and terrible as is this picture, I hold it to be strictly true of the overwhelming mass of professed Christians in America. They strain at a gnat, and swallow a camel. Could any thing be more true of our churches? They would be shocked at the proposition of fellowshipping a SHEEP-stealer; and at the same time they hug to their communion a MAN-stealer, and brand me with being an infidel, if I find fault with them for it. They attend with Pharisaical strictness to the outward forms of religion, and at the same time neglect the weightier matters of the law, judgment, mercy, and faith. They are always ready to sacrifice, but seldom to show mercy. They are they who are represented as professing to love God whom they have not seen, whilst they hate their brother whom they have seen. They love the heathen on the other side of the globe. They can pray for him, pay money to have the Bible put into his hand, and missionaries to instruct him; while they despise and totally neglect the heathen at their own doors.

Such is, very briefly, my view of the religion of this land; and to avoid any misunderstanding, growing out of the use of general terms, I mean by the religion of this land, that which is revealed in the words, deeds, and actions, of those bodies, North and South, calling themselves Christian churches, and yet in union with slaveholders. It is against religion, as presented by these bodies, that I have felt it my duty to testify.

I conclude these remarks by copying the following portrait of the religion of the South, (which is, by communion and fellowship, the religion of the North,) which I soberly affirm is "true to the life," and without caricature or the slightest exaggeration. It is said to have been drawn, several years before the present anti-slavery agitation began, by a northern Methodist preacher, who, while residing at the South, had an opportunity to see slaveholding morals, manners, and piety, with his own eyes. "Shall I not visit for these things? Saith the Lord. Shall not my soul be avenged on such a nation as this?"

Assignment

Respond to Douglass's criticism of the Church. Is it fair? Why or why not?

Two African-American children sitting on steps to porch, part of the Du Bois collection, 1899.

Photograph by George K. Warren, c1879. Four African-American women seated on steps of a building at Atlanta University, Georgia by Thomas E. Askew, 1899.

Chapter 12

REVIVALISM

First Thoughts . . .

"The power of God was wonderfully displayed; scores of sinners fell under the preaching, like men slain in mighty battle; Christians shouted aloud for joy," Peter Cartwright wrote. "I have seen more than a hundred sinners fall like dead men under one powerful sermon, and I have seen and heard more than five hundred Christians all shouting aloud the high praises of God at once; and I will venture to assert that many happy thousands were awakened and converted to God at these camp meetings." In 1801 more than 10,000 people gathered for two weeks of non-stop revival at Cane Ridge, near Lexington, Kentucky. American had never seen anything like it.

Chapter Learning Objectives . . .

Chapter 12 will analyze a unique American phenomenon: revivalism. From the beginning, Christianity in America has more or less embraced revivalism as a mode of church expansion, growth, and influence. We will examine this phenomenon and analyze its effect on Middle American culture.

As a result of this chapter study you will be able to:

1. Discuss the different components of revivalism, including conversion and response.

2. Analyze revivalism during the Second Great Awakening.

3. Differentiate between emotionalism and spiritual awakening in the Second Great Awakening.

4. Discuss Revivalism as a social movement.

5. Summarize Finney's views of salvation and debate whether or not his views are convincing.

COME TO THE WATER: AMERICAN REVIVALISM

The French social observer **Alexis de Tocqueville**, in his important book *Democracy in America* (1834), wrote, "The religious atmosphere of the country was the first thing that struck me on arrival in the United States."

What Tocqueville sensed was what all Americans know—that religion has played an important role in American history. In fact, it is doubtful that any serious scholar can understand American history without giving a great deal of attention to American religious history.

Tocqueville was observing the middle stages of the **Second Great Awakening**. Begun in 1800, the Second Great Awakening was at its peak in the early 1830s, when Tocqueville wrote his famous book. The form taken by this awakening was a veritable river of revivals, successively flowing across the country, energizing and focusing America in its pursuit of God. The phrase "religious revival" was originally coined in the 18th century to describe a new phenomenon in which churches experienced an unexpected "awakening" of spiritual concern, occasioned by a special and mysterious outpouring of God's saving grace, which led to unprecedented numbers of intense and "surprising conversions" that "revived" the piety and power of the churches. In the early 19th century, however, as "the revival" became a central instrument for provoking conversions, it became a controversial event (Scott).

Tocqueville found remarkable the seemingly endless number of sects into which American Christianity was divided, but, initially at least, they shared a commitment to revival. In *The Life of the Mind in America,* the historian Perry Miller observed, "In the larger perspective of American thinking, these divisions—though frequently argued with dismaying ferocity—are of little importance before the terrific universality of the Revival" (Miller, 7). As another historian explains, "The revival did not discriminate; those swept into the current were from all walks of life and religious backgrounds."

Alexis-Charles-Henri Clérel de Tocqueville by Théodore Chassériau, 1850.

Revivalism invites Americans to have a "personal relationship with Christ." It empowers Americans to think big. It creates a sort of national egalitarianism, movement toward equality for all.

The Second Great Awakening represents the contradiction that was so much a part of American religious history. For one thing, the Awakening was a revival—a phenomenon that we will describe in greater detail. On the other hand, the Awakening grew in the fragile air of pluralism, which was both the greatest strength and greatest challenge of American religious life. For instance, the Second Great

Awakening flourished in upstate New York, which was also the place where heretical **Mormonism**, the only indigenous American religion, originated.

From the beginning, Christianity in America has more or less embraced revivalism as a mode of church expansion, growth, and influence. We must be careful to define all our terms. **Revivalism,** according to historian D. E. Dieter, is "the movement within the Christian tradition which emphasizes the appeal of religion to the emotional and affectional nature of individuals as well as to their intellectual and rational nature. It believes that vital Christianity begins with a response of the whole being to the Gospel's call for repentance and spiritual rebirth by faith in Jesus Christ. This experience results in a personal relationship with God. Some have sought to make revivalism a purely American and even a predominantly frontier phenomenon."

Historian Geoff Waugh writes, "Revival must of necessity make an impact on the community and this is one means by which we may distinguish it from the more usual operations of the Holy Spirit. . . ." Roy Hession notes that the outward forms of revivals do, of course, differ considerably, but the inward and permanent content of them is always the same: a new experience of conviction of sin among the believers; a new vision of the Cross and of Jesus and of redemption; a new willingness on man's part for brokenness, repentance, confession, and restitution; a joyful experience of the power of the blood of Jesus to cleanse fully from sin and restore and heal all that sin has lost and broken; a new entering into the fullness of the Holy Spirit and of His power to do His own work through His people; and a new gathering in of the lost ones to Jesus.

Revivalism is not merely a Protestant phenomenon, as

The Mormon pioneers coming off Big Mountain into Mountain Dell, 1847.

witnessed by the great Catholic Charismatic revivals of the 1960s; however, revivalism, as it is manifested in America, is usually a Protestant phenomenon. An **Awakening** would be a revivalist period in American history that is of significant duration and effect.

Revival movements have their historical roots in Protestant, Puritan, pietistic reactions to the rationalism of the Enlightenment and the formalized, cold, institutional faith that characterized much of 17th-century Protestantism (Dieter). Their mode of attack has always been the revivalist (not necessarily didactic) sermon. Revivalist leaders discovered a more experiential element in Reformation faith that emphasized personal commitment and obedience to Christ and a life regenerated by the indwelling Holy Spirit. They also emphasized witness and missions as a primary responsibility of the individual Christian and the church. Subjective religious experience and the importance of the individual became a new force in renewing and expanding the church. These concerns gradually permeated much of Protestantism, especially the developing churches in America (Dieter).

American Revivalism has always been marked by an appeal for a personal, public response to the gospel. A key component of this response is called the conversion.

Professor Donald Scott, in an article entitled "Evangelicalism, Revivalism, and the Second Great Awakening," describes conversion this way:

The core of nineteenth-century evangelicalism was the experience of conversion. Conversion was compelled by a set of clear ideas about the innate

A Latter Day Saint with five wives and his mother by John P. Soule, c1885.

Princeton University, Haines Photo Company, c1909.

sinfulness of humans after Adam's fall, the omnipotence of God—His awful power and His mercy—and, finally, the promise of salvation for fallen humankind through Christ's death on the cross as the atonement for human sin. But what students need to understand is that conversion was an experience. It was not simply something that people believed—though belief or faith was essential to it—but something that happened to them, a real, intensely emotional event they went through and experienced as a profound psychological transformation which left them with a fundamentally altered sense of self, an identity as a new kind of Christian. As they interpreted it, they had undergone spiritual rebirth, the death of an old self and the birth of a new one that fundamentally transformed their sense of their relationship to the world.

Conversion consisted of a sequence of clearly mapped-out steps, each of which was accompanied by a powerful emotion that led the penitent from the terror of eternal damnation through redemption to the promise of heavenly salvation. The process of conversion characteristically began in a state of "concern" about the state of one's soul and "inquiry" into what were called the doctrines of salvation propelled by the question "what can I do to be saved?" This led to a state of acute spiritual "anxiety," marked by deep fear over the prospect of eternal damnation, which in turn grew into an unmistakable sense of "conviction," the heartfelt realization that one stood justly condemned for one's sins and deserved eternal damnation. Conviction was the terrifying point of recognition that no matter how much one might desire it, there was absolutely nothing one could do to earn salvation. But there was something the penitent could do, indeed, was bound to do. That was to fully repent

and surrender unconditionally to God's will to do with as He saw fit and to serve Him fully. It was this act of repentance, surrender, and dedication to serving His will that Finney meant when in his most famous sermon he insisted that "sinners [are] bound to change their own hearts." This moment of renunciation of sin and the abject surrender to the will to God was the moment of conversion, if it was to come, the moment at which, through the promise of Christ's atonement for human sin, a merciful God would bestow His grace upon the repentant sinner.

The initial signs of the 18th-century First Great Awakening occurred in the congregation of the Dutch Reformed pastor Theodore J. Frelinghuysen in northern New Jersey in 1725, a decade before John Wesley and George Whitefield began their preaching in England. In 1726 William Tennent, the Presbyterian leader of the Great Awakening, started his "log college" to prepare ministers who would call men and women to repentance (Dieter).

By the time George Whitefield began revivalist tours of the American colonies in 1738, Jonathan Edwards, the theologian of the colonial awakening, had already experienced revival in his Northampton, Massachusetts, Congregational church. Edwards accepted the validity of much of the religious emotion that accompanied the conversions among his parishioners and wrote in defense of the proper role of emotion in true religion. The revival continued to move south until it touched all the colonies. In England the

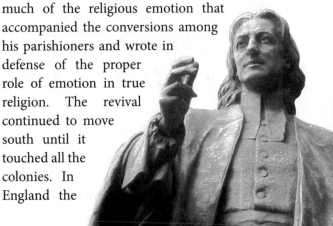

Statue of John Wesley, Melbourne, Australia

Hon. Theodore Frelinghuysen of N.J., photograph by Mathew Brady, c1855.

recognized leader of the "Evangelical Revival" was John Wesley, founder of Methodism and close friend of Whitefield. Whitefield had encouraged Wesley to take up the field preaching that brought the gospel directly to the masses of working people. (Note: while this discussion is general, it reflects insights and comments made by the historian D. E. Dieter.)

The success of Revivalism could not be doubted. People flocked to the churches in significant numbers. Revivalism brought unity to a colony divided by physical and cultural barriers.

The First Great Awakening demonstrated the general patterns that characterized all subsequent awakenings: prayer, inspired preaching, and subsequent manifestations of the Holy Spirt. However, it was the Second Great Awakening at the beginning of the 19th century that defined the theology and method of the tradition. The revival began at Hampden Sidney and Washington colleges in Virginia in 1787. It continued at Yale under Timothy Dwight and at Andover and Princeton at the end of the 18th century. It was popularized in the great camp meetings on the frontier.

Assignment

A. Church historian Ian Murray argues that there is a difference between revival and revivalism, a difference that has been lost to both American evangelicalism and academic historians. Genuine revival is the result of the activity of the Spirit of God in human lives and in human history, and is not under human control. Revivalism, in contrast, is the manifestation of human activism, energy, and organization and may exist where the Spirit of God is not active in any extraordinary way. Murray argues that the blurring of this distinction was accomplished during and after the Second Great Awakening in America in the first half of the 19th century, and that it came about under the influence of American Methodism and Presbyterian evangelist Charles G. Finney. It is the resultant emergence of revivalism that constitutes for Murray the marring of American evangelicalism (a review by Terry Chrisope).

Agree or disagree with Murray.

B. Central to revivalism is the concept of conversion. The first and perhaps most fundamental issue to be raised by this unit is that of the theology of conversion. It is a singularly American phenomenon in origin and duration. Prior to 1830 a Calvinistic conception of human inability and the necessity for the operation of divine grace prevailed among American Protestants except for the Methodists.

A corresponding understanding of revival as a sovereign outpouring of divine power accompanied this view. After 1830 the Methodist theology of conversion (known as Arminianism or semi-pelagianism) became gradually but widely accepted. This view sees conversion as dependent on the response of the autonomous human will rather than being the result of the special work of the Holy Spirit. This theology was associated with a new view of revivals, one which saw them as the product of the human means used to promote them. This revised understanding of conversion and revival had no more energetic proponent than Charles G. Finney, whose views came to prevail among American evangelical Protestants (a review by Terry Chrisope).

In what ways have contemporary understandings of conversion changed?

LESSON 2

REVIVALISM

The Cane Ridge, Kentucky, camp meeting in August 1801 became the most famous of all. The strange emotional phenomena that had shown themselves in the earlier colonial revival reappeared in intensified form. "Falling," "jerking," "rolling," and "dancing" exercises engaged many of the 20,000 worshipers present. These demonstrations moderated as the revival continued, but physical phenomena have always existed in some measure in popular revival movements (Dieter).

One historian explains:

The Presbyterians who organized these first camp meetings soon abandoned their use. The Methodists and Baptists, however, continued to use them. The ambience of the natural setting in which the camps were held, the release from the ordinary routines of home and church, the freedom to worship together in a less sectarian context, the family reunion, community center flavor, all contributed to a mystique that made the camp meeting a continuing factor in future revivalism. The frontier camp meetings declined by the time of the Civil War, but the Holiness revival which began to flourish after the Civil War utilized them extensively in both rural and urban settings.

Camp meetings eventually became more of a church family rally or reunion than a time for evangelistic outreach to the unchurched. In the 19th century, however, it was the evangelical tool of choice.

The most famous early 19th-century revivalist was Charles Grandison Finney. Finney took the rural camp meeting to the city. His success was partly due to new revivalist methods. Finney's new methods included expository preaching delivered without manuscript or notes. The public nature of the conversion experience was focused by the introduction of the anxious bench, forerunner of the altar call, by which the serious seeker made his intentions public. Finney's revivals completely transformed the fabric of American religious life. Shoe salesman Dwight L. Moody (left) dominated the revival movement after 1875. Moody, like Finney, brought revivalism to the city and merged it with powerful social movements that profoundly changed the social fabric of America. In fact, evangelical Christians became the great social reformers of the 19th and early 20th centuries.

Cane Ridge Meeting House. by W. R. Berry, 1882.

Professor Dieter writes:

Large audiences continued to attend the revival campaigns of William "Billy" Sunday, R. A. Torrey, Gypsy Smith, and others after the turn of the century. However, the change of national mood resulting from the economic upheavals that followed World War I, the persistent attacks of such social critics as H. L. Mencken, and the turn toward a gospel of social concern among the larger denominations led to a decline in the influence of revivalism in the churches and in American life. Nevertheless, the Pentecostal revival which spread swiftly from its center in Los Angeles after 1906 and the effective use of radio by Charles Fuller and other radio evangelists indicated the continuing strength of the revivalist tradition in the churches.

Perhaps the most famous revivalist was Billy Graham. Graham's success in working with a broad spectrum of Protestant churches as well as significant segments of Catholicism radically changed the direction of American revivalism. At the same time, Billy Graham (left) was an outspoken supporter of racial equality and social justice.

The success of Billy Graham evangelism assured the triumph of evangelical theology in American religion. Evangelicalism's commitment to the reliability and authority of Scripture and belief in the universal need for spiritual rebirth is the basis for the latter's direct call for repentance and faith in Christ.

In summary, America was founded by intensely religious people who expected and welcomed revivals that brought new converts and rededications. Three major revivals have occurred in American history: the First Great Awakening, the Second Great Awakening, and the Billy Graham Revivals. Along with each revival was an accompanying change in American society—thousands of people changed their behavior and outlook and, in the process, profoundly changed American history.

Assignment

A. Another important component of revivalism was the response. It is the issue of the altar call or invitation system (which is not synonymous with inviting people to come to Christ) that bothered the historian Ian Murray. Murray argues that the use of this device—calling on hearers to respond with some kind of physical movement, such as coming forward in a service—reflects a theology that replaces divine grace with a human ability that is strong enough to respond to God and the demands of the gospel. The older, Calvinistic theology denies any such ability, thus leaving the hearer shut up to divine grace as the only answer to his needs—a grace that must bestow a believing heart as well as forgiveness of sins. The new theology posits full human ability to respond any time one wills to do so; the only thing needed is the presentation to the hearer of the proper motivation to encourage and secure his response. With this view arose the direct appeal to "do something" physical, which is embodied in the altar call (a review by Terry Chrisope).

Argue for or against the altar call as a legitimate part of revivalism.

B. Alexis de Tocqueville states: "I was speaking of religion. Sunday is rigorously observed. I have seen streets barred off before churches during divine service; the law commands these things imperiously, and public opinion, much stronger than the law, obliges every one to show himself at church and to abstain from all diversion. And yet, either I am much mistaken or there is a great depth of doubt and indifference hidden under these external forms. No political passion mixes in with irreligion as with us, but for all that religion has no more power. It's a very strong impulsion which was given in former times and which is now diminishing every day. Faith is evidently inert. Go into the churches (I mean the Protestant ones) you will hear morality preached, of dogma not a word. Nothing which can at all shock the neighbour; nothing which can arouse the idea of dissent. The abstractions of dogma, the discussions especially appropriate to a religious doctrine, that's, however, what the human spirit loves to plunge into when a belief has seized it strongly. Of this character were the Americans themselves in former times."

Paraphrase Tocqueville. In what ways is Tocqueville quite contemporary in his discussion?

A CONTEMPORARY ACCOUNT OF A REVIVAL

The following is a contemporary account of a Charles Finney revival in Cincinnati, Ohio, by Mrs. Frances Trollope:

It was at the principal of the Presbyterian churches that I was twice witness to scenes that made me shudder; in describing one, I describe both, and every one; the same thing is constantly repeated.

It was in the middle of summer, but the service we were recommended to attend did not begin till it was dark. The church was well lighted, and crowded almost to suffocation. On entering, we found three priests standing side by side, in a sort of tribune, placed where the altar usually is, handsomely fitted up with crimson curtains, and elevated about as high as our pulpits. We took our places in a pew close to the rail which surrounded it.

The priest who stood in the middle was praying; the prayer was extravagantly vehement, and offensively familiar in expression; when this ended, a hymn was sung, and then another priest took the centre place, and preached. The sermon had considerable eloquence, but of a frightful kind. The preacher described, with ghastly minuteness, the last feeble fainting moments of human life, and then the gradual progress of decay after death, which he followed through every process up to the last loathsome stage of decomposition. Suddenly changing his tone, which had been that of sober accurate description, into the shrill voice of horror, he bent forward his head, as if to gaze on some object beneath the pulpit. And as Rebecca made known to Ivanhoe what she saw through the window, so the preacher made known to us what he saw in the pit that seemed to open before him. The device was certainly a happy one for giving effect to his description of hell. No image that fire, flame, brimstone,

Frances Trollope by Auguste Hervieu, c1832 (PD-US).

molten lead, or red-hot pincers could supply; with flesh, nerves, and sinews quivering under them, was omitted. The perspiration ran in streams from the face of the preacher; his eyes rolled, his lips were covered with foam, and every feature had the deep expression of horror it would have borne, had he, in truth, been gazing at the scene he described. The acting was excellent. At length he gave a languishing look to his supporters on each side, as if to express his feeble state, and then sat down, and wiped the drops of agony from his brow.

The other two priests arose, and began to sing a hymn. It was some seconds before the congregation could join as usual; every up-turned face looked pale and horror struck. When the singing ended, another took the centre place, and began in a sort of coaxing affectionate tone, to ask the congregation if what their dear brother had spoken had reached their hearts? Whether they would avoid the hell he had made them see? "Come, then!" he continued, stretching out his arms towards them, "come to us, and tell us so, and we will make you see Jesus, the dear gentle Jesus, who shall save you from it. But you must come to him! You must not be ashamed to come to him! This night you shall tell him that you are not ashamed of him; we will make way for you; we will clear the bench for anxious sinners to sit upon. Come, then! come to the anxious bench, and we will shew you Jesus! Come! Come! Come!"

Again a hymn was sung, and while it continued, one of the three was employed in clearing one or two long benches that went across the rail, sending the people back to the lower part of the church. The singing ceased, and again the people were invited, and exhorted not to be ashamed of Jesus, but to put themselves upon "the anxious benches," and lay their heads on his bosom. "Once more we will sing," he concluded, "that we may give you time." And again they sung a hymn.

And now in every part of the church a movement was perceptible, slight at first, but by degrees becoming more decided. Young girls arose, and sat down, and rose again; and then the pews opened, and several came tottering out, their hands clasped, their heads hanging on their bosoms, and every limb trembling, and still the hymn went on; but as the poor creatures approached the rail their sobs and groans became audible. They seated themselves on the "anxious benches"; the hymn ceased, and two of the three priests walked down from the tribune, and going, one to the right, and the other to the left, began whispering to the poor tremblers seated there. These whispers were inaudible to us, but the sobs and groans increased to a frightful excess. Young creatures, with features pale and distorted, fell on their knees on the pavement, and soon sunk forward on their faces; the most violent cries and shrieks followed, while from time to time a voice was heard in convulsive accents, exclaiming, "Oh Lord!" "Oh Lord Jesus!" "Help me, Jesus!" and the like.

Meanwhile the two priests continued to walk among them; they repeatedly mounted on the benches, and trumpet-mouthed proclaimed to the whole congregation, "the tidings of salvation," and then from every corner of the building arose in

Madison Square Presbyterian Church, New York City, photographer unknown, c1906

reply, short sharp cries of "Amen!" "Glory!" "Amen!" while the prostrate penitents continued to receive whispered comfortings, and from time to time a mystic caress. More than once I saw a young neck encircled by a reverent arm. Violent hysterics and convulsions seized many of them, and when the tumult was at the highest, the priest who remained above, again gave out a hymn as if to drown it.

It was a frightful sight to behold innocent young creatures, in the gay morning of existence, thus seized upon, horror struck, and rendered feeble and enervated forever. One young girl, apparently not more than fourteen, was supported in the arms of another, some years older; her face was pale as death; her eyes wide open, and perfectly devoid of meaning; her chin and bosom wet with slaver; she had every appearance of insanity. I saw a priest approach her, he took her delicate hand, "Jesus is with her! Bless the Lord!" he said, and passed on.

Assignment

What are Mrs. Trollope's criticisms and do they seem justified?

HISTORY MAKER: CHARLES FINNEY

In a time in history when so many important men and women lived—Abraham Lincoln, Andrew Jackson, Clara Barton—not one had an impact on as many people as Charles Finney. Finney, a lawyer turned Presbyterian preacher, literally converted thousands of people to the faith. But his ministry did much more than that: Finney would enter a town and scores of bars and other unsavory establishments would close. His ministry had an impact far beyond his words and actions. Praise be to God!

Generations of evangelists would emulate Finney's laudable example.

The following is a discussion of Finney's view of salvation:

Here I design to take a brief view of the gospel plan of salvation, and exhibit it especially in contrast with the original plan on which it was proposed to save mankind. Originally, the human race was put on the foundation of law for salvation; so that, if saved at all, they were to be saved on the ground of perfect and eternal obedience to the law of God. Adam was the natural head of the race. It has been supposed by many, that there was a covenant made with Adam such as this, that if he continued to obey the law for a limited period, all his posterity should be confirmed in holiness and happiness forever. What the reason is for this belief, I am unable to ascertain; I am not aware that the doctrine is taught in the Bible. And if it is true, the condition of mankind now, does not differ materially from what it was at first. If the salvation of the race originally turned wholly on the obedience of one man, I do not see how it could be called a covenant of works so far as the race is concerned. For if their weal or woe was suspended on the conduct of one head, it

Charles Grandison Finney, artist and date unknown (PD-US).

was a covenant of grace to them, in the same manner, that the present system is a covenant of grace. For according to that view, all that related to works depended on one man, just as it does under the gospel; and the rest of the race had no more to do with works, than they have now, but all that related to works was done by the representative. Now, I have supposed, and there is nothing in the Bible to the contrary, that if Adam had continued in obedience for ever, his posterity would have stood for ever on the same ground, and must have obeyed the law themselves for ever in order to be saved. It may have been, that if he had obeyed always, the natural influence of his example would have brought about such a state of things, that as a matter of fact all his posterity would have continued in holiness. But the salvation of each individual would still have depended on his own works. But if the works of the first father were to be so set to the account of the race, that on account of his obedience they were to be secured in holiness and happiness forever, I do not see wherein it differs materially from the covenant of grace, or the gospel.

As a matter of fact, Adam was the natural head of the human race, and his sin has involved them in its consequences, but not on the principle that his sin is literally accounted their sin. The truth is simply this; that from the relation in which he stood as their natural head, as a matter of fact his sin has resulted in the sin and ruin of his posterity. I suppose that mankind were originally all under a covenant of works, and that Adam was not so their head or representative, that his obedience or disobedience involved them irresistibly in sin and condemnation, irrespective of their own acts. As a fact it resulted so, that "by one man's disobedience many were made sinners;" as the apostle tells us in the 5th chapter of Romans. So that, when Adam had fallen, there was not the least hope, by the law, of saving any of mankind. Then was revealed THE PLAN, which had been provided in the counsels of eternity, on foresight of this event, for saving mankind by a proceeding of mere grace. Salvation was now placed on an entire new foundation, by a Covenant of Redemption. You will find this covenant in the 89th Psalm, and other places in the Old Testament. This, you will observe, is a covenant between the Father and the Son, regarding the salvation of mankind, and is the foundation of another covenant, the covenant of grace. In the covenant of redemption, man is no party at all, but merely the subject of the covenant; the parties being God the Father and the Son. In this covenant, the Son is made the head or representative of his people. Adam was the natural head of the human family, and Christ is the covenant head of his church.

On this covenant of redemption was founded the covenant of grace. In the covenant of redemption, the Son stipulated with the Father, to work out an atonement; and the Father stipulated that he should have a seed, or people, gathered out of the human race. The covenant of grace was made with men and was revealed to Adam, after the fall, and more fully revealed to Abraham. Of this covenant, Jesus Christ was to be the Mediator, or he that should administer it. It was a covenant of grace, in opposition to the original covenant of works, under which Adam and his posterity were placed at the beginning; and salvation was now to be by faith, instead of works, because the obedience and death of Jesus Christ were to be regarded as the reason why any individual was to be saved, and not each one's personal obedience. Not that his obedience was, strictly speaking, performed for us. As a man, he was under the necessity of obeying, for himself; because he had not put himself under the law, and if he did not obey it he became personally a transgressor. And yet there is a sense in which it may be said that his obedience is reckoned to our account. His obedience has so highly honored the law, and his death has so fully satisfied the demands of public justice, that grace (not justice,) has reckoned his righteousness to us. If he had obeyed the law strictly for us, and had owed no obedience for himself, but was at liberty to obey only for us, then I cannot see why justice should not have accounted his obedience to us, and we could have obtained salvation on the score of right, instead of asking it on the score of grace or favor. But it is only in this sense accounted ours, that he, being God and man, having voluntarily assumed our nature, and then voluntarily laying down his life to make atonement, casts such a glory on the law of God, that grace is willing to consider his obedience in such a sense ours, as, on his account, to treat us as if we were righteous.

Christ is also the covenant head of those that believe. He is not the natural head, as Adam was, but our covenant relation to him is such, that whatever is given to him is given to us. Whatever he is, both in his divine and human nature; whatever he has done, either as God or man, is given to us by covenant, or promise, and is absolutely ours. I want you should understand this. The church, as a body, has never yet understood the fullness and richness of this covenant, and that all there is in Christ is made over to us in the covenant of grace.

And here let me say, that we

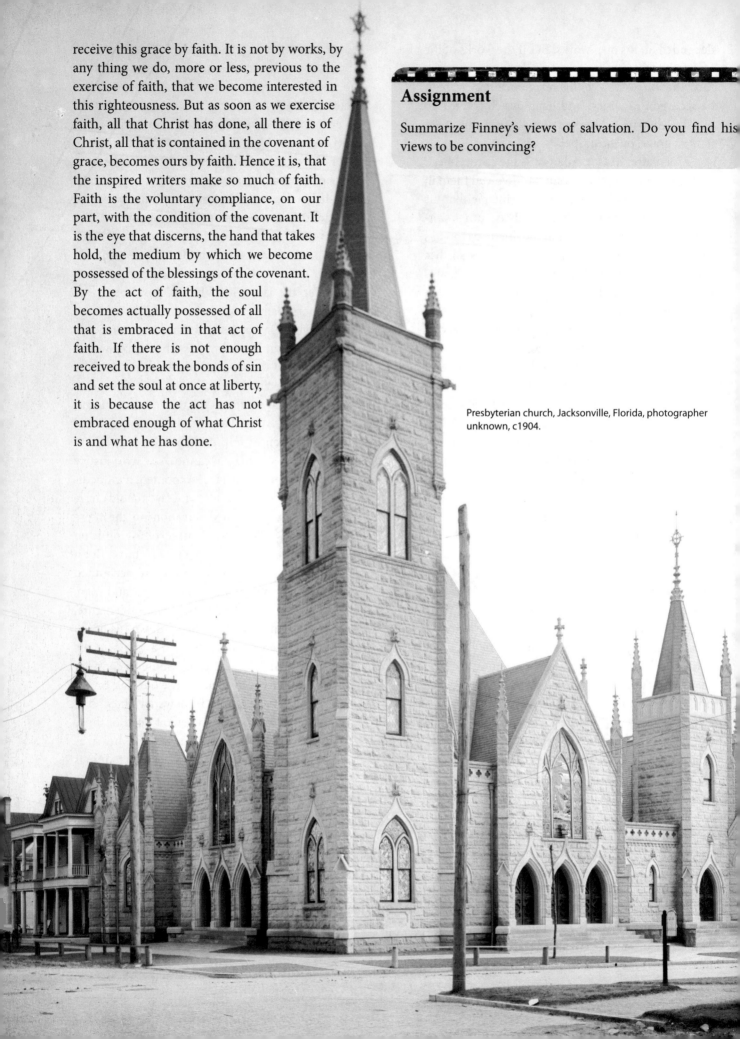

receive this grace by faith. It is not by works, by any thing we do, more or less, previous to the exercise of faith, that we become interested in this righteousness. But as soon as we exercise faith, all that Christ has done, all there is of Christ, all that is contained in the covenant of grace, becomes ours by faith. Hence it is, that the inspired writers make so much of faith. Faith is the voluntary compliance, on our part, with the condition of the covenant. It is the eye that discerns, the hand that takes hold, the medium by which we become possessed of the blessings of the covenant. By the act of faith, the soul becomes actually possessed of all that is embraced in that act of faith. If there is not enough received to break the bonds of sin and set the soul at once at liberty, it is because the act has not embraced enough of what Christ is and what he has done.

Assignment

Summarize Finney's views of salvation. Do you find his views to be convincing?

Presbyterian church, Jacksonville, Florida, photographer unknown, c1904.

CAUSES OF THE AMERICAN CIVIL WAR

First Thoughts . . .

With the end of the War of 1812, a wave of nationalism flooded the new nation. After the Mexican War in the 1840s, most Americans would have laughed if anyone suggested that we would be anything but one mighty, unified nation. Yet in 1861, Americans, North and South, who were experiencing unprecedented prosperity and good will, began fighting a civil war. How did this happen?

Chapter Learning Objectives . . .

For years the question "What caused the Civil War?" has puzzled historians. They suggest many reasons but what is the main cause? Slavery was the chief irritant but did not cause the conflict. In Chapter 13 we will study slavery but we will look at other mitigating causes of the great American Civil War: Nativism, Revivalism, Manifest Destiny.

The Civil War was caused because Southern and Northern Americans chose not to live together. Again, the operative word is chose. They chose to fight a war. The North and the South were always two nations, and by 1860 it was difficult to live together in the same house—but not impossible. They had solved their problems before—in 1820 and 1850 for instance. But, suddenly, in 1860, the political system failed. And when it did, war came. This terrible war lasted four years and cost more American lives than any war before or since.

As a result of this chapter you should be able to:

1. Discuss whether the American Civil War was avoidable or unavoidable.
2. Reflect upon why, especially among Southerners, the American Civil War has had such an enduring and profound impact.
3. Evaluate whether slavery expansion was the real cause of the Civil War.
4. Assess whether John Brown was a misunderstood patriot or a cold-blooded murderer.
5. Discuss the impact of 19th-century philosophers on world views.

THE COMING CRISIS: PART ONE

Mary Chestnut (right), a Southerner, wrote as the Civil War was beginning to unfold, "We [the North and the South] are divorced because we have hated each other so!" This hatred ultimately was a cause of a bloody and horrible civil war.

For years the question "What caused the Civil War?" has puzzled historians. They suggest many reasons but what is the main cause? Slavery was the chief irritant but did not cause the conflict. For example, both Rachel and Samuel Cormany, Civil War contemporaries, supported their government's efforts to quell the Southern rebellion. But neither of them was irritated by slavery. Rachel blamed the war on the "hotheadness of the South, and the invisibleness of the North." They were not in favor of freeing the slaves. They represented most of the North. In fact, there were many things that contributed to the Civil War—some more than others. Certainly slavery was a cause but not the sole cause.

The Civil War was caused because Southern and Northern Americans chose not to live together. Again, the operative word is chose. They chose to fight a war. The North and the South were always two nations, and by 1860 it was difficult to live together in the same house. But not impossible. They had solved their problems before—in 1820 and 1850 for instance. But suddenly, in 1860, the political system failed. And when it did, war came.

The Civil War was the fault of neither the North nor the South. Or rather, it was the fault of both! The combination of an expanding economy, a flood of immigrants, the Second Great Awakening, Manifest Destiny, and the failure of the American political system brought the young republic to the brink of Civil War. Ultimately, though, the failure of nerve manifested by American political leaders thrust the nation into its bloodiest war in American history.

A historian's assessment of the causes of the Civil War wrote:

When the Union was originally formed, the United States embraced too many degrees of latitude and longitude, and too many varieties of climate and production, to make it practicable to establish and administer justly one common government which should take charge of all the interests of society. To the wise men who were entrusted with the formation of that union and common government, it was obvious enough that each separate society should be entrusted with the management of its own peculiar interests, and that the united government should take charge only of those interests which were common and general (Hunter 1, 7–8).

What is ironic is that, in a way, the North and the South were fighting for the same thing. Both saw themselves preserving what was quintessentially American. The Confederacy was really fighting for the American dream as much as the Union! They saw themselves as the new patriots, the true "Americans." The South had some justification; many Founding Fathers owned slaves (Hunter 1, 9–10). Naturally, Northerners had the same argument and saw themselves as the true patriots. Their similar perspectives on this issue were further proof that North and South stood on common ground.

In other ways, though, by 1860, the North and South had nothing in common. The Civil War was a struggle between conflicting world views. Each section held to a belief system and increasingly felt alienated from the other. They disagreed over the power of the federal government; they disagreed over tariffs; they especially disagreed over slavery and its expansion westward (Williams 203). These disagreements were nothing new and did not bring a civil war. The war was avoidable. However, by the middle of the 19th century, these differing viewpoints, coupled with the almost violent change inflicted on America and the collapse of compromise as a viable option in the political arena, brought the young republic into a horrendous civil war. Americans chose to fight because they were unwilling to choose an alternative.

The first American to observe that the Civil War was unnecessary was former president Buchanan. He argued that the cause of the Civil War was to be found in "the long, active, and persistent hostility of the Northern Abolitionists, both in and out of Congress, against Southern slavery, until the final triumph of President Lincoln; and, on the other hand, the corresponding antagonism and violence with which the advocates of slavery resisted efforts, and vindicated its preservation and extension up till the period of secession." Buchanan's assumption that the war need not have taken place had it not been for Northern fanatics and, to a lesser extent, Southern extremists was a correct one. To put it another way, there was no substantive issue important enough in 1861 to necessitate a resort to arms; the war had been brought on by extremists on both sides. The moderate political center refused to solve the problem and left the solution to extremists. The extremists brought on a civil war.

Two Nations, Two Economies

I heard much of the extreme difficulty of ginning cotton, that is separating it from its seeds. . . . I involuntarily happened to be thinking on the subject and struck out a plan of a machine in my mind

A cotton gin on display at the Eli Whitney Museum.

. . . ' (qtd. Van Doren and McHenry 89).

The machine was the cotton gin, and the author of this letter was Eli Whitney. The cotton gin more than anything else made cotton a profitable business and assured its future in the Southern economy.

Originally cotton had been a minor crop because of the difficulty separating the fiber from the seeds. But in 1793 Eli Whitney's cotton gin solved this problem. In 1800 only about 70,000 bales of cotton were produced in the South. By 1825 cotton production increased 700 percent (Fenton 185). Demand for cotton of all sorts was growing, especially in England, where new textile factories, with their weaving and spinning machines, created an insatiable appetite. Demand and supply came together when Eli Whitney set his mind to the problem of short-staple cotton and its seeds (Nash, et al. 309). Eli Whitney supplied the technology for cotton to be king, and the industrial revolution supplied the market. By the early 19th century, British and American factories demanded more cotton. The expanding Southern plantation system was ready to supply that cotton.

In 1813 Boston Manufacturing Company opened the first textile factory to perform all cloth-making operations by power in Waltham, Massachusetts. Financed with large capital, the company recruited New England farm girls as operatives, boarded them in dormitories, and produced a standard coarse cotton cloth requiring minimal labor skill. Cotton mills began production in Massachusetts, with water-powered machinery; by 1826, in Lowell, one plant turned out 2 million yards of cloth annually (Van Doren and McHenry 128). Their production grew more and more over the next few years.

In 1828 a new sore spot appeared in North-South relations. That year Congress raised the tariff on imports, in order to protect native industry struggling to compete with European manufacturers. The South protested loudly over the tariff on the grounds that it favored the North at her expense. She was dependent almost wholly on the North and on Europe for manufactured goods, and while an increase in prices would enrich the North, it would mean a rise in the cost of living for the Southerners with no compensating increase in wealth.

Resentment reached its highest pitch in South Carolina, which at this particular time was experiencing a depression because of a drop in cotton prices. The state legislative body both met and threatened to nullify the act of Congress because it favored one section of the country at the expense of another. If carried out, this proposal would have placed the authority of a state over that of the federal government and would have made the Constitution useless.

The Nullification proceeding threw the country into turmoil. South Carolina, as a result, threatened to withdraw from the Union (Barnes 13). "We, therefore, the people of the state of South Carolina, in Convention assembled, do declare . . . that several acts of the Congress . . . are null, void, and no law, nor binding upon this state, its officers, or citizens" (Van Doren 146). This was not the first attempt at secession. New England states first suggested it as a possibility with the Hartford Convention Resolutions of 1815. But this was a more serious attempt and only the vigorous intervention of President Andrew Jackson stopped civil war from occurring.

Until the invention of the cotton gin, the North and the South were primarily farming communities. But the cotton gin brought new value on slaves, profit and demand in the South. The industrial revolution demanded workers and economic growth.

So going into the Civil War, America was two nations. Eli Whitney's inspiring ingenuity gave a tragic guarantee that the North would welcome the industrial revolution and the South would reject it. The North would go one way and the South another, and sooner or later they would collide.

Assignment

Was the conflict between the North and the South avoidable or unavoidable? Explain your answer.

THE COMING CRISIS: PART TWO

A Nation of Immigrants

Another change that provoked the Civil War was immigration. Immigrants furnished much of the labor that made the productive explosion possible and were also many of the consumers who made it profitable. The industrializing processes that were at work opened job opportunity and uprooted millions in Europe whose occupations became unneeded or whose land was confiscated by the more "efficient." The immigrants moved the United States population up from 4 million to 32 million in just 90 years. American culture simply molded itself around their presence (Weisberger 783).

Population growth can weaken the economy of a country that is limited in its natural and capital resources. The United States was not limited, therefore, the economy soared. (Fenton 280: Cooke 273). This was good. What was bad was that bad feelings grew among some Americans toward immigrants. That was called **Nativism**. At the same time, while millions of Americans flooded into Northern cities, very few came South. This only served to accentuate the growing differences between these two American sections. Foreign immigrants damaged an already enfeebled Whig party and created concern among many native-born Americans. To the average, hard-working Protestant American, the foreigners pouring into the cities and following the railroads westward spoke unfamiliar languages, wore dissimilar clothes, drank alcohol freely in the grogshops, and increased crime and pauperism. Worst of all, they attended Catholic churches, where the Latin mass and Eucharistic rituals offended those used to the Protestant worship. Furthermore they sent their children to their own schools. They also seemed content with lower standards of living and would work for lower pay and worse conditions than any American laborers, thus endangering American jobs.

Massive immigration then, like economic differences, was one of the causes of the Civil War. It brought instability

Immigrants at Ellis Island, Bains Collection, c1907.

to the North. At the same time, immigrants were flooding into the Western territories. These new Western immigrants had no wish to compete with slaves.

Slavery as a Cause but Not the Main Cause...

Rev. Abraham Essick, pastor of Chambersburg Lutheran Church, a moderate unionist, well-educated pastor, and a reliable witness, wrote a friend and admitted that slavery was an issue but not the most important issue. "Conservative men, who did all in their power to avert the collision before our flag was dishonoured [the fall of Ft. Sumter], are now burning with indignation. . . . The government must be sustained, rebellion suppressed, and the honor of the nation vindicated. May God defend the right!" He expressed no outrage at slavery and was more concerned about the honor and dignity of his nation and the breaking away of the South from that nation than any other issue (Abraham Essick, May 8, 1861). Other diarists concurred with Abraham Essick. James Lemuel Clark, a member of the Southern army, when he discussed the reasons he went to war with "Yankees," never mentioned slavery as a cause. In 1860, Cooke County, where James Lemuel Clark lived, had a population of nearly 4,000 white people and only 65 slaveowners! There were only 300 to 400 slaves and they were held by 10 slaveholders (Clark 20). Another Texan, William A. Fletcher, was delighted when he heard he could fight the Yankees. He even entertained a thought of arming the slaves to fight Yankees too (Fletcher 2)! Fletcher and Clark did not fight on the Southern side for slavery.

As one of the earliest attempts to make sense of this tragedy, the Southern Historical Society concluded in 1876:

The late civil war which raged in the United States has been very generally attributed to the abolition of slavery as its cause. When we consider how deeply the institutions of southern society and the operations of southern industry were founded in slavery, we must admit that this was cause enough to have produced such a result. But great and wide as was that cause in its far reaching effects, a close study of the history of the times will bring us to the

conclusion that it was the fear of a mischief far more extensive and deeper even than this which drove cool and reflecting minds in the South to believe that it was better to make the death struggle at once than submit tamely to what was inevitable, unless its coming could be averted by force. Men, too old to be driven blindly by passion, women, whose gentle and kindly instincts were deeply impressed by the horrors of war, and young men, with fortune and position yet to be won in an open and inviting field, if peace could be maintained so as to secure the opportunities of liberty and fair treatment, united in the common cause and determined to make a holocaust of all that was dear to them on the altars of war sooner than submit without resistance to the loss of liberty, honor and property by a cruel abuse of power and a breach of plighted faith on the part of those who had professed to enter with them into a union of justice and fraternal affection (Hunter 1).

Other evidence that slavery could not have been the cause of the Civil War was the issue of slavery in Brazil. Brazil and America were settled around the same time. Both had slavery. However,

Statue of Lincoln at the Lincoln Memorial located at the National Mall in Washington, D.C.

Brazil did not have a Civil War in order to rid themselves of this injustice (Degler, xviii). Therefore the presence of slavery, as controversial as it might be, as divisive as it may be, in no way assured that the United States would fight a civil war just as it did not cause a civil war in Brazil.

Slavery no doubt was an antiquated institution and eventually would cease. Very few Americans, North and South, doubted that. But virtually no one wanted to end it immediately—especially in the old South. However, slavery expansion—the expansion of slavery into new, free territories was a fiery issue. To Southerners, it was a constitutional right. To the North, it was a threat to free labor that was the bedrock of the industrial North.

What about slavery expansion? This issue is as heated as the issue of slavery. President Lincoln did not intend to stop slavery; what he didn't want was slavery expansion. He stated this in his first Inaugural Address, "Apprehension seems to exist among the people of the Southern states that, by accession of a republic administration, their property and their peace and personal security are to be endangered. There has never been any reasonable cause for such apprehension. Indeed, the most ample evidence to the contrary has all the while existed and been open to their inspection. It is found in nearly all the published speeches of him who now address you . . ." (Lincoln). What Lincoln said was that

Little Eva and Uncle Tom by Edwin Longsden Long, 1866 (PD-US).

there was no reason for the South to choose secession, for he by no means wanted the slaves free. Of course Lincoln changed later, but initially he, like the Republican Party, was opposed to slavery expansion, not to slavery (1860 Republican National Platform).

If slavery expansion threatened Northerners, the possibility of no slavery expansion infuriated Southerners. "The gospel of prosperity and the defense of bondage were inseparable in the minds of most slave holders. But when they made explicit reference to slavery, masters drew also from an intellectual tradition that reaffirmed their faith in the destiny of the white man as the harbinger of global wealth. In the antebellum South, racism and the gospel of prosperity were joined in symbiotic relation" (Oakes 130). The possibility of no slavery expansion was tantamount to commercial poverty in the mind of most Southerners. The more slave expansion, the more money for the slave holders. So Lincoln didn't want slavery expansion because that meant less money for the paid workers; and what the South wanted was more money. Of course the whole controversy about slavery was further exacerbated by Harriet Beecher Stowe's *Uncle Tom's Cabin*. Moderate Northerners thought that it was an exaggeration of slavery. Southerners thought that it was downright libelous! They hated Mrs. Stowe (McCullough 337). Many Southerners, like my great-great-great-uncle, Uncle Howard, fought for the South even though they had no or very few slaves.

Slavery, then, was an important cause of the Civil War. But it was not the most important cause. In fact, there was no substantive issue important enough in 1861 to fight a civil war. The war was brought on by extremism and misunderstandings on both sides (Grob and Billias 392).

Another contributing factor was the Second Great Awakening that spread across antebellum America, creating instability and heightened expectations.

Harriet Beecher Stowe, photographer unknown, c1870.

Fire Across the Land: The Second Great Awakening

While all this mix-up was occurring, there came the Second Great Awakening. This was precluded by what was called the Cane Ridge Revival in 1800. The Cane Ridge Revival was formed by a Presbyterian minister named James McGready. McGready preached against formality and the darkness of the churches. Many people were touched—even the "boldest most daring sinners in the county covered their faces and wept bitterly," and "many fell to the ground, and lay powerless, groaning, praying and crying for mercy." This was the beginning of a great change (Weisberger 24). The Revival of August 1801 at Cane Ridge was the climactic event of the Western Great Revival. It was estimated by military personnel that some 20,000 to 30,000 persons of all ages, representing various cultures and economic levels, traveled on foot and on horseback, many bringing wagons with tents and camping provisions. Because of the numbers of people attending and the length of the meeting, Cane Ridge has become the metaphor of the Great Revival. Historical accounts recall the contagious fervor that characterized the meetings that continued day and night. Descriptions abound of individuals, taken by great emotion, falling to the ground, crying aloud in prayer and song, and rising to exhort and assist others in their responses to the moment. Worship continued well into the week following the serving of Communion on Sunday, in fact, until provisions for humans and horses ran out. The sacramental gatherings of the Presbyterians, already undergoing transformation by the time of the August 1801 Cane Ridge Revival, contributed to the growing camp meeting revivals. Participation by Methodists added an emotional evangelical quality that Presbyterians had previously tried to hold in check. Baptists attended the meetings on a lesser scale, as the congregations were in revival paralleling that of their frontier peers. The American camp meeting and revival meeting were established as new norms for Protestants.

Then, in the 1820s Charles Finney held a series of revivals in New York State. Finney was known as a "soul winner" and a man who "made good" in his choice of work, which was to bring men to Christ (Weisberger 95; Ahlstrom 653). All this change made Americans more willing to follow their own wishes and not follow the government or other authority. By 1860 more Americans than ever had personal relationships with their God and wished to make personal decisions about where they lived and what they owned. In a real sense, then, when the North tried to take away the Southern slaves, the South saw it as a personal attack on their property and life. They were ready to do whatever was

Julia Ward Howe, most famous as the author of "The Battle Hymn of the Republic" photographer unknown, c1908.

necessary to protect those rights—even if it was rebellion against the government. At the same time, Northern Christians were prepared to force their Southern brothers to stay in the Union no matter what the cost. The religious revivals of the early and middle 19th century prepared them for this decision.

Assignment

A. In what way was slavery a cause but not the cause of the Civil War?

B. In what way was the Second Great Awakening a cause of the Civil War?

C. The Civil War is ubiquitous in the southern United States. When I was growing up in Arkansas in the 1950s I never heard "The Battle Hymn of the Republic" except on television. It was a "Yankee" song. The Fourth of July was hardly recognized; in fact, in Vicksburg, a town not too far south from my home town, the Fourth of July was not observed at all! Why has this war had such an enduring and profound impact on the South?

THE COMING CRISIS: PART THREE

Will Western States Be Free or Slave?

On top of all the revivals, the issue of slavery expansion, and the tariffs, there was also Manifest Destiny. The phrase "Manifest Destiny" was coined by **John L. O'Sullivan** (below), editor of the *Democratic Review*. It advanced the idea that America's superior culture and institutions gave us a God-given right to take over the entire continent (Nash, pp. 448). **Manifest Destiny** allowed the expansion west but did not cause it to happen. Occurrences in Texas triggered the government's determination to get possession of the territories west of the Mississippi River (Nash et al. 448).

Many people in the North opposed the Mexican War. They thought that it was a Southern plot to extend slavery. In 1846, David Wilmot, a congressman from Pennsylvania, introduced an amendment to a bill designed to appropriate $2 million for negotiating an agreement with Mexico. Part of his amendment suggested that slavery should be kept away from any territory acquired from Mexico. A bitter and prolonged debate broke out between those who were for slavery and those who were not. Finally, the Wilmot Proviso, as the amendment was called, was passed by the House of Representatives. However, it failed to pass the Senate (Fenton, 282–283). This debate showed how fragile the unity of North and South was. They were very close to fighting a war because they had no idea how to live together in peace.

Expansionism ran into problems when the nation discussed whether new states would be slave or free. This then led to the failure of the American political system to keep these two nations—North and South—one. Now nothing was working to unify the nations. There was no ground on which they could agree. In every issue, situation, and problem they were disagreeing.

No Way to Compromise

So what caused the Civil War? Why did Americans fight one another for four long years, at the cost of 600,000 lives? The American Civil War occurred because Americans allowed it. They let their differences be more important than their similarities. The government was no help.

Prior to the Civil War, Americans had done a lot of compromising. In 1820, there was the Missouri Compromise, when Congress took charge of the question of slavery in the territories by declaring it illegal in the huge region acquired by the Louisiana Purchase.

When Andrew Jackson was president (1829–1837), a sharp division arose between Northerners and Southerners over the tariff issue. The South favored free trade; the industrial North needed protection. Jackson confronted South Carolina and it backed down.

Next, President Polk's war with Mexico opened the slavery issue again. Should slavery be allowed in the new territories? The Wilmot Proviso (1846), which was supposed to have excluded slavery, became an irritating subject for both the North and the South. It was also being voted on again and again in Congress and successfully held off by Southerners. Abolitionists led by William Lloyd Garrison and others were popular in many Northern circles and called for the immediate emancipation of slaves with no compensation to slaveowners. However, the majority of Northern whites disliked blacks too and refused to support abolition; they did not want to allow slavery in the territories so that they would be preserved for white settlement based on Northern expectation: free labor, dignity of work, and economic progress (Multimedia Encyclopedia Online).

In 1848 northern dissatisfaction with the existing parties formed a new party—the Republican Party. By polling 300,000 votes for their candidate, Martin Van Buren, victory was denied to the Democrats, and the Whig Zachary Taylor was put in the White House. No one was happy, and the nation was ill-suited to handle the next crisis.

The Compromise of 1850 appeared to have settled the issue of slavery expansion by the principle of popular sovereignty, which said that the people who lived in the Mexican cession territories were to decide for themselves. A new Fugitive Slave Law was passed in 1850. This enraged Northerners—slaveowners could cross into the North and claim runaway slaves.

As the 1850s began, it seemed for a time that the issue of slavery and other sectional differences between North and South might eventually be reconciled. But as these substantial differences combined with the westward expansion of the American nation and the resulting conflict over the expansion of slavery, all attempts to compromise weakened and contrasting economic, political, and philosophical endeavor became more evident. The resulting civil war altered the American nation.

In 1860 the political system became dysfunctional. All consensus was lost. The American political system no longer functioned.

Charleston, S.C., November 8, 1860: "Yesterday on the train, just before we reached Fernandina, a woman called out: "That settles the hash." Tanny touched me on the shoulder and said: 'Lincoln's elected.' 'How do you know?' 'The man over there has a telegram.' The excitement was very great. Everybody was talking at the same time. One, a little more moved than the others, stood up and said despondently: 'The die is cast; stake is life or death.' 'Did you ever!' was the prevailing exclamation, and someone cried out: 'Now that the black radical Republicans have the power I suppose they will [John] Brown us all.' No doubt of it. I have always kept a journal after a fashion of my own, with dates and a line of poetry or prose, mere quotations, which I understood and no one else, and I have kept letters and extracts from the papers. From to-day forward I will tell the story in my own way."—Mary Chestnut

Southerners considered the rise of the Yankee-dominated Republican party with great apprehension. They were convinced that the party was secretly controlled by abolitionists (although most northerners loathed the abolitionists) and that Yankees believed in using government to administer their moralistic campaigns. Their fears were confirmed in 1859 when John Brown (left, PD-US) led a raid on the federal arsenal at Harpers Ferry, Va., hoping to encourage a slave uprise. His action—and his subsequent adoration by some northerners—helped convince southerners that emancipation of the slaves, if northerners attained authority of the country, was sooner or later inevitable. They then fought a war to protect their rights and property.

Again, all the different causes that led up to the American Civil War, the expanding of the economy, a flood of immigrants, the Second Great Awakening, Manifest Destiny, and the rise of Nativism—doomed the Republic to a Civil war. The war was essentially fought because the American political system failed to present a compromise that suited the North's demands as well as the South's. At the same time, massive immigration and Western expansion conspired to bring division in the nation. With no political consensus and cultural unanimity, the nation crumbled. The 1860s generation blundered into a needless war, because they played on emotions to gain votes rather than face the issues. Agitation over slavery led to mistaken and false sectional images and fanaticism (Crum 93). Therefore they fought it out in a great and awful civil war.

Assignment

A. Many historians argue that slavery expansion was the real cause of the Civil War. Argue in favor of this position.

B. Research the sad case of John Brown. Was he a misunderstood patriot or a cold-blooded murderer?

PHILOSOPHERS AND WORLD VIEWS

Arthur Schopenhauer (1788–1860)

Schopenhauer, often called the philosopher of pessimism, rejected Christianity and embraced eastern religions. Schopenhauer was a disciple of Immanual Kant, the greatest of German philosophers, who argued that knowledge was separate from experience. In fact, Kant and Schopenhauer argued that "it was that which exists independently of our perception, that which actually is." This was "the will." This all-encompassing human will is characterized by Schopenhauer as a blind striving power that "reveals itself to everyone directly as the in-itself of his own phenomenal being." Schopenhauer, with both a Romantic and Modern impulse, invited mankind to an arduous task: understanding experience separate from any outside force or reality (i.e., God). He and Kant differentiated between the will and action. The next step would be the relativism and nihilism of Nietzsche and Dewey.

Scholar Alex Scott wrote:

Schopenhauer believed that the will is the being-in-itself of everything in the world. The world as an idea is an objectification of the will. The will cannot be explained, nor can it be fully accounted for. The will is comprehensible insofar as it manifests itself in the world, but its inner nature cannot be adequately explained.

The will is beyond time and space, which together constitute a form of the principle of sufficient reason. The will is a unity, and not a plurality. The plurality of things in time and space represents an objectification of the will.

The will cannot be viewed as a necessary cause of its manifestations in the phenomenal world, because it is not governed by the principle of sufficient reason. The relationship between freedom and necessity is that between the will and its manifestations in time and space.

The will-in-itself cannot be defined as the will to do something. The will as a thing-in-itself does not have an object or purpose in its willing. The principle of motivation is a form of the principle of sufficient reason, which extends only to manifestations of the will.

According to Schopenhauer, the act of willing arises from need, and therefore from deprivation or suffering. The fulfillment of a wish ends the act of willing. But no obtained object of desire can give lasting satisfaction. Thus, what is necessary for knowledge of the Platonic Idea is pure contemplation, the absence of desire, the state of total dedication to perception, the transcendence of the subject-object relationship, and freedom from being confined by individuality.

Schopenhauer sees the gratification of a wish or desire as negative, in that it is only a temporary deliverance from deprivation and suffering. Happiness is negative, in that it does not provide lasting satisfaction. Because happiness is never lasting or complete, it is only the absence of true happiness that can become the subject of art.

Schopenhauer also says that freedom of the will is negative, because this freedom is merely the denial of necessity. The intellect is subservient to the will, in that it learns the decisions of the will only after the will has decided on a mode of action. The will is inaccessible to the intellect, and the intellect can only explore the motives for actions, which are manifestations of the will. Self-knowledge can reveal the motives for the act of willing. Knowledge of the self and of the phenomenal world can also influence the motives for action.

William Godwin (1756–1836)

For the first time in several hundred years, the philosopher William Godwin spoke seriously about a utopia. Most thinkers and writers had more or less given up pursuit of the whole ideal. Godwin's utopia was a society run by human nature, not by government. This view was classic anarchism. Godwin wanted to create a society with no laws or government at all. His view was that if mankind were unshackled from these things—laws, government, etc.—it would be able to reach its full potential. Like the philosopher Jean Jacques Rousseau, Godwin was critical of the political tradition of Hobbes and Locke. Unlike Rousseau, though, Godwin wanted no government at all. Subjective goodness and reason must supersede law and government. Only the Absurdism of Kurt Vonnegut, Jr., in the 20th century would approximate the radical thought of someone like Godwin.

The following passage is from *Political Justice*:

William Godwin, by Henry William Pickersgill, date unknown (PD-Art).

The rights of man have, like many other political and moral questions, furnished a topic of eager and pertinacious dispute more by a confused and inaccurate statement of the subject of enquiry than by any considerable difficulty attached to the subject itself.

The real or supposed rights of man are of two kinds, active and passive; the right in certain cases to do as we list; and the right we possess to the forbearance or assistance of other men. The first of these a just philosophy will probably induce us universally to explode.

There is no sphere in which a human being can be supposed to act, where one mode of proceeding will not, in every given instance, be more reasonable than any other mode. That mode the being is bound by every principle of justice to pursue.

Morality is nothing else but that system which teaches us to contribute, upon all occasions, to the extent our power, to the well-being and happiness of every intellectual and sensitive existence. But there is no action of our lives, which does not in some way affect that happiness. Our property, our time, and our faculties, may all of them be made to contribute to this end. The periods, which cannot be spent in the active production of happiness, may be spent in preparation. There is not one of our avocations or amusements, that does not, by its effects, render us more or less fit to contribute our quota to the general utility. If then every one of our actions fall within the province of morals, it follows that we have no rights in relation to the selecting them. No one will maintain, that we have a right to trespass upon the dictates of morality.

It has been observed by natural philosophers, that a single grain of land more or less in the structure of the earth, would have produced an infinite variation in its history. If this be true in inanimate nature, it is much more so in morals. The encounter of two persons of opposite sexes, so as to lead to the relation of marriage, in many cases obviously depends upon the most trivial circumstances, any one of which, being changed, the relation would not have taken place. Let the instance be the father and mother of Shakespeare. If they had not been connected, Shakespeare would never have been born. If any accident had happened to the wife during her pregnancy, if she had on any day set her foot half an inch too far, and fallen down a flight of stairs, if she had turned down one street instead of another, through which, it may be, some hideous object was passing, Shakespeare might never have come alive into the world. The determination of mind, in consequence of which the child contracts some of his earliest propensities, which call out his curiosity, industry, and ambition, or on the other hand leave him unobserving, indolent, and phlegmatic, is produced by circumstances so minute and subtle as in few instances to have been made the subject of history. The events which after wards produce his choice of a profession or pursuit, are not less precarious. Every one of these incidents, when it occurred, grew out of a series of incidents that had previously taken place. Everything is connected in the universe. If any man asserted that, if Alexander had not bathed in the river Cydnus, Shakespeare would never have written, it would be impossible to prove that his assertion was untrue.

To the inference we are deducing from this statement of facts, it may be objected "that it is true that all events in the universe are connected, and that the most memorable revolutions may depend for their existence upon trivial causes; but it is impossible for us to discern the remote bearings and subtle influences of our own actions; and by what we cannot discern it can never be required of us to regulate our conduct." This is no doubt true, but its force in the nature of an objection will be taken away if we consider, first, that, though our ignorance will justify us in neglecting that which, had we been better informed, we should have seen to be most beneficial, it can scarcely be considered as conferring on us an absolute right to incur that neglect. Secondly, even under the limited powers of our discernment, it will seldom happen to a man eminently conscientious and benevolent, to see no appearance of superiority, near or remote, direct or indirect, in favour of one side of any alternative proposed to his choice, rather than the other. We are bound to regulate ourselves by the best judgement we can exert. Thirdly, if anything remain to the active rights of man after this deduction, and if he be at liberty to regulate his conduct in any instance, independently of the dictates of morality, it will be, first, an imperfect, not an absolute right, the offspring of ignorance and imbecility; and, secondly, it will relate only to such insignificant matters, if such there be, as, after the best exercise of human judgment, cannot be discerned to have the remotest relation to the happiness of mankind."

Waterfall Berdan, also called the Tarsus River (Latin:Cydnus) by Nedim Ardoğa, 2010.

Assignment

A. What does Schopenhauer feel about ethical decisions? Is Schopenhauer's view Theistic?

B. Discuss Godwin's view of morality and why it is anti-Christian.

Abraham Lincoln, by Alexander Gardner, 1863.

Chapter 14

THE AMERICAN CIVIL WAR

First Thoughts . . .

"We have shared the incommunicable experience of war. We felt, we still feel, the passion of life to its top. In our youths, our hearts were touched by fire.

—Oliver Wendell Holmes

The American Civil War is something that Americans endured and reveled in. As the historian Shelby Foote says, "The Civil War was the last romantic war and the first modern war."

Chapter Learning Objectives . . .

In chapter 14 we will try to make sense of this horrible war that produced such carnage. We will examine battlefield strategy. We will see that it changed America forever: The results of the war were revolutionary in character. Slavery was abolished. The Union was declared to be perpetual and the right of a state to secede settled by the judgment of battle. The power and prestige of the federal government were enhanced beyond imagination.

As a result of this chapter you should be able to:

1. Describe each presidential administration from 1824–1860.
2. Compare the Northern and Southern views of the Union.
3. Evaluate whether the South really had a chance to win the war.
4. Predict what would have happened if the South had won the war.
5. Discuss the impact of unforgiveness on a person and on a nation.
6. Assess the impact of Abraham Lincoln on history.

PRESIDENTS

1825–1861

Research each of these presidents and write a paragraph describing what was most memorable about each one's administration. (The dates below represent their time in office.)

John Quincy Adams
1825–1829

Andrew Jackson
1829–1837

Martin Van Buren
1837–1841

William Henry Harrison
1841

James Tyler
1841–1845

James K. Polk
1845–1849

Zachary Taylor
1849–1850

Millard Fillmore
1850–1853

Franklin Pierce
1853–1857

THE AMERICAN CIVIL WAR

Before I departed to my Northern destination in 1976—Harvard University—to attend graduate school, my grandmother (affectionately called "Mammow") warned me, "Jimmy, go up there and be educated but stay away from Yankee ladies." More than 100 years after the Civil War ended, my grandmother still felt rancor and distrust against the North! This terrible conflict indelibly placed itself in the hearts of most Americans.

The American Civil War, 1861–1865, killed more Americans than any other war in history. From Ft. Sumter to Appomattox, 600,000 deaths and more than 1 million casualties, Americans killed one another in wholesale fashion.

"The irrepressible conflict is about to be visited upon us through the Black Republican nominee and his fanatical, diabolical Republican party," ran an appeal to the voters of South Carolina during the campaign of 1860. "If that calamity comes to pass," responded the governor of the state, "the answer should be a declaration of independence." Lincoln was elected and *The Charleston Mercury* reported, "The tea has been thrown overboard; the revolution of 1860 has been initiated." In the deep South there was unanimous support for secession" (Beard).

Within a month Florida, Georgia, Alabama, Mississippi, and Louisiana joined the "rebellion." In February, Texas followed. Virginia, hesitating until the bombardment of Fort Sumter, seceded in April; but 55 of the 143 delegates dissented, foreshadowing the creation of the new state of West Virginia, which Congress admitted to the Union in 1863. In May, North Carolina, Arkansas, and Tennessee announced their independence. They all joined together to form a new country, the Confederacy, whose capital city was Montgomery, Alabama, and whose new president was **Jefferson Davis**.

To the new Confederacy, the decision to leave the Union was natural and legal. The states joined the Union voluntarily and felt they had every right to leave the same Union.

Jefferson Davis, the first and only president of the Confederate States of America, photographer unknown, 1853 (PD-US).

In their mind, they were not creating a "civil war," but a second "American Revolution." And they had cause to think so. After all, the majority of American presidents had been Southerners. As far as they were concerned, the North—not the South—was straying from the Forefathers' original constitutional intentions.

Nonetheless, the task was daunting. The South consisted of 11 states in all, against 22 in the North; and a population of 9 million against 22 million; a land without great industries to produce war supplies, joined in battle against a nation already industrialized and fortified by property worth several billion dollars. Southern manpower, measured in numbers, was wholly inadequate to win independence. How did the South expect to win?

For one thing, the Confederacy did not think that they had to win; they only had to persevere until the North grew tired. They hoped, in vain, to carry the Confederacy as far as the Ohio River, and, with the aid of Missouri, to gain possession of the Mississippi Valley. In the second place, they expected to get help from Great Britain and other European nations—the exchange of cotton for war materials. "We just want to be left alone," Jefferson Davis proclaimed.

There were other grounds for confidence. Many of the best generals and many of the most competent junior officers in the regular U.S. Army were Southerners. Southerners seized vital military stores (a majority of well-stocked forts existed in the South). Finally, the South held the interior line and hoped that this would offset military inferiority. If Southern leaders could fight a fast war, they were sure that they could win.

The crisis at **Fort Sumter**, on April 12–14, 1861, forced President Lincoln to raise an army. Lincoln's first call for volunteers, issued on April 15, 1861, limited the number to 75,000, put their term of service at three months. No one thought the war would last long. "You people of the South don't know what you are doing. This country will be drenched in blood, and God only knows how it will end. It is all folly, madness, a crime against civilization! You people speak so lightly of war; you don't know what you're talking about. War is a terrible thing! You mistake, too, the people of the North. They are a peaceable people but an earnest people, and they will fight, too. They are not going to let this country be destroyed without a mighty effort to save it. . . . Besides, where are your men and appliances of war to contend against them? The North can make a steam engine, locomotive, or railway car; hardly a yard of cloth or pair of shoes can you make. You are rushing into war with one of the most powerful, ingeniously mechanical, and determined people on Earth— right at your doors. You are bound to fail. Only in your spirit and determination are you prepared for war. In all else you are totally unprepared, with a bad cause to start with. At first you will make headway, but as your limited resources begin to fail, shut out from the markets of Europe as you will be, your cause will begin to wane. If your people will

but stop and think, they must see in the end that you will surely fail" (William T. Sherman to a Southern friend).

War at that point, however, seemed inevitable. Charles and Mary Beard described its progression as follows:

The terrible defeat of the Yankees at Bull Run on July 21 revealed the shortsightedness of military planners. Early in August 1862, Lincoln ordered a draft of militiamen numbering 300,000 for nine months' service. Only about 87,000 soldiers were added to the army. Thus, in March, 1863, Lincoln signed the inevitable draft law; it enrolled in the national forces liable to military duty all able-bodied male citizens and persons of foreign birth who had declared their intention to become citizens, between the ages of twenty and forty-five years— with exemptions on grounds of physical weakness and dependency. Also, a draftee could buy his release. But it was the first **national draft** in history. Some Northerners resisted. In New York City, in July 1863, at least a thousand people were killed or wounded and more than a million dollars' worth of damage done to property by draft resisters. The draft temporarily interrupted by this outbreak was then resumed and carried out without further trouble.

Four days after his call for volunteers, April 19, 1861, President Lincoln issued a proclamation blockading the ports of the Southern Confederacy. The South never received foreign support or recognition.

There were many radical political decisions in the Civil War, some of which were illegal. In September 22, 1863, the **Emancipation Proclamation** announced that, unless the states in arms returned to the union by January 1, 1863, the fatal blow at their "peculiar institution" would be delivered. Southern leaders treated it with slight regard, and so on the date set the promise was fulfilled. The proclamation was issued as a war measure, adopted by the president as commander-in-chief of the armed forces, on grounds of military necessity. It did not abolish slavery. It simply emancipated slaves in the parts of the South that had not yet been conquered! Everywhere else slavery, as far as the Proclamation was concerned, remained lawful. Lincoln had no intentions of alienating the border slave states.

The broad outlines of military strategy followed by the commanders of the opposing forces are clear. The problem for the South was mainly one of defense, though even for defense swift and paralyzing strokes at the North were later deemed imperative measures. The problem of the North was one of invasion and conquest. Southern territory had to be invaded and Southern armies beaten on their own ground or worn down to exhaustion there.

In the execution of this undertaking, geography, as usual, played a significant part in the disposition of forces. The Appalachian ranges, stretching through the Confederacy to Northern Alabama, divided the campaigns into Eastern and Western theaters. Victory in the East promised the capture of the Confederate capital of Richmond, a stroke of moral worth, hardly to be overestimated. Victory in the West meant severing the Confederacy and opening the Mississippi Valley south to the Gulf.

The Western forces accomplished their task first. In February 1862, U. S. Grant captured Fort Donelson on the Tennessee River, rallied wavering unionists in Kentucky, forced the evacuation of Nashville, and opened the way for 200 miles into the Confederacy. At Shiloh, Murfreesboro, Vicksburg, Chickamauga, and Chattanooga, desperate fighting followed, and in spite of varying fortunes, it resulted in the retreat of Southern armies to the southeast into Georgia. By the middle of 1863, the Mississippi Valley was open to the Gulf, the initiative taken out of the hands of Southern commanders in the West, and the way prepared for Sherman's final stroke—the march from Atlanta to the sea—a maneuver executed with needless severity in the autumn of 1864.

For the almost unbroken succession of achievements in the West by Generals Grant, Sherman, Thomas, and Hooker against Albert Sidney Johnston, Bragg, Pemberton, and Hood, the Union forces in the East offered at first an almost equally unbroken series of misfortunes and disasters. Far

Union soldiers dead at Gettysburg, photographed by Timothy H. O'Sullivan, 1863

from capturing Richmond, they had been thrown on the defensive. General after general—McClellan, Pope, Burnside, Hooker, and Meade—was tried and found wanting. None of them could administer a crushing defeat to the Confederate troops, and more than once the Union soldiers were beaten in a fair battle. Second Battle of Bull Run, Fredericksburg, and Chancellorsville were all Union defeats. Union forces did succeed, however, in delivering a severe check to advancing Confederates under General Robert E. Lee, first at Antietam in September 1862 and then at Gettysburg in July 1863—checks reckoned as victories though in each instance the Confederates escaped. Not until the beginning of the next year, 1864, when General Grant, supplied with almost unlimited men and munitions, began his war of attrition on Lee's army, did the final phase of the war commence. General Lee, on April 9, 1865, seeing the futility of further conflict, surrendered an army still capable of hard fighting, at **Appomattox**, not far from the capital of the Confederacy.

Current "new" Appomattox Courthouse that was built in 1892 (CC BY-SA 3.0).

Assignment

A. Compare the Northern and Southern views of the Union.

B. Did the South really have a chance to win?

C. What do you think would have happened if the South had won the Civil War?

THE RESULTS OF THE AMERICAN CIVIL WAR

First and foremost, the war settled for all time the long dispute as to the nature of the federal system. The doctrine of state sovereignty was laid to rest. Never again could people think seriously that they could withdraw from the United States.

Measured in physical devastation and human lives, the American Civil War was the costliest war in the experience of the American people. When the war ended, 620,000 men (in a nation of 35 million people) had been killed and at least that many more had been wounded. The North lost a total of 364,000 (nearly one of every five Union soldiers) and the South 258,000 (nearly one of every four Confederate soldiers). More men died of disease and sickness than on the battlefield; the ratio was about four to one. The physical devastation was largely limited to the South, where almost all the fighting took place. Large sections of Richmond, Charleston, Atlanta, Mobile, and Vicksburg lay in ruins. The countryside through which the contending armies had passed was littered with gutted plantation houses and barns, burned bridges, and uprooted railroad lines. Many crops were destroyed or confiscated, and much livestock was slain. More than $4 billion worth of property had been wiped out through emancipation, the repudiation of Confederate bonds and currency, the confiscation of cotton, and war damage. The war settled the question of the permanence of the Union;

the doctrine of secession was discredited, and after 1865 states would find other ways to manifest their grievances.

The war expanded the authority of the federal government, with the executive branch in particular exercising broader jurisdiction and powers than at any previous time in the nation's history. The U.S. Congress, meanwhile, enacted much of the legislation to which the South had objected so strenuously before the war, including a homestead act, liberal appropriations for internal improvements, and the highest tariff duties in American history to that date. Economically, the war encouraged the mechanization of production and the accumulation of capital in the North. The needs of the armies in the field resulted in the mass production of processed foods, ready-made clothing, and shoes, and after the war, industry converted such production to civilian use. By 1865 the U.S. was on its way to becoming an industrial power. Finally, the American Civil War brought freedom to nearly 4 million blacks. But the attitudes that had sustained slavery in the South for more than 300 years did not end with the war, thereby creating tensions and problems that would persist into the 20th century (www.history.com).

Next to the vindication of national supremacy was the destruction of the planting aristocracy of the South. As historian Charles Beard explains, "The second and third came

King Cotton by J. C. Coovert, c1907

City Point, Virginia. Negro Soldier guarding 12-pdr. Napoleon cannons. Photographer unknown, 1865.

with the fourteenth (1868) and fifteenth (1870) amendments, giving the ballot to freedmen and excluding from public office the Confederate leaders—driving from the work of reconstruction the finest talents of the South. As if to add bitterness to gall and wormwood, the fourteenth amendment forbade the United States or any state to pay any debts incurred in aid of the Confederacy or in the emancipation of the slaves—plunging into utter bankruptcy the Southern financiers who had stripped their section of capital to support their cause. So the Southern planters found themselves excluded from public office and ruled over by their former bondmen under the tutelage of Republican leaders. Their labor system was wrecked and their money and bonds were as worthless as waste paper. The South was subject to the North. That which neither the Federalists nor the Whigs had been able to accomplish in the realm of statecraft was accomplished on the field of battle."

The wreck of the planting system was accompanied by a mighty upswing of Northern industry that discovered it did not need King Cotton after all. Moreover, it was henceforth to be well protected by tariffs. For many years before the war, the friends of protection had been on the defensive. The tariff act of 1857 imposed duties so low as to presage a tariff for revenue only. The war changed all that. The extraordinary military expenditures, requiring heavy taxes

on all sources, justified tariffs so high that even the most fervent American industrialist would blush. Liberal immigration policies supplied needed labor for this blossoming industry.

The Homestead Act of 1862, which stated that 40 acres of federal Western land was free for the taking, stimulated expansion. More and more federal projects emerged. After the Civil War, the United States was, and forever would be, a continental power of significant world importance.

Assignment

Read the essay/book review of *This Republic of Suffering*, by Drew Gilpin Faust on the following page.

A. Does this thesis ring true to you? Do you agree with this analysis?

B. What is the result of refusal to forgive?

Americans had never endured anything like the losses they suffered between 1861 and 1865 and have experienced nothing like them since. Two percent of the United States population died in uniform—620,000 men, North and South, roughly the same number as those lost in all of America's other wars from the Revolution through Iraq combined. The equivalent toll today would be eight million.

The lasting but little-understood impact of all that sacrifice is the subject of Drew Gilpin Faust's extraordinary new book, *This Republic of Suffering: Death and the American Civil War.* "Death created the modern American union," she writes, "not just by ensuring national survival, but by shaping enduring national structures and commitments." And she continues: "The work of death was Civil War America's most fundamental and most demanding undertaking." Her account of how that work was done, much of it gleaned from the letters of those who found themselves forced to do it, is too richly detailed and covers too much ground to be summarized easily. She overlooks nothing—from the unsettling enthusiasm some men showed for killing to the near-universal struggle for an answer to the question posed by the Confederate poet Sidney Lanier: "How does God have the heart to allow it?"

She begins with what she calls the "work" of dying. The faithful looked forward to what was called a Good Death, with time to see the end approaching, accept it and declare to friends and family members their belief in God and His promise of salvation. The battlefield brutally truncated that serene process, and soldiers and their families alike worried about what that might mean for their chances in the afterlife. Survivors tried to provide reassurance. When one Union soldier was killed during the siege of Richmond, a comrade told his mother that while her boy had died instantly and without the opportunity to declare his faith, he had told his fellow soldiers the previous summer that he "felt his sins were forgiven and that he was ready and resigned to the Lord's will and while talking he was so much overjoyed that he could hardly suppress his feelings of delight." But sometimes candor trumped comfort: one Georgia soldier worried in a letter home that while his dying brother had "said that he hoped he was prepared to meet his God in a better world than this," he was also aware "he had been a bad, bad, very bad boy."

In 1862 Congress empowered the president to purchase grounds for "a national cemetery for the soldiers who shall die in the service of their country" but provided him with no funds with which to buy it. By war's end, there were just five such cemeteries, three established by Union generals in the western theater, and two—Antietam and Gettysburg—paid for by states from which many of those killed there had come. Only after the war was over—and amid news reports that vengeful Southerners were desecrating Union graves—did Congress finally provide a national solution to what had become a national need. The Union dead were to be gathered from scores of Southern battlefields, identified when possible, then re-interred in burial grounds to be protected and maintained by the federal government. The ghastly work went on for six years, much of it performed by African-American soldiers. When the last body was reburied in 1871, 303,536 Union soldiers had been laid to rest in 74 national cemeteries at a cost of $4 million. Almost half remained nameless. "Such a consecration of a nation's power and resources to a sentiment, the world has never seen," wrote one of the officers charged with recovering the bodies.

Confederate corpses were barred. A Northern reporter walking a Southern battlefield stumbled upon the unburied skeletons of two soldiers. His local guide examined their uniform buttons. "They was No'th Carolinians," the man explained. "That's why they didn't bury 'em." Southern women saw to it that the Southern dead were reburied, but many of those who'd been hastily covered with earth during Confederate forays into the North were never found. As late as 1996, spring rains were still uncovering their bones near Gettysburg.

"The war's staggering human cost demanded a new sense of national destiny," Faust, now the president of Harvard University, writes, "one designed to ensure that lives had been sacrificed for appropriately lofty ends." Frederick Douglass thought freeing the slaves should have provided the "sacred significance" of all that loss. But, Faust continues, "the Dead became what their survivors chose to make them," and as the decades passed and memories blurred, "assumptions of racial hierarchy would unite whites North and South in a century-long abandonment of the emancipationist legacy." In the end, most Americans of my great-great-grandfather's generation—and their successors—allowed their shared memories of suffering to "establish sacrifice and its memorialization as the ground on which North and South would ultimately reunite." We might wish, with Frederick Douglass, that they had decided otherwise, but Drew Gilpin Faust's profoundly moving book helps us understand why they did not (Geoffrey C. Ward).

HISTORY MAKER: ABRAHAM LINCOLN

Of all the American presidents, Lincoln is probably the one about whom the most has been written. Certainly he is one of our most famous presidents. Encarta Encyclopedia states:

Many critical evaluations of his life have been published, but they have not diminished his stature, and he remains one of the foremost products of American democracy and an eloquent spokesman for its ideals. Abraham Lincoln is larger than life. He absorbs all of the history around him. Not only did he keep the Union together, but his compassion, forgiveness and foresight were a model for future generations. He was everyone's friend—including the South—even when it did not know it. There is some debate about whether or not he was a believer—he was not a regular churchgoer and he never spoke of a personal relationship with Jesus Christ. Nonetheless, he was an intensely religious man who advanced Judeo-Christian values in his words and actions. His most famous speech, virtually presented impromptu with a minimum of preparation, was the Gettysburg Address

Last photograph of Abraham Lincoln by Henry F. Warren, 1865 (PD-US).

The Gettysburg Address:

Fourscore and seven years ago our fathers brought forth on this continent, a new nation, conceived in Liberty, and dedicated to the proposition that all men are created equal. Now we are engaged in a great civil war, testing whether that nation or any nation so conceived and so dedicated, can long endure. We are met on a great battlefield of that war. We have come to dedicate a portion of that field as a final resting place for those who here gave their lives that that nation might live. It is altogether fitting and proper that we should do this. But, in a larger sense, we cannot dedicate—we cannot consecrate—we cannot hallow—this ground. The brave men, living and dead, who struggled here, have consecrated it, far above our poor power to add or detract. The world will little note, nor long remember what we say here, but it can never forget what they did here. It is for us the living, rather, to be dedicated here to the unfinished work which they who fought here have thus far so nobly advanced. It is rather for us to be here dedicated to the great task remaining before us—that from these honored dead we take increased devotion to that cause for which they gave the last full measure of devotion—that we here highly resolve that these dead shall not have died in vain—that this nation, under God, shall have a new birth of freedom—and that government of the people, by the people, for the people, shall not perish from the earth.

Lincoln's Second Inaugural Address (perhaps his most famous):

Fellow-Countrymen: At this second appearing to take the oath of the Presidential office there is less occasion for an extended address than there was at the first. Then a statement somewhat in detail of a course to be pursued seemed fitting and proper. Now, at the expiration of four years, during which public declarations have been constantly called forth on every point and phase of the great contest which still absorbs the attention and engrosses the energies of the nation, little that is new could be presented. The progress of our arms, upon which all else chiefly depends, is as well known to the public as to myself, and it is, I trust, reasonably satisfactory and encouraging to all. With high hope for the future, no prediction in regard to it is ventured.

On the occasion corresponding to this four years ago all thoughts were anxiously directed to an impending civil war. All dreaded it, all sought to avert it. While the inaugural address was being delivered from this place, devoted altogether to saving the Union without war, urgent agents were in the city seeking to destroy it without war—seeking to dissolve the Union and divine effects by negotiation. Both parties deprecated war, but one of them would make war rather than let the nation survive, and the other would accept war rather than let it perish, and the war came.

One-eighth of the whole population were colored slaves, not distributed generally over the Union, but localized in the southern part of it. These slaves constituted a peculiar and powerful interest. All knew that this interest was somehow the cause of the war. To strengthen, perpetuate, and extend this interest was the object for which the insurgents would rend the Union even by war, while the Government claimed no right to do more than to restrict the territorial enlargement of it. Neither party expected for the war the magnitude or the duration which it has already attained. Neither anticipated that the cause of the conflict might cease with or even before the conflict itself should cease. Each looked for an easier triumph, and a result less fundamental and astounding. Both read the same Bible and pray to the same God, and each invokes His aid against the other. It may seem strange that any men should dare to ask a just God's assistance in wringing their bread from the sweat of other men's faces, but let us judge not, that we be not judged. The prayers of both could not be answered. That of neither has been answered fully. The Almighty has His own purposes. "Woe unto the world because of offenses; for it must needs be that offenses come, but woe to that man by whom the offense cometh." If we shall suppose that American slavery is one of those offenses which, in the providence of God, must needs come, but which, having continued through His appointed time, He now wills to remove, and that He gives to both North and South this terrible war as the woe due to those by whom the offense came, shall we discern therein any departure from those divine attributes which the believers in a living God always ascribe to Him? Fondly do we hope, fervently do we pray, that this mighty scourge of war may speedily pass away. Yet, if God wills that it continue until all the wealth piled by the bondsman's two hundred and fifty years of unrequited toil shall be sunk, and until every drop of blood drawn with the lash shall be paid by another drawn with the sword, as was said three thousand years ago, so still it must be said "the judgments of the Lord are true and righteous altogether."

With malice toward none, with charity for all, with firmness in the right as God gives us to see the right, let us strive on to finish the work we are in, to bind up the nation's wounds, to care for him who shall have borne the battle and for his widow and his orphan, to do all which may achieve and cherish a just and lasting peace among ourselves and with all nations.

Assignment

Besides a well-crafted speech, Lincoln's Second Inaugural Address is one of the best theological speeches ever written by an American politician. Point out one or two theological themes in this speech, being careful to explain why it (they) is (are) theological and being careful to point out biblical references.

Lincoln's second inaugural address in 1865 at the almost completed Capitol building.

The Room in the McLean House, at Appomattox C.H., in which Gen. Lee surrendered to Gen. Grant. Library of Congress. Artist unknown, 1867. Pictured Left to Right: John Gibbon, George Armstrong Custer, Cyrus B. Comstock, Orville E. Babcock, Charles Marshall, Walter H. Taylor, Robert E. Lee, Philip Sheridan, Ulysses S. Grant, John Aaron Rawlins, Charles Griffin, unidentified, George Meade, Ely S. Parker, James W. Forsyth, Wesley Merritt, Theodore Shelton Bowers, Edward Ord. The man not identified in the picture's legend is thought to be General Joshua Chamberlain, a hero of Gettysburg who presided over the formal surrender of arms by Lee's Army of Northern Virginia on April 12, 1865.

Chapter 15

RECONSTRUCTION

First Thoughts . . .

Imagine what it was like to have been a Confederate soldier returning from the War. The outcome of the Civil War in the South was nothing short of a revolution. The government of the old order had been removed. To political chaos was added the devastation wrought in society by military operations. And to make things worse, the task of reconstruction was committed to political leaders from another section of the country, strangers to the life and traditions of the South.

Chapter Learning Objectives . . .

In chapter 15 we will look at a controversial historical figure of this period—Robert E. Lee. Then we will examine together the Reconstruction strategy employed by the victorious Union and ascertain its effectiveness.

As a result of this chapter you should be able to:

1. Evaluate whether Robert E. Lee was a great general, statesman, and human being, or a capable, egotistical, flawed military strategist?

2. Evaluate American Reconstruction policy.

3. Compare/contrast life for poor Southern whites before the Civil War and after Reconstruction.

4. Compare/contrast life for wealthy Southern whites before the Civil War and after Reconstruction.

5. Discuss the accomplishments and failures of President U. S. Grant's administration.

6. Analyze life for Southern blacks before the Civil War and after Reconstruction.

7. Examine fears of race mixing as an impediment to racial reconciliation.

ROBERT E. LEE

Robert E. Lee

Opinions about historical figures change as time passes. The following is an article by the historian James Taylor discussing the controversial general Robert E. Lee and how his impact on history has been debated by historians.

In the days and weeks that followed Robert E. Lee's death, the South held memorial services for its most respected soldier. In Richmond the crowd grew so large that the ceremony had to be moved to Monument Square. In Atlanta, an estimated ten thousand people gathered at city hall to hear a memorial address by Maj. Gen. John B. Gordon that left many in the audience in tears. The tributes were not all from the South. The *Montreal Telegraph* editorialized: "Posterity will rank Lee above Wellington or Napoleon, before Saxe or Turene, above Marlborough or Frederick, before Alexander or Caesar. . . . He has made his own name, and the Confederacy he served, immortal."

Some of Lee's admirers went further, infusing a spiritual quality to Lee's refusal of the command of a great Federal force in the spring of 1861. At the dedication of one monument to Lee, the principal orator recalled how Union General-in-Chief Winfield Scott had offered Lee the command of an army with which to conquer the South. Acceptance of Scott's offer meant honor, glory, and power. But, as one modern biographer wrote, Lee, Christlike, could not be tempted: "Since the Son of Man stood upon the Mount, and saw 'all the kingdoms of the world and the glory of them' stretched before him, and turned away . . . no follower of the meek and lowly Savior can have undergone [a] more trying ordeal."

Predictably, some of Lee's erstwhile enemies found such praise cloying, to say the least. General Ulysses S. Grant, during his trip around the world in the late 1870s, told a journalist that he never had the same regard for Lee as he had for Confederate General Joseph E. Johnston: "Lee was a good man, a fair commander, who had everything in his favor. . . Lee was of a slow, cautious nature, without imagination, or humor, always the same, with grave dignity. . . . Lee was a good deal of a headquarters general, from what I can hear and from what his officers say."

A few years later, in 1887, General William T. Sherman took exception to an article in *McMillan's Magazine* by the noted British officer Viscount Garnet Joseph Wolseley, a field marshal and later commander-in-chief who modernized the British army. Whereas Wolseley had argued that Lee was far more capable than his Federal opponents, Sherman contended in the *North American Review* that Lee's horizon never extended beyond Virginia: "He never rose to the grand problem which involved a continent and future generations."

Such views were very much in the minority at that time. A succession of chroniclers of the Lost Cause published books extolling Lee and his gallant army. Paradoxically, a running dispute about Lee's greatest defeat—Gettysburg—had the effect of further burnishing his reputation. In the years after the war, Lt. Gen. James Longstreet came under heavy criticism from former Confederates for his alleged slowness on the second, critical day of the battle. In an attempt to rebut his critics, Longstreet wrote a number of magazine articles in which he mixed praise for Lee with a picture of him as a rigid and unimaginative strategist. Lee, he contended, had agreed before the Gettysburg campaign that any battle fought in Pennsylvania should be fought

Portrait of General Robert E. Lee, by Julian Vannerson, 1863 (PD-US).

defensively. Longstreet told how he had suggested to Lee, after the first day at Gettysburg, that the Confederates forgo any frontal attack in favor of a move around the Army of the Potomac's left flank, only to be overruled by his commander.

Longstreet, who allied himself with the despised Republicans after the war, proved an inviting target for Lee's admirers. Major General Jubal A. Early, another of Lee's former corps commanders who was the president of the Southern Historical Society, led the counterattack. Charging Longstreet with having repeatedly placed obstacles in the way of Lee's plans in Pennsylvania, Early said of the mishandled Confederate attacks on the second day of Gettysburg that "either General Lee or General Longstreet was responsible for the remarkable delay that took place. . . . I choose to believe that it was not General Lee." So did most of Early's readers.

By the turn of the century Lee was receiving praise from the North as well as the South. Theodore Roosevelt wrote that, as a military commander, not even George Washington ranked with "the wonderful war-chief who for four years led the Army of Northern Virginia." Native Virginian Woodrow Wilson, then a history professor, called Lee "unapproachable in the history of our country." The centennial of Lee's birth fell in 1907, and for decades thereafter his birthday, January 19, would be a holiday in most states of the former Confederacy.

In 1912 popular historian Gamaliel Bradford published the widely acclaimed biography *Lee the American*, which enshrined Lee as a national, as well as a Southern, hero. Bradford sought to consider his subjects in terms of their character traits, and he found in Lee the finest qualities of the Old South: courage, dignity, and devotion to duty. When a national hall of fame was established at New York University in 1901, Lee was one of the first inductees.

The near-universal praise for Lee as a man and a soldier reached its zenith in the 1930s with the publication of Douglas Southall Freeman's epic four-volume biography, *R. E. Lee: A Biography*. A journalist by profession, Freeman was also a meticulous scholar and an unapologetic admirer of Lee. At first under contract for a 75,000-word biography, Freeman undertook instead a definitive work. In 1934, nineteen years after he had started in on Lee, the first two volumes appeared. The final two followed a year later. In 1935, Freeman was awarded the Pulitzer Prize for his biography.

Freeman saw Lee as a master of strategy who excelled at getting the most from his subordinate commanders and his soldiers. In the spring of 1862, Lee alone had seen how Maj. Gen. Thomas J. "Stonewall" Jackson's tiny army in the Shenandoah Valley could be the key to saving Richmond. In that summer's Seven Days' campaign, Lee had sought to seize the initiative wherever possible and to force the enemy to react. He had made the most of the intelligence resources available to him and routinely uncovered and exploited the weaknesses of enemy commanders. Lee's greatest victories—the Seven Days', Second Manassas, Chancellorsville—had been achieved in the face of great numerical odds. Five qualities, Freeman believed, made Lee a great commander: his interpretation of military intelligence, commitment to the offensive, careful choice of position, exact logistics, and daring.

Freeman reserved his greatest admiration for Lee's personal qualities. He had respect bordering on awe for the general's modesty, piety, consideration for his soldiers, and devotion to duty. What was the key to his subject's personality? Lee, Freeman concluded, was one of a small number of people "in whom there is no inconsistency to be explained, no enigma to be solved. What he seemed he was—a wholly human gentleman."

Freeman was a tough act to follow. In the latter half of the 20th century, however, the tide began to turn. In 1977, Thomas L. Connelly published a landmark study, *The Marble Man: Robert E. Lee and His Image in American Society*, which is really two books in one. The first relates the growth of the "Lee legend" in the South, the second presents the author's own insights into Lee's character. These insights, although heavily reliant on pop psychology, reflect a close examination of his subject.

Connelly insisted that the Lee cult was largely a postwar phenomenon. During the first years of the Civil War, most Southerners viewed Stonewall Jackson as the Confederacy's military genius. Lee, meanwhile, had to overcome the onus of his early setbacks in 1861 in western Virginia. Connelly, who downplays the devotion that Lee inspired in his soldiers, viewed the Lee legend as a response to the South's need to rationalize its defeat. Many Christians believed that there was a direct link between God's grace and one's success in earthly endeavors. Lee's sterling character was held up as proof that good men do not always succeed.

And what of Lee himself? In contrast to Freeman's view—that Lee was a model of simplicity and devoid of personality flaws—Connelly found his subject to be extraordinarily complex. Lee's life was replete with "frustration, self-doubt, and a feeling of failure." He suffered from the effects of an unsatisfactory marriage and protracted absences from his family. As for Lee's legendary self-control, Connelly saw it as "an almost mechanical device that suppressed his naturally strong temper and vibrant personality."

Five years after the appearance of *The Marble Man*, Lee's standing as a commander came under fire from authors with a different perspective. In *Attack and Die: Civil War Military Tactics and the Southern Heritage*, Grady McWhiney and Perry D. Jamieson took most of the South's military leaders to task for their aggressive battlefield tactics. The authors contended that the Confederate commitment to the tactical offensive, born of American successes in the Mexican War, destroyed the South's armies. According to McWhiney and Jamieson, Lee favored the tactical offensive and assumed it whenever he could. It brought him victories at Second Manassas and Chancellorsville but terrible defeats at Malvern Hill and Gettysburg.

As noted earlier, many factors contributed to the growth of the Lee legend. But there would have been no legend if Lee himself had not been almost universally admired by those who knew him best. His piety, in addition to his bravery and modesty, had a special appeal in the deeply religious South. The grim reality of defeat itself served to promote the Lee legend. The states of the former Confederacy not only had lost a generation of young men to war but had become the only part of the United States to experience military occupation. For many Southerners, Lee's character served somehow to validate the Confederate cause and to check any impulse to link the North's victory to God's will.

If we dispense with Lost Cause nostalgia, what can be said with some degree of objectivity of Lee the soldier? The core questions with respect to any commander are did he set reasonable objectives, and did he make the best use of the resources available to achieve them?

Lee's critics point out how reluctant he was to send any portion of his army to reinforce Confederate armies in the West. He had good reasons for his misgivings. In May 1863 he opposed the transfer of Maj. Gen. George E. Pickett's division to Mississippi, citing both his doubt that they could arrive in time to affect the Vicksburg campaign and his "uncertainty of its [the division's] application" under Lt. Gen. John C. Pemberton. Lee's reluctance appears prescient, for eight weeks later Pemberton surrendered Vicksburg to Grant. In September, Lee reluctantly agreed to the transfer of two of Longstreet's divisions to assist General Braxton Bragg and rejoiced in his subsequent victory at Chickamauga. Bragg, however, failed to follow up on his victory. Lee knew the men who led Confederate armies in the West, and he was properly, if privately, skeptical that they would put reinforcements from his army to better use than he himself would.

And what of Lee the man? At the core of Lee's personality, as many writers have noted, was his sense of duty. When, in his farewell address to his soldiers, Lee told them that they could take pride in "the consciousness of duty faithfully performed," he was according them the highest praise in his scale of values. To Lee, duty was not a burden but an opportunity. And war, however terrible, could be waged in accordance with Christian values.

Modest and selfless as a colonel in the U.S. Army, Lee did not change when he commanded an army of 90,000 men and his name was revered throughout the South. Small wonder that the South, in defeat, viewed him as the embodiment of all that had been good in the Lost Cause. A Virginia woman, who had been introduced to Lee while a young girl, never forgot the moment. "We had heard of God," she recalled, "but here was General Lee!"

Assignment

Was Robert E. Lee a great general, statesman, and human being, or was he a capable, egotistical, flawed military strategist? Defend your answer.

RECONSTRUCTION

At the end of the American Civil War, Mary Chestnut, a Southern aristocrat, observed, "There are sad changes in store for both races." Mary Chestnut's South had lost the Civil War. Now what? At the end of the Civil War, all Americans had to answer these questions:

1. What must the Confederate states do to be readmitted to the union?

2. Will Confederate leaders be punished as criminals?

3. What will be done with the former slaves?

4. What will happen to war veterans?

It was during the period called Reconstruction (1865–1877) that these questions were answered.

Responding to these questions, President Andrew Johnson and then Congress enacted legislation and policies that changed America forever. In a sense they determined that the Civil War was doomed to be fought over and over again for the next 150 years.

Northern politicians hoped to reconstruct Southern society, so that rights for former slaves were ensured, and a political base for the Republican Party could be formed. Southerners, especially ex-Confederates, hoped to regain some of the wealth and influence that they lost in the Civil War.

Caption: The Rail Splitter Repairing the Union. A political cartoon of Andrew Johnson and Abraham Lincoln from 1865, during the Reconstruction era of the United States (1863–1877)

President Lincoln organized a Reconstruction policy, but he didn't live to implement it (he was assassinated by John Wilkes Booth [below] in April 1865). Lincoln hoped to produce a speedy recovery for the South by inviting states to re-enter the Union if only 10 percent signed the loyalty oath.

Atlanta, Georgia, shortly after the end of the American Civil War showing the city's railroad roundhouse in ruins by George N. Barnard, 1866 (PD-US).

By January 1864, Tennessee, Louisiana, and Arkansas offered loyal state governments reinstatement on the basis of Lincoln's Reconstruction Plan. However, the radical Republican Congress had other plans. They believed that the South should be more severely punished for bringing the war to the nation and should be made to pay war costs. While agreeing with Lincoln that mass execution for treason was not in order, they did not want key Confederate political or military leaders to emerge as leaders of the post-war South.

Thus, with Lincoln's death, the stage was set for a struggle between the legislative and executive branches over Reconstruction. What ultimately occurred were two Reconstructions: one introduced by President Johnson and another promulgated by Congress.

Because Congress was adjourned when Lincoln was killed in 1865, President Andrew Johnson offered reconstruction to Southern states that was much like Lincoln's 10 percent plan. When Congress reconvened in December, most Southern states had accepted the President's requirements and re-entered the Union. They knew a good deal when they saw it! The problem is that the Southern states sent unrepentant, mostly ex-Confederate, all-white delegations to Congress for roll call, including representative Alexander Stephens (Georgia), the former Confederate vice president! Johnson made things even more intolerable to Congress by granting amnesty to thousands of ex-rebels, barring only those with sizable property holdings from taking oaths of allegiance.

Radical congressional Republicans wanted Southern states treated more like conquered provinces than wayward children. Among other things, they wished to ensure that mostly Republican blacks had civil rights, especially the vote. Therefore, Congress extended the controversial Freedman's Bureau. The Bureau gave black citizens the same rights as whites. Former Confederate officials were banned from holding elective office without Congressional pardon requiring two-thirds majority vote. Except for Tennessee, which had accepted the 14th amendment in 1866, the rest of the Confederacy was divided into five military districts, each governed by a major general, appointed by the President, empowered to bring offenders to trial and to punish them in order to maintain order. Each state was to call new constitutional conventions, elected by all adult males, excluding ex-Confederates. President Andrew Johnson consistently opposed these measures and, for that and other reasons, ultimately was impeached in February 1868. The Senate failed by one vote to convict and remove Johnson from office.

While Reconstruction was not officially over until 1877, the vituperative phase was behind Americans. (See A Timeline of Reconstruction chart in Appendix 1.)

Assassination of Lincoln, printed by Currier & Ives, 1865 (PD-US).

Assignment

After all is said and done, was the American Reconstruction policy a failure? Discuss what the American Reconstruction policies were. Next, discuss what its purposes were and state and defend whether or not it accomplished those purposes.

MORE QUESTIONS ON RECONSTRUCTION

Assignment

A. Complete the following chart.

Admendment	Substance	Date of Congressional Passage	Ratification Process	Implemented and Enforced
Thirteenth				
Fourteenth				
Fifteenth				

B. Compare/contrast life for poor and rich Southern whites before the Civil War and after Reconstruction.

Issue	Poor Southern Whites	Rich Southern Whites
Politics		
Economics		
Religion		

C. Discuss the accomplishments and failures of Ulysses S. Grant's administration.

At the heart of most Reconstruction discussions is the problem of race mixing.

The Senate as a court of impeachment for the trial of Andrew Johnson. Sketched by Theodore R. Davis, 1868 (PD-US).

RACE MIXING

It has always been difficult to know how many racially mixed Americans there are—since no marriage certificate, birth certificate, or census report reflected a category called "racially mixed" before the middle of the 20th century. In fact, before the 1940s, interracial marriage was against the law in most states. Since 1970, interracial dating and marriage has been an open and growing American phenomenon.

In American culture, race mixing has always been a social concern as much as a biological concern. The determination of boundaries between human groups in the United States has normally been a social one, but it is defined in racial terms. Americans have been quick to categorize people in biological terms: an multiracial person is very simply a black person. Social definition, though, has been more difficult to control. What does one do with a black and a white couple who decide to defy social customs and covenant together in marriage? Physical appearance informed, but ultimately a person gains status and identity according to which social group he belongs to. This social status, at least in America, is mostly defined according to racial criteria.

I think the most threatening and powerful image of race mixing to Reconstruction America was miscegenation. Yet, sexual intermingling between white and black races occurred with surprising frequency—especially in the Antebellum and Post-Civil War South. Today, one out of every nine African-American males marries a white woman.

Nevertheless, miscegenation was widespread in the antebellum South—especially in urban areas. In 1860, one-fourth of the African-American population of Charleston, South Carolina, was interracial. Freed African-American women in New Orleans outnumbered freed African-American men by more than two-to-one in 1850 when white men outnumbered white women by the same proportion. Historians are certain that miscegenation was widespread. In 1890, census statistics were suspect, but Federal enumerators counted 8.5 percent (or 37,200) of Mississippi's African-American population as interracial.

U.S. President Barack Obama is the son of a white American mother and a black Kenyan father, by Pete Souza, The Obama-Biden Transition Project (CC BY 3.0).

Census takers were instructed not only to count Negroes of "pure" or "mixed" blood, but to distinguish between African-Americans, mulattoes, quadroons, and octoroons. After 1920, census takers abandoned the task altogether and called all mixtures of races "blacks."

The notion of whites and blacks legally marrying was particularly onerous to many whites. In the context of a monogamous, nurturing marriage, people of color attained a legal equality. This was unacceptable to many prejudiced whites. Newspaper columnist Gary Wills observed in the late 1960s, "Americans do not like to think of their country as being white, but they are careful to keep it that way." The prospect that blacks and whites were equal in anything was too much for many white Americans to bear.

African-Americans learned race was a category of exclusion and prejudice—both in the society at large and in the Church in particular. It was a terrible lesson confirmed over and over again in American history. The American obsession and fears about racial mixing—especially in a sexual context—colored most of our national decisions about race. Whites were very happy to exploit black slaves sexually. Only when blacks openly dated and married whites in the late 1960s was there any problem with race-mixing in the white community. In fact, most scholars noted that there has been a preoccupation with interracial sexual relations for most of American history, but this concern was not articulated until whites and African-Americans were legally marrying at the end of the 20th century.

Interracial Marriage and the Bible

The argument that the Bible condemns interracial relationships can be simplified in three basic arguments. Using the Tower of Babel story (Genesis 11:1–9), opponents to interracial marriages argue that God does not want to dilute the races. However, a careful reading of this story reveals that such a position is spurious: God separated languages, not races.

Likewise, God wants to keep the races separated so that each race may distinctively offer praise in a unique manner (Revelation 1:7; 5:9). However, such passages can actually serve as a challenge for Christians to develop interracial churches. These verses show that Christ will be embraced by all—regardless of race or creed.

The Bible clearly teaches that there is neither Jew nor Greek in Christ Jesus (Galatians 3:28). Paul emphasized that three major first-century social distinctions no longer matter in Christ: ethnicity, socioeconomic status, and gender. To those I would add, by implication, race. First-century culture was, as 21st-century culture is, deeply divided along these lines. The Early Church struggled with these same issues, but Paul stressed, "You are one in Christ Jesus."

Sadly, the values of a society are reflected in the Church. The first-century church, as I mentioned above, struggled with many problems. For instance, Hellenist widows, traditionally neglected by the Jews, were now being neglected by Hebrew Christians (Acts 6:1). This was unacceptable behavior. Later in Church history, many Christians advocated and even promoted such evils as slavery, segregation, apartheid, and the Holocaust. If the Church can overcome such biases and divisions, we will truly manifest the kingdom of God on the earth, and the Church will grow—as it did in first-century Jerusalem (Acts 6:7).

Racism is very much alive in the American church. In spite of the above-mentioned biblical witnesses and others, such as the Old Testament justice teachings about including strangers, the Church remains a major segregated American institution. Studies have shown that individuals who were very active in their local churches dropped out when they entered an interracial marriage. Why? They did not feel welcome.

It seems quite clear that categories in marriage selection (other than a believer with a nonbeliever) are man-made and artificial.

Some will argue—based on 1 Corinthians 8—that Christians have to be sensitive to the mores and norms of society. And, even today, society, largely condemns interracial marriages. "Christians cannot afford to ignore society as it exists at any given time, nor can they ignore prejudice," the Christian counselor Dwight H. Small argues. Small opposes interracial society. But even he admits that there is no scriptural reason to do so! The Church conforms to society's morals at its own peril. While an interracial couple should be sensitive to societal concerns, they must not make lifelong decisions based on societal concerns.

Assignment

A. What does the Bible say about race mixing?

B. Compare life for Southern blacks before the Civil War and after Reconstruction.

Chapter 16

RECONSTRUCTION: PRIMARY SOURCES

First Thoughts . . .

Andrew Johnson made a courageous stand against the radical Republicans who sought to punish the recalcitrant South. Meanwhile, the Ku Klux Klan was more or less the law of the land. Who were the Klan? Noble Americans defending what was sacred, or hooded terrorists whose cowardly acts delayed inevitable reconciliation between the North and the South?

Chapter Learning Objectives . . .

In chapter 16 we will examine the lives of Andrew Johnson and Thaddeus Stevens and reflect upon their motivation and actions. Next, we will examine two primary sources and evaluate their veracity. Finally, we will examine several philosophers who formed the world views motivating Americans during the second half of the 19th century.

As a result of this chapter you should be able to:

1. Analyze President Andrew Johnson's handling of the Reconstruction policy.
2. Evaluate several different views of Reconstruction and decide which views are most credible.
3. Discuss Thaddeus Stevens' views on Reconstruction.
4. Analyze the impact of several different philosophers on world view formation in the 19th century.

ANDREW JOHNSON

Andrew Johnson's obituary in the *New York Times* (August 1, 1875):

Andrew Johnson, ex-President of the United States and member of the Senate from Tennessee, died at the house of his daughter, Mrs. W. R. Brown, near Elizabethtown, Carter County, Tenn., at 2 o'clock yesterday morning. The history this man leaves is a rare one. His career was remarkable, even in this country; it would have been quite impossible in any other. It presents the spectacle of a man who never went to school a day in his life rising from a humble beginning as a tailor's apprentice through a long succession of posts of civil responsibility to the highest office in the land, and evincing his continued hold upon the popular heart by a subsequent election to the Senate in the teeth of a bitter personal and political opposition. . . . Coming from a slave state and himself owning slaves, he held slavery to be protected by the Constitution and beyond the interference of Congress; nevertheless, he believed in its ultimate overthrow. He denounced the John Brown raid, and in those early mutterings of the coming tempest he urged concessions to the South to calm the rising discontent, and new guarantees for the protection of slavery.

It was in the era of the rebellion that Andrew Johnson achieved his greatest distinction. It was not necessary for him to weigh the chances of the coming struggle, or to nicely estimate its moral elements, like some others of the less radical class of Southern statesmen. He was by principle and training unreservedly for the right, and he declared without hesitation for the Union, and strove with all the strength of his rugged soul against the secession faction. . . . The remainder of his Presidential career is not especially noteworthy. He issued a full pardon to everybody who had taken part in the rebellion, on the 25th of December. . . . He was by

President Andrew Johnson, by Matthew Brady, c1870.

nature and temperament squarely disposed toward justice and the right, and was a determined warrior for his convictions. He erred from limitation of grasp and perception, perhaps, or through sore perplexity in trying times, but never weakly or consciously.

Johnson was born in North Carolina to a life of poverty. He was apprenticed to a tailor until he ran away to open his own tailor shop in Tennessee. He was the first president to be impeached and was acquitted in the Senate by just one vote. He was 17 years old before he learned to read, being taught by his wife. He is the only president not to have had any type of schooling. He resisted Congress's efforts to pass punitive restriction acts over his veto.

While Johnson could be stubborn and petty, he was a man of principle. For instance, he twice committed himself to a course of action that he knew would ruin his political career, but he did it anyway because he thought it was right. First, he championed the Union cause in a Confederate state knowing full well it could end his political career and also could alienate most of his family and friends. But he did it anyway because he thought it was right.

We read a lot about Robert E. Lee's decision to stay with Virginia when it seceded, but Andrew Johnson's decision to stay with the United States when Tennessee seceded is no less heroic. Secondly, he advanced a policy of forgiveness toward the defeated Confederate states. He knew that for-giveness—what Abraham Lincoln called "charity"—would do more to bring healing and peace than any Congressional action of retribution, however justified. He was indeed a man who was by nature and temperament squarely dis-posed toward justice and the right, and was a determined warrior for his convictions.

The following is an excerpt from Andrew Johnson's first (1865) annual talk to Congress (what we later called the State of The Union Address):

[Discussing the reentry of Confederate states into the Union] I know very well that this policy is attended with some risk; that for its success it requires at least the acquiescence of the States which it concerns; that it implies an invitation to those States, by renewing their allegiance to the United States, to resume their functions as States of the Union. But it is a risk that must be taken. In the choice of difficulties it is the smallest risk; and to diminish and if possible to remove all danger, I have felt it incumbent on me to assert one other power of the General Government—the power of pardon. As no State can throw a defense over the crime of treason, the power of pardon is exclusively vested in the executive government of the United States. In exercising that power I have taken every precaution to connect it with the clearest recogni-tion of the binding force of the laws of the United States and an unqualified acknowledgment of the great social change of condition in regard to slavery which has grown out of the war. . . .

The Johnson home in Greeneville, Tennessee, 1886, today restored and known as the Andrew Johnson National Historic Site. Hill & Ramkin Studio, 1886 (PD-US).

[Concerning the future of ex-slaves] I know that sincere philanthropy is earnest for the immediate realization of its remotest aims; but time is always an element in reform. It is one of the greatest acts on record to have brought 4,000,000 people into freedom. The career of free industry must be fairly opened to them, and then their future prosperity and condition must, after all, rest mainly on them-selves. If they fail, and so perish away, let us be careful that the failure shall not be attributable to any denial of justice.

What led to Johnson's impeachment? At the end of the Civil War, the physical destruction inflicted by the invading Union forces was enormous, and the old social and eco-nomic order founded on slavery had collapsed completely. The 11 Confederate states somehow had to be provided with loyal governments, and the role of the emancipated slaves in Southern society had to be established. Even before the war ended, President Lincoln began the task of restoration. Motivated by a desire to bring reconciliation, he issued on December 8, 1863, a proclamation of amnesty and recon-struction for those areas of the Confederacy occupied by Union armies. It offered pardon to any Confederate who would swear to support the Constitution and the Union. Once a group in any conquered state equal in number to one-tenth of that state's total vote in the presidential election of 1860 took the prescribed oath and organized a govern-ment that abolished slavery, he would grant that government executive recognition (see chapter 15). Lincoln's plan aroused the sharp opposition of the radicals in Congress. They passed (July 1864) the Wade-Davis Bill, which required 50 percent of a state's male voters to take a radical oath that they had never voluntarily supported the Confederacy. Lincoln's pocket veto kept the Wade-Davis Bill from becoming law, and he implemented his own plan. By the end of the war it had restored a few states. Congress, however, refused to seat the senators and congressmen elected from those states, and by the time of Lincoln's death there was acrimony between the executive and legislative branches.

Into this arena marched Andrew Johnson. Johnson at first pleased the radicals by publicly attacking the planter aristocracy and insisting that the rebellion must be punished. In fact, his amnesty proclamation (May 29, 1865) was more severe than Lincoln's; it disenfranchised all former military and civil officers of the Confederacy. The obvious intent was to accomplish a revolution in Southern society.

With Congress in adjournment from April to December 1865, Johnson put his plan into operation. Southern newly elected legislatures (excluding Mississippi) ratified the 13th Amendment guaranteeing freedom for African-Americans. By the end of 1865 every ex-Confederate state except Texas had reestablished civil government.

The control of whites over blacks, however, seemed to be restored, as each of the newly elected state legislatures enacted black codes denying African-Americans most of the civil and political rights enjoyed by whites. Many of the offices in the new governments, moreover, were won by disenfranchised Confederate leaders, and President Johnson, rather than ordering new elections, granted pardons on a large scale.

An outraged Congress believed that the fruits of victory were being lost by Johnson's lenient policy. As one historian explained, "When Congress convened (Dec. 4, 1865) it refused to seat the Southern representatives. Johnson responded by publicly attacking Republican leaders and vetoing their Reconstruction measures. His tactics drove the moderates into the radical camp. The Civil Rights Act (April 9, 1866), designed to protect African-Americans from legislation such as the black codes, and the Freedmen's Bureau Bill (July 16), extending the life of that organization (see Freedmen's Bureau), were both passed over Johnson's veto. Doubts as to the constitutionality of the Civil Rights Act led the radicals to incorporate (June 1866) most of its provisions in the Fourteenth Amendment (ratified 1868). The newly created Joint Committee on Reconstruction reported (April 28, 1866) that the ex-Confederate states were in a state of civil disorder, and hence, had not held valid elections. It also maintained that Reconstruction was a congressional, not an executive, function. The radicals solidified their position by winning the elections of 1866. When every Southern state (except Tennessee) refused to ratify the Fourteenth Amendment and protect the rights of its black citizens, the

Andrew Johnson, by William Sartain, c1865.

stage was set for more severe measures."

At that point Congress took over and enacted legislation that would ultimately lead to a confrontation that would result in a vote of impeachment of President Johnson. On March 2, 1867, Congress enacted the Reconstruction Act, which divided the South (excluding Tennessee) into five military districts in which the authority of the army commander was supreme. Former elected officials were removed. Johnson continued to oppose congressional policy, and when he insisted on the removal of the radical Secretary of War Edwin M. Stanton, in defiance of the Tenure of Office Act, the House impeached him (February 1868). The radicals in the Senate fell one vote short of convicting him.

Assignment

Summarize the previous quotes by President Andrew Johnson. Describe the context in which they were given.

PRIMARY SOURCES

Thomas Dixon's *The Clansman* presents racial conflict as an epic struggle, with the future of civilization at stake. Although Dixon (left) personally condemned slavery and Klan excesses after Reconstruction ended, he argued that blacks must be denied political equality because it leads to social equality and miscegenation, thus to the destruction of both family and civilized society. Throughout his work, white Southern women are the pillars of family life and society, the repositories of all human goodness.

An excerpt from *The Clansman*:

In the darkest hour of the life of the South, when her wounded people lay helpless amid rags and ashes under the beak and talon of the Vulture, suddenly from the mists of the mountains appeared a white cloud the size of a man's hand. It grew until its mantle of mystery enfolded the stricken earth and sky. An "Invisible Empire" had risen from the field of Death and challenged the Visible to mortal combat. How the young South, led by the reincarnated souls of the Clansmen of Old Scotland, went forth under this cover and against overwhelming odds, daring exile, imprisonment, and a felon's death, and saved the life of a people, forms one of the most dramatic chapters in the history of the Aryan race.

Assignment

Published in 1879, Albion Tourgee's *A Fool's Errand* was an enormously popular book in its time. It was based largely on Tourgee's actual experiences in Greensboro, North Carolina, during Reconstruction. *A Fool's Errand* is the fictional story of Northerner Comfort Servosse. He joins the Civil War on the Union side, then returns home after the war and moves his family to the South. He purchases a decayed plantation and almost immediately makes a name for himself as a radical Yankee—or carpetbagger—and arouses the hostility of the neighbors in the community.

Interspersed in this story are several digressions and conversations in which Servosse discusses the numerous problems of Reconstruction. Servosse is no radical Republican, but he does blame the federal government in Washington for some of the violence because it did not stop the violence.

On the following page are excerpts from *A Fool's Errand*.

A. Summarize Servosse's arguments.

B. Discuss at what points he disagrees with Thomas Dixon.

Excerpt from *A Fool's Errand* by Albion Tourgee:

The true object and purpose of Reconstruction should be (1) to secure the nation in the future from the perils of civil war, especially a war based upon the same underlying principles and causes as the one just concluded; (2) to secure a development homogeneous with that of the North, so as to render the country what it has never been heretofore—a nation. As an essential element of this, the bestowal of equal civil and political rights upon all men, without regard to previous rank or station, becomes imperative. It seems to be the Reconstruction Acts have made this postulate of greater importance than the result to which it is auxiliary. . . . I do not think the passions evoked by that struggle, based as it was upon a radical difference of development, and the ill-concealed hostility of many generations, can by any means be put out of sight in such a movement. I do not believe that those who have looked into each other's faces by the lurid light of battle are the fittest persons to devise and execute such rehabilitation, nor do I believe that a lately subject—race is likely to prove an emollient or a neutralizing element in this peaceful adjustment. . . .From a party standpoint, you will allow me to say that I do not think that a party composed of the elements which must constitute the bulk of our party in the South under the present plan of Reconstruction can ever be permanently successful. At least two-thirds of it must not only be poor and ignorant, but also inexperienced and despised. They are just freed from servitude; and the badge of that servitude, the leprosy of slavery, still clings to them. Politically they are unclean; and the contamination of their association will drive away from us the bulk of the brain, character, and experience which has hitherto ruled these States, and through them the nation. Not only this, but thousands of those who went with us in the late election will fall away when they find themselves and their families focused in the eye of public scorn and ridicule. You wise men who concocted these measures do not seem to have comprehended the fact that the brain and heart of the South—the pulpit, the bar, and the planters; a vast proportion of its best men, and almost every one of its women—cast in their lot with the late Confederacy with all the self-abandonment and

A. Tourgee (PD-US).

devotion of a people who fought for what they believed to be right. You do not realize that this feeling was intensified a thousand-fold by a prolonged and desperate struggle, and final defeat. You do not seem to appreciate the fact, which all history teaches, that there is no feeling in the human breast more blind and desperate in its manifestations, or so intense and ineradicable in its nature, as the bitter scorn of a long dominant race for one they have held in bondage. You deem this feeling insensate hate. You could not make a greater mistake. Hate is a sentiment mild and trivial in comparison with it. This embraces no element of individual or personal dislike, but is simply utter and thorough disgust and scorn for the race—except in what they consider its proper place—a feeling more fatal to any thing like democratic recognition of their rights as citizens than the most undying hate could be. A party builded upon ignorance, inexperience, and poverty, and mainly composed of a race of pariahs, who are marked and distinguished by their color, can not stand against intelligence, wealth, the pride of a conquered nation, and a race-prejudice whose intensity laughs to shame the exclusive haughtiness of the Brahmins. . . . The constitutions of the North had fostered individual independence, equal rights and power, and general intelligence among the masses. The township system had been the cause and consequence of this. Almost all offices were elective, and, except in rare instances, all men were electors. It developed democratic ideas and sentiments, and was a nursery of democratic freedom. In the South the reverse was true. The ballot and the jury-box were jealously guarded from the intrusion of the poor. Wealth was a prerequisite of official eligibility. It was a republic in name, but an oligarchy in fact. Its laws were framed and construed to this end. The land-holdings were enormous, and the bulk of those who cultivated the soil were not freeholders, but either slaves or renters. To my mind, the first great prerequisite of successful Reconstruction is to break down the legal barriers to a homogeneous development of the country; to so organize the new State governments that they will tend to encourage individual action, freedom of opinion, diversity of industry, and general education. . . .

VILLAIN OR HERO?

Excerpt from a speech delivered by the radical Republican Thaddeus Stevens (below), December 18, 1865:

The President assumes, what no one doubts, that the late rebel States have lost their constitutional relations to the Union, and are incapable of representation in Con-gress, except by permission of the Government. It matters but little, with this admission, whether you call them States out of the Union, and now conquered territories, or assert that because the Constitution forbids them to do what they did do, that they are therefore only dead as to all national and political action, and will remain so until the Government shall breathe into them the breath of life anew and permit them to occupy their former position. In other words, that they are not out of the Union, but are only dead carcasses lying within the Union. In either case, it is very plain that it requires the action of Congress to enable them to form a State government and send representatives to Congress. Nobody, I believe, pretends that with their old constitutions and frames of government they can be permitted to claim their old rights under the Constitution. They have torn their constitutional States into atoms, and built on their foundations fabrics of a totally different character.

Dead men cannot raise themselves. Dead States cannot restore their existence "as it was." Whose especial duty is it to do it? In whom does the Constitution place the power? Not in the judicial branch of Government, for it only adjudicates and does not prescribe laws. Not in the Executive, for he only executes and cannot make laws. Not in the Commander-in-Chief of the armies, for he can only hold them under military rule until the sovereign legislative power of the conqueror shall give them law. Unless the law of nations is a dead letter, the late war between two acknowledged belligerents severed their original compacts and broke all the ties that bound them together. The future condition of the conquered power depends on the will of the conqueror. They must come in as new states or remain as conquered provinces. Congress . . . is the only power that can act in the matter. Congress alone can do it. . . . Congress must create States and declare when they are entitled to be represented. Then each House must judge whether the members presenting themselves from a recognized State possess the requisite qualifications of age, residence, and citizenship; and whether the election and returns are according to law. . . .

The last speech on impeachment--Thaddeus Stevens closing the debate in the House, March 2., by Theodore R. Davis, Illus. in: Harper's Weekly, 1868 March 21, p. 180 (PD-US).

It is obvious from all this that the first duty of Congress is to pass a law declaring the condition of these outside or defunct States, and providing proper civil governments for them. Since the conquest they have been governed by martial law. Military rule is necessarily despotic, and ought not to exist longer than is absolutely necessary. As there are no symptoms that the people of these provinces will be prepared to participate in constitutional government for some years, I know of no arrangement so proper for them as territorial governments. There they can learn the principles of freedom and eat the fruit of foul rebellion. Under such governments, while electing members to the territorial Legislatures, they will necessarily mingle with those to whom Congress shall extend the right of suffrage. In Territories Congress fixes the qualifications of electors; and I know of no better place nor better occasion for the conquered rebels and the conqueror to practice justice to all men, and accustom themselves to make and obey equal laws. . They ought never to be recognized as capable of acting in the Union, or of being counted as valid States, until the Constitution shall have been so amended as to make it what its framers intended; and so as to secure perpetual ascendency to the party of the Union; and so as to render our republican Government firm and stable forever. The first of those amendments is to change the basis of representation among the States from Federal numbers to actual voters. . . . With the basis unchanged the 83 Southern members, with the Democrats that will in the best times be elected from the North, will always give a majority in Congress and in the Electoral college. . . . .I need not depict the ruin that would follow. . . But this is not all that we ought to do before inveterate rebels are invited to participate in our legislation. We have turned, or are about to turn, loose four million slaves without a hut to shelter them or a cent in their pockets. The infernal laws of slavery have prevented them from acquiring an education, understanding the common laws of contract, or of managing the ordinary business of life. This Congress is bound to provide for them until they can take care of themselves. If we do not furnish them with homesteads, and hedge them around with protective laws; if we leave them to the legislation of their late masters, we had better have left them in bondage. If we fail in this great duty now, when we have the power, we shall deserve and receive the execration of history and of all future ages.

Assignment

A. Discuss Mr. Stevens' view of Congress in policy making.

B. Carl Schurz (next page, above), special counsel to President Andrew Johnson, wrote the following report in December 1865 upon returning from a trip to the South. Compare and contrast Schurz's report with Stevens'.

Carl Schurz's report in December 1865:

"While the generosity and toleration shown by the Government to the people lately in rebellion have not met with a corresponding generosity shown by those people to the Government's friends, it has brought forth some results which, if properly developed, will become of value. It has facilitated the re-establishment of the forms of civil government, and led many of those who had been active in the rebellion to take part in the act of bringing back the States to their Constitutional relations; and if nothing else were necessary than the mere putting in operation of the mere machinery of government in point of form, and not also the acceptance of the results of the war and their development in point of spirit, these results, although as yet incomplete, might be called a satisfactory advance in the right direction. There is, at present, no danger of another insurrection against the authority of the United States on a large scale, and the people are willing to reconstruct their State governments, and to send their Senators and Representatives to Congress. But as to the moral value of these results, we must not indulge in any delusions. There are two principal points to which I beg to call your attention. In the first place, the rapid return to power and influence of so many of those who but recently were engaged in a bitter war against the Union, has had one effect which was certainly not originally contemplated by the Government. Treason does, under existing circumstances, not appear odious in the South. The people are not impressed with any sense of its criminality. And, secondly, there is, as yet, among the Southern people an utter absence of national feeling. I made it a business, while in the South, to watch the symptoms of "returning loyalty" as they appeared not only in private conversation, but in the public press and in the speeches delivered and the resolutions passed at Union meetings. Hardly ever was there an expression of hearty attachment to the great republic, or an appeal to the impulses of patriotism; but whenever submission to the National authority was declared and advocated, it was almost uniformly placed upon two principal grounds: That, under present circumstances, the Southern people could do no better; and then that submission was the only means by which they could rid themselves of the Federal soldiers and obtain once more control of their own affairs. Some of the speakers may have been inspired by higher motives, but upon these two arguments they had principally to rely whenever they wanted to make an impression upon the popular mind. . . . The solution of the social problem in the South, if left to the free action of the Southern people, will depend upon two things: (1) upon the ideas entertained by the whites, the "ruling class" of the problem, and the manner in which they act upon their ideas; and (2) upon the capacity and conduct of the colored people. I made it a special point in most of the conversations I had with Southern men to inquire into their views with regard to this subject. I found, indeed, some gentlemen of thought and liberal ideas who readily acknowledged the necessity of providing for the education of the colored people, and who declared themselves willing to cooperate to that end to the extent of their influence. Some planters thought of establishing schools on their estates, and others would have been glad to see measures taken to that effect by the people of the neighborhoods in which they lived.

Secretary of the Interior Carl Schurz cleans out the Indian Bureau at the Department of the Interior, by Thomas Nast, Harper's Weekly, January 26, 1878, p. 65. (Above left) Carl Schurz by M.B. Brady, 1877 (PD-US).

PHILOSOPHERS AND WORLD VIEWS

Arthur Schopenhauer (1788–1860)

Schopenhauer (right), often called the philosopher of pessimism, rejected Christianity and embraced eastern religions. Schopenhauer was a disciple of Immanual Kant, the greatest of German philosophers, who argued that knowledge was separate from experience. In fact, Kant and Schopenhauer argued that "it was that which exists independently of our perception, that which actually is." This was "the will." This all-encompassing human will is characterized by Schopenhauer as a blind striving power that "reveals itself to everyone directly as the in-itself of his own phenomenal being." Schopenhauer, with both a Romantic and a Modern impulse, invited mankind to an arduous task: understanding experience separate from any outside force or reality (i.e., God). He and Kant differentiated between the will and action. The next step would be the relativism and nihilism of Nietzsche and Dewey.

(PD-US).

Scholar Alex Scott wrote the following:

Schopenhauer believed that the will is the being-in-itself of everything in the world. The world as an idea is an objectification of the will. The will cannot be explained, nor can it be fully accounted for. The will is comprehensible insofar as it manifests itself in the world, but its inner nature cannot be adequately explained.

The will is beyond time and space, which together constitute a form of the principle of sufficient reason. The will is a unity, and not a plurality. The plurality of things in time and space represents an objectification of the will.

The will cannot be viewed as a necessary cause of its manifestations in the phenomenal world, because it is not governed by the principle of sufficient reason. The relationship between freedom and necessity is that between the will and its manifestations in time and space.

The will-in-itself cannot be defined as the will to do something. The will as a thing-in-itself does not have an object or purpose in its willing. The principle of motivation is a form of the principle of sufficient reason, which extends only to manifestations of the will.

According to Schopenhauer, the act of willing arises from need, and therefore from deprivation or suffering. The fulfillment of a wish ends the act of willing. But no obtained object of desire can give lasting satisfaction. Thus, what is necessary for knowledge of the Platonic Idea is pure contemplation, the absence of desire, the state of total dedication to perception, the transcendence of the subject-object relationship, and freedom from being confined by individuality.

Schopenhauer sees the gratification of a wish or desire as negative, in that it is only a temporary deliverance from deprivation and suffering. Happiness is negative, in that it does not provide lasting satisfaction. Because happiness is never lasting or complete, it is only the absence of true happiness that can become the subject of art.

Schopenhauer also says that freedom of the will is negative, because this freedom is merely the denial of necessity. The intellect is subservient to the will, in that it learns the decisions of the will only after the will has decided on a mode of action. The will is inaccessible to the intellect, and the intellect can only explore the motives for actions, which are manifestations of the will. Self-knowledge can reveal the motives for the act of willing. Knowledge of the self and of the phenomenal world can also influence the motives for action."

Friedrich Nietzsche (1844–1890)

Nietzsche (right) coined the phrase "God is dead." He said the only reality is this world of life and death, conflict and change, creation and destruction. For centuries, religious ideas had given meaning to life in the Western world; but as they appeared to Nietzsche to be collapsing, humanity faced a grave crisis of nihilism and despair. While I vociferously disagree with Nietzsche's vision, I like Nietzsche's honesty. His prophetic view is refreshing. Nietzsche took the hopeless vision of Naturalism and Social Darwinism to its natural conclusion. Nietzsche saw that a world where only power prevailed—a world without Christianity—would inevitably lead to totalitarianism and destruction. He saw, then, in the late 19th century that inevitably Western culture would create an Adolf Hitler or a Joseph Stalin. The basic character of life in this world is what Nietzsche called the "will to power." He admired those who were strong enough to face this reality, for they alone could live joyfully. But this "modern superman" lived without God and without any hope of salvation. Nietzsche was basically a naturalist: man is fundamentally only an animal who has developed in an unusual way. The "will to power" brings about new forms of competition and superiority, and can lead to a "superman" humanity.

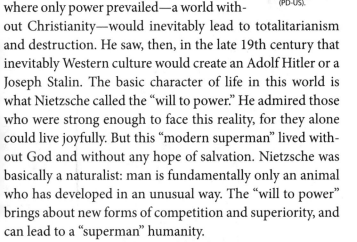

(PD-US).

A passage from Nietzsche's *Human, All Too Human*:

When we hear the ancient bells growling on a Sunday morning we ask ourselves: Is it really possible? This, for a Jew crucified two thousand years ago, who said he was God's son? The proof of such a claim is lacking. Certainly the Christian religion is an antiquity projected into our times from remote prehistory; and the fact that the claim is believed—whereas one is otherwise so strict in examining pretensions—is perhaps the most ancient piece of this heritage. A god who begets children with a mortal woman; a sage who bids men work no more, have no more courts, but look for the signs of the impending end of the world; a justice that accepts the innocent as a vicarious sacrifice; someone who orders his disciples to drink his blood; prayers for miraculous interventions; sins perpetrated against a god, atoned for by a god; fear of a beyond to which death is the portal; the form of the cross as a symbol in a time that no longer knows the function and ignominy of the cross—how ghoulishly all this touches us, as if from the tomb of a primeval past! Can one believe that such things are still believed?

After coming into contact with a religious man I always feel I must wash my hands.

— Friedrich Nietzsche

John Dewey (1859–1952)

John Dewey (left) was the pop psychologist of his age. His views were known as "pragmatism," which emphasizes action and results. According to Dewey, philosophy wasn't a system of beliefs but a practical, empirical method of inquiry. God was natural (not supernatural), ideal (not real). Ethical values described a thing's relationship to its environment (i.e., situational ethics). Inquiry must establish what is good as well as what we know (epistemology). Right and wrong, in other words, were not defined by the Word of God but by experience and practicality.

John Dewey at the University of Chicago, by Eva Watson-Schütze, 1902 (PD-US).

A passage from Dewey's *Constructive Conscious Control of the Individual*:

No one would deny that we ourselves enter as an agency into whatever is attempted and done by us. That is a truism. But the hardest thing to attend to is that which is closest to ourselves, that which is most constant and familiar. And this closest "something" is, precisely, ourselves, our own habits and ways of doing things as agencies in conditioning what is tried or done by us. Through modern science we have mastered to a wonderful extent the use of things as tools for accomplishing results upon and through other things. The result is all but a universal state of confusion, discontent, and strife.

The one factor which is the primary tool in the use of all these other tools—namely, ourselves—in other words, our own psycho-physical disposition, as the basic condition of our employment of all agencies and energies, has not even been studied as the central instrumentality. Is it not highly probable that this failure gives the explanation of why it is that in mastering physical forces we have ourselves been so largely mastered by them, until we find ourselves incompetent to direct the history and destiny of man.

Assignment

A. Many classic educators consider Dewey to be a great enemy of orthodox, Judeo-Christian education. Why?

B. Define "natural selection."

C. Why is this point of view unchristian?

D. Some philosophers and their theories are so bizarre that their theories can be easily rejected (e.g., Darwin and evolution). Nietzsche unnerves me. While he is wrong in his assessment of Christianity, his discernment about the future of Western culture is uncanny. The British historian Paul Johnson (*Modern Times*, p. 48) writes: "Among the advanced races, the decline and ultimately the collapse of the religious impulse would leave a huge vacuum. The history of modern times is in great part the history of how that vacuum is filled. Nietzsche rightly perceived that the most likely candidate would be what he called the 'Will to Power,' which offered a far more comprehensive and in the end more plausible explanation of human behavior than either Marx or Freud (right). In place of religious belief, there would be secular ideology. Those who once filled the ranks of the totalitarian clergy would become totalitarian politicians. And, above all, the Will to Power would produce a new kind of messiah, uninhibited by any religious sanctions whatever, and with an unappeasable appetite for controlling mankind. The end of the old order, with an unguided world adrift in a relativistic universe, was a summons to such gangster-statesmen to emerge. They were not slow to make their appearance."

But this is a new century. You are a new generation. What can you do to make sure that the "religious impulse will not collapse"?

E. Respond to Nietzsche's view of Christianity as presented in Human, all too Human.

Chapter 17

IMMIGRATION

First Thoughts . . .

Remember, remember always, that all of us . . . are descended from immigrants and revolutionists

—Franklin D. Roosevelt

All Americans, except Native Americans, have ancestors who are immigrants. We are a nation of immigrants. Imagine how it felt to be an immigrant and to arrive in this new nation.

Chapter Learning Objectives . . .

In chapter 17 we will cover immigration and its impact on American society. We will discuss the life of Albert Einstein, a vitally important immigrant, and his impact on world history.

As a result of this chapter you should be able to:

1. Understand the concept of "marginalization" and decide if such practices are sound.
2. Decide whether a national government has a legal or moral right to limit immigration for whatever reason it deems necessary and what criteria are acceptable.
3. Research your own family history and determine your own immigrant or Native American roots.
4. Consider different views on the question "Should all immigrants and their children be required to learn English?" Then, you will form your own opinion.
5. Analyze the value of Einstein to world history.
6. Discuss in great detail Marx's theory of society and class struggle.
7. Discuss why Marxism violates the gospel.

LESSON 1

THE HOME OF THE FREE

Immigration is the act or process of moving into another nation with the intention of living there permanently. The contrasting term **emigration** refers to moving from a nation permanently to another nation. Other than Native Americans, the fact is, every American family has immigrant roots. Some immigrants—African-American slaves —were forced to immigrate. Most immigrants, however, came voluntarily.

"Between 1815 and 1920, about 35 million men, women, and children migrated from Europe, Asia, Canada, and Mexico into the United States. From 1820–1860, for instance, 5 million immigrants came to America. However, from 1860–1900, 15 million immigrants arrived! Many of these migrants ultimately returned to their places of origin. For instance, in 1908 alone, 750,000 people left the United States. Most stayed, however" (Ed Fenton, et al., *A New History of the United States*).

What caused people to immigrate? There were several reasons. Some came to obtain political freedom. For instance, millions of Germans migrated in the middle of the 19th century to escape political unrest. Others came to practice their religion in a free environment. Notable among this group was the Russian Jewish community, made famous by the 20th-century Broadway play *Fiddler on the Roof*. Other reasons included economic opportunity and a desire to reunite with family members. Cheaper, faster, and safer modes of transportation brought millions to America's shores. Many immigrants arrived with high hopes. They were in the land of opportunity!

America needed and wanted immigrants. An expanding economy needed new workers; an almost limitless countryside needed more farmers. The construction of railroads from northeastern cities to the West opened large area of the nation to develop.

There were some attempts to stop immigration, but there were more attempts to limit immigration. Chinese immigration, for instance, was encouraged until the Continental Railroad was finished in 1869. In 1882, however, Chinese immigration was limited for the next 60 years. The era of mass immigration closed during the 1920s. Americans were suspicious of outsiders and sought to keep them out. Immigrants became the scapegoat for the growing dislocation of urbanization and, during the Great Depression, the challenges of unemployment. Ultimately, cooler heads prevailed and most Americans understood and valued the benefits of immigration.

It is impossible to make generalizations about immigrants. Each immigrant had his own unique experience. Thus it is impossible to describe a typical Italian, Irish, or German immigrant experience. Nonetheless, there are several generalizations that we can make. The experience of emigration inevitably weakened attachments to the villages and towns from which they emigrated. Inevitably, immigration caused the immigrant to have a strong attachment to his/her new adopted country. Nevertheless, immigrants often chose to remain among their own indigenous groups and resisted assimilation. Inevitably, immigrants participated vigorously in the society in which they lived. Finally, immigrant children usually resisted old cultural expectations—like learning the native language—and this caused tension in immigrant families (from Emily Balch's description of immigrant assimilation in *A New History of the United States*).

Immigration station, Angel Island, California by J.D. Givens, Library of Congress, 1863

Who were the immigrants? The following are charts examining European and other immigration from 1861-1930 (U.S. Bureau of the Census):

Period	Total Immigrants Admitted	Northern and Western Europe		Southern and Eastern Europe	
1861–1870	2,314,824	2,031,624	87.4%	33,628	1.4%
1871–1880	2,812,191	2,070,373	73.6%	201,889	7.2%
1881–1890	5,246,613	3,778,633	72.0%	958,413	18.3%
1891–1900	3,687,564	1,643,492	44.6%	1,915,486	51.9%
1901–1910	8,795,386	1,910,035	21.7%	3,379,126	51.9%
1911–1920	5,735,811	997,438	17.4%	1,193,830	58.9%
1921–1930	4,107, 209	1,284,023	31.3%	1,193,830	29.0%

Period	China	Japan	Canada	Mexico
1861–1870	64,301	186	153,878	2,191
1871–1880	123,201	149	383,640	5,162
1881–1890	61,711	2,270	393,304	1,913
1891–1900	14,799	25,942	3,311	971
1901–1910	20,605	129,797	179,226	49,642
1911–1920	21,278	83,837	742,185	219,004
1921–1930	29,907	33,462	942,515	459,287

What observations can you make from these charts? Where did most immigrants originate from? During which decade did immigration originate between two equal areas? Why did Chinese immigration begin vigorously during the decade 1861 to 1870? Why did that number drop precipitously in 1891–1900?

What did the immigrants do? The following is a chart examining the occupations of immigrants to the United States, 1860–1910 (Ernest Rubin, *Immigration and Economic Growth of the U.S.: 1790–1914*):

Decade	Agriculture	Skilled Labor	Unskilled Labor	Domestic Service	Professional	Misc.
1861–1870	17.6%	24.0%	42.4%	7.2%	0.8%	8.0%
1871–1880	18.2%	23.1%	41.9%	7.7%	1.4%	7.7%
1881–1890	14.0%	20.4%	50.2%	9.4%	1.1%	9.4%
1891–1900	11.4%	20.1%	47.0%	15.1%	0.9%	15.1%
1900–1910	24.3%	20.2%	34.8%	14.1%	1.5%	14.1%

Why was unskilled labor the largest immigration group consistently throughout this time period?

How well have immigrants assimilated in American society? America has never been a "melting pot." While assuming a national identity, especially in times of warfare, immigrants have maintained their ethnicity, even their native languages, while celebrating and participating in American institutions.

Assignment

Dr. Thomas Sowell argues in his book *The Economics and Politics of Race*, that cultural relativism, the notion that all ethnic and cultural differences are solely in the eye of the beholder, does not square with historical or contemporary reality. Sowell argues that to properly understand ethnicity, we must study the past and present political and economic experience of ethnic peoples. Having done so himself, Sowell says:

> The human race, throughout history, has differed greatly in its component parts. At various periods of history, some groups have been far ahead of others in certain areas.

What Sowell suggests is quite controversial. Instead of promoting institutions and social policies that encourage assimilation and blending of ethnic/immigrant groups, Sowell would concede that there are real advantages to keeping immigrant groups separate. Agree or disagree with Dr. Sowell.

Arriving at Ellis Island, Bain News Service, date unknown.

Ellis Island Immigration Museum as seen from the Circle Line Ferry from Battery Park to Liberty Island by Ken Thomas, 2005.

IMMIGRATION

A historical essay by Hasia Diner:

Millions of women and men from around the world have decided to immigrate to the United States—16 million to Ellis Island alone. That fact constitutes one of the central elements in the country's overall development, involving a process fundamental to its pre-national origins, its emergence as a new and independent nation, and its subsequent rise from being an Atlantic outpost to a world power, particularly in terms of its economic growth. Immigration has made the United States of America.

Like many other settler societies, the United States, before it achieved independence and afterward, relied on the flow of newcomers from abroad to people its relatively open and unsettled lands. It shared this historical reality with Canada, South Africa, Australia, New Zealand, and Argentina, among other nations.

In all of these cases the imperial powers that claimed these places had access to two of the three elements essential to fulfilling their goal of extracting natural resources from the colony. They had land and capital but lacked people to do the farming, lumbering, mining, hunting, and the like. Colonial administrators tried to use native labor, with greater or lesser success, and they abetted the escalation of the African slave trade, bringing millions of migrants, against their will, to these New World outposts.

Immigration, however, played a key role not only in making America's development possible but also in shaping the basic nature of the society. Its history falls into five distinct time periods, each of which involved varying rates of migration from distinctly different places in the world. Each reflected, and also shaped, much about the basic nature of American society and economy.

The first, and longest, era stretched from the 17th century through the early 19th century. Immigrants came from a range of places, including the German-speaking area of the Palatinate, France (Protestant Huguenots), and the Netherlands. Other immigrants were Jews, also from the Netherlands and from Poland, but most immigrants of this era tended to hail from the British Isles, with English, Scottish, Welsh, and Ulster Irish gravitating toward different colonies (later states) and regions.

These immigrants, usually referred to as settlers, opted in the main for farming, with the promise of cheap land a major draw for relatively impoverished northern and western Europeans who found themselves unable to take advantage of the modernization of their home economies. One group of immigrants deserves some special attention because their experience sheds much light on the forces impelling migration. In this era, considerable numbers of women and men came as indentured servants. They entered into contracts with employers who specified the time and conditions of labor in exchange for passage to the New World. While they endured harsh conditions during their time of service, as a result of their labors, they acquired ownership of small pieces of land that they could then work as independent yeoman farmers.

The numbers who came during this era were relatively small. That changed, however, by the 1820s. This period ushered in the first era of mass migration. From that decade through the 1880s, about 15 million immigrants made their way to the United States, many choosing agriculture in the Midwest and Northeast, while others flocked to cities like New York, Philadelphia, Boston, and Baltimore.

Actors in both Europe and the United States shaped this transition. The end of the Napoleonic Wars in Europe liberated young men from military service back home at the same time that industrialization and agricultural consolidation in England, Scandinavia, and much of central Europe transformed local economies and created a class of young people who could not earn a living in the new order. Demand for immigrant labor shot up with two major developments: the settlement of the American Midwest after the inauguration of the Erie Canal in 1825 and the related rise of the port of New York, and the first stirrings of industrial development in the United States, particularly in textile production, centered in New England.

Immigrants tended to cluster by group in particular neighborhoods, cities, and regions. The American Midwest, as it emerged in the middle of the 19th century as one of the world's most fertile agricultural regions, became home to tight-knit, relatively homogeneous communities of immigrants from Sweden, Norway, Denmark, Bohemia, and various regions of what in 1871 would become Germany.

This era saw the first large-scale arrival of Catholic immigrants to the largely Protestant United States, and these primarily Irish women and men inspired the nation's first serious bout of nativism, which combined an antipathy to immigrants in general with a fear of Catholicism and an aversion to the Irish. Particularly in the decades just before the U.S. Civil War (1861–1865), this nativism (or anti-immigration policy) spawned a powerful political movement and even a political party, the Know Nothings, which made anti-immigration and anti-Catholicism central to its political agenda. This period also witnessed the arrival of small numbers of Chinese men to the American West. Native-born Americans reacted intensely and negatively to their arrival, leading to the passage of the only piece of U.S. immigration legislation that specifically named a group as the focus of restrictive policy, the Chinese Exclusion Act of 1882.

Gradually over the course of the decades after the Civil War, as the sources of immigration shifted so too did the technology of ocean travel. Whereas previous immigrants had made their way to the United States via sail power, innovations in steam transportation made it possible for larger ships to bring larger loads of immigrants to the United States. The immigrants of this era tended to come from southern and eastern Europe, regions undergoing at the end of the 19th and beginning of the 20th centuries the same economic transitions that western and northern Europe had earlier experienced. As among the immigrants of the earlier period, young people predominated among the newcomers. This wave of migration, which constituted the third episode in the history of U.S. immigration, could better be referred to as a flood of immigrants, as nearly 25 million Europeans made the voyage. Italians, Greeks, Hungarians, Poles, and others speaking Slavic languages constituted the bulk of this migration. Included among them were 2.5 to 3 million Jews.

Each group evinced a distinctive migration pattern in terms of the gender balance within the migratory pool, the permanence of their migration, their literacy rates, the balance between adults and children, and the like. But they shared one overarching characteristic: They flocked to urban destinations and made up the bulk of the U.S. industrial labor pool, making possible the emergence of such industries as steel, coal, automobile, textile, and garment production, and enabling the United States to leap into the front ranks of the world's economic giants.

Their urban destinations, their numbers, and perhaps a fairly basic human antipathy towards foreigners led to the emergence of a second wave of organized xenophobia. By the 1890s, many Americans, particularly from the ranks of the well-off, white, native-born, considered immigration to pose a serious danger to the nation's health and security. In 1893 a group of them formed the Immigration Restriction League, and it, along with other similarly inclined organizations, began to press Congress for severe curtailment of foreign immigration.

Restriction proceeded piecemeal over the course of the late 19th and early 20th centuries, but immediately after the end of World War I (1914–1918) and into the early 1920s, Congress did change the nation's basic policy about immigration. The National Origins Act in 1921 (and its final form in 1924) not only restricted the number of immigrants who might enter the United States but also assigned slots according to quotas based on national origins. A complicated piece of legislation, it essentially gave preference to immigrants from northern and western Europe, severely limited the numbers from eastern and southern Europe, and declared all potential immigrants from Asia to be unworthy of entry into the United States.

The legislation excluded the Western Hemisphere from the quota system, and the 1920s ushered in the penultimate era in U.S. immigration history. Immigrants could and did move quite freely from Mexico, the Caribbean (including Jamaica, Barbados, and Haiti), and other parts of Central and South America. This era, which reflected the application of the 1924 legislation, lasted until 1965. During those 40 years, the United States began to admit, case by case, limited numbers of refugees. Jewish refugees from Nazi Germany before World War II, Jewish Holocaust survivors after the war, non-Jewish displaced persons fleeing Communist rule in eastern Europe, Hungarians seeking refuge after their failed uprising in 1956, and Cubans after the 1960 revolution managed to find haven in the United States because their plight moved the conscience of Americans, but the basic immigration law remained in place.

This all changed with passage of the Hart-Celler Act in 1965, a by-product of the civil rights revolution and a jewel in the crown of President Lyndon Johnson's Great Society programs. The measure had not been intended to stimulate immigration from Asia, the Middle East, Africa, and elsewhere in the developing world. Rather, by doing away with the racially based quota system, its authors had expected that immigrants would come from the "traditional" sending societies such as Italy and Poland, places that labored under very small quotas in the 1924 law. The law replaced the quotas with preference categories based on family relationships and job skills, giving particular preference to potential immigrants with relatives in the United States and with occupations deemed critical by the U.S. Department of Labor. But after 1970, following an initial influx from those European countries, immigrants began to hail from places like Korea, China, India, the Philippines, and Pakistan, as well as countries in Africa. By 2000 immigration to the United States had returned to its 1900 volume, and the United States once again became a nation formed and transformed by immigrants.

Now in the early 21st century, American society once again finds itself locked in a debate over immigration and the role of immigrants in American society. To some, the new immigrants have seemed unwilling or unable to assimilate into American society, too committed to maintaining their transnational connections, and too far removed from core American values. As in past eras, some critics of contemporary immigrants believe that the newcomers take jobs away from Americans and put undue burdens on the educational, welfare, and health care systems. Many participants in the debate consider a large number of illegal immigrants to pose a threat to the society's basic structure.

The immigrants, however, have supporters who point out that each new immigrant wave inspired fear, suspicion, and concern by Americans—including the children and grandchildren of earlier immigrants—and that Americans claimed, wrongly, that each group of newcomers would somehow not fit in and would remain wedded to their old and foreign ways. So too advocates of immigration and most historians of immigration argue that immigrants enrich the United States, in large measure because they provide valuable services to the nation.

In every era of U.S. history, from colonial times in the 17th century through the early 21st century, women and men from around the world have opted for the American experience. They arrived as foreigners, bearers of languages, cultures, and religions that at times seemed alien to America's essential core. Over time, as ideas about U.S. culture changed, the immigrants and their descendants simultaneously built ethnic communities and participated in American civic life, contributing to the nation as a whole.

Assignment

A. Does a national government have a legal or moral right to limit immigration for whatever reason it deems necessary? What criteria are acceptable?

B. Research your own family history and determine your own immigrant/Native American roots. Write a narration of your family from that beginning to today.

ALBERT EINSTEIN

It is ironical that a peace-loving man like Albert Einstein, a man who risked his life by signing a protest against German militarism in World War I, was, to a large degree, the grandfather (because Oppenheimer was the father) of the atomic bomb. Einstein was born in Ulm, Germany, but spent most of his life in Switzerland. He returned to Germany to teach in a German university. He stayed there until the Nazis rose to power in the early 1930s. He then emigrated to the United States. In 1919, while still in Germany, Einstein observed the bending of light near the sun at a solar eclipse. This helped him deduce the theory of relativity, $E=MC^2$. In early 1939, Einstein and several other scientists wrote President Franklin Roosevelt that Hitler was developing a terrible bomb and that America must do the same—and quickly! Roosevelt listened to Einstein and set up the Manhattan Project. To a large degree, then, the immigrant Einstein won World War II and made sure that democracy would win over tyranny. He was a great history maker!

A passage from Einstein's *Science, Philosophy, and Religion, A Symposium*:

Albert Einstein during a lecture in Vienna by Ferdinand Schmutzer, 1921 (PD-US).

The more a man is imbued with the ordered regularity of all events the firmer become his convictions that there is no room left by the side of this ordered regularity for causes of a different nature. For him neither the rule of human nor the rule of divine will exists as an independent cause of natural events. To be sure, the doctrine of a personal God interfering with natural events could never be refuted, in the real sense, by science, for this doctrine can always take refuge in those domains in which scientific knowledge has not yet been able to set foot. But I am convinced that such behavior on the part of representatives of religion would not only be unworthy but also fatal. For a doctrine which is to maintain itself not in clear light but only in the dark, will of necessity lose its effect on mankind, with incalculable harm to human progress. In their struggle for the ethical good, teachers of religion must have the stature to give up the doctrine of a personal God, that is, give up that source of fear and hope which in the past placed such vast power in the hands of priests. In their labors they will have to avail themselves of those forces which are capable of cultivating the Good, the True, and the Beautiful in humanity itself. This is, to be sure a more difficult but an incomparably more worthy task. . . ."

Albert Einstein receiving from Judge Phillip Forman his certificate of American citizenship by Al. Aumuller, 1940.

Albert Einstein to Guy H. Raner Jr., Sept. 28, 1949, from article by Michael R. Gilmore in *Skeptic* magazine, Vol. 5, No. 2, 1997:

> I have repeatedly said that in my opinion the idea of a personal God is a childlike one. You may call me an agnostic, but I do not share the crusading spirit of the professional atheist whose fervor is mostly due to a painful act of liberation from the fetters of religious indoctrination received in youth. I prefer an attitude of humility corresponding to the weakness of our intellectual understanding of nature and of our own being.

A passage from Einstein's *Out of My Later Years*:

> If this being is omnipotent, then every occurrence, including every human action, every human thought, and every human feeling and aspiration is also His work; how is it possible to think of holding men responsible for their deeds and thoughts before such an almighty Being? In giving out punishment and rewards He would to a certain extent be passing judgment on Himself. How can this be combined with the goodness and righteousness ascribed to Him?

> The idea of a personal God is an anthropological concept which I am unable to take seriously.
> — Albert Einstein, letter to Hoffman and Dukas, 1946

While I was at Princeton Theological Seminary in the early 1980s, my professor and good friend Dr. Donald McCleod told us a story about Einstein. "Professor Einstein," Dr. McCleod said, "loved Christmas. We would sing Christmas carols throughout the neighborhood [when McCleod himself was a student at Princeton]. Inevitably we would end at Professor Einstein's house [only a few blocks from Princeton]. As we began 'Silent Night' Professor Einstein would come out on his front porch and join us with his violin. Later we would all go in for hot chocolate."

Assignment

Albert Einstein may have been the smartest man who ever lived. Yet he missed the most important truth: the One and only Truth, the Way, and the Life—our Lord Jesus Christ. Pretend that you will be meeting Einstein in Princeton near the end of his life. What will you say? How will you refute his argument that there is no personal God?

Bernard Shaw: "Say, Einie, do you really think you understand yourself?" Dr. Einstein: "No, Bernie, do you?" by Oliver Herford, 1921.

LESSON 4

KARL MARX

G. W. F. Hegel had a great influence on Karl Marx. He created a vast speculative and idealistic philosophy in which truth is found not in the part but in the whole and is not absolute but relative. Hegel's famous "dialectic" is an argument for what he called the "struggle." Truth arises from the "struggle." For Hegel, history is a dynamic succession of novel and creative events, the gradual unfolding of reason.

I cannot imagine anyone having more influence on modern world view formation than Karl Marx. The father of Communism, Marx invited countless millions to an utopia that never fully materialized. Marx (right) argued that history flows inevitably toward a social revolution, which will result in a society without economic classes.

A passage from Marx's *Communist Manifesto*:

The history of all hitherto existing society is the history of class struggles. Freeman and slave, patrician and plebeian, lord and serf, guildmaster and journeyman, in a word, oppressor and oppressed, stood in constant opposition to one another, carried on an uninterrupted, now hidden, now open fight, a fight that each time ended, either in a revolutionary re-constitution of society at large, or in the common ruin of the contending classes. In the earlier epochs of history, we find almost everywhere a complicated arrangement of society into various orders, a manifold gradation of social rank. In ancient Rome we have patricians, knights, plebeians, slaves; in the Middle Ages, feudal lords, vassals, guildmasters, journeymen, apprentices, serfs; in almost all of these classes, again subordinate gradations. The modern bourgeois society that has sprouted from the ruins of feudal society has not done away with class antagonisms. It has but established new classes, new conditions of oppression, new forms of struggle in place of the old ones. Our epoch, the epoch of the bourgeoisie, possesses, however, this distinctive feature: it has simplified the class antagonisms. Society as a whole is more and more splitting up into two great hostile camps, into two great classes directly facing each other: Bourgeoisie and Proletariat.

(PD-US).

Assignment

A. Discuss in great detail Marx's theory of society and class struggle.

B. Karl Marx was greatly influenced by G. W. F. Hegel (1770–1831). For Hegel, history was a dynamic succession of novel and creative events, the gradual unfolding of reason. Hegel celebrated what he called the struggle. Truth unfolds in a dialectic. The dialectic comes from contradictions. He argues that truth is developed from contradictions. To Marx the struggle was between the bourgeoisie and the proletariat. The next result is that mankind no longer has absolute truth—truth lies between the struggle of contradictions (see the next page). Why is this view unacceptable to Christians?

Statue of Karl Marx, Berlin.

Chapter 18

THE GILDED AGE

First Thoughts . . .

Willa Cather, perhaps the most famous female writer of the so-called Gilded Age (that period in history from the end of the Civil War to World War I when America experienced unprecedented prosperity), wrote an insightful short story called "A Wagnerian Matinee" in which she described a hardened Western woman visiting her nephew in the East. While she is there, her nephew takes her to a Wagnerian Opera—a rare treat indeed for someone living in a prairie sod house in the 1880s. "The first number was the Tannhauser overture. When the horns drew out the first strain of the Pilgrim's chorus my Aunt Georgiana clutched my coat sleeve. Then it was I first realized that for her this broke a silence of thirty years; the inconceivable silence of the plains." Cather, in this short quote, captures the contradictions so evident in America during this strange Gilded Age, 1861–1917, when some Americans lived in filthy sod houses in Lincoln, Nebraska, and others in extravagant mansions in New York City.

Chapter Learning Objectives . . .

In Chapter 18, we will examine the Gilded Age, its robber barons and tycoons. Next, we will look closely at the rise of organized labor. Finally, we will see that while America was experiencing unparalleled prosperity at home, the country was also emerging at the beginning of the 20th century as a world power to be reckoned with.

As a result of this chapter you should be able to:

1. Discuss what sorts of changes occurred in antebellum America that set the stage for economic growth after the Civil War.

2. Analyze the Gilded Age, its opportunities and its problems.

3. Evaluate the post–Civil War labor movement.

4. Gauge the importance of Lenin to world history and world view formation.

5. Judge whether Carnegie and men like him (Frick, Rockefeller) were benevolent men or ruthless robber barons—or both.

THE GILDED AGE

The Gilded Age was a period of obscene materialism and blatant political corruption in U.S. history. It was a time of massive industrialization and serious social problems. At the same time, the Gilded Age ushered in the Moody Revivals in the Northeast and beyond. While industrial tycoons were squandering America's wealth, evangelical Christians in the name of Christ were tackling the most difficult urban problems this nation had ever known.

The period took its name from a novel by Mark Twain, *The Gilded Age* (1873). Predominately, the Gilded Age was a time of industrialization. In 1860, America was a rural society. Before 1861, most Americans were farmers. After 1917, most Americans were industrialized laborers. America became an urban society. In fact, for the first time since the time of Christ, the world was on its way to becoming an urban society. It was not to happen entirely until the end of the 20th century, but the dislocation and change of values were well underway by the end of the 19th century. In summary, by 1900, industrialization had transformed all aspects of American life.

Why did America industrialize so quickly after the Civil War? Other countries, like England, were heavily industrialized, but it had taken them a century or more to reach the mark that America reached in 40 years. Why? There were several reasons: cheap immigrant labor, new technology and inventions, seemingly endless natural resources, and readily available transportation.

The end of the 19th century also saw the beginning of **trusts**. In a trust, an aggressive group of business people, called trustees, acquire enough shares in several similar firms to control these companies and thereby control a particular market. Two examples were U.S. Steel, controlled by

Mark Twain in his later years by A.F. Bradley, 1907

Andrew Carnegie, and Standard Oil, controlled by John D. Rockefeller. Named after an 1873 social satire by Mark Twain and Charles Dudley Warner, the Gilded Age encompassed the years from the 1870s to 1900. Scholars tend to see the legacies of the Civil War and Reconstruction as important contributors to the transformations that took place in the last three decades of the 19th century. (This discussion is informed by Beard's Economic History of the United States).

The federal government was very business-friendly. **The Homestead Act (1862)** opened the West for settlement by individual farmers. Railroad expansion in combination with government land policies and the breaking of Native American resistance on the Plains in the 1870s and 1880s opened up the West for economic exploitation. Abundant natural resources and abundant cheap labor presaged an unprecedented economic boom.

Constitutional change, too, contributed to this process. Between 1875 and 1900 the Supreme Court removed many state laws restricting interstate commerce but also blocked federal attempts at regulation. The Interstate Commerce Commission was created in 1887, but its limited powers were further circumscribed by Court decisions. Legal change helped to create a political environment in which forces of social change could unfold.

There were many problems, though. Economic expansion came to a halt in the 1870s and crashed in the 1890s. In 1873, a credit scandal and the collapse of the Northern Pacific Railroad resulted in a recession from which the country finally recovered four years later in 1877. In May 1893, the collapse of the Pennsylvania and Reading Railroad led to a prolonged recession, at the height of which four million workers lost their jobs. Americans were not going to see something that bad again until the 1930s.

The Gilded Age had many contradictions. Along with the beginning of the modern American labor movement and a resurgence of the movement for women's rights, the age saw the implementation of **Jim Crow laws**, sanctioned by the Supreme Court's 1896 decision in **Plessy v. Ferguson**. The Gilded Age also witnessed the emergence of the United States as an imperialist foreign power. Desire for greatness on the seas, partially spawned by Alfred Thayer Mahan's *The Influence of Sea Power upon History* (1890), led the United States into war with Spain in 1898 and into a subsequent war in the Philippines from 1899 to 1902. The Gilded Age saw the birth pangs of the United States as a global power, an urban, industrial society, and a modern, liberal corporatist state. Many problems remained unsolved, however, for the Progressive Era and New Deal reform policies to address.

The first national labor organization, the Knights of Labor, organized in 1869, tried to include all workers. The Knights reached their greatest strength between 1884 and 1885, when railroad strikes raged, and then declined. As the Knights of Labor faded, a new federation of local and craft unions, the American Federation of Labor (AFL), was organized in 1886. Led from 1886 to 1924 by Samuel Gompers, an immigrant cigar maker from England, the AFL welcomed skilled workers, almost all of them men. The method most often employed by the unions to force an issue was the work stoppage or the strike. In the 1880s, a decade of 10,000

Dugout home from a homestead near Pie Town, New Mexico by Russell Lee 1940.

strikes and lockouts, workers often succeeded in averting wage reductions and winning shorter hours. Many of the strikes were violent. The Sherman Antitrust Act of 1890 declared illegal all strikes that hampered interstate commerce. Industrial workers of the late 19th century were often foreign-born. From 1865 to 1885, immigrants arrived mainly from northern and western Europe, as they had before the Civil War; the largest groups came from England, Ireland, Germany, and Scandinavia. From the mid-1880s until World War I began in 1914, the number of newcomers from southern, eastern, and central Europe increased. Many new immigrants were Slavs—Poles, Czechs, Russians, Ukrainians, Croatians—and others, including Jews, from the Austro-Hungarian and Russian empires. Among the new immigrants were also Greeks, Romanians, and Italians, mainly from southern Italy or Sicily. Record numbers of immigrants arrived in the United States, some 9 million from 1880 to 1900, and 13 million from 1900 to 1914. As immigration exploded, urban populations surged from 6 million in 1860 to 42 million in 1910. Big cities got bigger: Chicago tripled in size in the 1880s and 1890s. By 1900 three cities contained more than a million people: New York (3.5 million), Chicago (1.7 million), and Philadelphia (1.3 million). (This discussion is informed by www.answers.com)

Andrew Carnegie by Theodore C. Marceau, 1913 (PD-US).

Assignment

A. The following is a quote from Andrew Carnegie, "Wealth," *North American Review*, 148, no. 391 (June 1889): 653, 657–662:

This, then, is held to be the duty of the man of Wealth: First, to set an example of modest, unostentatious living, shunning display or extravagance; to provide moderately for the legitimate wants of those dependent upon him; and after doing so to consider all surplus revenues which come to him simply as trust funds, which he is called upon to administer, and strictly bound as a matter of duty to administer in the manner which, in his judgment, is best calculated to produce the most beneficial result for the community—the man of wealth thus becoming the sole agent and trustee for his poorer brethren, bringing to their service his superior wisdom, experience, and ability to administer—doing for them better than they would or could do for themselves.

Do you agree or disagree with this quote? Why or why not?

B. In the 1880s half the children born in Chicago did not live to celebrate their fifth birthday. Discuss why this occurred and offer some solutions in the context of the 1880s (i.e., do not offer a solution with 21st century technology).

C. What sort of changes occurred in antebellum America that set the stage for economic growth after the Civil War?

AMERICAN LABOR MOVEMENT

The American laborer began in the Commonwealth of Massachusetts when the first child labor law (1836) was passed, whereby employment of children under the age of 15 was forbidden in incorporated factories, unless they had attended school for three months the prior year of their employment. Generally speaking, the federal government was reticent to involve itself in labor relations. The government's willingness to intervene in dealing with poor working conditions in industrialized cities was greatly affected by the principles of laissez-faire, which stated that "the functions of the state should be limited to internal police and foreign protection— no public education, no limitation of hours of labor, no welfare legislation."

Labor then looked to itself for help. As the economy improved over the next few years, American labor took another direction: toward labor organizing. Several unions came into being, including the Order of the Knights of Labor. Founded in 1869, the Knights' goal was to increase negotiating powers by unionizing all American workers. The Knights of Labor, under the leadership of Pennsylvania machinist Terence V. Powderly, were essentially responsible for the Alien Contract Labor Law of 1885, which prohibited laborers migrating to America who had a contract to perform work.

Driven by wage cuts and poor working conditions, violent outbreaks of strikes and a long series of battles occurred all over the country during the 1870s. In 1877, around Pottsville, Pennsylvania, a secret miners' association called the Molly Maguires, mostly comprising Irish Catholics, burned buildings and murdered bosses who offended them.

By 1886, membership in the Knights of Labor had swollen to 700,000 workers and stood as a champion for the unskilled laborer. Unlike other labor unions, the Knights of Labor encouraged African-Americans to join, so that by 1886, approximately 60,000 African-Americans had become members.

The Knights of Labor participated in the famous Haymarket Square riot of 1886 in Chicago, along with trade unions, socialist unions, and "anarchists," where workers fought for the eight-hour day, and where a bomb and subsequent shooting resulted in the deaths of eight policemen and injuries to 67 others. Eight anarchists were jailed, tried, and convicted of murder, of which four were hanged.

The American Federation of Labor (A.F. of L.—now simply AFL) began that same year. The AFL was spearheaded by **Samuel Gompers** (left), a cigar maker by trade.

It was not until the Massachusetts' Ten-Hour Act (1874) went into effect that woman—and child—labor limits in factories were adequately enforced. But a New York act of 1883, which prohibited the manufacture of cigars in sweatshops, was overturned by the state's highest court, even though it had been sponsored by Theodore Roosevelt and signed by Governor Grover Cleveland. The court declared that government should not force workers to leave their homes to go to work and also should not interfere with the profitable use of real estate, without any compensation for the public good.

The Sherman Antitrust Act of 1890, which authorized federal action against any "combination in the form of trusts or otherwise, or conspiracy, in restraint of trade," was used as a blanket injunction against labor to break the current strike and others in the future. The Pullman Strike (1894) against the Great Northern Railway of Chicago, led by Eugene V. Debs, then president of the American Railway Union, was staged because of cuts in wages and continued high rents in company-owned housing. (This discussion was informed by an Internet article.)

Assignment

Why was the U.S. government generally opposed to the rise of labor unions?

HISTORICAL DEBATE

The rise of American industry and immigration labor in the decades following the Civil War had a profound and lasting effect on the American nation. (This discussion is informed by Gerald N. Grob and George Athan Billias, *Interpretations of American History: Patterns and Perspectives,* Vol. 2.) Industrialization had a fundamental effect on the way Americans saw their world. Traditionally Americans were accustomed to think in terms of individualistic values. The rise of industry itself was often rationalized in the ideology of the self-made man who claimed he attained success by virtue of his own talents, drive, and ambition. By the end of the 19th century, it was becoming more difficult to conceive of industrial progress solely in terms of the achievements of a few individuals (p. 229, Grob and Billias). The rise of the large, industrialized state flew in the face of individualism celebrated so lustily in the immigrant community. This argument is forcefully advanced by Kenneth E. Boulding. This loss of the so-called myth of hard work—that the sky was the limit if one was willing to work hard—was of great concern to late 19th century Americans. Because of greedy corporations and disparagement in wealth, was not American becoming like the feeble class-ridden society so many immigrants thought that they had left behind in Europe? Some historians like Vernon L. Parrington saw it that way. He wrote that America needed men who stood against the evil corporations who were "cesspools that were poisoning the national household" (Parrington, *Main Currents in American Thought,* 1927). John Hicks joined Parrington and celebrated the reform movements of the late 19th century. Many of the participants of these reform movements were immigrants. Hicks looked back to the Jeffersonian (i.e., Thomas Jefferson) agrarian tradition (Hicks, *The Populist Revolt,* 1931). Some historians disagreed with Hicks and Parrington. Notable among these was the Marxist John Chamberlain, who thought that Hicks and Parrington were naive and out of touch with reality. There never were any "good old days," Chamberlain argued (Chamberlain, *Farewell to Reform*). Criticisms increased as

Textile mill workers. Spinning machinery, by Lewis Wickes Hine, Macon, Georgia, 1909.

a new generation of historians wrote history. These Marxist historians naturally saw history developing along economic lines, not along ideological lines. They saw history as a class struggle, not as a struggle between ideologies (e.g., individualism vs. industrialization). These historians, writing in the Great Depression, criticized Hicks and Parrington for seeing history as a morality play where good always triumphed over evil. Left to their own designs, Chamberlain argued, men will always choose his own selfish, self-serving interests. The challenge to democracy posed by communism after World War II ensured that new historians would challenge Chamberlain and his Marxist friends.

Writing from a conservative point of view, these historians stressed the basic goodness of American society and the consensus that has characterized the American people throughout most of their history (Grob and Billias, p. 233). In other words, these historians argued, we should see American history in terms of consensus, not in terms of struggle (the heartbeat of Marxist historians). The leader of these anti-Marxists historians was Richard Hofstadter. The fierceness of the political struggles [in American history] has often been misleading; for the range of vision embraced by the primary contestants in the major parties has always been bounded by the horizons of property and enterprise. . . . The sanctity of private property, the right of the individual to dispose of and invest it, the value of opportunity, and the natural evolution of self-interest and self-assertion, within broad legal limits, into a beneficent social order have been staple tenets of the central faith in American political ideologies; these conceptions have been shared in large part by men as diverse as Jefferson, Jackson, Lincoln, Cleveland, Bryan, Wilson, and Hoover (Richard Hofstadter, *The American Political Tradition*).

Assignment

A. Remember a recent argument that you had with a brother or sister. Discuss how the "history" or retelling of that event differs between you and your sibling.

B. Which historian is correct? Hicks and Parrington? Chamberlain? Hofstadter? Defend your answer.

C. Discuss how movies have affected the way Americans view an issue (e.g., the movie *Bambi* vs. deer hunting).

Bethlehem Steel Works, a watercolor by Joseph Pennell, depicting Bethlehem Iron Company, Bethlehem, Pennsylvania, 1881 (PD-US).

VLADIMIR ILYICH LENIN

Vladimir Lenin's contribution to the modern world is that his world view actually was put into practice! Other philosophers talked about the world changing, but Lenin (left) actually brought it about through his actions as well as his words. I am speaking, of course, of the Russian Revolution in 1917 that literally changed the course of history. As philosopher Martyn Oliver states, "Lenin was impatient with Marxist [Karl Marx] theorizing, which, he believed, had spent too long discussing the perfect state of revolutionary consciousness among the working classes." Lenin did not believe that the working classes would have enough energy and expertise to start a revolution. They needed the help of an "elite" to guide them. In 1917, at the end of World War I, Lenin was able to gather and to motivate that same group of middle-class intellectuals who precipitated the Bolshevik (Communist) Revolution in Russia. Lenin, of course, was a Marxist/ Hegelian and believed that conflict among classes was both desirable and inevitable. He felt that the proletariat (workers) would ultimately win the day, and he sought to make sure that happened immediately and conclusively. He also believed strongly that once the workers' revolution began, it would not stop until it spread all over the world. He left a legacy that would impact America for years to come with the rise of communism and eventually the Cold War, which lasted from approximately 1946 to the early 1990s.

The following is an excerpt from Lenin's influential pamphlet "What Is to Be Done?"

I assert: that no movement can be durable without a stable organization of leaders to maintain continuity; that the more widely the masses are spontaneously drawn into the struggle and form the basis of the movement and participate in it, the more necessary is it to have such an organization, and the more stable must it be (for it is much easier for demagogues to sidetrack the more backward sections of the masses); that the organization must consist chiefly of persons engaged in revolutionary activities as a profession; that in a country with an autocratic government, the more we restrict the membership of this organization to persons who are engaged in revolutionary activities as a profession and who have been professionally trained in the art of combating the political police, the more difficult will it be to catch the organization, and the wider will be the circle of men and women of the working class or of other classes of society able to join the movement and perform active work in it. . . .

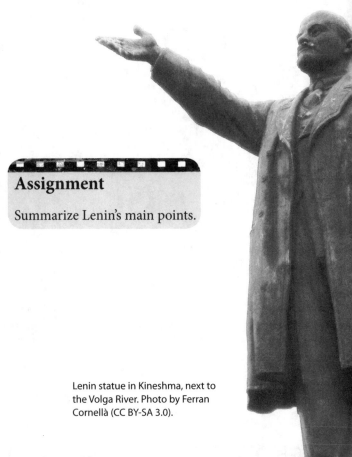

Lenin statue in Kineshma, next to the Volga River. Photo by Ferran Cornellà (CC BY-SA 3.0).

Assignment

Summarize Lenin's main points.

Chapter 19

THE GILDED AGE: PROBLEMS

First Thoughts . . .

"On May 31, 1889, an earthen dam on the Little Conemaugh River gave way after torrential rains and washed Johnstown, a small community east of Pittsburgh, Pennsylvania, off the face of the earth. The flood destroyed Johnstown, leaving 1,600 houses and 260 businesses demolished in its wake. At least 2,209 people lost their lives. All this was accumulated in one inextricable mass, which almost immediately caught fire from some stove which the waters had not touched. Hundreds of human beings, dead and alive, were caught in it, many by the lower part of the body only. Eyewitnesses describe the groans and cries which came from that vast holocaust for nearly the whole night as something fearful beyond all power of description" (eyewitness Rev. David Beale). The Gilded Age was full of glitter and extravagance, but, this week, we will look at the other side: the problems created during that age.

Chapter Learning Objectives . . .

In chapter 19 we will examine the Gilded Age from the common man's perspective. We will read about social welfare policies engendered by the Church. We will look at the Johnstown Flood as a case study of Gilded Age excesses. Next, we will look at the life of William Jennings Bryan, one of the great men of this era. Finally, we will read excerpts from philosophers who were impacting world views.

As a result of this chapter you should be able to:

1. Discuss how 19th-century Christian reformers pioneered social welfare technique and policy for their era.

2. Discuss the philosopher Proudhon's views of God and where his reasoning is flawed.

3. Learn about the Johnstown Flood of May 31, 1889.

4. Analyze William Jennings Bryan's "Cross of Gold" speech.

SOCIAL WELFARE AND CHRISTIANITY

By 1883, Thomas O'Donnell, an Irish immigrant, had lived in the United States for over a decade. He was 30 years old, married, with two children. His third child had died in 1882, and O'Donnell was still in debt for the funeral. Money was scarce, because O'Donnell was a textile worker in Fall River, Massachusetts, and not well educated. (This section is informed by Nash, Jeffrey, et al., *The American People,* Vol. II.)

O'Donnell and his family were barely getting by even though he worked every day and some nights. They were marginally Roman Catholic, but often attended revival meetings when they were held by the local Christian and Missionary Alliance Church. While they would never leave the Roman Catholic Church—mostly out of fear—they had already responded (more than once) to an evangelist's appeal to give "their hearts to the Lord."

The Church, especially the so-called Protestant Sunday schools—a sort of vacation Bible School—was vital to O'Donnell's family. When his paycheck came up a little short, he received a bag of groceries from a Salvation Army Station. Although O'Donnell never considered leaving the Roman Catholic Church, to a large degree, his life was indelibly improved by the kind acts of revivalist Christians in his neighborhood.

O'Donnell and thousands like him were part of the growing American urban working poor. Although no nationwide studies of poverty existed, estimates suggest that perhaps half of the American population was at poverty level. This "misery" was increasingly being concentrated in industrialized urban centers. Since its founding, the United States had changed from a rural to an urban nation. The most important city, for instance, New York, probably contained fewer than 22,000 people at the beginning of the American Revolution. In 1880, only 3.4 percent of the population lived in cities over a million. But, if one defines a city as having at least 100,000 people, the percentage of total population living in cities from 1850 to 1900 grew from 6 percent to almost 20

Rev. Russell Herman Conwell by Kúbey-Rembrandt Studios, c1922.

percent. And this figure is even more remarkable if one considers that urban growth from about 1750 to 1850 was only 5 percent to about 6 percent. This urban growth, to a large degree, was due to the Industrial Revolution.

Perhaps the most important development in American history during this period, however, was the flourishing of the revivalist movement. Norris Magnuson in his book *Salvation in the Slums: Evangelical Social Work 1865–1920* advanced an ambitious thesis: The pietistic, revivalistic, and holiness (as contrasted with later evangelical and Fundamentalist) Christian movements of the latter part of the 19th century were actively involving themselves in evangelical social work that was critical to the lives of thousands of average urban Americans. Christian urban missionaries/pioneers involved themselves in a wide range of social concerns (food, shelter, recreation, health, unemployment, and so forth). And that was before there was a positive liberal state in which the government funded most social welfare interventions.

Magnuson points out that revivalist movements like the Salvation Army, the Volunteers of America, the Christian and Missionary Alliance, and the "Rescue Movement" attempted some of the most ambitious and innovative urban redevelopment projects that America knew in the Gilded Age. Revivalistic social reformers were able to reinforce the already natural link between revivalism and social reform. The revivalists saw soul-salvation as the only hope for society, to be sure. But obedience to biblical injunctions to preach the gospel to all people, in the evangelical revivalist mind, also required a profound empathic identity with the poor.

This movement was unfortunately an aberration in the American religious scene. Remember that the famous Philadelphia Baptist preacher **Russell Conwell** (left) was preaching his famous sermon "Acres of Diamonds" to millions of people. Religious "giants" like Andrew Carnegie expressed the ethic most clearly in an article entitled "The Gospel of Wealth" (1889). In general, mainline Christianity praised wealth and unabashedly used it as a yardstick for spirituality. Riches were a sure sign of godliness, and they stressed the power of money to do good deeds.

This attitude is in direct contrast with that of men like **D. L. Moody** (above), who never made a general appeal for money. And, while the Revivalists did not extol poverty, they saw the poor as being victims of systemic evil rather than congenitally lazy people.

Moody, Gladden, and others became some of the best late 19th-century American social engineers. They understood firsthand the structural and environmental causes of poverty and social oppression. They offered, for their day, quite sophisticated and enlightened social welfare interventions. Fresh air programs, homes for single women, farm colonies—these were really very elaborate and in some cases expensive and very successful. While some of their programs were temporary, hand-out charity, some programs sincerely sought for more long-term solutions. Some programs sought to move folks out of the city to rural environments, and did betray a somewhat anti-urban bias, but other solutions offered amazing answers that celebrated the city and sought to rehabilitate it—not abandon the city.

These social welfare projects were by and large marked by lay participation and leadership. This was the last era in American history in which most social welfare reform occurred through "nonprofessional volunteers." After World War I, which was after Magnuson's period, paid social welfare professionals began to replace revivalist volunteer lay persons.

The Christian social movements were permeated with egalitarianism that affirmed the ministry of women and minorities. They transcended cultural barriers—race and class prejudice. Evangelistic movements of the last half of the 19th century embraced all humankind with surprising equanimity. This openness was far ahead of even the most ardent Progressive. Rescue workers accepted African-Americans and immigrants; they loved the prostitute and the unemployed. They opened their highest offices to women (especially in the Salvation Army). To these reformers race, creed, ethnicity, and sex were illegitimate categories by which to make judgments: the only legitimate categories were "saved" or "unsaved." And, because of this, they ministered without prejudice to the needs of all.

Far from being a hindrance to social Christianity, the revivalist and holiness faith produced extensive social programs and close identification with the poor. Joining in the plight of the "least of these," those evangelistic Christians found their Lord in the slums. The ugly, dilapidated parts of Chicago, New York, and Milwaukee became the Promised Land to the revivalists. They found their destiny with God among the poor and, by their dedication, graced an otherwise bleak American social scene.

But they were not sentimentalists. They saw that they were themselves part of the problem. They saw the heaviness of environmental pressure. They were some of the first American reformers who blamed the plight of the poor partly on environmental factors rather than exclusively on congenital flaws or sheer laziness.

Assignment

Evangelist D. L. Moody and Salvation Army founder William Booth were not only committed Christian leaders, they were also some of the best social welfare reformers of the 19th century. Today, Christian evangelicals are more or less absent from the social welfare arena. We evangelicals are practitioners, but rarely do we set policy or establish innovative interventions. Why?

PIERRE JOSEPH PROUDHON

Proudhon was the first philosopher to advance a world view called anarchy. Anarchy argues that all structure—social, political, and religious—is an impediment to the development of the human spirit and identity. It would be, as it were, the preview of later existentialist views of philosophers like Jean Paul Sartre. Proudhon mistrusted all authority. By the middle of the 19th century, Proudhon was the leading left intellectual in France or, for that matter, all of Europe, far surpassing Marx's notoriety. Proudhon was among the inventors of socialism, along wih Marx and Engels. Of these, Proudhon had the profoundest effect upon the workers' movement in the 19th century and his ideas influenced some of the most notable later anarchists, including Leo Tolstoy. His views, to say the least, were the antithesis of orthodox Christianity. "Man is by nature a sinner," Proudhon admitted, "that is to say not essentially a wrongdoer but rather wrongly made, and his destiny is perpetually to re-create his idea in himself." As the reader can see, this is one of the earliest attacks on the Christian concept of sin, and therefore redemption and responsibility. It was a hop, skip, and a jump to the nihilism later developed by Sigmund Freud and other humanist thinkers. Proudhon was the worst of both worlds. On one hand, he rejected the optimism of the Enlightenment but was unwilling to accept the structure of Hegel or Hobbes. He invited the world to chaos that was finally realized in the excesses of 1960s America. Spencer and other Darwinists loved his views—for they suggested that there could be order from chaos—the bedrock of evolutionary social and biological theory.

An excerpt from Proudhon's *A Theory of Capitalism*:

Before entering upon the subject-matter of these new memoirs, I must explain an hypothesis which will undoubtedly seem strange, but in the absence of which it is impossible for me to proceed intelligibly: I mean the hypothesis of a God. To suppose God, it will be said, is to deny him. Why do you not affirm him? Is it my fault if belief in Divinity has

Pierre-Joseph Proudhon by Gaspard-Félix Tournachon, 1862.

become a suspected opinion; if the bare suspicion of a Supreme Being is already noted as evidence of a weak mind; and if, of all philosophical Utopias, this is the only one which the world no longer tolerates? Is it my fault if hypocrisy and imbecility everywhere hide behind this holy formula? Let a public teacher suppose the existence, in the universe, of an unknown force governing suns and atoms, and keeping the whole machine in motion. With him this supposition, wholly gratuitous, is perfectly natural; it is received, encouraged: witness attraction—an hypothesis which will never be verified, and which, nevertheless, is the glory of its originator. But when, to explain the course of human events, I suppose, with all imaginable caution, the intervention of a God, I am sure to shock scientific gravity and offend critical ears: to so wonderful an extent has our piety discredited Providence, so many tricks have been played by means of this dogma or fiction by charlatans of every stamp! I have seen the theists of my time, and blasphemy has played over my lips; I have studied the belief of the people,—this people that Brydaine called the best friend of God,—and have shuddered at the negation which was about to escape me. Tormented by conflicting feelings, I appealed to reason; and it is reason which, amid so many dogmatic contradictions, now forces the hypothesis upon me. A priori dogmatism, applying itself to God, has proved fruitless: who knows whither the hypothesis, in its turn, will lead us? I will explain therefore how, studying in the silence of my heart, and far from every human consideration, the mystery of social revolutions.

God, the great unknown, has become for me an hypothesis,—I mean a necessary dialectical tool. I. If I follow the God-idea through its successive transformations, I find that this idea is preeminently social: I mean by this that it is much more a collective act of faith than an individual conception. Now, how and under what circumstances is this act of faith produced? This point it is important to determine. From the moral and intellectual point of view, society, or the collective man, is especially distinguished from the individual by spontaneity of action,—in other words, instinct. While the individual obeys, or imagines he obeys, only those motives of which he is fully conscious, and upon which he can at will decline or consent to act; while, in a word, he thinks himself free, and all the freer when he knows that he is possessed of keener reasoning faculties and larger information,—society is governed by impulses which, at first blush, exhibit no deliberation and design, but which gradually seem to be directed by a superior power, existing outside of society, and pushing it with irresistible might toward an unknown goal. The establishment of monarchies and republics, caste-distinctions, judicial institutions, etc., are so many manifestations of this social spontaneity, to note the effects of which is much easier than to point out its principle and show its cause. The whole effort, even of those who, following Bossuet, Vico, Herder, Hegel, have applied themselves to the philosophy of history, has

been hitherto to establish the presence of a providential destiny presiding over all the movements of man. And I observe, in this connection, that society never fails to evoke its genius previous to action: as if it wished the powers above to ordain what its own spontaneity has already resolved on. Lots, oracles, sacrifices, popular acclamation, public prayers, are the commonest forms of these tardy deliberations of society.

The **Anarchist movement** was popular in the late 19th-century labor movement in the United States. On May 3, 1886, a strike and mass demonstrations broke out at the McCormick Reaper plant in Chicago. In ugly scenes, strikers and their supporters were killed and injured by police deployed to control the crowd. To protest this brutality, local radicals called a mass meeting at the Haymarket Square for the following day, May 4. Somewhere in the region of 2,000 people attended to hear the speakers. The mayor of Chicago attended for a time and reported the meeting to be peaceful, which he would later testify to in court. After he had left, it began to rain and numbers began to dwindle, but as the last speaker was finishing a force of around 200 police appeared at Haymarket Square, demanding that the crowd disperse, although the meeting was all but over.

"Exactly what happened next is unclear, but as the police began to disperse the crowd, a bomb was thrown from the crowd that killed one officer. In the ensuing riot, at least four workers and several more police officers were killed, and many more injured. In the following few days most known radicals in Chicago were detained and there were raids on homes, union halls, and the offices of radical newspapers" (www.thumped.com/thepath/haymarket).

Assignment

Discuss Proudhon's views of God and why his reasoning is flawed.

A CASE STUDY:
THE JOHNSTOWN FLOOD

The Johnstown Flood is a perfect example of Gilded Age excesses gone awry. On May 31, 1889, Johnstown, Pennsylvania, was devastated by the worst flood in American history. Over 2,200 were dead, with many more homeless. With a population of 30,000, it was a growing and industrious community known for the quality of its steel. Founded in 1794, Johnstown began to prosper with the building of the Pennsylvania Mainline Canal in 1834 and the arrival of the Pennsylvania Railroad and the Cambria Iron Company in the 1850s. By the end of the Civil War, Johnstown was the largest producer of rolling steel in the world. Unfortunately, though, Johnstown was built on a flood plain at the fork of the Little Conemaugh and Stony Creek rivers. Because the growing city had narrowed the river banks to gain building space, the heavy annual rains had caused increased flooding in recent years. In fact, there was flooding almost every year—one or two inches in low-lying houses. But nothing big. That would change on May 31, 1889. Fourteen miles up the Little Conemaugh, three-mile-long Lake Conemaugh was held on the side of a mountain—450 feet higher than Johnstown—by the old South Fork Dam. At 4:07 p.m., after 14 inches of rain, on the wet afternoon of May 31, 1889, Johnstowners heard a low rumble that grew to a "roar like thunder." The earthen South Fork Dam had finally broken, sending 20 million tons of water crashing down the narrow valley. Boiling with huge chunks of debris, the wall of flood water grew at times to 60 feet high, tearing downhill at 40 miles per hour, leveling everything in its path. Those caught by the wave found themselves swept up in a torrent of oily, muddy water, surrounded by tons of grinding debris, which crushed some, provided rafts for others. Many became helplessly entangled in miles of barbed wire from the destroyed wire works. It was over in 10 minutes, but for some the worst was yet to come. Darkness fell, thousands were huddled in attics, others were floating on the debris, while many more had been swept downstream to the old Stone Bridge at the junction of the rivers. Piled up against the arches, much of the debris caught fire, entrapping forever 80 people who had survived the initial flood wave.

Many bodies were never identified, hundreds of the missing never found. The cleanup operation took years, with bodies being found months later, in a few cases, years after the flood. The city regained its population and rebuilt its manufacturing centers, but it was five years before Johnstown was fully recovered. In the aftermath, most survivors laid the blame for the dam's failure squarely at the feet of the members of the South Fork Fishing and Hunting Club, a resort for business tycoons. They had bought the abandoned reservoir, then repaired the old dam, raised the lake level, and built cottages and a clubhouse in their secretive retreat in the mountains. Members were wealthy Pittsburgh steel and coal industrialists, including Andrew Carnegie and Andrew Mellon. (Source: National Park Service—U.S. Dept. of the Interior.)

Assignment

In subsequent years, after the Johnstown Flood, there was a court case in which Johnstown plaintiffs filed a civil complaint against the South Fork club owners, claiming that the owners had been warned several times that the dam was not strong enough to withstand a torrential rain. The courts uniformly ruled in favor of the club owners. Was this a fair and legal outcome? Why or why not?

Main Street, Johnstown, after the flood, by E. Benjamin Andrews, 1912 (PD-US).

WILLIAM JENNINGS BRYAN

Despite a long and distinguished political career, William Jennings Bryan (right) is best known for the decisive defeats that he endured. He was nominated three times to represent the Democratic party as their presidential candidate. Three times he was defeated. But Bryan persevered. He spoke with candor and great inspiration. He was a very strong believer and his faith greatly affected his viewpoints. In 1896 he attacked the coinage of free silver and the end of the gold standard: "You shall not press down upon the brow of labor a crown of thorns. You shall not crucify mankind upon a cross of gold." In 1925 Bryan led the prosecution of John T. Scopes, a young biology teacher charged with breaking Tennessee law by teaching Darwin's theory of evolution.

"Cross of Gold" by William Jennings Bryan, campaign speech, 1896:

My friends, we declare that this nation is able to legislate for its own people on every question, without waiting for the aid or consent of any other nation on earth; and upon that issue we expect to carry every state of New York by saying that, when they are confronted with the proposition, they will declare that this nation is not able to attend to its own business. It is the issue of 1776 over again. Our ancestors, when but three millions in number, had the courage to declare their political independence of every other nation; shall we, their descendants, when we have grown to seventy millions, declare that we are less independent than our forefathers? No, my friends, that will never be the verdict of our people. Therefore, we care not upon what lines the battle is fought. If they say bimetallism is good, but that we cannot have it until other nations help us, we reply that, instead of having a gold standard because England has, we will restore bimetallism, and then let England have bimetallism because the United States has it. If they dare to come out in the open field and defend the gold standard as a good thing, we will fight to the uttermost. Having behind us the producing masses of this nation and the world, supported by the commercial interests, the laboring interests, and the toilers everywhere, we will answer their demand for a gold standard by saying to them: You shall not press down upon the brow of labor this crown of thorns; you shall not crucify mankind upon a cross of gold.

Bryan giving a speech during his 1908 run for the presidency, photographer unknown, 1908.

Assignment

Analyze the above quote and discuss why it was so effective.

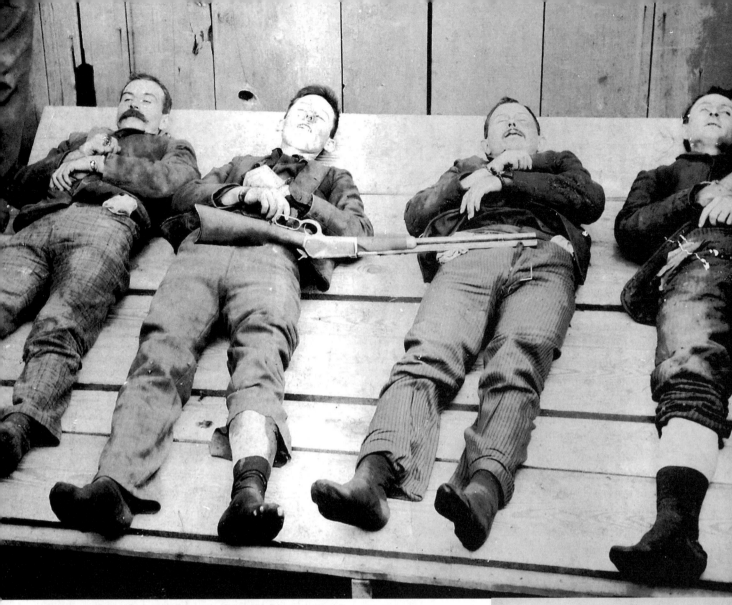

Dalton gang following the Coffeyville, Kansas, raid. Left to right: Bill Power; Bob Dalton; Grat Dalton, Dick Broadwell, photographer unknown, 1892 (PD-US).

Jesse James; last gun used, a 45 Schofield by Mesco Picture Corp, 1921.

Jesse James dead by R. Uhlman, 1882.

Chapter 20

THE WILD WEST

First Thoughts . . .

The Kiowa poet N. Scott Momaday remarked that the American West "is a place that has to be seen to be believed, and it may have to be believed in order to be seen." Ken Burns remarks, "In the West, everything seems somehow larger, grander, than life, and we now can see why so many different peoples have come to consider their own most innermost lives inextricably linked with it. Over the centuries, the West has been the repository of the dreams of an astonishing variety of people—and it has been on the long, dusty roads of the West that these dreams have crisscrossed and collided, transforming all who travelled along them, rewarding some while disappointing others." The West has been made into a morality tale too often. But it is really the story of men and women who moved to unknown territory to start a new life of hope and expectation.

Chapter Learning Objectives . . .

In chapter 20, we will examine the Wild West of truth, of legend. America without the West is unthinkable now. Yet there was nothing inevitable about our taking it. Native Americans had prior claim to its vastness, after all, and Europeans could quite easily have remained forever huddled east of the Mississippi. In resolving to move west and become a continental nation, we would exact a fearful price from those already living on the land. We will see that as we moved west we also became a different people, and it is no accident that that turbulent history—and the myths that have grown up around it—have made the West the most potent symbol of the nation as a whole, overseas as well as in our own hearts. (PBS Special "The West")

As a result of this chapter you should be able to:

1. Explain the historian Frederick Turner's thesis.

2. Write a history of your own town/community; discuss how it developed.

3. Learn from the Native American Geronimo.

4. Evaluate the American response to Native Americans.

5. Explore several outlaws.

6. Analyze Frances Willard's impact on history.

THE WILD WEST

In 1893, Frederick Jackson Turner gave an address to the American Historical Association entitled "The Significance of the Frontier in American History." In the address he stated that the frontier played a large part in the creation of American democracy. In fact, he argued that nothing was more influential in American history.

Turner was focused too much, perhaps, on one aspect of American history. However, one thing is certain: the movement westward helped America become the nation it is today. Vast open spaces, free or almost free land, Native Americans, cattle rustlers, desperados—they are all part of the story that we call the Wild West.

Americans moved westward from the time the Pilgrims landed on Plymouth Rock. It was part of our ethos.

One important help for this westward movement was the railroad. With the discovery of California gold in 1849, there was a need to connect California with the Eastern states. This need became acute with the advent of the Civil War. The answer seemed to be a railroad linking the two parts of the continent. Building a transcontinental system, however, was enormously complex and expensive. Tech-nologically, connecting the eastern and western terminuses of our country was similar to putting a man on the moon. In 1862 Congress agreed to lend hundreds of millions of dollars to two corporations—the Central Pacific in the West and the Union Pacific in the East—to construct the railroad. These companies were given little cash. However, they were given millions of acres of Western land to sell in order to pay back the loan. In effect, Western land was being used to pay for Western expansion.

With the help of thousands of Irish immigrant laborers, the Union Pacific Railroad was built westward from Omaha, Nebraska. At the same time, the Central Pacific was built eastward from northern California, edging over the Sierra Nevada through the efforts of Chinese workers imported for the job. Fighting hostile Native Americans, and horrible winters, the two railroad companies moved inexorably forward. In 1869 the two railroads joined at Promontory Summit, Utah.

Over the next 20 years, other transcontinental railroads were built: the Northern Pacific, the Great Northern, the Southern Pacific, the Atlantic and Pacific, and the Atchison, Topeka, and Santa Fe. Most were financed the same way—by massive gifts of public land that were subsequently turned into currency. Many other lines appeared, connecting the larger railroads and reaching into remote areas. Wherever the railroad went, small towns, industries, and cattle ranches were established (Stephen Ambrose, *The Transcontinental Railroad*).

Unlike Eastern towns, Western towns could be set up in organized, intentional patterns. Land was plentiful. Thanks to railroads, materials were plentiful too. Every town was set up in a rigid, symmetrical pattern. Even today towns like Abilene, Kansas, and Sacramento, California, have rectangular, well-organized streets in organized patterns. Town shapes developed in a way that functioned best. The earliest conception was a parallel arrangement with the railroad track as the axis of symmetry. This arrangement created two business streets, with buildings facing each other across railroad right-of-way. The wide strip provided symmetric town room for elevators, coal yards, cattle pens, and other businesses that needed direct access to the railroad. This industrial zone was considered undesirable for residential areas, and this is where the phrase "living on the wrong side of the tracks" arose. Rarely did both railroad-facing business streets develop equally; if First Avenue North was the major concentration, then First Avenue South became "the other (or the wrong) side of the tracks" with a row of saloons and cheap motels. This is the image we often see in Western movies (based on Internet articles).

Gold Prospector by Tony Oliver (CC BY 2.0).

Assignment

A. The following is a quote from Frederick Jackson Turner:

Ceremony for the driving of the golden spike at Promontory Summit, Utah; completion of the First Transcontinental Railroad by Andrew J Russell, 1869.

In a recent bulletin of the Superintendent of the Census for 1890 appear these significant words: "Up to and including 1880 the country had a frontier of settlement, but at present the unsettled area has been so broken into by isolated bodies of settlement that there can hardly be said to be a frontier line. In the discussion of its extent, its westward movement, etc., it can not, therefore, any longer have a place in the census reports." This brief official statement marks the closing of a great historic movement. Up to our own day American history has been in a large degree the history of the colonization of the Great West. The existence of an area of free land, its continuous recession, and the advance of American settlement westward, explain American development. Behind institutions, behind constitutional forms and modifications, lie the vital forces that call these organs into life and shape them to meet changing conditions. The peculiarity of American institutions is the fact that they have been compelled to adapt themselves to the changes of an expanding people—to the changes involved in crossing a continent, in winning a wilderness, and in developing at each area of this progress out of the primitive economic and political conditions of the frontier into the complexity of city life. Said Calhoun in 1817, "We are great, and rapidly—I was about to say fearfully—growing!" So saying, he touched the distinguishing feature of American life. All peoples show development; the germ theory of politics has been sufficiently emphasized. In the case of most nations, however, the development has occurred in a limited area; and if the nation has expanded, it has met other growing peoples whom it has conquered. But in the case of the United States we have a different phenomenon. Limiting our attention to the Atlantic coast, we have the familiar phenomenon of the evolution of institutions in a limited area, such as the rise of representative government; into complex organs; the progress from primitive industrial society, without division of labor, up to manufacturing civilization. But we have in addition to this a recurrence of the process of evolution in each western area reached in the process of expansion. Thus American development has exhibited not merely advance along a single line, but a return to primitive conditions on a continually advancing frontier line, and a new development for that area. American social development has been continually beginning over again on the frontier. This perennial rebirth, this fluidity of American life, this expansion westward with its new opportunities, its continuous touch with the simplicity of primitive society, furnish the forces dominating American character. The true point of view in the history of this nation is not the Atlantic coast, it is the Great West. Even the slavery struggle, which is made so exclusive an object of attention by writers . . . . occupies its important place in American history because of its relation to westward expansion."

Do you agree or disagree with this quote? Why or why not? Whether you agree or disagree, discuss other historical trends (e.g., military, economic, religious, etc.) that could explain the development of the American character.

B. Write a brief history of your own town/community. Discuss how the town developed. What industry or feature attracted settlers?

NATIVE AMERICANS

Railroad development and the resulting population growth all conspired to put tremendous stress on Native Americans. By the end of the 18th century the majority of Native Americans lived on reservations in the western United States. Generally, European Americans made no effort to assimilate Native Americans into American life, instead treating them as aliens and subversives. As General Sheridan observed, the only good Indian was a dead Indian. Therefore, the American military employed a systematic form of genocide unparalleled in American history.

It would be a mistake to think of Native American peoples as being one people, one nation. In fact, dozens of Native American tribes lived in the West, warred against one another—the Sioux and the Crows were mortal enemies—and manifested many different lifestyles. Some tribes, for instance, like the Sioux openly practiced polygamy. Other tribes, like the Cheyenne, practiced monogamy. Tribes like the Arapaho and Sioux, were hunters who depended on the 13 million buffalo that roamed the Great Plains. Most tribes in the Southwest, like the Apaches and Navajos, were hunters and farmers. In the Pacific Northwest, tribes like the Nez Perce were fishermen. Regardless of their lifestyle, however, every Native American community came under great stress when white American settlers moved west. Depleting natural resources, destroying the buffalo, and spreading disease, American settlers destroyed their Native American hosts.

Naturally, many Native Americans resisted white settlers. The most famous conflicts took place on the Great Plains, between Omaha, Nebraska, and Sacramento, California. Native Americans won some high-profile victories, including the defeat of George Custer on Montana's Little Bighorn River in 1876, but these were insignificant in the larger scheme of things. Native Americans were ultimately defeated and confined to reservations.

Government support given to Native Americans assigned to reservations was rarely adequate. Even that was compromised in 1887. Government policy tried to suppress native culture. The **Dawes Act of 1887** ended reservations and diminished the importance of the tribe/community by giving lands to individual tribal members. In 1934 the Wheeler-Howard Act preserved the remaining reservations, but the damage was done. Today very few Native Americans live among their own people groups.

Perhaps the most famous Native war chief was Geronimo. Geronimo (1829–1909) was chief of an Apache tribe in present-day Arizona. In 1876 the U.S. government attempted to move the Apaches from their traditional home to San Carlos, New Mexico. Geronimo then began a ten-year war against white settlements. In March 1886, the American general George Crook captured Geronimo and forced a treaty under which the Apaches would be relocated in Florida. Within a week Geronimo escaped. General Nelson Miles then pursued and captured Geronimo. Geronimo's wars were over. In fact, he converted to Christianity before he died in 1909.

The following is from Geronimo's autobiography:

About ten years later some more white men came. These were all warriors. They made their camp on the Gila River south of Hot Springs. At first they were friendly and we did not dislike them, but they were not as good as those who came first. After about a year some trouble arose between them and the Indians, and I took the war path as a warrior, not as a chief. I had not been wronged, but some of my people had been, and I fought with my tribe; for the soldiers and not the Indians were at fault.

Not long after this some of the officers of the United States troops invited our leaders to hold a conference at Apache Pass (Fort Bowie). Just before noon the Indians were shown into a tent and told that they would be given something to eat. When in the tent they were attacked by soldiers. Our chief, Mangus-Colorado, and several other warriors, by cutting through the tent, escaped; but most of the warriors were killed or captured. Among the Bedonkohe Apaches killed at this time were Sanza, Kladetahe, Niyokahe, and Gopi. After this treachery the Indians went back to the mountains and left the fort entirely alone. I do not think that the agent had anything to do with planning this, for he had always treated us well. I believe it was entirely planned by the soldiers.

From the very first the soldiers sent out to our western country, and the officers in charge of them, did not hesitate to wrong the Indians. They never explained to the Government when an Indian was wronged, but always reported the misdeeds of the Indians. Much that was done by mean white men was reported at Washington as the deeds of my people.

The Indians always tried to live peaceably with the white soldiers and settlers. One day during the time that the soldiers were stationed at Apache Pass I made a treaty with the post. This was done by shaking hands and promising to be brothers. Cochise and Mangus-Colorado did likewise. I do not know the name of the officer in command, but this was the first regiment that ever came to Apache Pass. This treaty was made about a year before we were attacked in a tent, as above related. In a few days after the attack at Apache Pass we organized in the mountains and returned to fight the soldiers. There were two tribes—the Bedonkohe and the Chokonen Apaches, both commanded by Cochise.

After a few days' skirmishing we attacked a freight train that was coming in with supplies for the Fort. We killed some of the men and captured the others. These prisoners our chief offered to trade for the Indians whom the soldiers had captured at the massacre in the tent. This the officers refused, so we killed our prisoners, disbanded, and went into hiding in the mountains. Of those who took part in this affair I am the only one now living.

In a few days troops were sent out to search for us, but as we were disbanded, it was, of course, impossible for them to locate any hostile camp. During the time they were searching for us many of our warriors (who were thought by the soldiers to be peaceable Indians) talked to the officers and men, advising them where they might find the camp they sought, and while they searched we watched them from our hiding places and laughed at their failures.

After this trouble all of the Indians agreed not to be friendly with the white men any more. There was no general engagement, but a long struggle followed. Sometimes we attacked the white men, sometimes they attacked us. First a few Indians would be killed and then a few soldiers. I think the killing was about equal on each side. The number killed in these troubles did not amount to much, but this treachery on the part of the soldiers had angered the Indians and revived memories of other wrongs, so that we never again trusted the United States troops.

Assignment

A. What did Geronimo (above) say was the primary reason whites and Native Americans did not get along? Does history support Geronimo's reason?

B. If Native Americans lived in valuable mining land, or on land vital to railroad expansion, should they have been relocated? If not, what should the American government have done?

LAWMEN AND OUTLAWS

The West, its reality and myth, has played an important role in the formation of the American ethos. The heroic deeds of those who moved west, from mountain men and cowboys to homesteaders and wild Indians, have been the subject of countless artistic expressions. Wyatt Earp, Wild Bill Hickock, Kit Carson, Jesse James, among others, are the stuff of legend. American movie stars, like John Wayne and Roy Rogers, have drawn their popularity from this mythology.

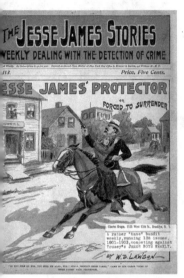

However, there is some truth in some of these legends. The "Wild" West invited individual expression and rugged individualism. Some of this free spirit was manifested in lawlessness. One particularly interesting outlaw was Billy the Kid. In 1878, Billy the Kid was capturing headlines across the American West. Three years later he was dead, shot down by lawman Pat Garrett.

Billy the Kid was born in the New York City slums, but his mother steadily worked her way west with her small family until they reached Silver City, New Mexico. There, the boy, accused of receiving stolen clothes, was jailed and escaped. Skipping to Arizona, he cowboyed, perhaps ran with rustlers, and committed his first authenticated killing. Billy fled Arizona. In 1876 or 1877, under the name of William H. Bonney, the then 17- or 18-year-old outlaw rode into Lincoln County, New Mexico. After the Apaches and plains Indians had been subdued, this 17-million-acre county had become the spoils in a violent struggle for economic and political control. Billy the Kid became notorious for his involvement in this conflict, which became known as the Lincoln County War (www.zianet.com). Billy the Kid represents the Wild West in its roughest style.

A contemporary of Billy the Kid was Jessie James. Of all the Wild West's legendary characters, few have attracted attention like the outlaw Jesse James. Some call him America's Robin Hood, while others see him as a cold-blooded killer. Jesse Woodson James was born in Kearney, Missouri, on September 5, 1847. His father, the Rev. Robert James, was a born-again Baptist minister.

During the Civil War, Jesse and his brother Frank rode with the Confederate Quantrill and participated in many bloody raids.

For the next 15 years after the Civil War, the James boys roamed throughout the U.S. robbing trains and banks of their gold, building a legend that was to live more than a century after Jesse's death in 1882 at the hands of Robert Ford. That legend was so pervasive that my own grandfather, Jesse Bayne, was named after Jesse James (www.ci.st-joseph.mo.us).

Assignment

Twice after Jesse James's death, Frank James was acquitted by juries for crimes he obviously committed. Why do Americans love to support the underdog, including convicted murderers like Jesse and Frank James?

FRANCES WILLARD

Westward expansion invited women to assume leadership in unprecedented proportions. One such woman was Frances Willard. Seven-year-old Frances Willard arrived in the Wisconsin Territory in 1846, and she lived most of her early life in the West. Her parents established a farmstead along the Rock River near Janesville. As busy as the pioneer Mrs. Willard was, she found time to homeschool Frances, who was a terrific student. Frances moved to northern Illinois at age 18.

Thanks to her parents' abiding faith and commitment to reform, in the 1870s Frances Willard emerged as a national leader within the temperance movement, an effort to limit the sale and consumption of alcoholic beverages. The temperance movement had been growing stronger in the United States for several decades, and in 1879, Willard was elected president of the Women's Christian Temperance Union (WCTU). Her leadership quickly made the WCTU an influential organization. Temperance supporters pointed to the financial and family problems often linked to the abuse of alcohol. Frances Willard also viewed temperance as part of a large social reform movement that could improve living conditions for women and make the United States a better place to live. She saw the home as the bedrock of the nation and saw herself as one of the guardians of this great institution. Through her writings she introduced thousands of women to other important social concerns: voting rights for women, safer conditions for American workers, world peace, and methods of improving the nation's schools. Willard died before many of the social reforms that she promoted became law, yet she inspired the generation of reformers who followed her. "The world is wide," Willard said, "and I will not waste my life in friction when it could be turned into momentum." She was surely a history maker (adapted from www.shsw.wisc.edu).

The following is the last formal speech that Frances Willard made before she died:

Reared in a Puritan home, I have never been inside

Frances Willard, May Wright Sewall Collection (Library of Congress), c1880 (PD-US)..

a theater a dozen times in all my life; but the other day I went to see 'The Sign of the Cross,' for I was told by those in whom I had the utmost confidence, that the play was a succession of scenes illustrating the sufferings of the early Christians under the tyrant Nero, and that no sermon could uplift the heart toward truer loyalty to Him who gave Himself for us. Believing as I do that my life has missed much by being shut out from the dramatic representations of the great scenes of history and life, and holding as I do that we Christians ought to discriminate between good and bad dramas, I went to see 'The Sign of the Cross;' and I frankly own it was to me a revelation of what the theatre might do to help humanity to the heights of purity and holiness. I could think of nothing but the Christians in Armenia, as scene after scene passed before us, full of that same utter devotion to Christ that they have sealed with their blood in this modern age, that was to witness, according to the prophecies of unbelievers, the downfall of Christianity; and as these devoted men, these saintly women, heroic youth and maidens with their heavenly faces, passed before us, I saw them often through my tears, and I never felt in my life such tender rejoicing to think that I, too, am a Christian and have been since the sweet years of my youth. I remembered the evening when in the old church at home I heard the invitation for those who would confess Christ to come forward and kneel at the altar; and if I ever thanked God for giving me courage to do so, it was in that theatre, as I remembered how I went straight to that altar without looking to the right or left, and though trembling so that I could feel my heart beat as I went forward, I was saying to myself, "He that confesseth me before men, him will I confess before my Father and the holy angels. The drama that can rejoice a human heart and renew its purpose, and vow still evermore to be a Christian, even though mine be the slowest foot in the last battalion of the wonderful militant army of Christ, is one that deserves well of all those who bear the Christian name; and I should feel it wrong not to make this frank admission, while I deprecate as strongly as anybody can, much that is put forward on the stage, and only hope that by the new discrimination constantly growing in the minds of Christian people, we may realize ere long that which has been the hope of the good since history began—namely, that the great heart of humanity may find in that union of music, picture, song, and the actual drama of life, passing before it, many of those lessons whereby we are lifted to a holier plane, delivered from the bondage of sense, and brought into harmony with God and His purposes of love toward all mankind. On my recent birthday, it came to me that I could gain no truer concept of God than by holding to the presence of Him who is the Way, Truth, and the Life; as ever tenderly smiling on me and saying, "Receive My spirit," and that in the halo round His head I saw the words, "With what measure ye mete, it shall be measured to you again." "Receive My spirit!" That is life's safest and most alluring voice,

but there will come a day when we shall utter those great words back again, "Lord Jesus, receive my spirit," and then the mystery of life, its discipline, its joys and grief, will end, and the glad mystery of death will work out the transfer to other realms of the Infinite Power." There will be other reforms and reformers when we are gone. Societies will be organized, and parties will divide on the right of men to make and carry deadly weapons, dynamite and other destructive agencies still more powerful, that human ingenuity will yet invent. They will divide on the question of the shambles, and there will be an army of earnest souls socially ostracized, as we are now, because they believe that the butcher should cease to kill and the sale of meat be placed under the ban of law. There will be a great movement to educate the people so that they will use neither tea, coffee, nor any of the numerous forms of anodynes and sedatives that are now tempting millions to deterioration and death, and which will more strongly affect the finer brain tissues of more highly developed men and women. Long after the triumph of the temperance reform has universally crystallized upon the statute books; long after the complete right of woman to herself and to the unlimited exercise of all her beneficent powers is regarded as a matter of course; long after the great trust of humanity takes to itself the earth and, the fullness thereof as the equal property of all, there will remain reforms as vital as any I have mentioned, and on them the people will group themselves in separate camps even as they do today. And it is not improbable that the chief value of the little work that we have tried to do on this small planet, lies in the fact that we have been, to some extent, attempered by it, we have become inured to contradiction, and may be useful either in coming invisibly to the help of those who toil in the reforms of the future, or we may be waging battles for God upon some other star.

Assignment

One Christian teacher observed that believers should be fervent disciples of Christ cleverly disguised as lawyers, doctors, housewives, etc. Explain how this quote summarizes the life of Frances Willard.

A young Oglala girl sitting in front of a tipi, with a puppy beside her, probably on or near Pine Ridge Reservation by John C. H. Grabill, 1891.

AFRICAN-AMERICAN HISTORY: THE GREAT MIGRATION

First Thoughts . . .

For many African-Americans, the years after the Civil War were much like the years before the War. While blacks were legally free, economically and socially they were still in bondage. "Jim Crow" laws made sure of this. The demon of racism manifested itself in unjust laws promulgated by white government to maintain its hegemony over its black population.

Chapter Learning Objectives . . .

In chapter 21 we will examine the state of race relations in the United States from 1865 to 1933. We will be disturbed by the continued injustice, inspired by the courage of men like Booker T. Washington, and challenged by the problems yet to be solved in this nation.

As a result of this chapter you should be able to:

1. Analyze the theory of "marginalization" where a minority group purposely decides to remain separate from mainstream culture.

2. Discuss theories advanced by African-American writers like Shelby Steele who called his community to assess the "content of its character."

3. Research the Great Migration and examine its effect on your community.

4. Understand why African-Americans were treated differently from other American ethnic groups.

5. Evaluate the movement in the Great Migration from rural Southern areas to Northern urban areas.

6. Analyze why the United States Supreme Court ignored Jim Crow laws for so many years.

THE GREAT MIGRATION

The Civil War changed little for many blacks, who, though legally free, were still in bondage economically and socially due to the **"Jim Crow" laws**. Racism manifested itself now in unjust laws promoted by white government to maintain dominance hegemony over the black population.

A sort of African-American revolution occurred in the early 20th century when millions of African-Americans migrated to Northern cities. The so-called Great Migration is one of the most powerful images of black resistance to racism. As surely as the Puritans left England to form a New Jerusalem in North America, many African-Americans left Alabama, Mississippi, and Arkansas to seek out a New Israel in Detroit, Chicago, and Boston. The Great Migration was the greatest transfer of a population group in world history. In the sense that African-Americans were leaving a place of unhappy circumstances to seek a better life elsewhere, it was also one of the greatest protest movements in world history.

Most African-Americans throughout this century have looked to the Northern urban setting as the "Promised Land." The North was African-America's "Diaspora."

Lucy Ariel Williams wrote:

Huh! de wurl' ain't flat
An' de wurl' ain't roun'
Jes' one long strip
Hangin' up an' down
Since Norf is up
an' Souf is down,
an' Hebben is up,
I'm upward boun'!

The first wave of migration occurred from about 1900 to 1940. From 1900 to 1955 most blacks moved from Southern agrarian centers to Northern cities. And, from 1955 to the present, rural areas continued the main source of African-Americans moving into cities. The migration, then, of African-Americans to Northern and Western cities was inexorable and unstoppable since before 1940.

The Great Migration to the North was primarily caused by the availability of jobs and the hope that racism would be absent or abated in the North. During World War I, and later when foreign immigration was severely limited by nativistic fears, jobs were abundantly available. Wages in the North were considerably higher than in the South. The welfare capitalism prevalent in a larger northern company were infinitely more appealing than the cotton mill in Macon, Georgia. And, Woolworths was a better place to buy something than the mom-and-pop store in Tupelo, Mississippi. This was part of the "pull" North. Racism, though, was never absent or abated.

At the same time, the "push" was a series of economic setbacks in the rural South—the boll weevil and tightened credit. By 1900 the mechanical cotton picker had made the sharecropper system obsolete. The sharecropper system began in the years after the Civil War as the means by which cotton planters' need for a great deal of cheap labor was satisfied. The issue of the labor supply was important because it was really the issue of race. Cotton planters no longer needed large numbers of African-American people to pick their cotton, and inevitably the nature of African-American society and of race relations changed. Racial relations, never

Jim Crow, published. by Hodgson, 111 Fleet Street & Turner & Fisher, c1835.

very good, became worse when whites no longer needed black labor. This partially explained the surge in nativism and increased Ku Klux Klan activity in the early 1920s.

Again, the demon of racism reared its ugly head in the Northern cities. African-Americans were as profitably exploited by white Northerners as they had been by white Southerners. This exploitation was painfully clear to the African-American community. Segregation assured that whites would retain some social status no matter what their socioeconomic situation. A South Carolina mill owner warned his white mill hands that manufacturers planned to place them "on the same basis as a free Negro." This owner was appealing to the whites' greatest fear: loss of independence by sinking to "Negro status."

Southern society at the beginning of the Great Migration was a feudal-like society, not unlike what existed before the Civil War. Every big farm was a fiefdom; sharecroppers lived their lives within a few miles of their homes. The sudden ending of slavery in 1865 did not mean an equally sudden end of fear on the part of African-Americans. Martin Luther King, Jr., on a visit to an Alabama plantation in 1965, was amazed to meet sharecroppers who had never seen United States currency. Education usually ended with the eighth grade. Many homes were rough two- or three-room shacks on the edge of a treeless cotton field. There was no plumbing, and the only heat came from a wood-burning stove. There was no electricity, usually the roof leaked, and families slept two and three to a bed. Most white Southerners made every effort to keep the African-American sharecropper system isolated from the rest of Southern society. Isolation enhanced control. Limited reward, control, and then exploitation emerged as inescapable themes of American racial history.

During the first half of the 20th century, race was essentially a Southern issue. After the Great Migration it was an American issue. The South, and only the South, had to deal with the contradictions of segregation. But the African-American migration to the city made segregation and racism national issues.

The African-American community demographic center shifted from a rural Southern base to an urban—Northern and Southern—base. But needs and wants remained the same. With this Great Migration came many dreams, hopes, and expectations that were not satisfied. And great anger resulted. The first great attempt of national assimilation occurred during the Great Migration. It was an unmitigated failure.

Life was not much better in the North. In many ways it was worse. In 1910, there were 10 million black heirs of the slave system. Many now lived in Northern cites. They occupied the bottom of the ladder of American society. They died younger, they were sick more, they were hungry most of the time. Many could not read, many did not have jobs. Northern migrations did not appreciably improve African-American life.

African-Americans in the city:

> A new type of Negro is evolving—a city Negro. He is being evolved out of those strangely divergent elements of the general background. And this is a fact overlooked by those students of human behavior. . . . In ten years, Negroes have been actually transported from one culture to another.
> —Charles S. Johnson, 1925

Charles Johnson knew that he was part of a cultural revolution—the Great Migration. This mass exodus brought increased hope that life would be better in the urban North. The deterioration of this hope was fertile ground for contemporary racial anger.

A scene in the ghetto, Hester Street by B.J. Falk, c1902.

The Northern city stood as a fitting symbol of this hope. American Northern cities stretched along a main street— there was no beginning or ending. The city with its myriad possibilities felt like it would be better than the rural South. The city, however, became a metaphor for what went wrong with race relations in America.

African-Americans moved to the urban setting only to find that the same problems that existed in Mississippi also existed in Detroit. This in fact was not lost on African-American leaders Martin Luther King and Malcolm X. They began their protest movements in the cities.

Slaves were brought to America primarily as agricultural workers in the rural South and as laborers and house servants in the urban North. After the American Revolution, the invention of the cotton gin increased the need for slaves. Before 1900 the African-American urban population grew very slowly, if at all, as European immigrants filled the need for unskilled labor. In the urban setting African-Americans were in competition with immigrants for jobs and opportunities. This competition explained why there was often friction between African-Americans and other urban immigrant groups for most of American history.

The life of antebellum African-American freemen in the city presaged later urban experience. Unable to vote, segregated in all sectors of public life, urban African-Americans had to look for their identity and well-being inside the African-American community itself. Thus, vital communities arose in places like Harlem in New York City as a result of ghettoization.

Ghettoization is a term that arose in the 20th century to describe the systematic accumulation of poor Americans into sections of urban America. The term became synonymous with poor housing and substandard living conditions, but it was much more. A ghetto was a breeding ground for crime, illegitimacy, and drug abuse. It maintained de facto segregation in most cities. Housing in the city was centered around three issues: adequacy, distribution, and safety. On all three issues ghetto housing came up short.

Within the ghetto some African-Americans forged strong community ties and nurtured cultural specialties. But, as we shall see, ghettoization overall had a devastating effect on most black Americans.

It was in the period from roughly 1870 to 1915 that most African-American ghettos were formed in the United States. From 1915 to the present these ghettos were expanded. Housing patterns, like all other parts of the African-American experience, were framed by racism. African-Americans continued to flood into the North during World War I. And this trend continued into the 1920s. Only 50 African-Americans, for instance, worked for the Ford Motor Company in 1916 Detroit. But there were 2,500 in 1920 and 10,000 in 1926. The African-American population of Chicago increased from 44,000 in 1910 to 234,000 in 1930. Cleveland's African-American population grew eightfold between 1910 and 1930 (Gary Nash, Julie Jeffrey, et al., *The American People: Creators of a Nation and a Society*, Vol. 2, p. 796). In 1940, 77 percent of African-Americans still lived in the South—49 percent in the rural South. But already millions were coming. The first wave of the Great Migration occurred from about 1900–1940. Between 1910 and 1970, 6.5 million African-Americans moved from the South to the North; 5 million of them moved after 1940, during the time of the mechanization of cotton farming. By 1970, African-American society had become decidedly northern and urban. Some scholars argue that toward the end of the Great Migration the main source was from Southern urban areas, and in the West, two main sources are the Northern urban areas and the western edge of the South.

There was no uniform way that African-American ghettos grew in the North. For instance, whereas the flat terrain of most Northern cities concentrated African-Americans into one or two large, homogeneous communities, Pittsburgh's hilly topography isolated them in six or seven communities. In Washington, D.C., the African-American community concentrated in adjacent alleys. And so forth. In general, African-Americans lived mainly in tenements and alley dwellings that they did not own. When they migrated from the South, they naturally settled in neighborhoods where other African-Americans lived—since many family members were part of these urban communities. Blacks who did own a home were often forced by economic circumstances to take in boarders. They clustered, too, in the city's lowest-paying, least-skilled occupations. Unlike their immigrant counterparts, they could not choose to live or work anywhere they wanted. African-Americans were barred from the city's economic mainstream, and they entered local industry only after the First World War.

Race relations in the city and country were framed by white supremacy. Social relations of slavery gave way to an informal code of exclusion and discrimination, which in turn evolved into legally and mandated separation and disenfranchisement. The essence of African-American life was pervasive powerlessness. There was an irony of accommodative resistance—the implications of compromises necessary to build institutions and to occupy anomalous roles—that touched every African-American life. They occupied a peculiar place in the South, and their acceptance of that place determined their survival. Every black American knew that this was true in the white South; what they did not anticipate was that racism also had a nefarious hold over the white North. Whether in the Southern countryside or in the Northern city, racism remained an inescapable demon.

At first, in Northern cities, African-American newcomers reveled in newfound freedom. But they were quickly absorbed into a deadly paradox: They could sit anywhere they wished on the trolley, but their children went to separate schools. In most cities they could vote, but there were no African-American candidates. They were accepted by relatives, but often rejected by other indigenous African-Americans and nearly always rejected by other immigrant groups. Education was better; housing was better; jobs were better. But the dream was compromised by hostility and prejudice. By the middle 1960s, the dream had soured altogether.

And the Klan was present in the North too. For instance, Robert and Helen Lynd's seminal social history study of Middletown, New York, showed that with the rise of the Klan in the 1920s and with the increase of ethnic and racial migration, racism was very much present. "Negroes are allowed under protest in the schools but not in the larger motion picture houses or in Y.M.C.A. or Y.W.C.A.... Negro children must play in their own restricted corner of the Park." In the local newspaper, Middletown black news was featured separately from Middletown white news. Northern urban society clearly saw two Americas emerging as surely as two had existed in the Southern agrarian society. White privilege in the North was as strong as it was in the South.

Racism mitigated any economic gains that were everywhere available in the capitalistic society arising in most cities. If an African-American migrant was fortunate enough to possess a skilled trade and could gain entrance to the union controlling the craft—which was doubtful—then he might prosper. But even the adequately compensated artisan or industrial worker had to return each night to live in the least desirable section of the city. Gains in industry by African-Americans during World War I and the 1920s were substantial, but after World War I, and during the Great Depression, African-Americans were the first ones to be let go.

African-Americans, in another way, were out of step with other labor developments. For instance, while other Northern workers were shifting from manual to nonmanual employment, from blue-collar to white-collar work, African-Americans did not share in much of this upward mobility. The number of African-Americans in white-collar

An African-American man drinking at a "colored" drinking fountain in Oklahoma City, Oklahoma by Russell Lee CC-BY-SA 3.0, 1939.

jobs was 2.8 percent in 1910, 3.8 percent in 1920, and by 1930, 4.6 percent In fact, by 1930, over two-thirds of the African-American population was still working in unskilled jobs. There was no ethnic group in such a position. As the African-American community braced for the Great Depression, it found itself in a particularly vulnerable position.

African-American patron going in colored entrance of the Crescent Theatre in Belzoni, Mississippi, on a Saturday afternoon by Marion Post Wolcott CC-BY-SA 3.0, 1939.

Assignment

A. Research the Great Migration and examine its effect on your community.

B. African-Americans, 1865-1900, were treated much differently from other American ethnic groups. While other groups inhabited ethnic enclaves, their residence was commonly limited to two or at most three generations. Then they could blend into American culture. African-Americans, however, could not do that. Race and racial discrimination were a ubiquitous reality for blacks throughout their American experience. Whether it was 1767 Philadelphia, 1876 Atlanta, 1890 Detroit, 1920 Chicago, or 1950 Cleveland, the urban African-American experience was structured by discrimination, unequal competition, and a lack of political rights. All advances in standard of living, housing, and political power were inevitably mitigated by racism. The city taught African-Americans an unforgettable lesson: racial discrimination could never be escaped. This was a bitter pill for the African-American community to swallow. Why have African-Americans been treated differently from other ethnic groups?

C. Most African-Americans moved from Southern farms to Northern ghettos. While the ghetto served as a springboard for other ethnic groups, the blacks rarely managed to escape it. The increase in residential segregation that accompanied black ghetto development was, again, dramatic in the 20th century. Although there were black enclaves in many cities in the 19th century, in no case was the overwhelming majority of a city's black population concentrated in one neighborhood with densities of 75 percent to 90 percent. Instead, blacks inhabited several neighborhoods in modest numbers and shared territory with nonblack groups. But in the 20th century, while ethnics were enjoying residential dispersion, blacks were being funneled into Watts and other ghettos. For no other group in America has residential segregation increased so uniformly. Why?

D. African-Americans in post–Civil War America were marginalized—or placed outside mainstream American society. Professor Sang Lee, Princeton Theological Seminary, using the works of H. Richard Niebuhr as a reference point, argued that minorities are now and always were treated in a "marginal" way in American society and therefore should interpret reality through this reality. He calls the "marginalized community" to "free our churches, at least once in a while, from their captivity under idolatrous ethnocentrism wherever it may be found, so that our churches will become the household of God where all peoples, black and white, yellow and brown, will be affirmed in the beauty of their particularity and not in the delusion of any one's superiority" (from *The Princeton Seminary Bulletin*, January 1995). Dr. Lee's application to the African-American experience is obvious. In other words, Dr. Lee suggests that African-Americans simply should give up on trying to integrate into American society and create their own segregated institutions. Agree or disagree.

E. The African-American writer Shelby Steele offers fresh perspectives, too, on the African-American experience. Steele argues that if America is ever to achieve true racial harmony, its citizens must start by examining their own attitudes and preconceptions. Steele argues that the American racial problem is both a white and a black problem. Agree or disagree.

BOOKER T. WASHINGTON

Booker Taliaferro Washington was the foremost African-American educator of the late 19th and early 20th centuries. Born a slave on a small farm in the Virginia backcountry, he moved with his family after emancipation to work in the salt furnaces and coal mines of West Virginia. After completing a secondary education at Hampton Institute, he taught school and experimented briefly with law and the ministry. In 1881 he founded Tuskegee Normal and Industrial Institute in Alabama. Washington defied many African-American and white leaders alike by advocating self-sufficiency among African-Americans.

A passage from Washington's *The Awakening of the Negro*:

First, it must be borne in mind that we have in the South a peculiar and unprecedented state of things. It is of the utmost importance that our energy be given to meeting conditions that exist right about us rather than conditions that existed centuries ago or that exist in countries a thousand miles away. What are the cardinal needs among the seven millions of colored people in the South, most of whom are to be found on the plantations? Roughly, these needs may be stated as food, clothing, shelter, education, proper habits, and a settlement of race relations. The seven millions of colored people of the South cannot be reached directly by any missionary agency, but they can be reached by sending out among them strong selected young men and women, with the proper training of head, hand, and heart, who will live among these masses and show them how to lift themselves up.

"Atlanta Compromise Address" by Booker T. Washington (1856–1915):

Mr. President and Gentlemen of the Board of Directors and Citizens:

Booker T. Washington by Harris & Ewing, 1905 (PD-US).

One-third of the population of the South is of the Negro race. No enterprise seeking the material, civil, or moral welfare of this section can disregard this element of our population and reach the highest success. I but convey to you, Mr. President and Directors, the sentiment of the masses of my race when I say that in no way have the value and manhood of the American Negro been more fittingly and generously recognized than by the managers of this magnificent Exposition at every stage of its progress. It is a recognition that will do more to cement the friendship of the two races than any occurrence since the dawn of our freedom.

Not only this, but the opportunity here afforded will awaken among us a new era of industrial progress. Ignorant and inexperienced, it is not strange that in the first years of our new life we began at the top instead of at the bottom; that a seat in Congress or the state legislature was more sought than real estate or industrial skill; that the political convention or stump speaking had more attractions than starting a dairy farm or truck garden.

A ship lost at sea for many days suddenly sighted a friendly vessel. From the mast of the unfortunate vessel was seen a signal, "Water, water; we die of thirst!" The answer from the friendly vessel at once came back, "Cast down your bucket where you are." A second time the signal, "Water, water; send us water!" ran up from the distressed vessel, and was answered, "Cast down your bucket where you are." And a third and fourth signal for water was answered, "Cast down your bucket where you are." The captain of the distressed vessel, at last heeding the injunction, cast down his bucket, and it came up full of fresh, sparkling water from the mouth of the Amazon River. To those of my race who depend on bettering their condition in a

Booker Washington and Theodore Roosevelt at Tuskegee Institute, photographer unknown, 1905.

foreign land or who underestimate the importance of cultivating friendly relations with the Southern white man, who is their next-door neighbor, I would say: "Cast down your bucket where you are"—cast it down in making friends in every manly way of the people of all races by whom we are surrounded.

Cast it down in agriculture, mechanics, in commerce, in domestic service, and in the professions. And in this connection it is well to bear in mind that whatever other sins the South may be called to bear, when it comes to business, pure and simple, it is in the South that the Negro is given a man's chance in the commercial world, and in nothing is

Residence of Booker T. Washington, Tuskegee Institute, Alabama, photographer unknown, c1906.

this Exposition more eloquent than in emphasizing this chance. Our greatest danger is that in the great leap from slavery to freedom we may overlook the fact that the masses of us are to live by the productions of our hands, and fail to keep in mind that we shall prosper in proportion as we learn to dignify and glorify common labour, and put brains and skill into the common occupations of life; shall prosper in proportion as we learn to draw the line between the superficial and the substantial, the ornamental gewgaws of life and the useful. No race can prosper till it learns that there is as much

Washington's wealthy friends included Andrew Carnegie and Robert C. Ogden, seen here in 1906 while visiting Tuskegee Institute by Frances Benjamin Johnston, 1906

dignity in tilling a field as in writing a poem. It is at the bottom of life we must begin, and not at the top. Nor should we permit our grievances to overshadow our opportunities.

To those of the white race who look to the incoming of those of foreign birth and strange tongue and habits for the prosperity of the South, were I permitted I would repeat what I say to my own race, "Cast down your bucket where you are." Cast it down among the eight millions of Negroes whose habits you know, whose fidelity and love you have tested in days when to have proved treacherous meant the ruin of your firesides. Cast down your bucket among these people who have, without strikes and labour wars, tilled your fields, cleared your forests, builded your railroads and cities, and brought forth treasures from the bowels of the earth, and helped make possible this magnificent representation of the progress of the South. Casting down your bucket among my people, helping and encouraging them as you are doing on these grounds, and to education of head, hand, and heart, you will find that they will buy your surplus land, make blossom the waste places in your fields, and run your factories. While doing this, you can be sure in the future, as in the past, that you and your families will be surrounded by the most patient, faithful, law-abiding, and unresentful people that the world has seen.

As we have proved our loyalty to you in the past, in nursing your children, watching by the sick-bed of your mothers and fathers, and often

following them with tear-dimmed eyes to their graves, so in the future, in our humble way, we shall stand by you with a devotion that no foreigner can approach, ready to lay down our lives, if need be, in defense of yours, interlacing our industrial, commercial, civil, and religious life with yours in a way that shall make the interests of both races one. In all things that are purely social we can be as separate as the fingers, yet one as the hand in all things essential to mutual progress.

There is no defense or security for any of us except in the highest intelligence and development of all. If anywhere there are efforts tending to curtail the fullest growth of the Negro, let these efforts be turned into stimulating, encouraging, and making him the most useful and intelligent citizen. Effort or means so invested will pay a thousand per cent interest. These efforts will be twice blessed—"blessing him that gives and him that takes."

There is no escape through law of man or God from the inevitable: The laws of changeless justice bind oppressor with oppressed; And close as sin and suffering joined; We march to fate abreast.

Nearly sixteen millions of hands will aid you in pulling the load upward, or they will pull against you the load downward. We shall constitute one-third and more of the ignorance and crime of the South, or one-third its intelligence and progress; we shall contribute one-third to the business and industrial prosperity of the South, or we shall prove a veritable body of death, stagnating, depressing, retarding every effort to advance the body politic.

Gentlemen of the Exposition, as we present to you our humble effort at an exhibition of our progress, you must not expect overmuch. Starting thirty years ago with ownership here and there in a few quilts and pumpkins and chickens (gathered from miscellaneous sources), remember the path that has led from these to the inventions and production of agricultural implements, buggies, steam-engines, newspapers, books, statuary, carving, paintings, the management of drug stores and banks, has not been trodden without contact with thorns and thistles. While we take pride in what we exhibit as a result of our independent efforts, we do not for a moment forget that our part in this exhibition would fall far short of your expectations but for the constant help that has come to our educational life, not only from the Southern states, but especially from Northern philanthropists, who have made their gifts a constant stream of blessing and encouragement.

The wisest among my race understand that the agitation of questions of social equality is the extremest folly, and that progress in the enjoyment of all the privileges that will come to us must be the result of severe and constant struggle rather than of artificial forcing. No race that has anything to contribute to the markets of the world is long in any degree ostracized. It is important and right that all privileges of the law be ours, but it is vastly more important that we be prepared for the exercise of these privileges. The opportunity to earn a dollar in a factory just now is worth infinitely more than the opportunity to spend a dollar in an opera-house.

In conclusion, may I repeat that nothing in thirty years has given us more hope and encouragement, and drawn us so near to you of the white race, as this opportunity offered by the Exposition; and here bending, as it were, over the altar that represents the results of the struggles of your race and mine, both starting practically empty-handed three decades ago, I pledge that in your effort to work out the great and intricate problem which God has laid at the doors of the South, you shall have at all times the patient, sympathetic help of my race; only let this be constantly in mind, that, while from representations in these buildings of the product of field, of forest, of mine, of factory, letters, and art, much good will come, yet far above and beyond material benefits will be that higher good, that, let us pray God, will come, in a blotting out of sectional differences and racial animosities and suspicions, in a

W. E. B. Du Bois (1868–1963), cofounder of the National Association for the Advancement of Colored People (NAACP) by Cornelius Marion (C.M.) Battey, 1918 (PD-US).

determination to administer absolute justice, in a willing obedience among all classes to the mandates of law. This, coupled with our material prosperity, will bring into our beloved South a new heaven and a new earth.

Assignment

W. E. B. Du Bois, another African-American leader, and contemporary of Booker T. Washington, was greatly bothered by the above speech, and other things that Washington wrote. Du Bois felt that Washington was too "accommodating" to white Americans. "When Mr. Washington apologizes for injustice, he does not rightly value the privilege and duty of voting, belittles the emasculating effects of caste distinctions, and opposes the higher training and ambition of our higher minds." Do you agree or disagree?

PRIMARY SOURCES

The following is a letter written by an African-American:

Lutcher, Louisiana, May 13, 1917

Dear Sir: I have been reading the *Chicago Defender* and seeing so many advertisements about the work in the north I thought to write you concerning my condition. I am working hard in the south and can hardly earn a living. I have a wife and one child and can hardly feed them. I thought to write and ask you for some information concerning how to get a pass for myself and family. I don't want to leave my family behind as I cant hardly make a living for them right here with them and I know they would fare hard if I would leave them. If there are any agents in the south there haven't been any of them to Lutcher if they would come here they would get at least fifty men. Please sir let me hear from you as quick as possible. Now this is all. Please don't publish my letter, I was out in town today talking to some of the men and they say if they could get passes that 30 or 40 of them would come. But they haven't got the money and they don't know how to come. But they are good strong and able working men. If you will instruct me I will instruct the other men how to come as they all want to work. Please don't publish this because we have to whisper this around among ourselves because the white folks are angry now because the negroes are going north.

The following are examples of Jim Crow Laws:

(Created after the Civil War by Southern states to control African-Americans)

> No person or corporation shall require any white female nurse to nurse in wards or rooms in hospitals, either public or private, in which negro men are placed.
>
> Alabama

All passenger stations in this state operated by any motor transportation company shall have separate waiting rooms or space and separate ticket windows for the white and colored races.

Alabama

It shall be unlawful to conduct a restaurant or other place for the serving of food in the city, at which white and colored people are served in the same room, unless such white and colored persons are effectually separated by a solid partition extending from the floor upward to a distance of seven feet or higher, and unless a separate entrance from the street is provided for each compartment.

Alabama

All marriages between a white person and a negro, or between a white person and a person of negro descent to the fourth generation inclusive, are hereby forever prohibited.

Florida

The schools for white children and the schools for negro children shall be conducted separately.

Florida

Every person ... operating ... any public hall, theatre, opera house, motion picture show or any place of public entertainment or public assemblage which is attended by both white and colored persons, shall separate the white race and the colored race and shall set apart and designate...certain seats therein to be occupied by white persons and a portion thereof, or certain seats therein, to be occupied by colored persons.

Virginia

About lynching, by Robert L. Zangrando:

Between 1882 (when reliable statistics were first collected) and 1968 (when the classic forms of lynching had disappeared), 4,743 persons died of lynching, 3,446 of them black men and women. Mississippi (539 black victims, 42 white) led this grim parade of death, followed by Georgia (492, 39), Texas (352, 141), Louisiana (335, 56), and Alabama (299, 48). From 1882 to 1901, the annual number nationally usually exceeded 100; 1892 had a record 230 deaths (161 black, 69 white). Although lynchings declined somewhat in the twentieth century, there were still 97 in 1908 (89 black, 8 white), 83 in the racially troubled postwar year of 1919 (76, 7, plus some 25 race riots), 30 in 1926 (23, 7), and 28 in 1933 (24, 4).

A man lynched from a tree. LOC, 1925 (PD-US).

Drinking fountain on the Halifax County Courthouse (North Carolina). Photo by John Vachon for U.S. Farm Security Administration, 1938 (PD-US).

Editorial cartoon criticizing the usage of literacy tests for African Americans as a qualification to vote. Cartoon shows Uncle Sam writing on wall, "Eddikashun qualifukashun. The Black man orter be eddikated afore he kin vote with US Wites, signed Mr. Solid South." Illustration in: *Harper's Weekly*, v. 23 (1879 Jan. 18), p. 52 (PD-US).

Several Tuskegee airmen. at Ramitelli, Italy, by the Tuskegee Airmen 332nd Fighter Group pilots, 1945 (PD-US).

Assignment

A. Write a letter of response to the Louisiana African-American (page 255) seeking work in the North.

B. Why would white Southerners lynch defenseless African-Americans?

C. Why did the United States Supreme Court ignore the Jim Crow laws, Lutcher, for so many years?

HISTORICAL DEBATE

The historical debate about African-Americans is as full of emotion as American society itself is. As long as the United States continues to be race-conscious, African-American history will be full of acrimony and recrimination. It can be argued that no white American historian can accurately portray African-American history—perhaps all are tainted by prejudice. That may be true. What do you think? Clearly, though, there are several emerging themes in African-American history.

First there was the period of paternalism—1865–1920. Historians in this era saw African-Americans as docile, benevolent wards of American whites. Typically, slavery is seen as a positive institution that benefitted both whites and African-Americans. Reconstruction was an unmitigated disaster. The second was the period of transition—1920s to 1950s—when the attitudes of scholars toward African-Americans began to change and racist views were no longer accepted. This generation of historians argued that African-American slaves were treated poorly in antebellum and Reconstruction America. This group refused to accept the notion that African-Americans were inherently inferior. They argued forcefully that African-Americans were then and always had been victims of prejudice. The third was the period of maturation—the 1950s and 1960s—when white liberal scholars intentionally ferreted out prejudice in American history. This generation of historians sought to make race a secondary issue, if not absent from historical discussions. The fourth was the period of accommodation—the 1970s to the present—when historians recognized that African-American history was a subculture and needed to be examined separately from white American history (Grob and Billias 127). During this period several African-American historians dominated the scene and moved the discussion toward more African-American nationalistic themes. They argued that race has been and always will be a part of American history, and historians refuse to discuss it at their own peril.

African-American Historical Debate Summary

Paternalism 1865–1920	Transition 1920–1950	Maturation 1950–1970	Accmmodation 1970–Present
African-Americans are perceived as being inferior to whites.	African-Americans are beginning to be seen separately from white history.	African-Americans are finally seen as victims of prejudice.	African-Americans are studied separately from white history.

Assignment

Summarize the different ways that historians have presented African-American history.

Company D, 8th Illinois Volunteer Regiment, Photographer unknown, 1899.

Chapter 22

AMERICA BECOMES A WORLD POWER

First Thoughts . . .

Imagine being born in the 1830s when virtually no one in America had heard of the Philippines, only to find your nation is fighting a war there 70 years later! You would have lived through some of the most aggressive expansionism in American history. Expansionism has enjoyed a long and colorful life in the history of the USA. In its broadest application, expansionism is the concept of expanding the geographic holdings of a given country, either by attempting to annex surrounding territory or by gaining control of lands that are located far away from the mother country. Often expansionism includes military aggression, with the idea of establishing political hegemony over a new area.

Chapter Learning Objectives . . .

In chapter 22 we will examine America's inexorable path to world power, 1865–1917. We will see America fight its first Vietnam-type "police action" in the Philippines and annex territory in Hawaii. We will join Teddy Roosevelt and his Rough Riders as they storm San Juan Hill. Finally, we will pause to evaluate whether our expansionist policies were motivated by God or by greed.

As a result of this chapter you should be able to:

1. Evaluate a popular 19th-century view that white Europeans had a "white man's burden" to share their so-called superior culture with perceived "unfortunate" people groups around the world.

2. Discuss conditions under which a nation has the duty or right to invade or to take over another country or culture.

3. Discover arguments Americans offered in support of imperialism and foreign expansion.

4. Discuss how Christians can share their faith without forcing their culture on unevangelized people groups.

5. Evaluate primary source letters from American soldiers in the Philippine insurrection.

6. Compare the "police action" in the Philippines in 1900 to the "police action" in Vietnam from 1965 to 1975.

7. Analyze anti-Catholicism in American foreign policy from 1900 to 1912.

8. Summarize former President Teddy Roosevelt's speech on the Monroe Doctrine.

AMERICA BECOMES A WORLD POWER

During the last quarter of the 19th century, the United States emerged as a world power. Its industrial and agricultural productivity, large size, growing population, and modern navy gave it a prominence that could not be ignored. In 25 years America became a dominant power in both the Caribbean (Cuba, Puerto Rico) and the Pacific (the Philippines). At the same time, America was to fight and lose its first Vietnam-type war.

Historians Charles and Mary Beard argue that Americans were always a "world power":

It has now become a fashion, sanctioned by wide usage and by eminent historians, to speak of America, triumphant over Spain and possessed of new colonies, as entering the twentieth century in the rôle of "a world power," for the first time. Perhaps at this late day, it is useless to protest against the currency of the idea. Nevertheless, the truth is that from the fateful moment in March 1775 when Edmund Burke unfolded to his colleagues in the British Parliament the resources of an invincible America, down to the settlement at Versailles in 1919 closing the drama of the World War, this nation has been a world power, influencing by its example, by its institutions, by its wealth, trade, and arms the course of international affairs. And it should be said also that neither in the field of commercial enterprise nor in that of diplomacy has it been wanting in spirit or ingenuity.

When John Hay, Secretary of State, heard that an American citizen, Perdicaris, had been seized by Raisuli, a Moroccan bandit, in 1904, he wired his brusque message: "We want Perdicaris alive or Raisuli dead." This was but an echo of Commodore Decatur's equally characteristic answer, "Not a minute," given nearly a hundred years before to the pirates of Algiers begging for time to consider

Mary Ritter Beard of New York, photographer unknown, 1914.

whether they would cease preying upon American merchantmen. Was it not as early as 1844 that the American commissioner, Caleb Cushing, taking advantage of the British Opium War on China, negotiated with the Celestial Empire a successful commercial treaty? Did he not then exultantly exclaim: "The laws of the Union follow its citizens and its banner protects them even within the domain of the Chinese Empire"? Was it not almost half a century before the battle of Manila Bay in 1898, that Commodore Perry with an adequate naval force "gently coerced Japan into friendship with us," leading all the nations of the earth in the opening of that empire to the trade of the Occident? Nor is it inappropriate in this connection to recall the fact that the Monroe Doctrine celebrates in 1923 its hundredth anniversary.

Several times in the last part of the 19th century Americans had to decide whether or not to participate in global expansion. There were some major concerns. For one thing, some Americans still felt antipathy toward Europe. The American Revolution was scarcely a century away from their memory. Americans felt natural affinity with colonized people groups since they themselves were once a colony. Besides, America has always taken the side of the underdog. Some even wondered if America's democratic institutions were compatible with an overseas empire and the large military establishment that would be required to maintain it (Billias, et al., p. 173). Others rejected the concept of empire because they opposed bringing under the American flag racial and ethnic groups they deemed inferior.

At the same time, Americans wanted a piece of the imperialist pie. European competitors were grabbing the best seaports and market locations and some Americans felt that they needed to be in the action, while other Americans did not want to assume the hated role of colonial power.

European nations had no pangs of conscience. They were dominating with reckless abandon the whole African continent and making inroads into Asia. France was dominating North Africa. England was everywhere in Africa and Germany and had established a presence in East Africa.

America, though, hesitated. Even when instability in Latin America invited an American intervention, she hesitated. Until the last two years of the 19th century America sent no armies or navies to try to gain territory or win influence in Latin America (this discussion is informed by Ed Fenton, *A New History of the United States*).

This was to change during the Spanish-American war, a topic to which we will return later.

Before America was prepared to participate in colonial expansion she needed an ideology of expansion. This took two decidedly different directions.

First, there was the so-called Anglo-Saxon Mission or the White Man's Burden.

The Reverend Josiah Strong, a leader in American missions, best expressed this view:

The two great needs of mankind are, first, a pure, spiritual Christianity, and second, civil liberty. It follows, then, that the Anglo-Saxon, as the great representative of these two ideas, is divinely commissioned to be his brother's keeper. Add to this the fact of his rapidly increasing strength in modern times, and we have well-nigh a demonstration of his destiny.

"Uncle Sam's New Class in the Art of Self-Government." Harper's Weekly, August 27, 1898.

Connected to the notion of white man's burden was the idea of Social Darwinism. Namely, uncivilized nations (according to Western standards) exhibited behaviors of inferiority that invited judgment calls. If nations differed little from animals preying on one another, shouldn't more civilized nations take over? After all, survival of the fittest ideas demanded that the best, the strongest, the most capable dominate the weaker. The advancement of superior culture demanded it.

Next, there were several opportunities that arose at the end of the 19th century. In 1867, America purchased Alaska from Russia. In 1879, it joined England and Germany in an agreement to provide military protection for the Samoan Islands in the South Pacific. Later, America acquired a naval base at Pearl Harbor, Hawaii (Fenton p. 537).

With a naval base in the Pacific it was patently obvious that a canal must be built between the Atlantic and the Pacific Ocean. This was to be discussed for several years, but it was President Theodore Roosevelt who ultimately championed the cause and made it happen.

Politics, of course, had a great impact on foreign policy. In particular, President William McKinley led America into war, into the next destiny, and into unbridled imperialism. McKinley was elected president in 1896. He grew up in the

Midwest. Deeply attached to his mother, who was a committed Christian, he gave his heart to Christ when he was very young. He devoted himself to the Lord's purposes, and to a great extent, he was a believer cleverly disguised as president! McKinley's first term coincided with a movement away from isolationism, which advocated staying out of foreign entanglements. As foreign trade grew, so did demands for foreign territory and a larger navy, so that markets could more easily be developed and controlled. When there was unrest in Cuba, McKinley saw this as an opportunity to insinuate an American presence into Latin America. Although McKinley wanted peace, he made little effort to curb the growing demand for Cuban intervention. Yellow or exaggerated journalism, especially in New York newspapers owned by the competing publishers Joseph Pulitzer and William Randolph Hearst, was enormously successful in creating demand for U.S. intervention in Cuba. Theodore Roosevelt, McKinley's assistant secretary of the navy, also supported intervention. On February 15, 1898, the American battleship *Maine* exploded in the harbor at Havana, Cuba, and 266 men died. No one knew who—if anyone—caused the explosion, but most Americans felt certain that it was the work of Spain. Further study in 1976 showed conclusively that the explosion was a spontaneous combustion in the coal room, but Congress, on April 25, 1898, declared war on Spain.

The Spanish-American War was a splendid little war where more soldiers died of yellow fever than of combat. It lasted less than four months, from April to August 1898. Two American victories, one by Admiral George Dewey at Manila Bay in the Philippines and the other by Admiral William Sampson at Santiago Bay in Cuba, quickly terminated hostilities. The United States acquired Guam, the Philippines, and Puerto Rico. However, many Filipinos resented American presence as much as Spanish. As a result, a costly guerrilla war was fought for three years. The Philippine action was unfortunate—a sideshow, really. After several million dollars and countless lives lost, the conflict ended with a partial American victory in 1902.

At the same time, several Pacific Ocean acquisitions were obtained. McKinley supported the annexation of

Assassination of President McKinley by T. D. Walker, c1905.

Hawaii in 1898. In 1899, by agreement with Britain and Germany, the United States also acquired the island of Tutuila in Samoa Islands. McKinley further consolidated the nation's position in East Asia with the Open Door Policy, which announced that all nations should have equal access to China's markets. This lead to an armed conflict called the Boxer Rebellion. President McKinley was assassinated in 1901 and Vice President Theodore Roosevelt became president.

The year 1900 marked the beginning of a new century full of hope and optimism. Clearly America was on the go.

A bump in the road was the Philippine Insurrection. A particularly controversial event in American history was the Philippine–American War, also known as the Philippine War of Independence or the Philippine Insurrection (1899-1902). It was an armed military conflict between the Philippines and the United States that arose from the struggle of the First Philippine Republic to gain independence following annexation (to annex means to "own" a territory) by the United States at the end of the Spanish American War. The war was part of a series of conflicts in the Philippine struggle for independence, preceded by the Philippine Revolution and the Spanish-American War.

The conflict began on June 2, 1899, when the Philippines declared war against the United States, and it ended on July

4, 1902, after President Emilio Aguinaldo's surrender. However, guerilla fighters continued to harass Americans. This continued until 1913. This was the first time, but not the last time, that American became entangled in nation building across the globe.

Opposition to the war inspired Mark Twain to found the Anti-Imperialist League on June 15, 1898. The war had a devastating effect on the Philippine people but did not generate much opposition at home. There were almost a million casualties. Americans sustained 8,000 casualties.

Such unfortunate losses did not stop American expansionist ambitions. Americans were, as Teddy Roosevelt said, "walking softly and carrying a big stick." Roosevelt formed a new policy called the New Nationalism. He gave part of the speech that follows before union veterans of the Grand Army of the Republic in 1910 (Fenton, 515).

A part of Theodore Roosevelt's speech before union veterans of the Grand Army of the Republic in 1910:

> One of the main objectives in every wise struggle for human betterment has been to achieve equality. In the struggle for this goal, nations rise from barbarism to civilization. . . The New Nationalism puts the national interests before sectional or personal interests (Fenton, 515).

Roosevelt was a very popular president. His popularity allowed him to take America places that she had never been—particularly in foreign policy. He advanced the imperialist aims of McKinley. In particular, he introduced the Roosevelt Corollary, which updated and strengthened the Monroe Doctrine's rejection of possible European claims to territory in the Americas. Roosevelt made it clear that America was committed to keeping the peace and status quo whatever the cost. With that in mind, Roosevelt oversaw the construction of the Panama Canal. Still, the United States carefully avoided foreign alliances—especially those with European powers. Subsequent administrations were not so blessed as Roosevelt's administration—Taft found himself drawn into several Latin American wars. The same was true for Woodrow Wilson, who was drawn into a "police action" in Mexico.

World War I, 1914–1918, was initially perceived as a European war. Americans wanted nothing to do with it. Once committed to going to war, though, in 1917, America intended to make the world—using Woodrow Wilson's words—"safe for democracy." We will discuss this in greater detail in our next chapter.

Virtually no one wanted to go to war in 1914 and it was not clear whose side to join anyway. Americans were sympathetic toward England and her allies, but millions of Americans were of German descent. Support for the allies was never a foregone conclusion. However, by 1917, unrestricted submarine warfare and German mistakes made American participation on the allied side inevitable. While casualties on the American side were relatively light when compared to other allied casualties—more Americans died in the 1919 flu epidemic—Americans nonetheless were horrified and resolved never again to be involved in foreign wars. This view was further cemented when Woodrow Wilson was humiliated at the infamous Treaty of Versailles. In fact, Congress refused to ratify the Treaty of Versailles and made its own peace with Germany. This movement toward isolationism ushered in the excesses and hedonism of the 1920s.

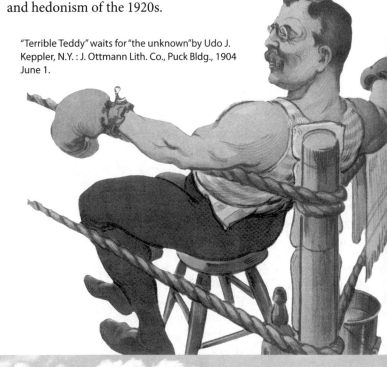

"Terrible Teddy" waits for "the unknown" by Udo J. Keppler, N.Y. : J. Ottmann Lith. Co., Puck Bldg., 1904 June 1.

Panorama of Pacific entrance of the canal. Left: Pacific and Puente de las Americas (Pan American Highway); far right: Miraflores locks (CC BY 2.0).

Assignment

A. Published in *McClure's Magazine* in February of 1899, Rudyard Kipling's poem "The White Man's Burden" appeared at a critical moment in the debate about imperialism within the United States. The Philippine-American War began on February 4, and two days later the U.S. Senate ratified the Treaty of Paris that officially ended the Spanish-American War, ceded Puerto Rico, Guam, and the Philippines to the United States, and placed Cuba under U.S. control. Although Kipling's poem mixed exhortation to empire with sober warnings of the costs involved, imperialists within the United States latched on to the phrase "white man's burden" as a euphemism for imperialism that seemed to justify the policy as a noble enterprise (Jim Zwick).

In the post–modern era of equality and individualism it is easy to discount the above statement as archaic, self-serving, and naive. Yet to millions of Americans in 1899 it made a great deal of sense. I want you to take a position with which you do not agree: support Kipling's argument.

Write a letter to a friend supporting Kipling's view.

The White Man's Burden
by Rudyard Kipling
McClure's Magazine 12 (Feb. 1899)

Take up the White Man's burden–
    Send forth the best ye breed—
Go, bind your sons to exile
    To serve your captives' need;
To wait, in heavy harness,
    On fluttered folk and wild—
Your new-caught sullen peoples,
    Half devil and half child.

Take up the White Man's burden—
    In patience to abide,
To veil the threat of terror
    And check the show of pride;
By open speech and simple,
    An hundred times made plain,
To seek another's profit
    And work another's gain.

Take up the White Man's burden—
    The savage wars of peace—
Fill full the mouth of Famine,
    And bid the sickness cease;

And when your goal is nearest
    (The end for others sought)
Watch sloth and heathen folly
    Bring all your hope to nought.

Take up the White Man's burden—
    No iron rule of kings,
But toil of serf and sweeper—
    The tale of common things.
The ports ye shall not enter,
    The roads ye shall not tread,
Go, make them with your living
    And mark them with your dead.

Take up the White Man's burden,
    And reap his old reward—
The blame of those ye better
    The hate of those ye guard—
The cry of hosts ye humour
    (Ah, slowly!) toward the light:—
"Why brought ye us from bondage,
    Our loved Egyptian night?"

Take up the White Man's burden—
    Ye dare not stoop to less—
Nor call too loud on Freedom
    To cloak your weariness.
By all ye will or whisper,
    By all ye leave or do,
The silent sullen peoples
    Shall weigh your God and you.

Take up the White Man's burden!
    Have done with childish days—
The lightly-proffered laurel,
    The easy ungrudged praise:
Comes now, to search your manhood
    Through all the thankless years,
Cold, edged with dear-bought wisdom,
    The judgment of your peers.

B. Next, write a letter to a friend criticizing Kipling's poem.

C. Under what conditions does a nation have the duty or right to invade or to take over another country or culture?

D. The Bible teaches that Jesus Christ is the only Savior for mankind. Given that fact, is expansion into another country for the purpose of sharing the faith justifiable? Should a Christian impose his faith on other people even if they do not want to be converted?

PRESIDENT THEODORE ROOSEVELT

The Roosevelt Corollary to the Monroe Doctrine by Roosevelt, 1904:

It is not true that the United States feels any land hunger or entertains any projects as regards the other nations of the Western Hemisphere save such as are for their welfare. All that this country desires is to see the neighboring countries stable, orderly, and prosperous. Any country whose people conduct themselves well can count upon our hearty friendship. If a nation shows that it knows how to act with reasonable efficiency and decency in social and political matters, if it keeps order and pays its obligations, it need fear no interference from the United States. Chronic wrongdoing, or an impotence which results in a general loosening of the ties of civilized society, may in America, as elsewhere, ultimately require intervention by some civilized nation, and in the Western Hemisphere the adherence of the United States to the Monroe Doctrine may lead the United States, however reluctantly, in flagrant cases of such wrongdoing or impotence, to the exercise of an international police power.

If every country washed by the Caribbean Sea would show the progress in stable and just civilization which with the aid of the Platt amendment Cuba has shown since our troops left the island, and which so many of the republics in both Americas are constantly and brilliantly showing, all question of interference by this Nation with their affairs would be at an end. Our interests and those of our southern neighbors are in reality identical. They have great natural riches, and if within their borders the reign of law and justice obtains, prosperity is sure to come to them. While they thus obey the primary laws of civilized society they may rest assured that they will be treated by us in a spirit of cordial and helpful sympathy.

President Theodore Roosevelt by the Pach Brothers, 1906.

We would interfere with them only in the last resort, and then only if it became evident that their inability or unwillingness to do justice at home and abroad had violated the rights of the United States or had invited foreign aggression to the detriment of the entire body of American nations. It is a mere truism to say that every nation, whether in America or anywhere else, which desires to maintain its freedom, its independence, must ultimately realize that the right of such independence can not be separated from the responsibility of making good use of it.

Charge of the Rough Riders at San Juan Hill by Frederic Remington. In reality, they assaulte[d] San Juan Heights and the portion later calle[d] "Kettle Hill" by the Americans, c1909 (PD-US[).]

In asserting the Monroe Doctrine, in taking such steps as we have taken in regard to Cuba, Venezuela, and Panama, and in endeavoring to circumscribe the theater of war in the Far East, and to secure the open door in China, we have acted in our own interest as well as in the interest of humanity at large. There are, however, cases in which, while our own interests are not greatly involved, strong appeal is made to our sympathies. . . . In extreme cases action may be justifiable and proper. What form the action shall take must depend upon the circumstances of the case; that is, upon the degree of the atrocity and upon our power to remedy it.

Assignment

To whom was President Roosevelt addressing this 190[4] speech and what major points was he making?

Roosevelt and his "Rough Riders" taken by William Dinwiddie, capturing San Juan Hill, the bloodiest campaign of the war (PD-US).

PRIMARY SOURCES

During the U.S. war in the Philippines between 1899 and 1904 (which grew out of the Spanish-American War that had erupted in 1898), ordinary American soldiers shared the nationalist zeal of their commanders and pursued the Filipino "enemy" with brutality and sometimes outright lawlessness. Racism, which flourished in the United States during that period, led American soldiers to repeatedly assert their desire "to get at the niggers." The following are excerpts from letters by American soldiers in the Philippines writing home about the Philippine Insurrection. Published in 1899 by the Anti-Imperialist League, it bore the provocative subtitle: "Being Materials for a History of a War of Criminal Aggression."

Insurgent (Filipino) soldiers in the Philippines by US Army Signal Corps, 1899

Private Fred B. Hinchman, Company A, United States Engineers, writes from Manila, February 22:

At 1:30 o'clock the general gave me a memorandum with regard to sending out a Tennessee battalion to the line. He tersely put it that "they were looking for a fight." At the Puente Colgante [suspension bridge] I met one of our company, who told me that the Fourteenth and Washingtons were driving all before them, and taking no prisoners. This is now our rule of procedure for cause. After delivering my message I had not walked a block when I heard shots down the street. Hurrying forward, I found a group of our men taking pot-shots across the river, into a bamboo thicket, at about 1,200 yards. I longed to join them, but had my reply to take back, and that, of course, was the first thing to attend to. I reached the office at 3 p.m., just in time to see a platoon of the Washingtons, with about fifty prisoners, who had been taken before they learned how not to take them.

Arthur H. Vickers, sergeant in the First Nebraska Regiment:

I am not afraid, and am always ready to do my duty, but I would like someone to tell me what we are fighting for.

General Reeve, lately colonel of the 13th Minnesota Regiment:

I deprecate this war, this slaughter of our own boys and of the Filipinos, because it seems to me that we are doing something that is contrary to our principles in the past. Certainly we are doing something that we should have shrunk from not so very long ago.

Sergeant Elliott, of Company G, Kansas Regiment:

Most of the general officers think it will take years, and a large force of soldiers, to thoroughly subjugate the natives. And the unpleasant feature of this is that unless the conditions change radically there will be few soldiers who will care to stay there.

There's no use trying to conceal the fact that many of the men over there now, especially the volunteers, are homesick, and tired of fighting way off there, with nothing in particular to gain. There is not one man in the whole army now in the Philippines who would not willingly give up his life for the flag if it was necessary, but it isn't pleasant to think about dying at the hands of a foe little better than a savage, and so far away from home. And the thought of its not ending for several years is not an especially pleasant one, either.

Guy Williams, of the Iowa Regiment:

The soldiers made short work of the whole thing. They looted every house, and found almost everything, from a pair of wooden shoes up to a piano, and they carried everything off or destroyed it. Talk of the natives plundering the towns: I don't think they are in it with the Fiftieth Iowa.

Charles Bremer, of Minneapolis, Kansas:

Company I had taken a few prisoners, and stopped. The colonel ordered them up in to line time after time, and finally sent Captain Bishop back to start them. There occurred the hardest sight I ever saw. They had four prisoners, and didn't know what to do with them. They asked Captain Bishop what to do, and he said: You know the orders, and four natives fell dead.

Sylvester Walker, of the Twenty-third Regulars, February 20:

There has not been a night for the last ten days we have not had fighting. Our force is too weak, and we cannot spare any more men, and will have to wait for more troops. Then we will have hard fighting, for there are so many that, no matter how many we kill or capture, it doesn't seem to lessen their number.

Assignment

A. First, react to these letters. How do they make you feel about the war in the Philippines? If you were a congressman, would it cause you to withdraw your support? Next, argue against U.S. policy in the Philippines, circa 1900.

B. Argue that the preceding quotes are inflammatory and not indicative of what truly happened in the Philippines. You will need to do some research to answer this question.

C. Compare the "police action" in the Philippines in 1900 to the "police action" in Vietnam from 1965 to 1975.

Police Action	War in the Philippines	War in Vietnam
Years of duration		
Combatants		
Goals		
Response in U.S.		
Outcome		

MORE PRIMARY SOURCES

Assignment

A. In the following passage, Rev. Strong, a pastor, is quoting Charles Darwin (below) to support his argument that American Christian whites are a superior race and obligated to share their largesse with less fortunate people groups. In what ways is this quote by a churchman a warning of what might be a problem for Christianity in other areas? In other words, by quoting Darwin, in what ways is Rev. Strong opening Pandora's Box, so to speak?

Josiah Strong, an advocate of imperialism and American expansionism, wrote:

Mr. Darwin is not only disposed to see, in the superior vigor of our people, an illustration of his favorite theory of natural selection, but even intimates that the world's history thus far has been simply preparatory for our future, and tributary to it. He says: "There is apparently much truth in the belief that the wonderful progress of the United States, as well as the character of the people, are the results of natural selection; for the more energetic, restless, and courageous men from all parts of Europe have emigrated during the last ten or twelve generations to that great country, and have there succeeded best. Looking at the distant future, I do not think that the Rev. Mr. Zincke takes an exaggerated view when he says: 'All other series of events—as that which resulted in the culture of mind in Greece, and that which resulted in the Empire of Rome—only appear to have purpose and value when viewed in connection with, or rather as subsidiary to, the great stream of Anglo-Saxon emigration to the West.'"

B. Both Cuba and the Philippines were Roman Catholic nations. Some Protestant Americans argued that America should conquer these and other Roman Catholic nations so that Protestant "truth" could be reasserted. Agree or disagree with the following assessment of Roman Catholicism.

One Protestant contemporary wrote:

Let it be remembered, it is the boast of Rome that she never changes. The principles of Gregory VII and Innocent III [these popes asserted Roman-Catholic dominance over all faiths] are still the principles of the Roman-Catholic Church. And had she but the power, she would put them in practice with as much vigor now as in past centuries. Protestants little know what they are doing when they propose to accept the aid of Rome in the work of Sunday exaltation. While they are bent upon the accomplishment of their purpose, Rome is aiming to re-establish her power, to recover her lost supremacy. Let the principle once be established in the United States that the church may employ or control the power of the state; that religious observances may be enforced by secular laws; in short, that the authority of church and state is to dominate the conscience, and the triumph of Rome in this country is assured.

God's Word has given warning of the impending danger; let this be unheeded, and the Protestant world will learn what the purposes of Rome really are, only when it is too late to escape the snare. She is silently growing into power. Her doctrines are exerting their influence in legislative halls, in the churches, and in the hearts of men. She is piling up her lofty and massive structures in the secret recesses of which her former persecutions will be repeated. Stealthily and unexpectedly she is strengthening her forces to further her own ends when the time shall come for her to strike. All that she desires is vantage ground, and this is already being given her. We shall soon see and shall feel what the purpose of the Roman element is. Whoever shall believe and obey the word of God will thereby incur reproach and persecution."

Oregon Volunteer Infantry on firing line, March 14, 1899 (PD-US). (Inset) Wounded American soldiers, Santa Mesa, Mania, 1899.

WORLD WAR I AND THE ROARING '20s

First Thoughts . . .

Now things accelerate. From the relatively negative experience that World War I brought to America, to the revolutionary 1920s, and then the sobering Great Depression, these momentous events all occurred in one lifetime! Americans were born in dirty back-room shacks and died in antiseptic hospitals. Americans went to church in buggies and 30 years later they are flying airplanes across the country. What an age!

Chapter Learning Objectives . . .

In chapter 23 we will examine how America was drawn into World War I. We will visit the kaleidoscopic world of 1920 flappers. Finally, we will taste the dust whirling across the Great Plains and feel the throes of poverty grabbing most Americans.

As a result of this chapter you should be able to:

1. Discuss the steps that led America to enter a war (i.e., World War I) that she initially had no intentions of entering.

2. Argue when/if war is justified.

3. Discuss what positive and negative effects public education had on American families.

4. Evaluate what role technological developments (e.g., iPods) have played in the lives of teenagers today compared with the roles the automobile, movies, telephone, and radio played in the lives of teens in the 1920s.

5. Analyze why some Christian public figures like William Jennings Bryan are treated shabbily by the press.

6. Delineate the causes of the Great Depression.

7. Speculate what it would be like if your family suddenly lost all its income.

WORLD WAR I

A few years ago, while my wife and her mother vigorously reconnoitered and then exploited local shopping opportunities in a Scottish highland community, my father-in-law and I walked around the same quaint village. In the center of this small community—no more than 1,200 people—there was the obligatory World War I monument. We see the same sort of thing in America, so I was not at first particularly impressed. For instance, in my hometown there is a memorial to American war dead in the center of our town square. In fact, there is a list of American World War veterans on the wall at our local post office too. While waiting for stamps, I read through the names almost every day. The ones who died have a small, impressive gold star next to their names. Only two names have gold stars.

However, on the monument in the central square of this beautiful Scottish village, there were 128 names. This community of about 850, during World War I, lost 128 of its citizens in that war. The implication is that twice as many were permanently maimed. Indeed, on one summer day in 1916, along the Somme river in northern France, some towns lost their entire local soccer team and most of the volunteer fire company. Suppose there were about 425 men who lived in this community in 1914. By 1918 more than 250 of them had been killed or wounded. Can you imagine the impact World War I had on the small, backwater Scottish community I visited? It had lost almost half its male population. As I traveled across Scotland, many other towns had similar stories to tell. Time after time such carnage is unique to European communities; there is nothing to compare in American history.

For the last time, during World War I, the British army recruited its regiments by county and town, but the trend was exaggerated in the Kitchener armies recruited for World War I. The British army made a promise very early on, when

World War I Veteran's Parade, Bain Collection, date unknown.

they weren't sure how many volunteers they were going to get, that if a volunteer joined up as part of a group, the group would be kept together. The phrase was: "Join up with your pals or your chums, your friends." This certainly maintained morale and increased recruitment numbers—until entire groups were killed together on some nameless battlefield in France.

Of the 65 million men who participated in the war, more than 10 million were killed and more than 20 million wounded. The term "World War I" did not come into general use until after World War II. Before that, the war was known as the "Great War." World War I was the first total war. No war had been quite like it. All the participating countries mobilized all their resources to achieve victory on the battlefield. The home front, then, became as important as the battlefield. In fact, in some places in France, the home front was only a few miles behind the war front.

What caused this conflagration to spread all over the world?

By 1900, the world was changing with increasing speed and pronounced intensity that was sheer fancy. Space, time, and physical dimensions had been transformed in a way that a century before, no one could have imagined. Telephones defied time and space to take the human voice instantly across time and space. Cities were lit by electricity all the time. There was less darkness by 1900 than in any previous century. It did not take 80 days to travel around the world; 80 hours was a possibility. Indeed there were limitless possibilities—mankind could even travel under the ocean.

People were moving from the farm to the city. Advances in medicine and surplus led to a substantial population explosion, so that by 1914, countries had a surplus of young men to throw into the war engine. The expansion of education, the expansion of entertainments, the emergence of the film industry, newsreels—all brought to masses of people visions of worlds they had never thought available. All this progress conspired to give people realistic reasons to hope that things would be better tomorrow than they were today.

It could also mean intense frustration for those poor people who did not participate in this progress. Inequality and injustice among classes had always existed. However, with the advent of the national media, people now knew about it. And this suddenly mattered a whole lot. People wanted more things and more control over their lives.

The industrial revolution had increased productivity and made possible a flourishing military. Europe knew the industrial basis of military power. In order to provide for the

President Woodrow Wilson, Harris & Ewing Collection, c1912.

steel and the machinery necessary to stand up to the powers of the day, countries knew that they had to grow economically if they were to have military power. And the converse was also true. If they wished to have military power, they needed to build a strong, thriving industrial infrastructure. Nations—no matter how large—that did not have a strong industrial base lost wars. This was why Russia with its massive army and large land mass lost to lowly Japan in 1905. The same was true 30 years earlier when industrial Germany defeated agrarian France in the Franco-Prussian War of 1870. This was a fundamental anxiety that plagued all European nations and contributed in no small way to the War when it finally came less than two decades into the new century. The instability of European life arose because Germany grew too rapidly for the old political structures, and nobody knew how to change them, short of war.

Once a nation felt it was threatened, it had to move quickly to meet the challenge. In the European industrial states, the nation that mobilized first usually won the resulting war. Thus, small conflict could easily become big world wars.

That is exactly what happened in an obscure part of the Balkans.

In the summer of 1914, a Serbian nationalist—a citizen of the aging Austro-Hungarian Empire—assassinated the

Archduke Francis Ferdinand, the heir to the throne of Austria-Hungary. Germany, perhaps foolishly, issued a blank check to Austria-Hungary and said it would support her no matter what. Russia, whose ally was Serbia, said the same thing. Then, everyone rushed to declare war on each other so that they could mobilize first. Quickly a local, insignificant conflict became a world war.

On June 28, the heir to the Austro-Hungarian throne was assassinated at Sarajevo, the capital of Bosnia, an Austrian province occupied mainly by Serbs. With a view to stopping Serbian agitation for independence, Austria-Hungary laid the blame for this incident on the government of Serbia (which was indeed responsible) and made impossible demands. Austro-Hungarian ally Germany proposed that the issue should be regarded as "an affair which should be settled solely between Austria-Hungary and Serbia," meaning that Serbia was doomed. Russia was an ally of Serbia. Great Britain proposed a settlement by mediation, but she, too, was an ally of Russia and France. Germany backed up Austria to the limit. That made the war inevitable. By the first five days of August, 1914 a world war was underway.

While President Woodrow Wilson promptly proclaimed the neutrality of the United States, the large majority of the American people were without doubt on the side of Great Britain and France. To them the invasion of the little kingdom of Belgium and the horrors that accompanied German occupation were terrible in the extreme.

Germany announced on and after February 18, 1915, the whole of the English Channel and the waters around Great Britain would be deemed a war zone and that every enemy ship would be destroyed. The response of the United States to the German order was swift and direct. On February 10, 1915, it warned Germany that if her commanders destroyed American lives and ships in obedience to that decree, the action would "be very hard indeed to reconcile with the friendly relations happily subsisting between the two governments." On the morning of May 1, 1915, the *Lusitania*, a British steamer, sailed from New York for Liverpool. On May 7, without warning, the ship was struck by two torpedoes and in a few minutes went down by the bow, carrying to death 1,153 persons, including 114 American men, women, and

German U-boat exhibited in London after the First World War, 1918.

children. The *Lusitania* in fact, was carrying munitions but this mattered very little to the outraged American public.

After President Wilson was reelected in 1916, he addressed "peace notes" to the European belligerents. None of the belligerents took these efforts seriously. Most ignored them.

Meanwhile, Germany renewed its aggressive submarine campaign. Between February 26 and April 2, six American merchant vessels were torpedoed, in most cases without any warning and without regard to the loss of American lives. President Wilson therefore called upon Congress to answer the German challenge. The reply of Congress on April 6 was a resolution, passed with only a few dissenting votes, declaring the existence of a state of war with Germany. Austria-Hungary at once severed diplomatic relations with the United States; but it was not until December 7 that Congress, acting on the president's advice, declared war also on that "vassal of the German government."

In many addresses at the beginning and during the course of the war, President Wilson stated the purposes that actuated our government in taking up arms. He first made it clear that it was a war of self-defense. "The military masters of Germany," he exclaimed, "denied us the right to be neutral."

In a message read to Congress on January 8, 1918,

The Lusitania at the end of the first leg of her maiden voyage, New York City, by N. W. Penfield, 1907.

Brigadier General John Pershing at General Headquarters in Chaumont, France, by 2d Lt. L. J. Rode, 1918.

President Wilson laid down his famous "fourteen points" summarizing the ideals for which Americans were fighting. They included open treaties of peace, openly arrived at; absolute freedom of navigation upon the seas; the removal, as far as possible, of trade barriers among nations; reduction of armaments; adjustment of colonial claims in the interest of the populations concerned; fair and friendly treatment of Russia; the restoration of Belgium; righting the wrong done to France in 1871 in the matter of Alsace-Lorraine; adjustment of Italian frontiers along the lines of nationality; more liberty for the peoples of Austria-Hungary; the restoration of Serbia and Romania; the readjustment of the Turkish Empire; an independent Poland; and an association of nations to afford mutual guarantees to all states great and small. On a later occasion President Wilson elaborated the last point, namely, the formation of a league of nations to guarantee peace and establish justice among the powers of the world.

On June 13, 1917, General John J. Pershing, chosen head of the American Expeditionary Forces, reached Paris and began preparations for the arrival of our troops. In June, the vanguard of the army reached France. A slow and steady stream followed. The army was enlarged from about 190,000 men to 3,665,000, of whom more than 2 million were in France when the armistice was signed (Guttenberg Archives).

On January 18, 1919, a conference of the Allied and Associated Powers assembled to pronounce judgment upon the German empire and its defeated satellites: Austria-Hungary, Bulgaria, and Turkey. The treaty was a harsh arrangement for the Central Powers. Germany was reduced by the cession of Alsace-Lorraine to France and the loss of several other provinces. Austria-Hungary was dissolved and dismembered. Russia was reduced by the creation of new states on the west. Bulgaria was stripped of her gains in the recent Balkan wars. Turkey was dismembered. Nine new independent states were created: Poland, Finland, Lithuania, Latvia, Estonia, Ukraine, Czechoslovakia, Armenia, and Hedjaz. Italy, Greece, Romania, and Serbia were enlarged by cessions of territory, and Serbia was transformed into the great state of Yugoslavia. A League of Nations was formed, but the United States Senate refused to support an American presence. This was a terrible blow to President Wilson.

Assignment

A. Discuss the steps that led America to enter a war (i.e., World War I) that she initially had no intentions of entering.

B. Identify U.S. goals that were/were not accomplished in World War I.

C. Reinhold Niebuhr, a famous theologian, initially embraced pacifism because, he argued, that World War I was a senseless war. However later he changed his mind and argued that at times war was necessary. In particular, he argued that while a man may be moral alone, in a crowd or in society he can become evil. The evil that a nation produces may demand that mankind devote itself to destroying that evil, and, if necessary, that evil nation. Niebuhr argued that war was justified—his expression is "just war"—when the evil could not be removed any other way except by force. Based on Niebuhr, the Bible, and your own views, what makes armed conflict justifiable? Once you have established your own moral baseline, discuss whether or not America was morally justified in participating in World War I; World War II; the 2001–2002 Afghan Conflict.

HISTORICAL DEBATE

Was America justified in her domination in the Philippines and Latin American countries? Were her policies a form of altruism or aggression? The debate among historians about American imperialism was in reality not merely an interpretation of the past—it was more a vision of what America ought to be (Grob, et al., p. 173). What caused America to suddenly abandon its isolationism in the post–Civil War era and to embrace imperialism? Some historians argue that it was because of economics. American business needed new markets that the American navy provided. Other historians saw imperialism as a fleeting aberration—an opportunity that arose after an unexpectedly quick military victory in the Spanish-American War. Several other historians argued that the emergence of social Darwinism provided Americans with an intellectual reason to pursue her imperialist aims. Other historians argue that World War I was an extension of imperialist policies. All of the above arguments more or less agree that imperialism grew out of domestic considerations —not foreign influences.

Assignment

Was America's involvement in World War I an extension of American expansionism? Or was it a reluctant response to a world crisis? What do you think?

"A Venerable Orang-outang", a caricature of Charles Darwin as an ape published in The Hornet, a satirical magazine, 1871 (PD-US).

PERILS OF PROSPERITY

During the 1920s, the United States experienced unparalleled prosperity. The benefits of the 19th-century industrial revolution were paying off. After World War I a postwar boom began that continued unabated until the 1929 stock market collapse. The 1920s marked the climax of the "second industrial revolution."

During the last half of the 19th century, American industry had primarily manufactured goods intended for other producers. By 1920 industry was focusing on goods and consumables such as silk stockings, washing machines, and cars (Nash, et al., *The American People*). Powering this great revolution was electricity. The technology surrounding electricity advanced as radically as space technology in the middle decades of the 20th century. Electricity has had as profound an effect on American culture as any technology in modern times.

Where electricity could not take Americans, the gasoline-powered engine did. Americans had a love affair with the auto from the beginning. There were 8,000 motor vehicles in 1900 and nearly a million in 1912. By 1929 Americans were purchasing 4.5 million cars, and by the end of that year 27 million were registered (Nash, et al., p. 787). The automobile caused American cities to expand beyond their natural barriers. Great distances could be covered by automobiles in a relatively short amount of time. For one thing, Americans could live in the suburbs and work in the cities. The census of 1920 indicated that for the first time, more Americans lived in and near cities than in the country. These advances, however, created problems.

Modern technologies, like radio and movies, promoted a national secular culture. This new culture emphasized consumption and pleasure, not discipline and sacrifice. Religious and moral values were under attack. The most famous example of this attack was the famous Scopes trial in 1925. John Scopes, a young biology teacher, broke a Tennessee law and taught evolution in his classes. He was arrested and a famous trial was held in Dayton, Tennessee. While Scopes was convicted, Fundamentalist Christianity was ridiculed. For the first time, Americans were publicly invited to mock their faith. It would not be the last time.

In 1900 Americans were regularly connected only to close friends and family. The only connection to the outside world was through an occasional old newspaper and low-circulation magazine. In spite of military victories all over the globe, Americans simply did not have a global perspective.

In a sense, World War I changed all that. It was hard to keep a farm boy home after he had seen Paris! At the same time, technological innovations brought radical changes too. By 1940, network radio linked millions of listeners together. Mass transportation, the telephone, and the automobile made it possible for people to communicate while living great distances apart (Fenton, *A New American History*, p. 561). The Sears & Roebuck catalogue and mail order catalogues like it created a common fashion culture. Americans, for the first time, regardless of socio-economic status, could wear the same type of underwear and hats! National magazines were read by millions of readers, who saw the same photographs and read the same stories. In darkened movie houses patrons cried through the same scenes, in the same movies (Fenton, p. 561). Americans, then, for the first time, had a national cultural identity as well as a national political identity.

In the middle of the 1920s, two young sociologists, Robert and Helen Lynd, made a city the object of their study and suggested certain sociological commonalities. They found some astounding statistics, values, and attitudes. For one thing, for the first time in American history, Americans no longer wished to have six or eight children. On the contrary, Americans sought to have two or three children. Quality of life issues were suddenly more important than child-bearing. The shift was from the Victorian image of child-bearing to the modern image of child-rearing (Fenton, p. 563). The former dominance of the home in the child's life was threatened. Young people spent less time in the home than their parents who grew up in the 1890s. The growth of suburbs and residential cities offered less yard space. Most important, however, was the growth of public education.

The lure of the kindergarten to four- and five-year-olds was irresistible. The invention of the high school was even more influential. Athletics, dramatics, societies all conspired to compromise the American family. Young people now drove automobiles. They participated in "dates," which replaced older notions of "courtship." As a result, the rate of out-of-wedlock pregnancies skyrocketed.

As historians put it:

The more sophisticated social life of today has brought with it another "problem" much discussed by parents. This problem is the apparently increasing relaxation of some of the traditional prohibitions upon the approaches of boys and girls to each other's persons. Here again new inventions of the last 35 years have played a part. In 1890 a "well-brought-up" boy and girl were commonly forbidden to sit together in the dark. But motion pictures and the automobile have lifted this taboo, and, once lifted, it is easy for the practice to become widely extended. Buggy-riding in 1890 allowed only a narrow range of mobility. Three to eight were generally accepted hours for riding, and being out after 8:30 without a chaperone was forbidden. In an auto, however, a party may go to a city halfway across the state in an afternoon or evening. And un-chaperoned automobile parties as late as midnight, while subject to criticism, are not exceptional" (Lynd & Lynd, quoted in Fenton, p. 564).

Not all cultural advances were bad. Young people and parents, for the first time in some cases, openly discussed private and personal issues. A more democratic form of relationship arose. Death from disease decreased. Everyone had more leisure time.

The following is a summary of the 1920s:

1920	Census reports that half the United States' population lives in cities. KDKA (the first commercial radio station) begins broadcasting in Pittsburgh.
1923	The Senate orders investigation of leasing of Teapot Dome oil reserves. President Warren G. Harding dies.
1924	National Origins Act puts quota on immigration.
1925	Scopes Trial.
1927	Charles Lindbergh flies nonstop across the Atlantic Ocean. Warner Brothers releases the first talking movie.
1929	The Stock Market crashes.

Assignment

A. Public education became widespread in the United States in the 1920s. What positive and negative effects did public education have on the American family?

B. What did the automobile, the movies, and the radio do to 1920 culture? How did these inventions affect parents' ability to control the experiences of young people?

C. How important to your life is the freedom of choice that modern technology has brought? What are the costs of this technology in human and psychological terms?

D. What technological developments (e.g., iPods) have played a role in the lives of teenagers today similar to the role played by the automobile, movies, telephone, and radio of the 1920s?

E. The whole concept of a "teenager" is a relatively late phenomenon. In fact, the word did not even enter the English language until the mid-1930s. Trace the growth of that word and speculate on why our culture felt it necessary to categorize this special group of people.

THE GREAT DEPRESSION

President Herbert Hoover had been in office only seven months when the stock market crashed. This great crash ended the Roaring 20s. The Great Depression followed. The American dream seemed to have gone sour. Most Americans blamed themselves for the Depression. Americans believed that if they worked hard enough they would prosper. This was no longer possible for millions of Americans. The Great Depression destroyed America's confidence in the future.

There had been recessions and depressions in American history but nothing close to what Americans experience in the 1930s.

In spite of President Hoover's innovative efforts, the Great Depression only worsened. When Franklin D. Roosevelt became president in 1932, Americans were ready for a change.

The Great Depression lasted from 1929 to the beginning of America's involvement in World War II (1941). Roosevelt attacked the Great Depression forcefully and with innovative tactics. His politics of intervention can be divided into two phases. He promised a "new deal" for the American people. The first was from 1933 to 1935 and focused mainly on helping the poor and unemployed. Roosevelt authorized, with Congressional support, massive spending to employ millions of people. These projects included the Civilian Conservation Corps (CCC) and the Tennessee Valley Authority (TVA). While Roosevelt did not implement socialism, he did superimpose a welfare state on a capitalistic society with controversial results.

The so-called second new deal occurred from 1935 to 1937. During this period, Roosevelt emphasized social reform and social justice. To accomplish his goals, he established the Works Progress Administration (WPA), which helped many poor people and built massive projects (like the Blue Ridge Parkway in Virginia). Next, he enacted the Social Security Act, which provided a safety net and retirement income for workers.

Finally, in 1937–1938, Roosevelt implemented a third

Herbert Hoover, photographer unknown, c1928.

new deal. He did this primarily to help homeless farmers and agricultural workers.

What caused the Great Depression?

1. Stock Market Crash of 1929 and bank failures destroyed most of America's liquid income and savings.

2. Americans stopped spending money. This accentuated the problem. Inventory accumulated. The unemployment rate rose above 25 percent which meant, of course, even less spending to help alleviate the economic situation.

3. American economic policy with Europe: a huge tariff was imposed against European imports that ultimately caused European governments to retaliate by not selling American goods.

4. Drought conditions: lowered productivity in the Midwest.

The following is a summary of the 1930s:

1932 Roosevelt is elected president.

1933 Roosevelt declares a bank holiday.

1933 Tennessee Valley Authority begins reclamation of farmland.

1933 Civilian Conversation Corps is established.

1933 Congress passes agricultural Adjustment Act.

1934 Congress passes National Industrial Recovery Act.

1935 Roosevelt establishes Works Progress Administration.

1935 Congress passes the Social Security Act.

1939 World War II begins in Europe.

The New Deal failed to stop the Great Depression. Only World War II could end the Depression. However, the New Deal convinced most Americans that their government had a moral and legal right to intervene in public and private affairs if the general good of the public demanded it. America, for better or for worse, was never to be the same.

Roosevelt and Hoover on Inauguration Day, Photograph from Architect of the Capitol, AOC no. 18241, 1933.

Assignment

A. What were the causes of the Great Depression?

B. When only 2 percent of Americans owned stock, why did America sink deeper and deeper into depression after the stock market collapsed?

C. If your family suddenly lost all its income, how would your life be affected?

Migrant Mother depicts destitute pea pickers in California, centering on Florence Owens Thompson, age 32, a mother of seven children, in Nipomo, California, by Dorothea Lange, 1936.

Chapter 24

AMERICAN LIFE: 1900–1940

First Thoughts . . .

By 1900 Americans were reading under electric lights and looking optimistically to the future. They fought and won a war but were ready to start a new decade separated from the Europe that had claimed so many of their farm boys on the plains of Ypres, Belgium. The unparalleled prosperity of the 1920s led to the worst economic collapse in the history of America. By 1940, things were improving but only at the horrible price of another European war. Yet through it all, Americans lived, endured, and persevered. This chapter is the story of our grandparents and great-grandparents, who lived during these most Spartan of all America's years.

Chapter Learning Objectives . . .

In chapter 24, we will meet Billy Sunday, one of many evangelists who captivated the public imagination and led many Americans to faith in Christ. Then we will examine the historical debate surrounding the New Deal: Was it a good or a bad thing for America? Next, we will examine the world views that significantly impacted the lives of millions of Americans. Finally, we will examine primary source material from my own grandmother, Helen Stobaugh, a true flapper, who raised a family in these turbulent times.

As a result of this chapter you should be able to:

1. Describe someone whom God has used in a major way to encourage you in your walk with the Lord.

2. Evaluate the effectiveness of the New Deal.

3. Contrast Karl Schmitt's view of power and government with a biblical understanding of the same.

4. Evaluate whether Simone de Beauvoir was a threat to a Christian view of femininity.

5. Discuss ways in which Martin Heidegger's world view clashed with Christianity.

6. Interview a relative and record an oral history.

BILLY SUNDAY

Billy Sunday was one of the greatest evangelists of all times. He was also one of the best shortstops in professional baseball. Controversial to the core, Billy often combined a solid gospel message with a radical patriotism. From famous ballplayer to famous evangelist, Billy Sunday is still remembered today for his energetic preaching style and large, successful evangelistic campaigns across the United States. In his lifetime, Billy Sunday addressed over 100 million people without the aid of loud speakers, TV, or radio. Hundreds of thousands made commitments to Jesus Christ because of the efforts of Billy Sunday!

Sunday was well known before he felt called into the ministry. He gained nationwide recognition for becoming the first player to run the bases in 14 seconds, and set records for stealing bases.

Shortly after being "saved" through the outreach of the Pacific Garden Mission in Chicago, Sunday turned down a $400-per-month baseball salary (at a time when the average worker made $480 per year) for an $84-per-month ministry position. Ball teams later offered $500 a month and even $2000 a month, but Sunday remained committed to his ministry for God. Later in life he was offered $1 million to be in the movies, but again declined in order to continue the evangelistic ministry God had called him to. He died after a heart attack in 1935 at age 73.

There is a story saying that when Billy Sunday was converted and joined the church, a Christian man put his arm on the young man's shoulder and said, "William, there are three simple rules I can give to you, and if you will hold to them you will never write 'backslider' after your name. Take 15 minutes each day to listen to God talking to you; take 15 minutes each day to talk to God; take 15 minutes each day to talk to others about God." This young convert was deeply impressed and determined to make these the rules of his life. From that day onward throughout his life he made it a rule to spend the first moments of his day alone with God and God's Word. Before he read a letter, looked at a paper or even read a telegram, he went first to the Bible so that the first impression of the day might be what he got directly from God (www. billysunday.org/).

A portion of Sunday's famous "Booze Sermon" preached in Boston, Massachusetts:

I am the sworn, eternal, and uncompromising enemy of the liquor traffic. I have been, and will go on, fighting that damnable, dirty, rotten business with all the power at my command. I shall ask no quarter from that gang, and they shall get none from me.

After all is said that can be said on the liquor traffic, its influence is degrading on the individual, the family, politics and business and upon everything that you touch in this old world. For the time has long gone by when there is any ground for arguments of its ill effects. All are agreed on that point. There is just one prime reason why the saloon has not been knocked into hell, and that is the false statement "that the saloons are needed to help lighten the taxes." I challenge you to show me where the saloon has ever helped business, education, church morals, or anything we hold dear.

You listen today and if I can't peel the bark off that damnable fallacy I will pack my trunk and leave. I say that is the biggest lie ever belched out. The wholesale and retail trade in Iowa pays every year at least $500,000 in licenses. Then, if there were no drawback, it ought to reduce the taxation 25 cents per capita. If the saloon is necessary to pay the taxes, and if they pay $500,000 in taxes, it ought to reduce them 25 cents a head. But no, the whiskey business has increased taxes $1,900,000 instead of reducing them, and I defy any whiskey man on God's dirt to show one town that has the saloon where the taxes are lower than where they do not have the saloon. I defy you to show me an instance.

Billy Sunday with Mrs. Sunday photographed at the White House today where they called on President Coolidge, photographer unknown, c1923.

Some Christian leaders criticized Billy Sunday for putting too much emphasis on social policy (e.g., prohibition) and not putting enough emphasis on the gospel message. Preaching on inebriation is well and good, they argued, but it will not get a person into heaven. What do you think?

Helen Thompson Sunday—affectionately called Ma Sunday by friends and family—lived quite a few years beyond her husband. During those years she devoted herself to her family, and to other young evangelists just starting out. One of these young men was a skinny boy from North Carolina. His first name was also Billy. His last name was Graham.

Assignment

Describe someone whom God has used in a major way to encourage you in your walk with the Lord.

HISTORICAL DEBATE

Franklin D. Roosevelt, if he was anything, was controversial. To his friends Roosevelt was a genius/innovator who skillfully guided America through some of her darkest days. To his enemies Roosevelt was a megalomaniac who destroyed ingenuity and free enterprise and replaced them with a welfare state. Historian Rexford G. Tugwell argued that Roosevelt did not go far enough—he should have given up on capitalism altogether and formed a socialist state. Henry Steele Commager argued that Roosevelt's policy was really not radical at all—it was in the spirit and ideology of early reform movements. In that sense, Commager, and then Arthur M. Schlessinger, Jr., thought that Roosevelt was pretty well on target and did what he needed to do. They argued, furthermore, it was very much an "American" solution to the problems facing the Great Depression generation. Former President Herbert Hoover and John T. Flynn wrote historical accounts of the New Deal, however, that were not flattering at all. They argued that Roosevelt had substituted for the free enterprise system one that operated upon "permanent crises" (Grob & Billias, p. 292). Richard Hofstadter, while disagreeing with Schlessinger and Hoover, saw Roosevelt's policy as being something entirely new in American history. But Hofstadter nonetheless argued that it was a good idea. "The New Deal, and the thinking it engendered," wrote Hofstadter, "represented the triumph of economic emergency and human needs over inherited notions and inhibitions."

Franklin D. Roosevelt by Elias Goldensky, 1933.

In brief, Billias and Grob describe the debate about Roosevelt in this way:

> The problem of understanding and assessing the achievements of the New Deal and its place in American history, therefore, is one whose answer will largely be determined by a series of prior assumptions about the nature of the American past and the nation's ideals in both the present and the future. To those historians whose view is that America is founded upon an atomistic philosophy—that the nation's greatness arose from the achievements of talented and ambitious individuals and was not always related to the activities of government—the New Deal will always appear as a movement alien and hostile to traditional values. . . . On the other hand, to those scholars who adhere to a corporate philosophy—that society is more than a mere aggregate of private individuals and that a

modern complex industrial economy requires a certain amount of public regulation as well as government reform—the New Deal becomes a political movement inspired by proper ideals. Instead of being an aberration in terms of the American political tradition, the New Deal was a movement consonant with previous struggles for justice and equality. Finally, to those historians who maintain that only a radical restructuring of American society could eliminate poverty, racism, war, and equality, the New Deal appears as a palliative or sham designed to gloss over fundamental defects" (Grob & Billias, p. 301).

Summary of Historical Theories about the New Deal

The New Deal was fundamentally flawed. It is a radical departure from American traditions of individual initiative and free enterprise.

The New Deal was not radical at all. It was promulgated in the same spirit of the reform movements of the middle 19th century and early 20th century.

The New Deal was fundamentally flawed, to be sure. But it was flawed because it did not go far enough. It should have taken America to a socialism utopia waiting just over the horizon.

Assignment

Which theory do you find most plausible? Why?

San Francisco, California. After 44 years of Republican administration, California gets a Democratic administration. The California "New Deal" faces same opposition as the national "New Deal", by Dorothea Lange, 1939.

PHILOSOPHERS AND WORLD VIEWS

Karl Schmitt (1888–1985)

Schmitt was a German theologian who was one of the most brilliant but disturbing philosophers of the 20th century. Schmitt, like so many brilliant men at the turn of the century, considered entering the priesthood. However, the disillusioning effect of World War I forced him to question his faith. As a result, he rejected God. Schmitt championed real politics, or in German, real politik. Schmitt openly advocated an authoritarian regime since he saw it as the only alternative to morality that, in his opinion, invited vacillation and equivocation. The state is bound by no law; thus, the individuals running the state are also not bound by any law or moral constraints. The implications are obvious. Schmitt openly supported Adolf Hitler (Oliver, *History of Philosophy*).

Simone de Beauvoir (1908–1986)

Simone de Beauvoir did more to influence modern views of women than any other single person. Her views deeply damaged the Judeo-Christian understanding of femininity. Beauvoir, working from a philosophy called existentialism, argued that women should gain their identity from their self or individuality—not from a role (e.g., in a family) or from the Bible. Especially not from the Bible. The Bible, according to de Beauvoir, was a draconian document that effectively made women subservient to male domination. She stated that throughout history women were seen as the "Other" of man. In other words, women wrongly derived their essential being from someone or something outside themselves. This, of course, was very wrong according to de Beauvoir, for whom marriage was a contract of subjugation in which the woman was bound by her unavoidable duties as a wife. This was wrong, Beauvoir argued. The woman needed to take control of her own life and this could not

Wife and child of tobacco sharecropper. Person County, North Carolina by Dorothea Lange, 1939.

happen as long as she remained in a role of servant to the man. She could not do that, de Beauvoir argued. Simone de Beauvoir and her followers devoted their lives to removing institutions and ideologies that restricted women's freedom.

A passage by Simone de Beauvoir:

She [the wife] is defined and differentiated with reference to man and not he with reference to her; she is the incidental, the inessential as opposed to the essential. He is the Subject, he is the Absolute—she is the Other . . . being codified by man, decrees that woman is inferior: she can do away with this inferiority only by destroying the male's superiority. Those interested in perpetuating present conditions are always in tears about the marvelous past that is about to disappear, without having so much as a smile for the young future. . . . It's frightening to think that you mark your children merely by being yourself. . . . It seems unfair. You can't assume the responsibility for everything you do—or don't do . . . the torment that so many young women know, bound hand and foot by love and motherhood without having forgotten their former dreams.

Martin Heidegger (1889–1976)

Heidegger supported Idealism, a philosophical school that argued that reality is an entirely cerebral affair, an affair of the mind. In other words, objects have innate quality separate from their physical reality. This concept is very similar to Plato's view of the form.

Another German philosopher, Heidegger, like Schmitt, joined the Nazi Party and openly supported Hitler. Heidegger was one of the first philosophers who would be called postmodern. Postmodernism is a philosophical movement that opposes those philosophies that it believes are typically modern, i.e., those centered around the European Enlightenment. It is therefore opposed to the idea that there can be a universal rationality or an object theory of knowledge, or in general, that there can be permanent foundations of human knowledge. For most postmodern philosophers, human thought and knowledge is thoroughly historical and contingent (*The History of Philosophy*). Martin Heidegger (1889–1976) explored the nature of Being, not through intuition but through interpretation and understanding of the "primary sources" of consciousness, as found in ordinary life. He believed that the essence of human being is not consciousness but existence, not theory but praxis—and he underlined the importance of Being and language.

The scholar Martyn Oliver describes Martin Heidegger in this way:

Heidegger believed that when we are born we are thrown into a world with pre-established norms and standards which include the tools we use to describe ourselves and our relation to the world. We are not born innately with the instruments of rationality. But Heidegger is presenting much more than a simple nurture over nature argument. For Heidegger, language is not just a medium through which we express our imperfect views of the world, it is the world. To believe otherwise is to believe that somehow nature and truth have a language which was somehow bestowed upon us rather than invented. For Heidegger, a consideration of the way we understand the world will shatter our assumed certainties. We cannot describe the world without recourse to metaphor and storytelling. When we give meanings we inevitably do so in certain contexts, otherwise they are meaningless.

Where shall we seek Nothing? Where shall we find Nothing? In order to find something must we not know beforehand that it is there? Indeed we must! First and foremost we can only look if we have pre-supposed the presence of a thing to be looked for. But the thing we are looking for is Nothing. Is there after all a seeking without presupposition, a seeking complemented by a pure finding?

—Heidegger

www.members.aol.com/KatharenaE/private/
PhiloHeid/heid.html

Assignment

A. Contrast Schmitt's view of power and government with a biblical understanding of the same.

B. Why was Simone de Beauvoir's world view such a threat to Christian views of femininity?

C. In what ways does Heidegger's world view clash with Christian Theism?

ORAL HISTORY: HELEN PARRIS STOBAUGH

Helen Parris Stobaugh, whom I affectionately call "Mamaw," was born at the beginning of the 20th century and died close to its end. The following excerpts are about her life. The first concerns her ancestors and childhood. The second is about her marriage to her first husband, whom she married when she was 15 and divorced when she was 16. Mamaw was, by her own admission, a wild flapper of the 1920s!

Mamaw was truly an iconoclast. She was the first unrepentant divorced woman my small Southern railroad town had ever known. Her first husband abused her once and she nearly killed him. In fact, she would have killed him but the shotgun with which she shot him was loaded with number eight shot and only crippled him for life. "He didn't hit me that hard," she reverently quipped, "or I would have killed him." She merely walked away from the marriage and the man. It was beneath her to file for divorce, but Judge Merritt knew what she wanted—everyone did—so he filed and granted divorce within the week. Her first husband never remarried and suffered in ebullient regret for the rest of his life—for he remained in love with Helen. For penance, he became a United Methodist pastor.

Mamaw was an enigma who greatly bothered our arcane Southern society. She cared nothing about what others thought—except to irritate potential critics. For instance, Mamaw, a fourth generation Methodist, loved to visit the Presbyterian church because the pastor's wife wore stylish dresses. Mamaw wore scandalous short dresses, and while she refused to inhale, she nonetheless carried a lit cigarette in her right hand to pique scurrilous busybodies.

Nonetheless, she had to be punished. When she was banished from the country club, most felt that she was sufficiently castigated. To be banned from the country club and its social events and dinner parties was social suicide. But she was not penitent. In fact, when she married my grandfather—the wealthiest and most eligible bachelor—the town was only too happy to invite my grandmother back into the

Helen Parris Stobaugh by author, 1978.

country club. She refused, and all her offspring and generations following grew up as pariahs—without the benefit of Southern country club amenities. Mamaw allegedly never again set a foot in the Desha County Country Club—although she loved to have garden parties and social events in her house.

Assignment

Interview an elderly relative and ask him or her to discuss what it was like growing up in the 20th century.

Chapter 25

WORLD WAR II AND BEYOND

First Thoughts . . .

"In 1941, 14-year-old Carolyn Gregory Perkins lived in Osborne, KS. The family had moved from their family farm outside of town when her father was forced to sell it because of the Depression. Carolyn was a freshman in high school. The strongest memory she has about what she heard was the surprise and shock expressed by the adults. The next day the entire school was called to an assembly in the auditorium of the high school. On the stage was a radio and the students listened as President Roosevelt asked Congress for a declaration of war against the Japanese. 'I knew things were serious because my parents were so worried, but the whole thing became real for me when my brother was sent overseas'"(National Archives). Pearl Harbor was one of those watershed dates that changed the lives of millions of Americans and changed the world for all time.

Chapter Learning Objectives . . .

In chapter 25, we will review the causes of World War II and America's ultimate intervention in this conflict. Next, we will examine the tragedy of the Holocaust. Finally, we will explore the roots of the Cold War and its ultimate resolution.

As a result of this chapter you should be able to:

1. Evaluate the causes of World War II.
2. Discuss the internment of Japanese-Americans.
3. Analyze the causes of the Holocaust.
4. Evaluate the roots of the Cold War and why America ultimately won this conflict.
5. Discuss America's intervention in the Korean War.

REMEMBER PEARL HARBOR

There are many excellent resources on the causes of World War II. One of the best is by historian Jen Rosenberg.

Rosenberg discusses the beginning of World War II in Europe:

Adolf Hitler wanted more land, especially in the east, to expand Germany according to the Nazi policy of 'lebensraum' [territory for political and economic expansion]. Hitler (left) used the harsh limitations that were set against Germany in the Versailles Treaty as a pretext for Germany's right to acquire land where German-speaking people lived. Germany successfully used this reasoning to envelop two entire countries without starting a war. Why was Germany allowed to take over both Austria and Czechoslovakia without a fight? The simple reason is that Great Britain and France did not want to repeat the bloodshed of World War I. They believed, wrongly as it turned out, they could avoid another world war by appeasing Hitler with a few concessions (such as Austria and Czechoslovakia). Great Britain and France had not clearly understood that Hitler's goal of land acquisition was much, much larger than any one country. After having gained both Austria and Czechoslovakia, Hitler was confident that he could again move east, this time acquiring Poland without having to fight Britain and France. (To eliminate the possibility of the Soviet Union fighting if Poland were attacked, Hitler made a pact with the Soviet Union—the Nazi-Soviet Non-Aggression Pact. So that Germany did not officially seem the aggressor (which it was), Hitler needed an excuse for entering/attacking Poland. It was Heinrich Himmler who came up with the idea; thus the plan was code named Operation Himmler.

On the night of August 31, 1939, Nazis took an unknown prisoner from one of their concentration camps, dressed him in a Polish uniform, took him to the town of Gleiwitz (on the border of Poland and Germany), and then shot him. The staged scene with the dead prisoner dressed in a Polish uniform was supposed to appear as a Polish attack against a German radio station. Hitler used the staged attack as the excuse to invade Poland.

At 4:45 on the morning of September 1, 1939 (the morning following the staged attack), German troops entered Poland. The sudden, immense attack by the Germans was called a Blitzkrieg ("lightning war"). The German air attack hit so quickly that most of Poland's air force was destroyed while still on the ground. To hinder Polish mobilization, the Germans bombed bridges and roads. Groups of marching soldiers were machine-gunned from the air. But the Germans did not just aim for soldiers, they also shot at civilians. Groups of fleeing civilians often found themselves under attack. The more confusion and chaos the Germans could create, the slower Poland could mobilize its forces.

Using 62 divisions, six of which were armored and ten mechanized, the Germans invaded Poland by land. Poland was not defenseless, but they could not compete with Germany's motorized army. With only 40 divisions, none of which were armored, and with nearly their entire air force demolished, the Poles were at a severe disadvantage—Polish cavalry were no match for German tanks. On September 1, the beginning of the German attack, Great Britain and France sent Hitler an ultimatum—withdraw

German forces from Poland or Great Britain and France would go to war against Germany.

On September 3, with Germany's forces penetrating deeper into Poland, Great Britain and France both declared war on Germany. World War II had begun.

It may have begun in Europe, but 1939 Depression-era America was not yet ready to fight. Preoccupied with domestic problems, Americans had no intention of entering another European War—as we had in 1917. Let the Europeans fight their own war! These Americans were called "Isolationists" and without a doubt they were the majority of Americans.

The outbreak of World War II in Europe proved to be an important turning point in the development of American foreign policy. This was a shift back to the America of the 1870s (see Foreign Expansion unit), which now wished to be left alone and out of European politics. Most American sympathies, however, lay with the underdogs—Great Britain and France—and it was difficult to remain neutral, especially after France fell in 1940 and Great Britain was about to fall. German submarine warfare also complicated matters. Still, in 1941, America officially was neutral.

The situation in Asia was no better. In the early 1930s Japan began her conquest of China and vigorously continued her efforts in 1937 with her attack on Nanking, called "the rape of Nanking." President Roosevelt responded slowly to these threats. His domestic problems were all he could bear, and besides, from the beginning, Roosevelt saw

Hitler as a greater threat. Roosevelt supported nonviolent means to control Japanese aggression. By 1941, America had imposed an embargo on certain goods —notably scrap iron. These measures persuaded Japan to take a great gamble: Japan could either retreat from her world conquest and lose face, or she could make a bold gamble and attack the U.S. She chose the latter course of action.

On December 7, 1941, America was attacked at Pearl Harbor by the Empire of Japan. The next day, December 8, 1941, the same day that the U.S. declared war on Japan, Germany declared war on America. Now the whole world was at war!

The Japanese attack on American soil at Pearl Harbor motivated America in a way no one expected. America brought her entire industrial might to bear on the Axis powers (Japan-Italy-Germany). After four long, terrible years, in August 1945, World War II ended with America and her allies the victors.

From 1941 to 1945 Americans, many of whom had never been 25 miles from home, visited places halfway around the world—Hamburg, Manila, Honolulu, and Casablanca. This world war changed Americans in ways no one had ever predicted. We were forever part of the world community. Isolationism was no longer an option.

One group who experienced this change was the

Japanese-Americans. During the early years of the war most Americans were afraid that Japan or Germany might invade the United States. Such thoughts seem ludicrous to us today, but to our parents and grandparents, it was a real possibility. The federal government felt that it needed to relocate thousands of Japanese-Americans. They were resettled away from the Pacific coast. This was, of course, a tragic mistake, but at the time the decision had widespread support from most Americans.

The war required a massive effort on the part of all Americans. More than 12 million Americans served in the armed forces. The total number of dead, wounded, or missing was 1 million (Fenton, et al., p. 624). Those who stayed at home had to adjust themselves to a strikingly different style of life. The economy was closely controlled by the federal government. Food, fuel, and other strategic raw materials were rationed. Women replaced their soldier-husbands in factories and other workplaces. America would never be the same again.

The world would never be the same again. More than 46 million people died in World War II. Six million of these casualties were Jewish people murdered by the Nazis in a systematic attempt to destroy European Jewry.

The word *holocaust* literally means "massive destruction by fire." The word *Shoah*, meaning "widespread disaster," is the modern Hebrew equivalent. The Holocaust was the murder of approximately six million Jews by the Nazis and their collaborators. Between the German invasion of the Soviet Union in the summer of 1941 and the end of the war in Europe in May 1945, Nazi Germany and its accomplices strove to murder every Jew under their domination. They very nearly succeeded. Today there are virtually no Jewish people living in Poland; before World War II there were millions. Almost all the Jewish children of Europe died—four out of five (80 percent). The Jews were not the only victims—other individuals and groups were persecuted and murdered during this period, but the Jews were the only group that the Nazis sought to destroy entirely. (See World War II Timeline in Appendix.)

By the end of the Second World War, in 1945, the Nazi regime and its accomplices had physically annihilated about 11.5 million people: 6 million Jews and 5.5 million non-Jews and undesirable "others"—mentally ill, disabled, political opponents, homosexuals, Slavs, Gypsies, Jehovah's Witnesses, and Pentecostals (history1900s.about.com).

Assignment

A. What were the causes of World War II?

B. Why did America hesitate to enter into the war?

C. Was the internment of Japanese-Americans justified? Why or why not?

Sailors in a motor launch rescue a man overboard from the water alongside the burning West Virginia during or shortly after the Japanese air raid on Pearl Harbor, 1941.

THE HOLOCAUST

The Holocaust was the systematic, state-sponsored murder of approximately six million Jews by the Nazi regime and its collaborators from 1933 to 1945. The National Socialist Party, Nazis, who came to power in Germany in January 1933, believed that Jews, deemed "inferior," were an alien threat to the so-called German self-proclaimed, superior Aryan racial community.

During the era of the Holocaust, German authorities also targeted other groups because of their perceived "racial inferiority": Roma (Gypsies), the disabled, and some of the Slavic peoples (Poles, Russians, and others). Other groups were persecuted on political, ideological, and behavioral grounds, among them Communists, Pentecostals, Socialists, Jehovah's Witnesses, and homosexuals.

In 1933, the Jewish population of Europe stood at over eight million. Most European Jews lived in countries that Nazi Germany would occupy or influence during World War II. By 1945, the Germans and their collaborators had killed nearly two out of three European Jews as part of the "Final Solution," the Nazi policy to murder the Jews of Europe. Almost eight out of ten Jewish children younger than five were killed.

Jewish slave laborers in the Buchenwald concentration camp near Jena, Germany, by Private H. Miller (Army), 1945.

Following the invasion of the Soviet Union in June 1941, Einsatzgruppen (mobile killing units) initiated mass-murder operations against Jewish people and Gypsies. Between 1941 and 1944, Nazi German authorities deported millions of Jews from Germany, from occupied territories, and from the countries of many of its Axis allies to ghettos and to killing centers, often called extermination camps, where they were murdered in specially developed gassing facilities (e.g., Auschwitz, Treblinka).

Assignment

A. Although the Holocaust and the Nazi assault on humanity took place during World War II, the war was not the cause of the Holocaust. Genocide is the last step in a continuum of actions taken by those who are prejudiced. The first step of this continuum is discrimination —treating certain groups of people as inferior to others. The second step is isolation, such as the physical segregation of minorities in ghettos or setting up separate schools. The third step is persecution, followed by dehumanization and violence. Genocide is the deliberate and systematic extermination of a group of people. How could this have happened? (This question was partly taken from an internet site).

B. In the 1960s, a disturbing study was conducted on ex-concentration camp prison guards. They had participated in the worst crime ever committed on humanity, yet their lives seemed normal. There was no high rate of cancer, divorce, or early deaths. A similar study was conducted on concentration camp survivors. The opposite results were true: Their rate of cancer, suicide, divorce, and early death was significantly higher than that of the general population. The study offered some surprising reasons for why this was so. What do you think those reasons were?

C. What were the causes of the Holocaust?

THE COLD WAR

The "hot" war ended in September 1945, but a "cold" war began soon after.

The Yalta conference is often cited as the beginning of the Cold War. This meeting of the "Big Three" at the former palace of Czar Nicholas on the Crimean southern shore of the Black Sea took place February 4–11, 1945.

Stalin's army had reached the Oder River and was poised for the final attack on Berlin, but Stalin on February 3 had ordered his leading general, Zhukov, to pause while the conference was in session. His occupation of Poland was complete, and he possessed command of the largest army in Europe, 12 million soldiers in 300 divisions. Eisenhower's 4 million men in 85 divisions were still west of the Rhine. Strategic bombing had devastated German cities, and the last untouched major city in Germany would be destroyed February 13 when Churchill sent his bombers over Dresden. Roosevelt appeared weak and tired in photos of the Yalta conference, and he would present his Yalta report to Congress March 1 sitting down. In two months, he would be dead of a massive cerebral hemorrhage. His physician, Dr. Howard Bruenn, has written that

Dresden, 1945—over ninety percent of the city center, was destroyed by G. Beyer, 1945 (Bundesarchiv, Bild 183-11408-0005 / Unknown / CC-BY-SA).

although FDR suffered from high blood pressure, there was no evidence that his health impaired his judgment at Yalta. Critics would accuse Roosevelt of a sellout at Yalta, of giving away Eastern Europe to Stalin, of "secret deals" with a ruthless dictator.

Bert Andrews in the *New York Herald Examiner* wrote about four secret deals: Russia's demand for $20 billion in reparations from Germany, for Poland to the Curzon line, for three seats in the United Nations, for territory in the Far East including Outer Mongolia, south Sakhalin Island, the Kuriles. Stalin did not hold free elections in Eastern Europe, and the American press turned increasingly hostile to Russia. However, as Robert Dallek has pointed out in *Franklin Roosevelt and American Foreign Policy*, FDR was hoping the future United Nations organization would be the place to deal with Stalin, not at Yalta. He told Adolf Berle, "I didn't say the result was good. I said it was the best I could do." Both Roosevelt and Churchill recognized the reality of Soviet power in 1945 (qtd. verbatim americanhistory.com/).

Sir Winston Churchill by the United Nations Information Office, New York, 1942 (PD-US).

The so-called Cold War continued unabated from 1945 until 1991. The war had several phases:

	Negotiations 1945	World War II ends and the allies disagree about the way post-war Europe should appear. The Soviet Union sets up the "iron curtain" around eastern Europe.
	Demonstration 1946	The Cold War transformed Harry Truman. He had overcome the hostile attacks of the 80th Congress, threats from Josef Stalin, the takeover of Czechoslovakia, the blockade of Berlin, strikes and economic reconversion problems at home, and a public image of a not-very-serious president. Most importantly was that he listened to his advisers, especially George Marshall, and supported their hard-line advice and policies.
	Containment 1947–1949	By 1947 American policy toward communism was known as "containment." Truman committed American resources to any nation who was opposed to Communism. To that end, America supported the French in Indochina (i.e., Vietnam), the Nationalist Chinese as opposed to Communist Chinese, and South Korea as opposed to North Korea.
	Coercion 1950–1968	America fights a war against North Korea, joins the race to the moon, and enters the Vietnam War. Again, America chooses to confront Communism wherever it shows its face.
	Detente 1968–1980	With the end of the Vietnam War, President Nixon invites a cooling of relations with the Soviet Union, which was exhausted by the expensive arms race. Ultimately, all parties were discouraged by Detente, and it was abandoned by President Ronald Reagan.
	Confrontation 1980–1985	President Ronald Reagan forces the Soviet Union to enter a costly arms race. The Soviet Union could not sustain this economic pressure. As a result, major divisions emerged in the communist bloc (CC BY-SA 3.0).
	Glasnost 1985–1989	By this point, it was clear to the Soviet Union that accommodation and reform were necessary or the country's economy would collapse (CC BY 2.0).
	Revolution 1989–1991	The Berlin War falls and Communism ends in the Soviet Union (CC BY-SA 3.0).

Assignment

What were the roots of the Cold War and why did America ultimately win this conflict?

KOREAN WAR

Douglas MacArthur at the front lines above Suwon, Korea , accompanied by Courtney Whtney, Matthew B. Ridgway, William B. Kean, and others. Photo by USASC, 1951 (PD-US).

Korean civilians pass an M-46 tank by Major R. V. Spencer, 1951.

The Korean War has been called the "Forgotten War," historically overshadowed by World War II and Vietnam, though it figures prominently in the development of events. The Korean War was one of the first hot wars of the Cold War and involved many of the great personalities of the era: Truman, MacArthur, Mao, and Stalin.

The Korean War began in the early hours of June 25, 1950, when North Korean troops crossed the 38th parallel and invaded South Korea. The South Korean army was driven south to the end of the peninsula. Only when the U.S. Army intervened could the Communist forces be stopped. The war involved some of the most difficult fighting ever experienced by American soldiers—and some of the worst conditions. Within three years, 34,000 American servicemen lost their lives—most of them during the first critical year. This was a significantly higher figure per year than the almost 60,000 American casualties spread over ten years in Vietnam.

There were both great trials and epic accomplishments during the Korean war: the humiliating retreat of inexperienced U.S. soldiers in the opening days of the war; the brilliant Inchon landings masterminded by General Douglas MacArthur; and the grittiness revealed near the Chosin Reservoir by the 1st Marine Division surrounded by a massive Chinese force.

Although an armistice was signed in 1953 between the U.S., China, and North Korea, South Korea refused to sign it, leaving the two Koreas in a state of war to the present.

Assignment

Do you think America's intervention in the Korean War was or was not a good idea? Why or why not?

THE VIETNAM WAR

First Thoughts . . .

The Vietnam War was a long, bloody conflict that ended with the United States' first major military upset. It had huge ramifications nationally and globally. In spite of that loss, however, America won the Cold War. Thanks to history makers like Lech Walesa, the Berlin Wall came down!

Chapter Learning Objectives . . .

In chapter 26 we will explore the causes and results of the longest of American wars: the Vietnam War. We will also examine the life of Lech Walesa. Finally, we will explore the impact of several philosophers and the impact they have had on America from 1940 to the present.

As a result of this chapter you should be able to:

1. Give a brief history of American involvement in the Vietnam War and discuss why we lost this war.
2. Discuss how Lech Walesa's faith influenced his decision to take a stand against communism.
3. Evaluate several historical theories of what caused the Cold War.
4. Analyze Jean-Paul Sartre's influence on history.
5. Discuss, in light of the Holocaust, why God allows bad things to happen to good people.

WAR IN VIETNAM

The Vietnam War (although it was never formally a "war") was waged for control of South Vietnam by North Vietnam and its allies against South Vietnam, the United States, and their allies between 1962 and 1975. While there had been earlier U.S. involvement, such as support for the French in the 1950s, the Vietnam War, in terms of U.S. armed intervention, began in 1962 with direct support to the South Vietnamese Army of the Republic of Viet Nam (ARVN), and ended with the last U.S. bombing of North Vietnam in late 1972. At various times, the U.S. and ARVN forces were supported by Australian, South Korean, New Zealand, Thai, and Filipino troops.

The principal opposition was the North Vietnamese People's Army of Viet Nam (PAVN) and the Viet Cong (VC) military wing of the National Front for the Liberation of South Vietnam (NLF).

U.S. military advisers had been present in the south since 1955, but they began to accompany South Vietnamese combat troops in 1962. The Gulf of Tonkin incident in 1964 signaled the beginning of open combat involvement, although the overt part was initially limited to air attacks and local security for air bases in the South.

A U.S. B-66 Destroyer and four F-105 Thunderchiefs dropping bombs on North Vietnam by Lt. Col. Cecil J. Poss, 20th TRS on RF-101C, USAF, 1966.

Major introductions of U.S. ground combat troops came in 1965, generally increasing until 1968, when the policy of **Vietnamization** went into effect. As Vietnamization began, and the Paris Peace Talks were completed in 1972, the U.S. role changed again, South Vietnam fought its own ground war, with U.S. ground combat troops withdrawing between 1968 and 1972, and the last air attacks occurring in 1972. After that, the U.S. provided limited replacements of supplies, and maintained a large diplomatic Defense Attaché Office that monitored the ARVN until the fall of South Vietnam in 1975.

After the U.S. withdrawal, South Vietnam collapsed, having been invaded by the DRV in 1975. Memorable pictures of desperate people clinging to helicopters reflect the evacuation of diplomatic, military, and intelligence personnel, and some Vietnamese allies. Other than for the immediate security of the evacuation, no U.S. combat troops or aircraft had been in South Vietnam since 60 days after the signing of the peace treaty in Paris.

A UH-1D helicopter piloted by Maj. Bruce P. Crandall climbs skyward after discharging a load of US infantrymen on a search and destroy mission by the U.S. Army, c1960.

Assignment

Give a brief history of American involvement in the Vietnam War and discuss why we lost this war.

HISTORY MAKER: LECH WALESA

The most important cause of the end of the Cold War was not President Ronald Reagan or President George Bush or Premier Mikhail Gorbachev or Pope John Paul II. It was the grassroots resistance to communism by the people of Eastern Europe. Movements like Solidarity were the real reason that communist governments found themselves undermined and vulnerable, and it was the mass of working men and women in Europe that made possible the free elections, the collapse of the Berlin Wall, and the disappearance of the Iron Curtain that signified the end of the Cold War. It was also the prayer and fasting of a great number of Christian believers, inside and outside the Iron Curtain. Lech Walsea was the leader of the Solidarity resistance. Walesa organized the shipyard and dock workers into a powerful labor movement that was suppressed December 13, 1981, when General Wojciech Jaruzeluski declared martial law. However, it continued to grow as an underground anti-communist organization. Walesa received secret aid from Pope John Paul II, the Reagan administration, and the AFL-CIO in the United States led by Lane Kirkland. The printing press proved to be a more powerful weapon than the sword, as Poland was deluged with books, magazines, newspapers, video documentaries, and radio broadcasts. Reagan lifted U.S. sanctions against Poland on February 19, 1987, and the Pope praised Solidarity on his trip to Poland in June. At

Lech Walesa by MEDEF, (((CC BY-SA 2.0), 2009.

Gorbachev's urging, on April 5, 1989, the Polish Communist government legalized Solidarity. Within a year communist rule ended in Eastern Europe and the Soviet Union (americanhistory.com). Walesa, who is still alive, is also a committed Christian believer. "In myself I am nothing," he has noted. "It all comes from God and the Virgin Mary." A devout Catholic, he wears a likeness of Poland's patron, the Black Madonna of Czestochowa, in his lapel and seldom misses morning Mass. In fact, he has his own chaplain who travels with him and serves as an adviser.

Polish Round Table Talks took place in Warsaw, Poland, 1989.

Assignment

Discuss how Lech Walesa's faith influenced his decision to take a stand against communism.

HISTORICAL DEBATE

After World War II, America faced challenges it had never known. (This discussion is informed by Gerald N. Grob and George Athan Billias, *Interpretations of American History: Patterns and Perspectives*, Vol. 2.) By 1945 the United States was the strongest nation in the world. Americans looked to the future with hope and optimism; however, all these hopes were dashed with the advent of Soviet imperialism. The tyranny of Nazi fascism was quickly replaced by Soviet hegemony. Two developments within the context of World War II determined the direction the Cold War would take. One was the toppling of five nations from the ranks of first-rate powers (Germany, Japan, Italy, France, and Great Britain). This left only two superpowers (the U.S. and Soviet Union). The second development was the technological revolution in warfare (Grob, et al., p. 373). For the first time in history a country had the technological means to destroy world civilization.

Historians argued energetically about the origins of the Cold War, and their views crystallized around three theories:

1 The traditional school argued that Soviet aggression and imperialism was the fundamental cause of the Cold War.

2 The revisionist school was reticent to place all the blame on the Soviet Union. Many revisionists came to the conclusion that the United States expansionist ambition was partly responsible for the Cold War. In fact, revisionist historians blamed both American and Soviet leaders for the Cold War.

3 The new left school found America exclusively responsible for the Cold War, since the Cold War offered Americans a chance to expand their economic hegemony over the world and Americans pursued their selfish aims with ingenuity and enthusiasm.

Assignment

Which cause(s) of the Cold War seem most plausible to you? Defend your answer.

PHILOSOPHERS AND WORLD VIEWS

Jean-Paul Sartre (1905–1980)

"There are two kinds of existentialists; first, those who are Christian . . . and on the other hand the atheistic existentialists, among whom . . . I class myself. What they have in common is that they think that existence precedes essence, or, if you prefer, that subjectivity must be the turning point." This quote by the philosopher Jean-Paul Sartre captures, in broad relief, the philosophical bent of this thoroughly modern Existentialist. Existentialism is a world view/philosophy that argues that each individual is his own world. Existence precedes essence. "Freedom is existence," Sartre writes, "and in it existence precedes essence." This means that what we do, how we act in our life, determines our apparent "qualities." It is not that someone tells the truth because he is honest, but rather he defines himself as honest by telling the truth again and again (http://www.imagi-nation.com). "I am a professor in a way different than the way I am six feet tall, or the way a table is a table. The table simply is; I exist by defining myself in the world at each moment." Freedom is the central and unique potentiality that makes us uniquely human. Therefore, to abdicate that role, and to submit oneself to a higher authority—e.g., God—is to act in an inhuman way. Yet, humans are hopelessly lost—without direction and without real choices. "I am my choices," Sartre writes. "I cannot not choose. If I do not choose, that is still a choice. If faced with inevitable circumstances, we still choose how we are in those circumstances." We are condemned because we did not create ourselves. We must choose and act from within whatever situation we find ourselves.

Jean-Paul Sartre wrote:

Existentialism is nothing less than an attempt to draw all the consequences of a coherent atheistic position. It isn't trying to plunge man into despair at all. But if one calls every attitude of unbelief despair, like the Christians, then the word is not being used in its original sense. Existentialism isn't

Jean-Paul Sartre, photographer unknown, c1950 (PD-AR-Photo).

so atheistic that it wears itself out showing that God doesn't exist. Rather, it declares that even if God did exist, that would change nothing. There you've got our point of view. Not that we believe that God exists, but we think that the problem of His existence is not the issue. In this sense, existentialism is optimistic, a doctrine of action, and it is plain dishonesty for Christians to make no distinction between their own despair and ours and then to call us despairing. If man, as the Existentialist conceives him, is indefinable, it is because at first he is nothing. Only afterward will he be something, and he himself will have made what he will be. Thus there is no human nature, since there is no God to conceive it. Not only is man what he conceives himself to be, but he is also only what he wills himself to be after this thrust toward existence. . . . The existentialist . . . thinks it very distressing that God does not exist, because all possibility of finding values in a heaven of ideas disappears along with Him; there can no longer be a priori of God, since there is no infinite and perfect consciousness to think it. Nowhere is it written that the Good exists, that we must be honest, that we must not lie; because the fact is that we are on a plane where there are only men. Dostoevsky said, If God didn't exist, everything would be possible. That is the very starting point of existentialism. Indeed, everything is permissible if God does not exist, and as a result man is forlorn, because neither within him nor without does he find anything to cling to.

Elie Wiesel (1928–)

Elie Wiesel was born in 1928 and lived through one of the most horrible periods in history. During World War II, he, with his family and other Jews from Romania, were sent to Auschwitz concentration camp where his parents and little sister were gassed and cremated. Wiesel and his two older sisters survived. But Wiesel's faith and heart were broken. "My God died," Wiesel said, "in the fires of Auschwitz." Wiesel changed from a devout Jew to a broken, bitter young man who doubted his belief in God. If there is a God, how could He allow this to happen, he wonders. Elie Wiesel speaks for a generation of 20th century people who doubt the existence of God.

Elie Wiesel, by David Shankbone, (CC BY-SA 3.0), 2010.

Assignment

A. Sartre in one sense is a quintessential modern. He invites the reader to think through his life in a rational way. On the other hand, his writings presage postmodernism. Postmodernism is opposed to universal rationalism or objective views of knowledge. Postmodernism purports to be a movement that is centered in the subjective and relative. Why is someone like Jean-Paul Sartre such a great threat to the 21st century Christian? At what points does his world view clash with Christianity?

B. Discuss why Sartre's world view would be so appealing to a Naturalist.

C. Sartre's play "No Exit" describes hell. Hell, to the self-actualized Sartre, is a place where people spend an eternity with other people whom they despise. "There's no need for red-hot pokers. Hell is—other people!" How is this different from the Christian view of hell?

D. What does one say to a person like Wiesel? Why does God allow bad things to happen to innocent, even good people?

AFRICAN-AMERICAN HISTORY: NATIONALISM

First Thoughts . . .

Americans learned in the last half of the 20th century that no one can escape the effects of racism. Some of us who lived in the South during that era started the first grade in segregated schools and graduated from high school in integrated schools. The effect that the Civil Rights struggle had on the American nation would be hard to exaggerate! New heroes emerged—for example Martin Luther King, Jr. Forty years later, for the first time in history, an African-American was elected president of the United States!

Chapter Learning Objectives . . .

In chapter 27, we will examine the inexorable progress that African-Americans made in American society from 1933 to the present. We will speculate about possible racial reconciliation strategies that have yet to be fully realized.

As a result of this chapter you should be able to:

1. Define racism and prejudice.

2. Discuss the impact that welfare has had on African-American families.

3. Analyze why the African-American community turned to violence in the 1960s.

4. Discuss why some African-Americans turned to separatism as an alternative to assimilation.

5. List events, legislation, and tactics that advanced African-American rights between 1960 and the present.

BLACK NATIONALISM

There is much that needs to be forgiven. Before I become too mawkish, let me share the devastating result of 300 years of white racism:

African-American Demographic Statistics:

◆ Infants born to African-American teenage girls have a 50 percent higher mortality rate than those of the general population.

◆ 50 percent of African-American teens are unemployed (triple the rate of whites).

◆ 25 percent of African-American men aged 20 through 64 are unemployed.

◆ One-third of African-Americans live below the poverty line.

◆ 25 percent of African-American males 16 through 30 are in our prison system.

◆ 64 percent of the prison population is African-American (and yet African-Americans account for only 12 percent of the general population).

◆ 600,000 African-Americans are in prisons, as opposed to 400,000 in college.

◆ Two-thirds of African-American children are born to unwed mothers.

◆ 2.6 million of 4.6 million African-American families are headed by single women.

◆ Homicide is the leading cause of death for African-American males aged 15 through 44.

◆ Suicide is the second. (John M. Perkins, *Beyond Charity: The Call to Christian Community Development*)

When white people talk about racism they define it in personal terms—individual attitudes, actions, perceptions, stereotypes, relationships. When African-Americans talk about racism they define it in systemic terms—how the systems of police, education, health care, business, church, etc., respond to them as a whole.

An African American boy outside of Cincinnati, Ohio by John Vachon, c1942 (LOC-image).

In 1969 William Grier wrote:

We weep for the true victim, the African-American. His wounds are deep. . . .For white Americans to understand the life of the African-American man, it must be recognized that so much time has passed and so little has changed.

So much time had passed and so little had changed. By the middle of the 20th century most African-Americans felt they'd had enough, so they joined together to form their own nation.

Black nationalism was a movement among African-Americans whose primary purpose was to define and to celebrate African-American culture and heritage. The early civil rights movement sought to assimilate blacks into American society; black nationalism oftentimes sought to bring blacks out of American culture. Black nationalism engaged white America and gained civil rights for blacks. To black nationalists, American democracy was a modern form of tyranny inflicted on the black minority by the white majority.

I use "Black Nationalism" and "Black Power" interchangeably. I also include within Black Nationalism the Black Muslim movement.

Genesis of Black Nationalism

Black nationalism had been a part of the African-American vision since Frederick Douglass urged blacks to follow the examples of modern Jews in Europe and America, who, by emphasizing group solidarity and pride, improved their status. Likewise, Booker T. Washington offered a nonviolent celebration of "blackness" and called for his country to embrace a form of separatism and black pride.

W. E. B. Du Bois called his race to Black Nationalism:

The Negro is a sort of seventh son, born with a veil, and gifted with second-sight in this American world—a world which yields him no true self-consciousness, but only lets him see himself through the revelation of the other world. It is a peculiar sensation, this double-consciousness, this sense of always looking at one's self through the eyes of others, of measuring one's soul by the tape of the world that looks on in amused contempt and pity. One ever feels his twoness—an American, a Negro; two souls, two thoughts, two unreconciled strivings; two warring ideals in one dark body, whose dogged strength alone keeps it from being torn asunder.

Black nationalism flowered in the 1960s under the leadership of Malcolm X. The civil rights movement increased expectations and black pride. Black nationalism grew out of this optimism and in reaction to it. In other words, black nationalists felt that the Civil Rights movement did not go far enough to improve black conditions. Black nationalism grew in what was perhaps the most disappointing period in African-American history: the previous 35 years (1930–1965). For it was during this period that the Civil Rights movement brought increased expectations and profound disappointment—both at the

Malcolm X, by Ed Ford (CC BY-SA 3.0), 1964

same time.

The most impressive areas of racial solidarity occurred during 1967 in the political arena. The election of African-American mayors in several urban areas was evidence that African-Americans were gaining ground in American society. However, gains by the civil rights movement were mitigated by unemployment, by welfare, and by persistent racism. Civil Rights gains were important; but many American hearts remained unchanged.

Black nationalist strategies called for the development of African-American–controlled economic and political institutions. These institutions assured cultural preservation. Violence was not ruled out as a tactic to obtain desired ends.

Assignment

A. Define racism and prejudice. Are these two concepts different?

B. Some people argue that an African-American person (i.e., the victim) cannot be racist. They argue that a victim has no "power" to be racist. What do you think? Agree or disagree and offer evidence to support your decision.

SEPARATISM

Separatism—intentional separation from white American-dominated culture and retreat into pan–African-American nationalistic culture—was the main tactic embraced by black nationalism. Separatism was not a new tactic. Black slaves early learned to avoid the "Big House" and the "white master." By the 1960s black leaders, many of whom were very angry, urged fellow African-Americans to live outside mainstream, mostly white American culture. Black nationalism grew out of a belief that African-Americans had a distinct culture and this distinctiveness needed to be expressed. This was vividly evidenced at the **1968 Olympics**.

Separatism had several common themes. First, slavery and discrimination were more than aberrations or anomalies in the American ethos. They were fundamental to what it meant to be a white American. Second, African-Americans assumed a position of moral authority, in some cases moral superiority, which made them in some way the true examples of American virtue. Third, because of racism, white America was failing its God-given task to be a city on a hill. And, finally, some African-Americans concluded that attempts at reconciliation were too late, that white America's apostasy was too great to be redeemed. The only thing left for African-Americans was to preserve their own culture and to separate themselves from malevolent white America.

The preservation of this culture was a weighty matter. The African-American writer Bell Hooks wrote: "This experience of relational love, of a beloved Black community, I long to know again. . . . Feelings of connection that held Black people together are swiftly eroding. Assimilation rooted in internalized racism further separates us." In Paul Marshall's novel *Praisesong for the Widow*, a black couple becomes so intent on prospering economically in the white world that they lose their sense of identity and history. Motivated by many such situations, black nationalists decided that the only way they could preserve African-American culture was to withdraw from white American culture.

African-Americans had always been aware of a special connection with each other. Now, in the '60s, African-American professionals volunteered their time to support African-Americans in the ghetto. Many African-Americans refused to move out of the ghetto, even when they were financially able to do so, because they wanted to remain in their own community. Milkman in Toni Morrison's book *Song of Solomon* describes white/black relations in this way: "Look. It's the condition our condition is in. Everybody wants the life of a black man. Everyone. White men want us dead or quiet—which is the same thing as dead." Deep in the heart of African-Americans circa 1965 was an increasing frustration with white society. At the same time there was a growing African-American anger. Black Americans were willing to die in vast numbers for their cause, and many did.

Violence

Black nationalism was mostly nonviolent. However, some African-American leaders were extremely angry. To these people, gradualism was anathema. It suggested that races could coexist at the very time many were suggesting that the races should remain separate.

In *The Fire Next Time* (1962) James Baldwin wrote of the "rope, fire, torture, castration, infanticide, rape . . . fear by day and night, fear as deep as the marrow of the bone." By 1970, many African-American thinkers, religious leaders, social workers, and politicians were outraged. In fact, hatred ran so deep in African-American culture that the struggle became the end itself—instead of a means to an end.

Five days after the great 1967 Newark race riots, the National Conference on Black Power held an auspicious conference that marked a dramatic change in African-American resistance strategies. A seminal paper was presented by Adelaide Cromwell Hill entitled "What is Africa to us?" Hill made this haunting observation: "On this soil, the Negro has never been given an opportunity to name himself." Black leaders vigorously called their people to resist white cultural encroachments. For the first time, violence was openly sanctioned. The Black Nationalist movement was a Black Power movement.

In Pittsburgh an inflammatory pamphlet, "The Black Mood in Pittsburgh," was widely read in the African-American community. "Black is anger, Tom," it proclaims. This pamphlet called for a "Burn Day." "Black Power cannot mean only a black sheriff in the sovereign state of Alabama . . . . Black Power is the power to control our lives," LeRoi Jones wrote in 1971. "We can have nothing without power." Black Power consciously tied its views to the historical reality of America prejudice. Part of the Black Power movement was trying to ameliorate its race through community-based interventions. But, from the beginning, black organizers saw themselves as soldiers in a war against white domination.

White America was a culture that for 300 years dominated and controlled, not nurtured and comforted. Black nationalists now decided to wage war on that society. They felt they had no choice.

What caused the black community to move from non-violent resistance to violent resistance? There were isolated instances of African-American violence before (e.g., Nat Turner Slave Revolt), but nothing like the violence manifested in the summer of 1968. The black community moved from nonviolent resistance to violent resistance because African-Americans saw themselves in an intolerable state of shame. This violence was precipitated by the April assassination of Martin Luther King, Jr., but frustration had been brewing in the African-American heart for years. Violence was inevitably seen as a course of last resort—the black community understood that it was their community that was being destroyed, not the predominately white community—but it became necessary because they felt they had no choice. To the African-American community, the 1968 riots were retributive justice. To most whites this violence was a wake-up call.

African-American violence increased even more with the assassination of Martin Luther King, Jr. For many African-Americans, King's assassination sealed the demise of nonviolent resistance as a viable means of achieving equality for black America. But, as early as 1962, with the murder of James Meredith, African-American leaders like Stokely Carmichael were calling for a more radical response to racism. Stokely Carmichael and Charles V. Hamilton had a powerful vision: Pan-African Nationalism and Separatism. Carmichael's vision was decidedly political.

Aftermath from the riots in Washington D.C. following the assasination of Martin Luther King Jr. by Warren K. Leffler, (CC BY-SA 3.0), 1968.

A similar vision arose that emphasized the cultural uniqueness of African-American culture. From this perspective, in 1966, the Black Panthers were founded by African-American nationalists Huey Newton and Bobby Seale. Sympathetic to this movement included radicals like H. Rap Brown. Brown spoke with great pain and anger. "Separate but equal is cool with me. What's the big kick about going to school with white folks? . . . We stand for the transformation of the decadent, reactionary, racist system that exists at this time. . . . We don't like the system. We want to negate the system."

The Black Panther Party of Self Defense was an organized movement designed to spread a message of pride and empowerment to African-Americans. Their tactics were openly aggressive, and violent if necessary (as contrasted with the National Association for the advancement of Colored People [NAACP] and the Southern Christian Leadership Conference). The Black Panthers wanted immediate results and were not willing to wait for legal and legislative processes. They wanted revolution not gradualism. The Black Panthers did not allow radical whites to belong to their organization. The Black Panthers, which was an uncharacteristic phenomenon for any Black Power movement. Black Power advocates were calling for educational segregation.

Black Panthers were more than just urban guerrillas. They set up community-based medical testing for sickle-cell anemia and lead poisoning, registered voters, and organized food giveaways. Now blacks did not have to rely on whites for anything. All their programs promoted an old tactic first suggested by white supremacists: segregation. They urged the African-American community to form a separate nation in the United States. They excluded themselves from white America.

Malcolm X and Louis Farrakhan began the controversial Nation of Islam or African-American Muslims. The idea of returning to Islam as the ancestral religion of African-Americans was not new. In the 1920s Marcus Garvey suggested that Blacks reject white institutions—including its religions—and form their own. But now, Farrakhan and Malcolm X connected Christianity to white hatred. "A White Man's Heaven Is an African-American Man's Hell" is the national anthem of the Nation of Islam. Farrakhan saw a vast white conspiracy seeking to conceal the glorious past of African-Americans, and the Nation of

101st Airborne Division escort the Little Rock Nine students into the all-white Central High School in Little Rock, Arkansas by the U.S. Army, (CC BY-SA 3.0), 1957

Islam sought to set the record straight. Sharod Baker, a Columbia University student, and a member of the Nation of Islam, recently stated, "I don't think there's anything wrong with saying I hate them [whites]. They have caused me harm over and over, and I wish they are [were] dead."

In contrast, Martin Luther King, Jr., called for reconciliation and nonviolence, assimilation and peaceful coexistence. Toward the end of his life, King shifted somewhat toward separatist tactics, but he never embraced violence. He stressed the unity of society and wanted to gain those ends through nonviolent means. "African-Americans should have the same right to vote, the same access to education, and the same economic opportunities as every other American," King argued. "They have the same goal as every other immigrant group—full assimilation into American life." King gave both African-Americans and whites hope that the race problem in America could be solved. But when African-Americans saw that assimilation was not working, some embraced "tribalism."

Another Black Power champion was Stokely Carmichael (mentioned earlier), chairman of the Student Nonviolent Coordinating Committee.

The SNCC was founded in Raleigh, North Carolina, in April 1960 at the suggestion of Martin Luther King, Jr., as a student arm of the Southern Christian Leadership Conference. The SNCC's objective was defined as integration through nonviolent protest, all of which was incorporated into the Mississippi Freedom Summer Project launched in 1964. The SNCC formally adopted a black-consciousness philosophy and a separatist stance. African-American resistance was clearly defined as pro-black and anti-white. Northern white activists were expelled and the group broke with Martin Luther King, Jr. The organization faded from the public eye by 1969, but its causes were embraced by nationalistic groups. The Black Panthers, too, were disbanded by the middle of the 1970s, but during this decade they captured the African-American social agenda and deeply impacted African-American society. Any racial discussion that speaks of "black power," "black identity," or "black self-determination" traces its genesis to the black nationalistic movement.

The 1960s marked a shift in resistance: from nonviolence to violence, from gradualism to immediatism, from desegregation to separatism. This shift clearly marked a new challenge for racial reconciliation proponents. In the mid-1970s fully 30 percent of black Americans felt that violence could be necessary to bring change and 8 percent were sure that it would be necessary. Little has changed since then. Similar studies and articles today confirm that those

Crowds surrounding the Reflecting Pool, during the 1963 March on Washington by Warren K. Leffler (CC BY-SA 3.0).

fears still exist among many African-Americans.

By the 1990s, within the African-American community the marriage of race and power was secure. Equality was no longer a goal: empowerment was. Now the movement wanted more than a piece of the pie—they wanted to be in charge. After so much misery and given the failure of the white church to address the needs of the African-American urban community, who can blame them? The Black Power movement encouraged a permanent state of rage. "Anytime you make race a source of power," a Black Power leader wrote, "you are going to guarantee suffering, misery, and inequality. . . . We are going to have power because we are black!" Many African-Americans today, influenced by black nationalism, argue that the distribution of power in American society has become the single issue of overriding importance to the upward progress of African-Americans. From 1965 to the present every item on the black agenda has been judged by whether or not it added to the economic or political empowerment of black people. In effect, Martin Luther King's dialogue of justice for all—whites and blacks—has been cast into the conflagration of empowerment. The triumph of black nationalism made black anger an indelible part of the racial reconciliation quest.

Today, the politics of difference has led to an establishment of "grievance identities." The African-American community has documented the grievance of their group, testifying to its abiding alienation.

While predominantly white colleges and universities now enroll a majority of the more than 1.3 million black college students, the fact is there is not much race mixing really occurring. Racism divides and conquers still. "We have a campus of 25,000 students and there is no mixing across cultural and racial lines. . . . Even during a campus rally for racial unity all the blacks cluster together and all the whites cluster together."

No one can deny that the Civil Rights initiatives in the 1960s brought substantial improvements to the African-American community. In 2008, for the first time in history, an African-American was elected president of the United States. As a result of these encouraging developments, many black Americans developed what some historians call a "black revolution in expectations." African-Americans no longer felt that they had to put up with the humiliation of second-class citizenship. The jury is still out regarding the actual racial progress being made. (See "Important Dates and Events in Black History" in Appendix One.)

Assignment

A. Did the New Deal and its welfare assistance harm African-Americans?

B. How did separatism affect the Christian church during the 1960s?

Black Panther convention, Lincoln Memorial, Washington D.C. by Thomas O'Halloran and Warren K. Leffler, (CC BY-SA 3.0), 1970.

RACIAL ANGER

Racial anger has become indelibly connected to the American ethos. Many African-Americans, in particular, are very angry. They are angry because they feel that the American dream has eluded them. They are angry because they are constantly being judged, harassed, and discriminated against because of their race. After such hopeful beginnings in the Great Migration, many find themselves held prisoner in unwholesome ghettos. White racism created a cycle of poverty in northern urban ghettos, constructing with it a de facto segregation that remains.

A result of African-American ghettoization was the denial of meaningful upward mobility. This was a unique element of American urban history. Other ethnic groups (e.g., Chicanos, Puerto Ricans, Asians) fared better in the upward mobility trek than did African-Americans. The ghetto became the unavoidable symbol of the failure of white America to overcome its racial divisiveness. As the African-American ghetto rapidly declined throughout the 20th century and industrialization took hold, likewise the African-American businessman and skilled craftsman disappeared from the American city. By the 1930s and 1940s, the goods and services once provided by neighbors were supplanted by mass retail outlets—a trend that continues today. In spite of affirmative action, federal job training programs, and ameliorated relationships with predominantly white unions, the number and proportion of African-American skilled workers continued to decline, assuring that the black community would continue to hold the lowest economic level of American society.

Some African-American enclaves existed in white suburbs, but whites were by far the majority presence in American suburbs. As African-American intellectuals like Fulwood remind us, money and education do not fully mitigate white privilege and white racism.

The African-American community is not without its strengths—witness the great Harlem Renaissance—but the strengths were constantly compromised by institutional racism manifested by almost all aspects of Northern urban

Participants, some carrying American flags, marching in the civil rights march from Selma to Montgomery, Alabama by Peter Pettus, 1965 (PD-US).

white society. Ethnicity, class formation, political power—all of these forces were overshadowed by racism. Racism was not competing with ethnicity and other forces—it was overwhelming them all!

May 17, 1954, Brown vs. The Board of Education, was a momentous day in the history of the world: a nation voluntarily acknowledged and repudiated its own oppression of part of its own people. Martin Luther King and nonviolent passive resistance allowed the protestors to retain their "innocence." King's vision is truly a moral vision undaunted by racial parochialism.

In the late '60s, suddenly a sharp racial consciousness emerged to compete with the moral consciousness that was part of earlier civil rights issues. Whites were no longer welcome in the movement, and a vocal "African-American power" minority gained control of the movement. It was from this phase—the Black Power phase—that black separatist organizations arose.

There was a time when African-Americans expected to solve the racial problem. Now, after the violence of the previous 30 years, it was difficult for Americans even to discuss the topic. The problem was that Americans sought racial, not moral, power, which led the African-American

Civil rights march on Washington, D.C. showing civil rights leaders, including Martin Luther King, Jr., surrounded by crowds carrying signs. by Warren K. Leffler, (CC BY-SA 3.0), 1963

Community into a series of contradictions: Moral power precluded racial power as a means to power. The civil rights movement sought equality by demanding that racism cease to be a significant category. Now, the Black Power movement was demanding that race must be a ubiquitous category. Thus, Black Power, grasping for political and economic power rather than justice, became itself unjust.

By the 1990s, the marriage of race and power was secure. Equality was no longer a goal: empowerment was. Now the movement wanted a piece of the pie. The Black Power movement encouraged a permanent state of rage and seeing themselves as vicitms.

By the 1980s, the "politics of difference" (Shelby Steele's term) led to an establishment of "grievance identities." Now the African-American community gained identity according to grievances committed by the dominant group. They sought to document the grievances of their group, testifying to its abiding alienation. African-American and whites alike were punished for not recognizing and accepting this litany of grievances.

Much of the black community's world view grew out of this feeling of anger and alienation. Listen to the rhetoric of a black leader, Cenie J. Williams, Jr. "The thrust of Black people in the late '50s and in the '60s for black power is viewed by our racist oppressors as a most serious challenge to the continuation of the white power dynamic in this area of the world and indirectly throughout the world." Dr. Farris Page, an African-American psychologist at the Children's Home Society, discussed adoption of black children by white families: "I have a young child who's in a school with only two or three black kids to a class and the impact is very, very tremendous. . . . The issues of race and color and hair are prevalent for black children in black homes. And they're going to be magnified in a white home." Dr. Page implied that racism is a dominant category. Clearly this rhetoric exhibited a politics of difference and rage.

Within the civil rights movement and the black community in general was a profound discouragement. In

African-American communities there was no doubt a loss of any optimism concerning the future. Racism had taken its toll.

Chief Justice Thurgood Marshall during the U.S. Bicentennial Celebration:

In this bicentennial year, we may not all participate in the festivities with flag-waving fervor. Some may more quietly commemorate the suffering, struggle, and sacrifice that has triumphed over much of what is wrong with the original document [the U.S. Constitution], and observe the anniversary with hopes not realized and promises not fulfilled.

African-American culture had grown terribly disillusioned by the late 1990s. Jim Crow laws had soured life in the South. De facto segregation had undermined attempts at advancement in the urban North. In reality, as Thomas Sowell explained, there is far less residential segregation in the northern city before the advent of aggressive government intervention than there is after the rise of the positive liberal state. Government intervention, too, had failed the African-American community. This was evidenced by the tremendous, widespread decline of many African-American urban families. The African-American immigrant experienced rejection from the Northern white and in some cases the Northern indigenous African-American family. The African-American family, then, had found the Promised Land to be another empty dream.

Chief Justice Thurgood Marshall, photographer unknown, (CC BY-SA 3.0), 1976.

In one way we end this narrative on a dreary note, for we have made almost no progress in race relations in the last 350 years. Viktor E. Frankl (left, by Prof. Dr. Franz Vesely), a survivor of the Nazi concentration camps, observes, "A man who could not see the end of his 'provisional existence' was not able to aim at an ultimate existence." Nietzsche observed, "He who has a why to live can bear with almost any how." The black community had lost a "how" and a "why."

Race should not be a source of power and advantage or disadvantage in a Christian, free society. The civil rights movement in its early and middle years offered the best way out of America's racial impasse. It embodied a moral vision. And it was a very important step forward for all Americans. The civil rights movement thankfully removed many of the racist systemic problems in white America. However, much work remains. Racial reconciliation will require more than systemic change: it will require that human hearts are changed, and human hearts are changed by the power of the Holy Spirit.

Assignment

A. Why did the African-American community turn to violence in the 1960s?

B. At first, African-American resistance was decidedly Christian. The Christian church, in fact, continues to be the basis of most African-American resistance. Martin Luther King, Jr., for instance, was a pastor. However, in the 1960s, black nationalism began to take over the black rights movement. Why did the Christian church lose so much ground?

ORAL HISTORY

Dwight Washington, a high school scholar and track star, had a conversion experience at one of our revival services. This was an aberration, to say the least. There existed, however in our church a well-defined, strongly held white Christian racial orthodoxy that supported racism.

Pastor Garner predicted that America was the probable site of the coming millennium. For many African-American believers, however, America was not the Promised Land—it was Egypt. No doubt Dwight felt some hesitation when he attended our church. I never told anyone, but I had invited him.

I knew that people like Uncle George—the Grand Wizard of the Klan—would not approve, but I felt that Dwight's life required a radical intervention. The problem was, Dwight was converted on Wednesday night and thought he would visit us again on Sunday morning. He foolishly thought that since Jesus loved him all the time, and we appeared to love him on Wednesday night, we would love him on Sunday morning too, so he came.

So, he attended our Sunday morning worship service.

Only one African-American had ever attended our church on Sunday morning. A new paper mill executive, Marcus Danforth, sought to transfer his membership from another Methodist church in Chicago, Illinois. Mrs. Ollie Smith fainted outright when Marcus sat in her deceased husband's pew.

Marcus never visited our church again. After Uncle George and his friends visited Marcus one evening and burned a cross in his finely landscaped lawn, and after his children were not allowed to play in the local little league, Marcus quickly transferred to Idaho Falls, Idaho.

Dwight arrived promptly at 10:45 and shook Tommy Somerville's hand. Without looking up, Tommy Somerville, who ushered the faithful to their pews, handed Dwight a bulletin. Dwight smiled. Mr. Somerville was speechless, but Dwight did not wait for Mr. Somerville to escort him to his seat; Dwight sat in T-Bone Arnold's seat.

Ten minutes later, arriving late from a fishing trip to Kate Adams Lake, T-Bone appeared noticeably irritated. Dwight was no doubt going to use the pew hymnal that was dedicated to his uncle Harry Arnold. This was T-Bone's favorite hymnal and no one used it but T-Bone. Everyone in my church knew that.

T-Bone growled (literally) but eventually sat next to the Widow Adams, whose false teeth inevitably leaped from her mouth during the second hymn. T-Bone grimaced and carefully placed his *Hymns of Praise* in a position to catch the widow's teeth. The first hymn was everyone's favorite, "Holy! Holy! Holy!"

Before the end of the first verse, Mr. Somerville politely asked Dwight to leave because folks like him should go to their own churches. Dwight lowered his head and walked away from our church and Jesus.

Garner saw everything and was obviously displeased. Not that he castigated us. We could handle that. We enjoyed pastors who scolded us for our sins. We tolerated, even enjoyed his paternalistic diatribes. No, Garner did the intolerable: He wept. Right in the middle of morning worship, right where great preachers like Muzon Mann had labored, where our children were baptized, Garner wept! Right in the middle of morning worship, as if it was part of the liturgy, he started crying! Not loud, uncontrollable sobs, but quiet, deep crying. Old Man Henley, senile and almost deaf, remembering the last time he cried—when his wife died—started crying too. And then the children started. My cousin Ronny, our organist, sensing Brother Garner's impropriety, judiciously played the last hymn.

Assignment

Write an account of your own history, based on an event in your life that had emotional significance.

Chapter 28

AFRICAN-AMERICAN HISTORY: FREE AT LAST

First Thoughts . . .

"But one hundred years later, we must face the tragic fact that the Negro is still not free. One hundred years later, the life of the Negro is still sadly crippled by the manacles of segregation and the chains of discrimination." Martin Luther King, Jr., spoke these words in 1963. Was he right? If so, have things changed?

Chapter Learning Objectives . . .

If history is anything, it is personal. For many of us, African-American history during this time period is more than a hypothetical look at theories and facts. We lived that history and it is, painfully, still with us. In chapter 28, we will examine the life of the great history maker Martin Luther King, Jr. We will look at two other African-American leaders, and finally, we will read a personal, oral history. Oral histories can invite us to look again at this incredible part of the American story.

As a result of this chapter you should be able to:

1. Evaluate how King's speech is full of hope to both black and white Americans.

2. Discuss a memorable situation in which you experienced racism.

3. Reflect upon whether an African-American can also exhibit racism.

4. Compare and contrast the ways that Malcolm X and John Perkins approached racial reconciliation.

5. Analyze the impact of enlightenment programs upon African-American families.

HISTORY MAKER: MARTIN LUTHER KING, JR.

Martin Luther King, Jr., (1929-1968), civil rights leader, American humanitarian, pastor, and Nobel Peace Prize winner, was one of the premier history makers of the 20th century. He was not only one of the principal leaders of the American civil rights movement, he was also a prominent advocate of nonviolent protest. King's nonviolent challenges to racial discrimination persuaded many white Americans to support the cause of civil rights in the United States. Perhaps no other leader had more influence on the advancement of justice in the 20th century than Martin King.

"I Have a Dream" by Martin Luther King, Jr., Washington D.C., August 28, 1963:

Five score years ago, a great American, in whose symbolic shadow we stand, signed the Emancipation Proclamation. This momentous decree came as a great beacon light of hope to millions of Negro slaves who had been seared in the flames of withering injustice. It came as a joyous daybreak to end the long night of captivity.

But one hundred years later, we must face the tragic fact that the Negro is still not free. One hundred years later, the life of the Negro is still sadly crippled by the manacles of segregation and the chains of discrimination. One hundred years later, the Negro lives on a lonely island of poverty in the midst of a vast ocean of material prosperity. One hundred years later, the Negro is still languishing in the corners of American society and finds himself an exile in his own land. So we have come here today to dramatize an appalling condition.

In a sense we have come to our nation's capital to cash a check. When the architects of our republic wrote the magnificent words of the Constitution and the Declaration of Independence, they were signing a promissory note to which every American

Martin Luther King, Jr. by Dick DeMarsico, (CC BY-SA 3.0), 1964.

was to fall heir. This note was a promise that all men would be guaranteed the inalienable rights of life, liberty, and the pursuit of happiness.

It is obvious today that America has defaulted on this promissory note insofar as her citizens of color are concerned. Instead of honoring this sacred obligation, America has given the Negro people a bad check which has come back marked "insufficient funds." But we refuse to believe that the bank of justice is bankrupt. We refuse to believe that there are insufficient funds in the great vaults of opportunity of this nation. So we have come to cash this check—a check that will give us upon demand the riches of freedom and the security of justice. We have also come to this hallowed spot to remind

America of the fierce urgency of now. This is no time to engage in the luxury of cooling off or to take the tranquilizing drug of gradualism. Now is the time to rise from the dark and desolate valley of segregation to the sunlit path of racial justice. Now is the time to open the doors of opportunity to all of God's children. Now is the time to lift our nation from the quicksands of racial injustice to the solid rock of brotherhood.

It would be fatal for the nation to overlook the urgency of the moment and to underestimate the determination of the Negro. This sweltering summer of the Negro's legitimate discontent will not pass until there is an invigorating autumn of freedom and equality. Nineteen sixty-three is not an end, but a beginning. Those who hope that the Negro needed to blow off steam and will now be content will have a rude awakening if the nation returns to business as usual. There will be neither rest nor tranquility in America until the Negro is granted his citizenship rights. The whirlwinds of revolt will continue to shake the foundations of our nation until the bright day of justice emerges.

But there is something that I must say to my people who stand on the warm threshold which leads into the palace of justice. In the process of gaining our rightful place we must not be guilty of wrongful deeds. Let us not seek to satisfy our thirst for freedom by drinking from the cup of bitterness and hatred.

We must forever conduct our struggle on the high plane of dignity and discipline. We must not allow our creative protest to degenerate into physical violence. Again and again we must rise to the majestic heights of meeting physical force with soul force. The marvelous new militancy which has engulfed the Negro community must not lead us to distrust of all white people, for many of our white brothers, as evidenced by their presence here today, have come to realize that their destiny is tied up with our destiny and their freedom is inextricably bound to our freedom. We cannot walk alone.

And as we walk, we must make the pledge that we shall march ahead. We cannot turn back. There are those who are asking the devotees of civil rights, "When will you be satisfied?" We can never be satisfied as long as our bodies, heavy with the fatigue of travel, cannot gain lodging in the motels of the highways and the hotels of the cities. We cannot be satisfied as long as the Negro's basic mobility is from a smaller ghetto to a larger one. We can never be satisfied as long as a Negro in Mississippi cannot vote and a Negro in New York believes he has nothing for which to vote. No, no, we are not satisfied, and we will not be satisfied until justice rolls down like waters and righteousness like a mighty stream.

I am not unmindful that some of you have come here out of great trials and tribulations. Some of you have come fresh from narrow cells. Some of you have come from areas where your quest for freedom left you battered by the storms of persecution and staggered by the winds of police brutality. You have been the veterans of creative suffering. Continue to work with the faith that unearned suffering is redemptive.

Go back to Mississippi, go back to Alabama, go back to Georgia, go back to Louisiana, go back to the slums and ghettos of our northern cities, knowing that somehow this situation can and will be changed. Let us not wallow in the valley of despair.

I say to you today, my friends, that in spite of the difficulties and frustrations of the moment, I still have a dream. It is a dream deeply rooted in the American dream.

I have a dream that one day this nation will rise up and live out the true meaning of its creed: "We hold these truths to be self-evident: that all men are created equal."

I have a dream that one day on the red hills of

Statue of Dr. Martin Luther King, Jr., in the Kelly Ingram Park, Birmingham, Alabama.

Georgia the sons of former slaves and the sons of former slaveowners will be able to sit down together at a table of brotherhood.

I have a dream that one day even the state of Mississippi, a desert state, sweltering with the heat of injustice and oppression, will be transformed into an oasis of freedom and justice.

I have a dream that my four children will one day live in a nation where they will not be judged by the color of their skin but by the content of their character.

I have a dream today.

I have a dream that one day the state of Alabama, whose governor's lips are presently dripping with the words of interposition and nullification, will be transformed into a situation where little black boys and black girls will be able to join hands with little white boys and white girls and walk together as sisters and brothers.

I have a dream today.

I have a dream that one day every valley shall be exalted, every hill and mountain shall be made low, the rough places will be made plain, and the crooked places will be made straight, and the glory of the Lord shall be revealed, and all flesh shall see it together.

This is our hope. This is the faith with which I return to the South. With this faith we will be able to hew out of the mountain of despair a stone of hope. With this faith we will be able to transform the jangling discords of our nation into a beautiful symphony of brotherhood. With this faith we will be able to work together, to pray together, to struggle together, to go to jail together, to stand up for freedom together, knowing that we will be free one day.

This will be the day when all of God's children will be able to sing with a new meaning, "My country, 'tis of thee, sweet land of liberty, of thee I sing. Land where my fathers died, land of the pilgrim's pride, from every mountainside, let freedom ring."

And if America is to be a great nation this must become true. So let freedom ring from the prodigious hilltops of New Hampshire. Let freedom ring from the mighty mountains of New York. Let freedom ring from the heightening Alleghenies of Pennsylvania! Let freedom ring from the snow-capped Rockies of Colorado! Let freedom ring from the curvaceous peaks of California! But not only that; let freedom ring from Stone Mountain of

Martin Luther King, Jr. (left) and Malcolm X, Both men had come to hear the Senate debate on the Civil Rights Act of 1964. This was the only time the two men ever met; their meeting lasted only one minute, by Marion S. Trikosko, U.S. News & World Report Magazine, 1964.

Georgia! Let freedom ring from Lookout Mountain of Tennessee! Let freedom ring from every hill and every molehill of Mississippi. From every mountainside, let freedom ring.

When we let freedom ring, when we let it ring from every village and every hamlet, from every state and every city, we will be able to speed up that day when all of God's children, black men and white men, Jews and Gentiles, Protestants and Catholics, will be able to join hands and sing in the words of the old Negro spiritual, "Free at last! free at last! thank God Almighty, we are free at last!"

Assignment

A. What rhetorical techniques does King use to inspire and to persuade his audience?

B. In what way is this speech a word of hope to both black and white Americans?

TWO DIFFERENT VIEWS

John Perkins (1930–):

John Perkins (below) is an outspoken born-again Christian who unapologetically argues that faith in Christ is the hope of both the white and black communities. John Perkins and his family have been ministering among the poor for the last 40 years. In 1960 John Perkins, his wife Vera Mae, and their children left a "successful" life in California and moved back to Mendenhall, Mississippi to begin ministry. John Perkins is a man who overcame oppression and prejudice with forgiveness and reconciliation. The urban poor are oppressed, observes Perkins, but not always in the ways normally thought. They oppress themselves by clinging to their role as "victims." From the wisdom gained in his many years of working with both black and white church leaders, Perkins helps readers rethink their assumptions about what inner-city ministry should be and relates what the Bible says it is (www.mbc-tmm.org).

Black nationalist leader Marcus Garvey, a national hero of Jamaica, from the George Grantham Bain Collection. LOC, 1924 (PS-US).

Malcolm X (1925–1965):

Malcom X (right) had a very sad childhood that no doubt colored his later views. Malcolm X was born Malcolm Little on May 19, 1925, in Omaha, Nebraska. His mother, Louise Norton Little, was a homemaker occupied with the family's eight children. His father, Earl Little, was an outspoken Baptist minister and avid supporter of black nationalist leader Marcus Garvey. Earl's civil rights activism prompted death threats from the white supremacist organization Black Legion, forcing the family to relocate twice before Malcolm's fourth birthday. Nonetheless, Malcolm was taught the gospel and some people think that he made a commitment to Christ. Regardless of the Littles' efforts to elude the Black Legion, in 1929 their Lansing, Michigan, home was burned to the ground, and two years later Earl's mutilated body was found lying across the town's trolley tracks. Police ruled both accidents, but the Littles were certain that members of the Black Legion were responsible. Louise had an emotional breakdown several years after the death of her husband and was committed to a mental institution. Her children were split up among various foster homes and orphanages. By the early 1950s Little was converted to Islam and took the name Malcolm X. For the remainder of his life Malcolm X devoted himself to promoting black nationalism and violence (www.cmgww.com).

Assignment

Compare and contrast the ways that Malcolm X and John Perkins approached racial reconciliation.

THE WELFARE STATE

One of the most vigorous targets of racism is the American urban black family. And for good reason. The black American family, as well as the black American church, has been the cornerstone of African-American society for centuries.

Among African-American activists, by 1968 there was an open admission that the African-American family was in very serious trouble. (It has only gotten worse in the years since then.)

Many urban black families were devastated by racism and attempts to remove racism—like entitlement programs. In spite of the fact that the government provided unprecedented resources for children, the well-being of African-American children has declined steadily since the '60s.

The primary cause of broken African-American families has been the disappearance of a two-parent household. Three out of four teenage suicides occur in households where a parent has been absent. Eighty percent of adolescents in psychiatric hospitals come from broken homes. Tracking studies indicate that five of six adolescents caught up in the criminal-justice system come from families in which a parent (usually the father) has been absent. In 1988 a government survey of 17,000 children found, according to one analyst, that "children living apart from a biological parent were 20 percent to 40 percent more vulnerable to sickness."

The reasons for the demise of many African-American families were multi-faceted and complicated. Whatever the reasons, though, the net result was even more black rage.

The Great Depression was a pivotal event in the African-American family history because it spawned the great American welfare state. The welfare state would be another great disappointment for the African-American community. The first child of the welfare state was the New Deal. The New Deal was a mixed blessing to most blacks and eventually proved to be a disaster. Clearly federal economic intervention—the welfare state—failed the African-American community.

With the rise of the positive liberal state, the African-American community allied itself with the American liberal agenda. The black community looked now to the federal government as its savior. It was not until the late 1960s that the many African-Americans abandoned this basically humanistic agenda in favor of a black nationalistic agenda. Within many parts of the African-American community it was too late. Welfare dependency had demoralized, impoverished, and devastated the African-American community like nothing else ever had. The New Deal represented a new way of doing business: The federal government assumed the major role of taking care of the American poor, of which African-American representation was a disproportionate part.

Relief giving served the larger economic and political ends of America. President Franklin D. Roosevelt, for instance, saw all America benefiting if the poor and destitute benefited. This view prevailed in the American political mind for half a century. Within the last few years, this thesis has been seriously challenged by black intellectuals. Relief arrangements were initiated or expanded during occasional outbreaks of civil disorder to placate the disgruntled masses. Social welfare, as it was conceived and implemented in American history, was not much different from other governmental initiatives. It was a way to control, to placate, to appease. This fact became increasingly evident to the African-American community in the late 1960s.

President Roosevelt never envisioned that things would go so far. Welfare was originally intended only for widows and divorcees. Frances Perkins, Roosevelt's labor secretary, nearly excluded unwed mothers on moral grounds. At the time, no one imagined that out-of-wedlock pregnancies would burgeon as they have. No one thought that the government would ever intervene so strenuously as it has over the last 30 years. Personal accountability and social responsibility could not be passed on to the state. The results of trying to do so were disastrous.

There were great promises, though, that the African-American community implicitly embraced. The black community entrusted its future to the American political, legal, and social welfare systems. The previous generation had gone to the city to seek justice; this generation was putting its future in the hands of the federal government.

While many African-Americans were helped by government programs like President Johnson's Great Society, gains were short-lived and inadequate. African-Americans received less assistance than they needed. The government never attacked the real cause of African-American poverty: racism. Housing, job, and social opportunities were being sabotaged by racism. Entitled programs delayed genuine racial progress by masking the real problem.

For the African-American community, at least, the New Deal was woefully inadequate. The Welfare State did not provide sufficient employment or housing, but it stimulated hope in abundance. That was the rub. When, in the late '80s, the black community discovered that the welfare state had devastated its care-giving infrastructure, it was furious.

The effect of the positive liberal state was disastrous on the African-American community. Some scholars—many of whom are African-American—are offering an almost "doomsday" appraisal of American society. They argue that our social welfare policies are moving the African-American community toward a sort of "dystopia," defined in Webster as a situation "in which conditions and the quality of life are dreadful." Murray reminded us in an October 1993 *Wall Street Journal* article entitled "The Coming White Underclass" that the Negative Liberal State—at least in the area of welfare reform—has been an unmitigated disaster. Murray recalled that when New York Senator Daniel Patrick Moynihan wrote his 1965 warning about the disintegration of the African-American family, 26 percent of African-American births were to unwed mothers. Today, that figure has soared to 68 percent and even higher (nearly 80 percent) in innercity neighborhoods. As a result, as John Perkins also argued, African-Americans were literally killing themselves.

From 1932 to 1995 the social welfare system became a runaway train on which the government has spent over $5 trillion since 1965. If all this money had given us happy, healthy families, it would have been worth it. But the opposite was true. It consigned untold millions of children to lives of bitterness and failure. This has been particularly true among African-American families. The failure of the welfare state again generated anger among the African-American community.

2009 Inaugural Parade. Michelle and Barack Obama watch the parade from the viewing stand in front of the White House, Washington, D.C. by Carol M. Highsmith, 2009.

It was in the ghetto where most African-Americans found themselves moving into the welfare web. The central core of the American city remained the entry point for black immigrants. Decaying structures, slum conditions, massive unemployment, and African-American ghettos became underclass colonies for African-Americans. To the African-American, the ghetto represented a shattered dream. It also became a hothouse for unhealthy, welfare-dependent, single-parent African-American families.

The African-American family has been devastated primarily by the loss of the nuclear, two-parent family. By 1994 the number of illegitimate births grew to 40 percent and—an even more alarming figure—27 percent of pregnancies were aborted. "Now, I don't care what your position is, whether you're pro-choice or anti-abortion—that's too many," President Clinton told the National Baptist Convention U.S.A. Having a baby out of wedlock was "simply not right," he said. "You shouldn't have a baby before you're ready, and you shouldn't have a baby when you're not married." The welfare state, by removing initiative and by rewarding illegitimacy, encouraged single families. Absent fathers, single families, are more fertile ground for dysfunctional family development. The loss of fathers in African-American families because of welfare dependency has had the most devastating effect on the black community.

"Children who do not live with a mother and a father are more likely to be high school dropouts, more likely to abuse drugs and alcohol, and more likely to be dependent on welfare than children who live with both biological parents,"

Human Services Chief Louis Sullivan said in October 1994. Psychologists pointed out that fathers were not simply substitute mothers. Fathers tended to be stronger disciplinarians than mothers, and that was particularly true for boys. Boys were much less likely to develop good self-control when fathers were not present. But, as Senator Daniel Patrick Moynihan pointed out in 1965, a man, already suffering from his failure as a provider, was further demeaned by becoming dependent on the woman who gets the welfare check. As a result, many African-American men turned to violence to gain self-esteem. Roughly 40 percent of young African-American men ages 17 to 35 were in prison, on probation, or on the dole.

Of course the real victims were children. Single-parent households statistically were usually poorer than two-parent households. In 1993, 46.1 percent of the 8.8 million female-headed families with children lived in poverty, compared with only 9.0 percent of the 26.1 million married couple families with children. Of 1.6 million families headed by unmarried men only 22.5 percent lived in poverty. Out of 69.3 million children younger than 18, 15.7 million—one in four—are poor. Most of these poor children were born out of wedlock to African-American women. This fact was not lost on many blacks.

Clearly single parenthood exacerbated poverty, but would marriage cure it? Yes. Research suggested that over 60 percent of poor children in mother-only families would be lifted out of poverty if they were in two-parent households. More African-American children were raised in single-parent homes than in two-parent homes, and federal welfare was doing nothing to encourage a change. It was doing just the opposite.

Would money help the problem? "Unless we slow down these social trends—out-of-wedlock births, crime, drugs, the breakdown of values—government money was not going to do much," says Gary Bauer of the Family Research Council. Bauer concludes by saying, "Kids are not in poverty because Washington was not spending more money."

"Programs like AFDC combined with food stamps and housing assistance, although meant for good, have broken up more families than slavery ever did. As a result of these broken families, children were being raised without fathers in the house. This single fact contributes more than anything to the chaotic atmosphere in our inner cities," writes Rev. John Perkins, a pioneer of African-American self-help programs, in *Policy Review,* a publication of the Heritage Foundation.

The overall failure of the American welfare system has disillusioned the African-American community. Legal barriers between the races no doubt fell in the last 30 years. But in many ways African-Americans are worse off today than they ever were.

Roosevelt's New Deal and Johnson's Great Society failed, on one hand, because they ignored the most fundamental need of all disadvantaged people: employment. But on the other hand, I think that they failed because these programs were not able fundamentally to change the American character. The welfare state was devastating to the African-American community because it fostered dependency. It broke down the infrastructure that sustained the African-American community without replacing it with an efficacious alternative.

Welfare had done more than that. It masked the real problem: racism. Racism had attacked the most vulnerable and important victim to date: the African-American family. Racism, ironically, used entitlement programs to claim more victims. The fact is, economic progress is not enough. It will never be enough. Until human hearts and systems of injustice change, the African-American situation in America will not be significantly improved. Welfare, then, has served only to delay real racial progress and reconciliation.

Assignment

Entitlement programs (i.e., welfare), according to African-American scholars Thomas Sowell and Charles Murray, have greatly harmed the African-American community by creating dependency upon the federal government. Agree or disagree with this argument.

ORAL HISTORY

In John Milton's description of hell in *Paradise Lost*, there is a brilliant image of both utter darkness and the burning fire of God's judgment juxtaposed in the same place, much as sin and love coexist in one's heart: "In utter darkness, their portion set/As far removed from God and light of Heaven." Then, Milton (left) lights the fires of hell with hatred, rebellion, and prejudice. "The unconquerable will,/And study of revenge, immortal hate,/And courage never to submit or yield."

"Better to reign in Hell than serve in Heaven," Satan cries to God from the floor of hell. I felt and saw the cosmological battle between good and evil on the horizon of my property and in the center of my heart.

"And crown thy good with brotherhood,/From sea to shining sea."

I was angry. And scared. I should have known that there was trouble coming. Two weeks earlier I had heard that a giant Klu Klux Klan unity rally would be held near my farm. "It was the only public event that you could still attend and not see a single dirty, filthy, stinking nigger!" an advertising bulletin announced.

"Well, that is comforting," I snickered, "I do not think my two daughters and my son—the only African Americans who lived within 10 miles of the rally—would want to go anyway."

There was an inordinate amount of traffic in the late afternoon—cars with out-of-state license plates, cars that stopped and whose occupants stepped out to look at my registered Suffolk sheep and, to my horror, at my children playing in the background. My wife, Karen, gathered our little ones and took them into the house—but where could we be safe? My daughter's bedroom was next to a window

Klu Klux Klan, National Photo Company Collection, c1921.

whose glass could easily be shattered by an angry Klansman's 30-30 rifle. Assured of the veracity of our cause, but afraid of a thoughtless, perhaps inebriated, Klansmen's angry rifle shot, we waited for the dawn.

I had met my antagonist at his father's funeral a few weeks earlier, before I knew that he was the Imperial Wizard of the Invisible Kingdom of my unpretentious neighborhood, committed to ridding our neighborhood of "niggers," Jews, and other "undesirables." As far as I knew my three children and one man were the only African-Americans in our area, and I knew of only one Jewish family. But the Grand Dragon was nothing more to me than the distraught son of a good man who had recently died. Joe, his father, had died of cancer. The night of Joe's death I held his hand and led him to Christ. So I felt nothing but pity for his sheepish son with his head bowed. He had no idea I harbored "subversive minorities" on my farm, and I had no idea he was the esteemed leader of the local imperial kingdom.

On this eerie fall night I had the distinct feeling that I still did not know him and he did not know me either. And I still felt sorry for him, but we were more alike than he knew.

My three adopted, interracial children were my promised land. They were my new time, my new land, my new chance. They were more than my son and daughters: they were God's invitation to me to experience wholeness and new life. You know, what I have learned, and what my Ku Klux Klan neighbor needs to learn, is that being prejudiced is as bad as having others express prejudice against you. People know what Martin Luther King, Jr., did for my African-American neighbors, but do they understand what he did for me—a prejudiced white Southerner who hated African-Americans? King showed me a way home—a way to put an end to this hatred and hopelessness.

"Oh beautiful for patriot dream/That sees beyond the years." I had pleaded with my neighbors not to go to the rally. "It is like going to a pornographic movie. You really don't need to go and see what is happening to know that it is evil," I said.

But they went. By the hundreds they went. "I am not for the violence," they sheepishly explained. "But, you know, what they say makes sense."

What do they say? "The . . . hordes have overrun all of America's major cities, and turned them into jungles, unfit for human habitation," a Ku Klux Klan broadside reads. Yes, it makes sense. That makes their actions even more evil. No, my community has played the harlot.

Klu Klux Klan parade in Washington, D.C., National Photo Company Collection, 1926.

My family, thanks to the watchful eye of the FBI and the grace of God, survived that evening. My story is the American Story. It is the story of racism and what its resulting anger can do to one family.

Assignment

Is there a minority group living in your community or a nearby town? Describe their neighborhood, behavior, economic and educational opportunities, and relationships with other races or ethnic groups in the area. How do you feel about them? How do your thoughts and actions toward them compare with Jesus' teachings about love and kindness?

Chapter 29

CULTURE WARS: 1950s TO THE PRESENT

First Thoughts . . .

So bye-bye, Miss American pie.
Drove my Chevy to the levee,
But the levee was dry.
And them good old boys were drinkin' whiskey and rye,
Singin', "This'll be the day that I die.
This'll be the day that I die."

Don McClean's lyrics in his 1971 folk song capture the essence of an era marked by nihilism and revolution. It was an era of irresponsible excess and flamboyance. It was also an era that took us to the moon and discovered a cure for polio. It is in the essence of these contradictions that we find ourselves from 1950 to the present.

Chapter Learning Objectives . . .

As we look at the United States from 1950 to the present, we will see 70 million children from the post–World War II baby boom become teenagers and young adults. These young people, and then young adults, will lead America from the conservative '50s to the extravagant, narcissistic new century. American life. No longer content to be reflections of preceding generations, young people want change. Many of the revolutionary ideas that began in these decades are continuing to evolve today.

As a result of this chapter you should be able to:

1. Discuss the causes and results of the counter-revolution of the 1950s and 1960s.

2. Discuss the culture wars that have been raging since the 1960s.

3. Trace the loss of "consensus" in American political and cultural history.

4. Evaluate whether there is a message that the Church needs to hear from contemporary culture.

CULTURE WARS: PART ONE

The decade of the 1960s was a time of unprecedented subjectivity and hedonism. America lost its way in the cultural wilderness and is still wandering.

While a cold war raged overseas, a culture war broke out at home. During the 1950s, Americans experienced unprecedented prosperity. This prosperity invited most Americans to a new form of conservatism that posited the viewpoint that "if it works, don't fix it." Therefore, conformity and uniformity were watchmen on the walls of early 1950 American culture. One social historian explains, "Everyone preferred group norms and cultural icons rather than experiencing the uncomfortableness of nonconformity." The camaraderie and community engendered by World War II invited Americans to embrace the security of group conformity. They were to abandon it with reckless haste in the 1960s.

Most Americans craved the security of the simpler world of the 1930s rather than the uncomfortable, risky, unknown world that was to come. Post–World War II Americans preferred to maintain old, traditional values, not to invent new ones. This included job choices and home life. Though men and women had been forced into new employment patterns during World War II, once the war was over, traditional roles were reaffirmed. As soon as the War ended, returning soldiers expected to be the breadwinners. Many women returned to their former roles as housewives. Even those who remained in other jobs saw themselves primarily as wives and mothers.

Sociologist David Riesman observed the importance of peer-group expectations in his influential book *The Lonely Crowd* (1950). He called this new society "other-directed," and maintained that such societies led to stability as well as conformity. Television contributed to the homogenizing trend by providing young and old with a shared experience reflecting accepted social patterns. Radio and then television created an American culture that competed with local culture. This new ubiquitous culture invited conformity (from *An Outline of American History*).

But not all Americans, particularly young Americans, conformed to such cultural norms. A number of writers and other artists rebelled against conventional values. Stressing spontaneity and spirituality, they asserted intuition over reason, mysticism over denominational religion. This new world view was reminiscent of the Transcendental movement of the previous century. These new cultural rebels went out of their way to challenge the patterns of respectability and shock the rest of the culture.

Their literary work displayed their penchant for nonconformity. Jack Kerouac (left, CC BY-SA 2.0) typed his best-selling novel *On the Road* (1959) on a 75-meter roll of paper. Lacking accepted punctuation and paragraph structure, the book glorified the possibilities of the free life. Poet Allen Ginsberg gained similar notoriety for his poem "Howl," a scathing critique of modern, mechanized civilization (from *An Outline of American History*). The movie *The Blob* (1958) broke new ground when Steve McQueen and his teenage friends, unable to rely on adult superiors, took matters into their own hands, broke the law, and ultimately figured

Senator John F. Kennedy and Vice President Richard M. Nixon during the first televised U.S. presidential debate, photographer unknown, 1960

out themselves how to kill this monster. The viewer knew without any doubt that youth unencumbered by adult supervision was the hope for America's future.

This was only the beginning. Elvis Presley, who to later generations seemed fairly tame, in fact revolutionized non-conformity music in the '50s. Born in Tupelo, Mississippi, Elvis Presley popularized African-American soul music and took it a step further. He in effect helped create a new music genre: rock and roll. Presley shocked Americans with his unconventional hairstyle, seductive lyrics, and undulating hips.

Some painters of the '40s and '50s, like Jackson Pollock, discarded easels and laid out gigantic canvases on the floor, then applied paint, sand, and other materials in wild splashes of color. Akin to Dadaism (which peaked between 1916 and 1920) and Surrealism (which started in the 1920s), this new abstract, called "modern art," invited the participant to new levels of subjectivity and narcissism. Meaning resided in the viewer, not in the artists, and Americans could find meaning in their own experiences rather than in socially accepted norms and rituals. All of these artists and authors, whatever the medium, provided fertile ground for the more radical social revolutions of the 1960s.

Photograph promoting the film *Jailhouse Rock* depicts singer Elvis Presley, Metro-Goldwyn-Mayer, Inc., 1957.

The '60s was an era when individualism was deified. But the greatest changes were evident in government participation in the daily lives of individuals. By 1960 government had become an increasingly powerful force in people's lives. During the 1930s, the president initiated legislation and worked closely with Congress to ease the trauma of the Great Depression. New executive agencies were created to deal with many aspects of American life. The number of civilians employed by the federal government rose from 1 million to 3.8 million during World War II, then stabilized at 2.5 million throughout the 1950s. Federal expenditures, which had stood at $3.1 billion in 1929, increased to $75 billion in 1953 and passed $150 billion in the 1960s. With the creation of more aggressive racial equality social policy and legislation, the United States government became even more ubiquitous in American lives. This intervention was debated, but nowhere hotly contested: most Americans accepted that fact that there were problems in the 1960s that could not be solved without government help (from *Outline of American History*).

The youngest man ever to win the presidency was 43-year-old John F. Kennedy. For the first time, television played a major role in national politics. In a series of televised debates with opponent Richard Nixon, Kennedy was poised, comely, and erudite. These debates provided the margin of victory that Kennedy needed to win the 1960 election. For the first time since the presidency of Abraham Lincoln, during Kennedy's 1,000 days in office, America enjoyed a young family and an energetic leader. However, though President Kennedy was immensely popular, he in fact offered little new legislation or executive leadership before he was assassinated just three years into his term.

Lyndon Johnson, a Texan who was majority leader in the Senate before becoming Kennedy's vice president, was a masterful politician. Johnson, lacking Kennedy's charisma, nonetheless possessed the political skills to advance an aggressive, even radical social agenda. He had been schooled in Congress, where he developed an extraordinary ability to get things done. He could plead, cajole, or threaten as necessary to achieve his ends. As president, he wanted to use his power aggressively to

John F. Kennedy, photograph in the Oval Office by Cecil Stoughton, 1963.

Portrait of President Lyndon B. Johnson by Yoichi R. Okamoto, White House Press Office, 1969

eliminate poverty and spread the benefits of prosperity to all (from *Outline of American History*).

Johnson took office determined to secure the measures that Kennedy had sought. As one historian explains, "Immediate priorities were bills to reduce taxes and guarantee civil rights. Using his skills of persuasion and calling on the legislators' respect for the slain president, in 1964 Johnson succeeded in gaining passage of the Civil Rights Bill. Introduced by Kennedy, it was the most far-reaching piece of civil rights legislation enacted since Reconstruction. Soon Johnson addressed other issues as well. By the spring of 1964, he had begun to use the name 'Great Society' to describe his reform program, and that term received even more play after his landslide victory over conservative Republican Barry Goldwater in the presidential election of that year."

The **Great Society** was the greatest burst of legislative activity since the New Deal. This legislation permanently radicalized American society. Many argue, however, that ultimately the Great Society failed miserably. America faced in the 1970s the same problems Johnson confronted in the 1960s.

Assignment

A. During the 1950s and 1960s, increasing numbers of married women entered the labor force, but in 1963 the average working woman only earned 63 percent of what a man made. That year author Betty Friedan published *The Feminine Mystique*, an explosive critique of middle-class patterns that helped millions of women articulate a pervasive sense of discontent. Arguing that women often had no outlets for expression other than "finding a husband and bearing children," Friedan encouraged readers to seek new roles and responsibilities, to seek their own personal and professional identities rather than have them defined by the outside, male-dominated society. React to Frieden's views.

B. Why were Americans ready for change in the 1950s and 1960s?

CULTURE WARS: PART TWO

The next twist in history has shocked a generation of Americans.

(1992) William Clinton is elected President.

(1998) President Clinton's affair with Whitehouse intern Monica Lewinski is exposed.

(2001) George W. Bush takes office. September 11. Terrorists hijack four airliners full of passengers and fly them into both of the World Trade Towers, the Pentagon, and the ground.

A conservative reaction to the radicalism of the 1960s and 1970s was inevitable (thank God!). This conservative upsurge had many sources. A large group of evangelical Christians—some of whom were called the Moral Majority—were particularly concerned about an increase in immoral behavior. Some of you may remember the laudable (in my opinion) effect men of God like Jerry Falwell and Pat Robertson had on the Republican Party.

Another galvanizing issue for conservatives was one of the most divisive and morally reprehensible issues of the time: abortion. Opposition to the 1973 Supreme Court decision, Roe v. Wade, which upheld a woman's right to an abortion, brought together a wide array of organizations and individuals. They included, but were not limited to, large numbers of Catholics, political conservatives, and religious fundamentalists, most of whom regarded abortion under virtually any circumstances as tantamount to murder. They were prepared to organize in support of politicians who agreed with their position—and against those who disagreed with it. Pro-choice and antiabortion demonstrations became a fixture of the political landscape (from *An Outline of American History*).

The figure who drew all these disparate strands together was Ronald Reagan. Reagan, born in Illinois, achieved stardom as an actor in Hollywood movies and television before turning to politics. He first achieved political prominence

James Earl "Jimmy" Carter, Department of Defense. Department of the Navy. Naval Photographic Center, 1977.

with a nationwide televised speech in 1964 in support of Barry Goldwater. In 1966 Reagan won the governorship of California, owing to a wave of voter reaction against the student rebellion at the University of California-Berkeley, and served until 1975. He narrowly missed winning the Republican nomination for president in 1976 before succeeding in 1980 and going on to win the presidency from Jimmy Carter. Reagan won overwhelming reelection in 1984 against Carter's vice president, Walter Mondale (from *An Outline of American History*).

As one historian explains, President Reagan's unflagging optimism and his ability to celebrate the achievements and aspirations of the American people persisted throughout his two terms in office. He was a figure of reassurance and stability for many Americans. Despite his propensity for misstatements, Reagan was known as the "Great Communicator," primarily for his mastery of television. For many, he recalled the prosperity and relative social tranquility of the 1950s—an era dominated by another genial public personality who evoked widespread affection, President Dwight Eisenhower.

President Reagan enjoyed unusually high popularity at the end of his second term in office, but under the terms of the U.S. Constitution he could not run again in 1988. He certainly wanted to do so! His vice president during all eight years of his presidency, George H. W. Bush, was elected the 41st president of the United States.

Bush campaigned by promising voters a continuation of the prosperity Reagan had brought; he also argued that his expertise could better support a strong defense for the United States than that of the Democratic Party's candidate, Michael Dukakis. Dukakis, the governor of Massachusetts, claimed that less fortunate Americans were hurting economically and that the government had to help those people while simultaneously bringing the federal debt and defense spending under control. The public was much more engaged, however, by Bush's economic message: a promise of no new taxes. In the balloting, Bush finished with a 54-to-46-percent popular vote margin.

Because of an ailing economy, Bill Clinton was elected president in 1990. While America experienced significant prosperity in his two-term tenure, we also experienced unprecedented political and moral abuse of the office. It was, as former Education Secretary William Bennett wrote, a time of "the Death of Outrage."

Official Portrait of President Ronald Reagan, photographer unknown, 1983.

Assignment

A. Many were aroused by the publication in 1962 of Rachel Carson's book *Silent Spring*, which pointed to the ravages of chemical pesticides, particularly DDT. Public concern about the environment continued to increase throughout the 1960s as many became aware of other pollutants surrounding them—automobile emissions, industrial wastes, oil spills—that threatened their health and the beauty of their surroundings. On April 22, 1970, schools and communities across the United States celebrated Earth Day. "Teach-ins" educated Americans about the dangers of environmental pollution. While we all applaud these efforts to a certain extent, what dangers are inherent to this sort of "new Romanticism?"

B. Speculate upon why President George W. Bush (2001–2009) had become so unpopular by the time he left office.

Ronald Reagan sculpture in Presidents Park, Black Hills, South Dakota.

MORE QUESTIONS

Assignment

A. Trace the loss of a "consensus" in American political and cultural history from 1950 to 1980.

B. When the term "ecology" became popular, many resisted proposed measures to clean up the nation's air and water. Solutions would cost money for businesses and individuals, and force changes in the way people lived or worked. However, in 1970, Congress amended the Clean Air Act of 1967 to develop uniform national air-quality standards. It also passed the Water Quality Improvement Act, which made cleaning up offshore oil spills the responsibility of the polluter. Then, in 1970, the Environmental Protection Agency was created as an independent federal agency to spearhead the effort to bring abuses under control. In light of the BP ecological disaster in 2010, do you think the government should be even more aggressive in regulatory legislation concerning the environment? Why do you believe that a government should be or should not be involved in environmental regulation?

Jellyfish in an Aquarium by Rebecca White, 2011

THE DEATH OF OUTRAGE

The following is an essay from William Bennett's description of his book *The Death of Outrage* (1998):

Bill Clinton is completing the second year of his second term. Why not let these matters go? Instead of keeping the nation's attention focused on scandals and squalid acts, why not move on to other issues? Why not just look away?

The answer to these questions is that on Bill Clinton's behalf, in his defense, many bad ideas are being put into widespread circulation. It is said that private character has virtually no impact on governing character; that what matters above all is a healthy economy; that moral authority is defined solely by how well a president deals with public policy matters; that America needs to become more European (read: more "sophisticated") in its attitude toward sex; that lies about sex, even under oath, don't really matter; that we shouldn't be "judgmental"; that it is inappropriate to make preliminary judgments about the president's conduct because he hasn't been found guilty in a court of law; and so forth.

If these arguments take root in American soil—if they become the coin of the public realm—we will have validated them, and we will come to rue the day we did. These arguments define us down; they assume a lower common denominator of behavior and leadership than we Americans ought to accept. And if we do accept it, we will have committed an unthinking act of moral and intellectual disarmament. In the realm of American ideals and the great tradition of public debate, the high ground will have been lost. And when we need to rely again on this high ground—as surely we will need to—we will find it drained of its compelling moral power. In that sense, then, the arguments invoked by Bill Clinton and his defenders represent an assault on American ideals, even if you assume the president did nothing improper. So the arguments need to be challenged.

I believe these arguments are also a threat to our understanding of American self-government. It demands active participation in, and finally, reasoned judgments on,

Official White House photo of President Bill Clinton by Bob McNeely, 1993

important civic matters. "Judgment" is a word that is out of favor these days, but it remains a cornerstone of democratic self-government. It is what enables us to hold ourselves, and our leaders, to high standards. It is how we distinguish between right and wrong, noble and base, honor and dishonor. We cannot ignore that responsibility, or foist it on others. It is the price—sometimes the exacting price—of citizenship in a democracy. The most popular arguments made by the president's supporters invite us to abandon that participation, those standards, and the practice of making those distinctions.

Bill Clinton's presidency is also defining public morality down. Civilized society must give public affirmation to principles and standards, categorical norms, notions of right and wrong. Even though public figures often fall short of these standards—and we know and we expect some will—it is nevertheless crucial that we pay tribute to them. When Senator Gary Hart withdrew from the 1988 presidential contest because of his relationship with Donna Rice, he told his staff, "Through thoughtlessness and misjudgment I've let each of you down. And I deeply regret that." By saying what he said, by withdrawing from the race, Senator Hart affirmed public standards. President Clinton, by contrast, expresses no regret, no remorse, no contrition—even as he uses his public office to further his private ends. On every scandal, what he says or intimates always amounts to one of the following: "It doesn't matter. I wasn't involved. My political enemies are to blame. I have nothing more to say. The rules don't apply to me. There are no consequences to my actions. It's irrelevant. My only responsibility is to do the people's business." This is moral bankruptcy, and it is damaging our country, its standards, and our self-respect.

Once in a great while a single national event provides insight into where we are and who we are and what we esteem. The Clinton presidency has provided us with a window onto our times, our moral order, our understanding of citizenship. The many Clinton scandals tell us, in a way few other events can, where we are in our public philosophy. They reveal insights into how we view politics and power; virtue and vice; public trust and respect for the law; sexual morality and standards of personal conduct.

America's professional opinion classes—journalists, columnists, and commentators—have produced truckloads of words, both spoken and written, about the Clinton scandals. Some of them are excellent, and I have mined them for this book. What I hope to do is to put things in a broader context, explaining their implications for our national political life and for the lessons we teach our young.

My goal is also to give public expression to people's private concerns. Many Americans have an intuitive understanding that something is deeply troubling about President Clinton's conduct and the defenses offered on his behalf. But Bill Clinton and his supporters have skillfully deflected criticism by changing the subject. They have persuaded many in the middle that the sophisticated thing is to dismiss the scandalous as irrelevant. My purpose in this book is to speak citizen to citizen to those in the middle—not to "preach to the converted," but to speak to the troubled. I believe that public opinion has not yet hardened on these matters and that people are still open to evidence, facts,

Clinton with President Barack Obama by a White House photographer, 2010.

persuasion, and an appeal to reason and the rule of law. This book is presented in that spirit.

This is a short book. It is not a systematic work of moral philosophy. Its aim is much more limited: to respond to an urgent public matter now before the American people—in a manner, I trust, that is informed by sound reasoning. In what follows I take the words of the president and his defenders seriously, examining them, and asking the reader to judge whether the conclusions that flow from them are true or false, good or harmful. In the end this book rests on the venerable idea that moral good and moral harm are very real things, and moral good or moral harm can come to a society by what it esteems and by what it disdains.

Many people have been persuaded to take a benign view of the Clinton presidency on the basis of arguments that have attained an almost talismanic stature but that in my judgment are deeply wrong and deeply pernicious. We need to say no to those arguments as loudly as we can—and yes to the American ideals they endanger."

Assignment

A. What is the "death of outrage" that Bennett describes?

B. What message does the Church need to give to contemporary culture, which, by all accounts, is becoming hostile, even anti-Christian? Is the world simply the enemy who needs to be brought into faith, or can we learn something from this post-Christian world?

The Beatles were representative of a huge shift in entertainment and culture which has continued to evolve through the next five decades and even today. They wave to fans after arriving at Kennedy Airport, United Press International, photographer unknown, 1964.

Chapter 30

CONTEMPORARY SOCIAL HISTORY

First Thoughts . . .

"The path America is traveling today is happy-go-lucky nihilism," former Attorney General Robert Bork argues. "God and religion have long since dropped out of the public discourse, to our nation's folly." In particular, the secularization of issues is seen in the abortion question, which Bork says is now largely performed as a matter of convenience and has nothing to do with medical reasons in the majority of cases. He believes this is an issue that "ought to have a religious dimension." This is only one of many cultural maladies afflicting our nation. In this chapter, we will examine again, in greater depth, the genesis of the culture war facing the new generation of Americans growing up at the begining of this century. In order to do this, we will have to look at the social lives of Americans from 1950 to the present.

Chapter Learning Objectives . . .

We will examine the 1950s as a beginning point for the culture wars described in the previous chapter. Next, we will examine the home school movement—perhaps the most revolutionary cultural development of the 20th century. We will examine the effect of television on American culture, and finally, we will be inspired by the life of history maker Rev. Billy Graham, perhaps the most influential American from 1950 to the present.

As a result of this chapter you should be able to:

1. Describe what a social historian can learn from a picture of a 1950 woman.

2. Evaluate an essay about homeschooling as a cultural revolution.

3. Analyze Neil Postman's argument that television is "dumbing down" American culture.

4. Discuss the influence of evangelist Billy Graham in American history.

A CASE STUDY:
SOCIAL HISTORY IN THE '50s

There are different ways to write history. Some historians emphasize the political side of history—who was in power and who was not. Other historians look at all the wars—who won them and who didn't. Still others look at the economic side of history—who made money and who didn't. Finally, social historians look at the lives of people living this history—what they ate and drank, what they did for entertainment, and so forth. This chapter is a social history of America—the story of the American people and how they lived from 1950 to 2010.

The end of World War II brought thousands of young veterans back to America to continue their lives. American industry abandoned wartime industries to meet peacetime needs. Americans, for their part, began buying goods with reckless abandon, goods not available during the war, which created more jobs.

At the same time, traditional values had a revival among all Americans. For one thing, the addition of the phrase "under God" was added to the Pledge of Allegiance. Churches were full. Men wore gray flannel suits and women wore dresses and high heels. Families vacationed together at national parks and the new Disneyland. Gender roles were strongly held, girls played with Barbie dolls, boys with Davy Crockett rifles. Drive-in movies became popular for families and

teens. Highways were built to take people quickly from one place to another, bypassing small towns and helping to create shopping malls. Toys like Hula Hoops® and Silly Putty® flew off the market shelves.

Missionaries to Hawaii in the 1700s, who saw the hula dance there, named the toy the Hula Hoop®. Though the hoops were wildly popular in the U.S., Japan banned them. The Soviet Union said the Hula Hoop® toy was an example of the "emptiness of American culture." Wham-O manufactured 20,000 hoops a day at the peak of Hula Hoop® popularity. The plastic tubing used for all Hula Hoop® toys ever produced would stretch around the earth more than five times.

Television created an American mass-media culture. Whether one lived in Topeka, Kansas, or New York City, one saw the same programs, same commercials. Television promoted the ideal family. People began to accept what was heard and seen on television because they were eyewitnesses to events as never before. Coonskin hats were a huge fad in the 1950s, all due to Fess Parker's portrayal of Davy Crockett. I had one and even wore it to bed! In 1954, black-and-white broadcasts became color broadcasts. Shows like *The Honeymooners, Lassie, Father Knows Best, The Adventures of Ozzie and Harriet, Flash Gordon*, and *I Love Lucy* drew thousands of viewers and transformed America.

Assignment

Look up some Coca-Cola ads from the 1950s that have teens in them (on the Internet, in books, or old magazines), and describe what a social historian could learn from the images.

HOMESCHOOLING

From about late '70s to the present, home education, or homeschooling emerged in American social life. Homeschooling is to teach your children at home, or be taught at home rather than in the public or private school systems. By 2010 there were about 2.5 million homeschoolers in America.

While they are less than 1 percent of American students, homeschoolers are having a disproportionate impact on American life. For one thing, they are dominating college admission scores and descending in droves on the most prestigious college in the country, which positions them to be among the next culture creators of American social life.

As sociologist Peter Berger accurately observes, evangelicals (and Christian homeschoolers) generally subscribe to two strongly held propositions: that a return to Christian values is necessary if the moral confusion of our time is to be overcome, and that the Enlightenment is to be blamed for much of the confusion of our time. In fact, Christian homeschooling, along with other strains of evangelicalism, is one of the most potent anti-**Enlightenment** movements in world history. I most assuredly did not say "anti-intellectual." Christian homeschoolers argue that the excessives of Enlightenment rationalism have sabotaged the certitude of traditional ethics and Christian theism that so strongly influenced Western culture long before the formidable onslaught of the likes of **David Hume**.

Higher test scores and functional family units are only two reasons that homeschoolers are capturing the elite culture of America. *The Washington Post* in 1993 coyly observed that evangelicals are "largely poor, uneducated, and easy to command." And, among our own, evangelical professor Mark Noll unkindly observed, "The scandal of the evangelical mind is that there is not much of an evangelical mind." Indeed. Not anymore. Today, more than ever, in the garb of Christian homeschooling, evangelicalism has gained new life. By sidestepping the Enlightenment, Christian homeschooling has opened up a whole new arena for debate. While conceding that faith is not a makeshift bridge to overcome some **Kierkegaardian** gap between beliefs and evidence, homeschooling posits that it still is important that we look beyond our experience for reality. Human needs and aspirations are greater than the world can satisfy, so it is reasonable to look elsewhere for that satisfaction. Worth is the highest and best reality (a decidedly anti-Enlightenment notion) and its genesis and maintenance come exclusively from relationship with God alone. Homeschooling families, with their sacrificial love for one another and the extravagant gift of time to one another, offer a radical path into this new way of looking at reality.

Christian homeschooling, then, moves backward to a time when intellectualism was not separate from religion. It blows the claims of the Enlightenment to bits. Homeschooling has brought back stability into the lives of millions of Americans, while the majority of Americans are living in a context of clashing reactivities where (as Kenneth J. Gergen explains) the very ground of meaning, the foundations and structures of thought, language, and social discourse are up for grabs, where the very concepts of personhood, spirituality, truth, integrity, and objectivity are all being demolished, breaking up, giving way.

Homeschoolers are building a new generation of **culture creators** the old-fashioned way: parents stay home and love the kids and in the process lay their lives down for all our futures. Homeschooling. Millions strong. Unpretentious to a fault, this new cultural revolution is inviting Americans back to traditional truths that have been with us always and others that need to be rediscovered. Homeschooling has invited Americans to a comfortable marriage of intellectualism and transcendentalism that fares our culture and our nation well in the years ahead. In that sense, then, perhaps homeschooling families are the new patriots, the hope for our weary nation and our dysfunctional culture (Jim Stobaugh, crosswalk.com).

Assignment

In what way is homeschooling a cultural revolution?

"PEEKABOO WORLD"

The following is a passage from *Amusing Ourselves to Death* **(1987) by Neal Postman:**

Television has become, so to speak, the background radiation of the social and intellectual universe, the all-but-imperceptible residue of the electronic big bang of a century past, so familiar and so thoroughly integrated with American culture that we no longer hear its faint hissing in the background or see the flickering gray light. This, in turn, means that its epistemology goes largely unnoticed. And the peekaboo world it has constructed around us no longer seems even strange.

There is no more disturbing consequence of the electronic and graphic revolution than this: that the world as given to us through television seems natural, not bizarre. For the loss of the sense of the strange is a sign of adjustment, and the extent to which we have adjusted is a measure of the extent to which we have changed. Our culture's adjustment to the epistemology of television is by now almost complete; we have so thoroughly accepted its definitions of truth, knowledge, and reality that irrelevance seems to us to be filled with import, and incoherence seems eminently sane.

It is my object in the rest of this book to make the epistemology of television visible again. I will try to demonstrate by concrete example . . . that television's conversations promote incoherence and triviality . . . and that television speaks in only one persistent voice—the voice of entertainment. Beyond that, I will try to demonstrate that to enter the great television conversation, one American cultural institution after another is learning to speak its terms. Television, in other words, is transforming our culture into one vast arena for show business. It is entirely possible, of course, that in the end we shall find that delightful, and decide we like it just fine.

Family watching television by Evert F. Baumgardner, (CC BY-SA 3.0), 1958.

Assignment

A. Postman writes, "We are by now into a second generation of children for whom television has been their first and most accessible teacher and, for many, their most reliable companion and friend. To put it plainly, television is the command center of the new epistemology. . . . There is no subject of public interest. . . that does not find its way into television. Which means that all public understanding of these subjects is shaped by the biases of television. . . . Television has gradually become our culture."

Do you share Postman's concern? What long-term problems may arise from too much television watching?

B. Postman's main concern with television is that it ties learning to entertainment and undermines other forms of knowledge acquisition (e.g., reading the Bible). Speculate upon why this concerns him so much.

BILLY GRAHAM

"I intend to go anywhere, sponsored by anybody, to preach the gospel of Christ. When God gets ready to shake America, He may not take the Ph.D. and the D.D. God may choose a country boy . . . and I pray that He would. . . . There are no strings attached to my message. . . . The one badge of Christian discipleship is not orthodoxy but love. Christians are not limited to any church. The only question is: are you committed to Christ?" So spoke perhaps the greatest man of the 20th century. Graham was raised on a dairy farm in Charlotte, North Carolina. Graham made his "commitment to Christ" at age 16 through the ministry of a traveling evangelist, Mordecai Ham. He and Ruth McCue Bell met as students at Wheaton College and were married in 1943, the year he graduated. Billy Graham has preached the gospel of Christ in person to more than 80 million people and to countless millions more over the airwaves and in films. Likewise, he was an advisor to every living president from 1950 to 2008.

Billy Graham by Warren K. Leffler, 1966 (CC BY-SA 3.0).

Assignment

Imagine that there had never been a Billy Graham. In what ways would America have been different?

President Barack Obama meets with Rev. Billy Graham at his house in Montreat, N.C. Official White House Photo by Pete Souza, (CC BY-SA 3.0), 2010.

Drive-in theaters were part of America's culture during the '50s and '60s.

Chapter 31

LATE 20TH CENTURY WORLD VIEWS

First Thoughts . . .

At the end of the 20th century, America was at a major crossroads. Throughout the century, more technological advances had been made than in all of preceding history. Computers, the Internet, and other modern technology radically altered daily lives. Increased globalization, specifically Americanization, had occurred. It has caused anti-Western and anti-American feelings in parts of the world, especially the Middle East. But the great battlefields have not occurred among warring nations but now among competing world views.

Chapter Learning Objectives . . .

We will examine two competing philosophers, C. S. Lewis and Alfred North Whitehead, both offering alternative views of mankind and God. In that context, we will meet a great man of God, and history maker, Charles Fuller. Finally, we will look at Pax Americana, the American Peace, and predict what the world will look like in the next 25 years.

As a result of this chapter you should be able to:

1. Explain why "concept process" is heretical.

2. Evaluate the importance of C. S. Lewis to modern world view formation.

3. Discuss the importance of Charles Fuller to history.

4. Explain the advantages and disadvantages of being the most powerful nation on earth.

5. Predict how America will look in 25 and 50 years.

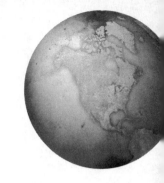

PHILOSOPHERS AND WORLD VIEW

C.S. Lewis (1898–1963)

Along with George MacDonald, C. S. Lewis (below, by Arthur Strong, 1947) was one of the most prolific writers of this generation. Perhaps no single Christian writer has done more to speak persuasively to the non-Christian world than C.S. Lewis. "In our world," said Eustace, 'a star is a huge ball of flaming gas.' Even in our world, my son, that is not what a star is, but only what it is made of."

The following is a passage from *Mere Christianity*:

"I am ready to accept Jesus as a great moral teacher, but I don't accept his claim to be God." That is the one thing we must not say. A man who was merely a man and said the sort of things Jesus said would not be a great moral teacher. He would be either a lunatic—on a level with the man who says he is a poached egg—or else he would be the Devil of Hell. You must make your choice. Either this man was, and is, the Son of God; or else a madman or something worse. You can shut Him up for a fool, you can spit at Him and kill Him as a demon, or you can fall at His feet and call Him Lord and God. But let us not come with any patronizing nonsense about his being a great human teacher. He has not left that open to us.

Alfred North Whitehead (1861–1947)

Whitehead was a metaphysician (i.e., scientist/philospher who studies the universe) whose world view requires God (if a decidedly anemic God), and who respects the cultural role of religious institutions. Contrasted to Existentialists and Naturalists, Whitehead preferred to work within society's institutions. Nonetheless, Whitehead (right, stanford.edu) appealed to direct experience. Like many Romantics, Whitehead saw harmony in nature and all human experience. Similar to the Empiricists, Whitehead leaned toward rationalism. Whitehead's story is a modern story—he became an agnostic. He also took some radical tangents in his world view. In his book *Process and Reality*, A. N. Whitehead abandoned the notion, strong in Western philosophy since Plato, that what is most unchanging is most real. Instead he conceived the structure of reality in dynamic terms. Whitehead set out a radical metaphysics based not on entities but on events—on an infinite series of "actual occasions." Reality was not based on Platonic "forms" but on "fluid experience." All entities are "momentary constituents of the processes of reality"; unchangingness is a property of what is "dead, past, abstract, or purely formal." The emphasis is on becoming, on development in time, rather than on static being, and by implication, absolute truth. Whitehead embraced the modernist notion of process thought. The central metaphor for process thought is that of organism, rather than that of machine. The formation of each event is a function of the nature of the entities involved, their context and interdependence in a way more characteristic of biological organisms than of inanimate objects; their "experience" and their effort to "fulfill their possibilities to the full" in the given event; language deriving not merely from biology but from the analogy of human mentality. Whitehead's agnosticism is most evident in his understanding of suffering. God "the fellow-sufferer who understands," who does not coerce but merely seeks to persuade other beings in the direction of love, seems profoundly attractive in the light of the Holocaust. Process schemes subvert the notion of the omnipotence of God, and therefore escape some of these tensions.

The following is a passage from *Modes of Thought* by A. N. Whitehead (1938):

Mathematics in its widest signification is the development of all types of formal, necessary, deductive reasoning. The reasoning is formal in the sense that the meaning of propositions forms no part of the investigation. The sole concern of mathematics is the inference of proposition from proposition. . . . The ideal of mathematics should be to erect a calculus to facilitate reasoning in connection with every providence of thought, or external experience, in which the succession of thoughts, or of events can be definitely ascertained and precisely stated. So that all serious thought which is not philosophy, or inductive reasoning, or imaginative literature, shall be mathematics developed by means of a calculus.

The characteristics of life are absolute self-enjoyment, creative activity [fusing the past and the possible in a new unity, a new creation], aim, the enjoyment of emotion, derived from the past and aimed at the future. It is the enjoyment of emotion which was then, which is now, and which will be then. This vector character is of the essence of such entertainment. The emotion transcends the present in two ways. It issues from, and it issues towards. It is received, it is enjoyed, and it is passed along, from moment to moment. . .

In so far as conceptual mentality does not intervene, the grand patterns pervading the environment are passed on with the inherited modes of adjustment. Here we find the patterns of activity studied by physicists and chemists. In the case of inorganic nature any sporadic flashes are inoperative so far as our powers of discernment are concerned. The lowest stages of effective mentality, controlled by the inheritance of physical pattern, involves the faint direction of emphasis by unconscious ideal aim. The various examples of the higher forms of life exhibit the variety of grades of effectiveness of mentality. In the social habits of animals, there is evidence of flashes of mentality in the past which have degenerated into physical habits. Finally in the higher animals and more particularly in mankind, we have clear evidence of mentality habitually effective. In our own experience, our knowledge consciously entertained and systematized can only mean such mentality, directly observed.

[God is] creative in the only sense in which creation is given any meaning by our experience. To create is to mold the course of events into correspondence with an idea. Men thus literally create each other when they mold each other's character by education and friendship. Thus the paradoxes of timeless purpose, together with those of non-sensitive ("impassive") love, and of action without reaction, are done away with once for all.

Assignment

A. Research the conversion of Chuck Colson and discuss how *Mere Christianity* brought him to the Lord.

B. Discuss the heretical notions of Whitehead's process thought. Where are evidences of process thought in Modernism?

CHARLES FULLER

Charles Fuller (below) was born in Los Angeles, California. After graduating from Pomona College in 1910 and then stuying at the Bible Institute of Los Angeles (now Biola University), he later became chairman of the board. Initially a Presbyterian, he became a Baptist minister in 1925.

He was famous as the radio host and speaker of the *Old-Fashioned Revival Hour*, a weekly Sunday broadcast that aired from 1937 to 1968. From 1941 through 1958, audiences attended services that were broadcast live on the radio from the Long Beach Municipal Auditorium. The broadcasts were also noted for the music, featuring the *Old-Fashioned Revival Hour* choir and quartet, accompanied by organist George Broadbent and pianist Rudy Atwood.

Fuller also founded Fuller Theological Seminary in Pasadena, California, in 1947. Charles Fuller died in 1968 shortly after his final broadcast of the *Old-Fashioned Revival Hour*. He is buried at Forest Lawn Memorial Park in Glendale, California. Charles Fuller was indeed one of the great evangelical leaders of the 20th century. The following are some quotes from his original papers. You become the historian and judge who this man is!

A conversation with Harold Ockenga (the founder of *Christianity Today* Magazine) on April 18, 1946:

Discussing Fuller Seminary: "We find there are some scholarly men to be had, few of whom have the spiritual qualities which we believe to be necessary for teachers in this school. . . . But I believe that God has for us, somewhere, scholarly men who are deeply spiritual and who have great vision."

"It may be God's plan that later you should take over the presidency of this school. . . . We shall be praying very definitely about this, that if it is God's will, He shall so impress you."

Ockenga to Fuller, October 31, 1946:

"We are on the eve of the Great Revival."

Fuller to Ockenga November 17, 1949:

Billy Graham is soon to be on the East Coast for a revival. Fuller speaks highly of this young man. "Billy Graham's meetings will close Sunday night. He has had a wonderful series of meetings, and I am sure he will prove a blessing in Boston too."

Assignment

A. Dr. Fuller was undeniably one of the greatest evangelical theologians of the 20th century. Yet, he also had his dark nights. According to a letter that his wife Grace wrote on April 15, 1948, to evangelical leader Harold Ockenga, "Charles had had something like a nervous breakdown." While no one would claim that Dr. Fuller was anything but a great man, why is it that sometimes great men and women of God still succumb to pressures and collapse?

B. Describe someone like Dr. Fuller who has had a great impact on your life.

PAX AMERICANA

Pax Americana is the term describing a relative military peace in the Western world, resulting from the power enjoyed by the United States of America starting around the end of World War II. Today, America is still the most powerful nation on earth.

Since the end of the Cold War, many Americans have regarded the United States as the only superpower. After 1990, America's political status has been a strong capitalist presence in virtually every geopolitical theater in the world. America has strong ties with Western Europe, Latin America, British Commonwealth, and several East Asian countries. Arguably, from 1945 to today, America has wielded influence by supporting right-wing dictatorships in undeveloped countries and democracies in developed countries. America is, then, a nation builder.

Today, America has the largest economy in the world. America has large resources of minerals and timber, a large modern farming industry and an equally large industrial base. The U.S. dollar is still the dominant world reserve currency.

America's military is second to none. America has the world's largest navy. America had the largest nuclear arsenal in the world during the first half of the Cold War. America has one of the largest, best equipped armies in the world. America has the most advanced air force in the world. America possesses a global intelligence network (CIA).

America's cultural impact is everywhere. American TV, American movies, and American fashion dominate world culture. American pop icons such as Elvis Presley, Michael Jackson, and Madonna are global celebrities.

The decade from 2000 to 2010 was marked generally by an escalation of the social issues from the end of the 1990s—the rise of terrorism, the expansion of telecommunications with mobile phones, and the Internet.

Perhaps nothing has influenced America, and the world, more than the advent of the computer and the

USS Carl Vinson (CVN-70) is the third United States Navy Nimitz class supercarrier and is named after Carl Vinson, a Congressman from Georgia (PD-US).

Internet. People can now transfer and receive vast amounts of information freely and quickly. During the late 1990s, both Internet directories and search engines were popular—Yahoo! (founded 1995) and Altavista (founded 1995) were the respective industry leaders. By late 2001, the directory model had begun to give way to search engines, tracking the rise of Google (founded 1998), which had developed new approaches to relevancy ranking.

The rapid development of Asia's economic and political potential, with China experiencing immense economic growth, has greatly impacted American foreign policy. But the greatest overseas market for American industry is in India.

In spite of the terrorist attacks on September 11, 2001, America remains the most influential political, military, and social force in the world.

Assignment

Discuss the advantages and disadvantages of being the most powerful nation on earth.

THE NEXT TWENTY-FIVE YEARS

Historian Ed Fenton wrote the following essay in 1975:

Prediction is risky, particularly in a world where one scientific advance can change a whole era. Still some trends seem certain. Take the nature of the American people, for instance. By the year 2000, despite a declining birth rate, the present 200 million people will have grown to 300 million. Many Americans will live well beyond retirement age . . . many beyond age 80. Population rates will increase in the West. . . . The computer will transform America. . . . Third world countries will emerge as new world powers. As the world's richest nation, the United States will face the responsibilities of power in a world where other nations, disturbed by our dominance, will grasp every opportunity to force us to face our human responsibilities. If we are impatient, we can set off an atomic war. The exodus from farms to cities is almost over. Americans will move back into rural areas. Government will grow astronomically. The environment will become more of an issue than ever. . . . The energy crisis of 1974–75 will be repeated in the next few decades.

Assignment

A. In what way(s) was Professor Fenton accurate in his 1975 predictions? Inaccurate?

B. What do you think America will be like in 2050? 2075?

Chapter 32

WAR ON
TERRORISM

First Thoughts . . .

The New York Times (Oct. 7, 2001) stated, "Perhaps the most admirable part of the response to the conflict that began on Sept. 11 has been a general reluctance to call it a religious war." Officials and commentators stressed that this is not a battle between Islam and Christianity. Really? The War on Terrorism is a religious war. The religious dimension of this conflict is central to its meaning. Osama bin Laden is a religious leader before he is anything else. Although some Muslim leaders have criticized the terrorists, and Saudi Arabia's rulers have distanced themselves from the militants, other Muslims in the Middle East and elsewhere did not denounce these acts; some were conspicuously silent or have indeed celebrated them.

Chapter Learning Objectives . . .

We will examine the War on Terrorism. We will examine its roots, the actual beginning of the war on September 11, 2001, and President Bush's response. Along the way we will compare Christianity with Islam and speculate upon ways that these two faiths can live in peace.

As a result of this chapter you should be able to:

1. Analyze the roots of terrorism.
2. Discuss the causes of September 11, 2001, and how the U.S.A. responded.
3. Evaluate the Bush Principles.
4. Contrast a passage in the Koran with a passage from the Bible.
5. Summarize Marvin Olasky's article on September 11, 2001.

THE WAR ON TERRORISM

On September 11, 2001, 19 men hijacked four commercial airplanes. Two of the planes were deliberately crashed into the twin towers of the World Trade Center in New York City, one was deliberately crashed into the Pentagon in Washington, D.C., and the fourth crashed into a field in rural Western Pennsylvania, presumably on its way to a fourth symbolic target: the White House or the U.S. Capitol Building. Strong evidence suggested that Osama bin Laden, a Saudi Arabian citizen living in Afghanistan, was behind the attacks. In 2003 bin Laden became the head of a terrorist organization known as al-Qaeda (Arabic for "the base").

It would be difficult to overstate the magnitude of the simultaneous attacks and their psychological impact on the history of the world. The September 11 attacks instantly moved international terrorism and national security concerns to the top of the U.S. agenda and drove the United States headlong into a war against terrorism.

International terrorism, however, predated September 11, 2001. Four major incidents of international terrorism against U.S. interests since the mid-1990s involved bombings: the Khobar Tower in Dharan, Saudi Arabia; the U.S. embassy in Nairobi, Kenya; the U.S. embassy in Dares Salaam, Tanzania; and the USS *Cole* in the port of Aden, Yemen. These attacks abroad made headlines around the world and commanded massive investigative efforts by the U.S. government.

From 1998 to 2000, President Clinton pursued a policy of economic sanctions against the Taliban and sent numerous messages to the de facto government of Afghanistan demanding that it deliver bin Laden for trial in the United States. The Clinton administration quickly became frustrated by the Taliban's lack of cooperation. Although the administration deliberately raised the specter of military confrontation, ultimately it chose to step back for a variety of reasons.

Osama bin Laden himself couldn't have been clearer about the religious underpinnings of his campaign of terror.

Plumes of smoke billow from the World Trade Center towers in New York City after a Boeing 767 hits each tower during the September 11 attacks by Michael Foran (Flickr user), (CC BY 2.0), 2001.

In 1998, he told his followers, "The call to wage war against America was made because America has spearheaded the crusade against the Islamic nation, sending tens of thousands of its troops to the land of the two holy mosques over and above its meddling in its affairs and its politics and its support of the oppressive, corrupt, and tyrannical regime that is in control." Notice the use of the word "crusade," an explicitly religious term, and one that simply ignores the fact that the last few major American interventions abroad—in Kuwait, Somalia, and the Balkans—were all conducted in defense of Muslims (*The New York Times*, Oct. 7, 2001). This is a religious war against "unbelief and unbelievers," in bin Laden's words. "The ruling to kill the Americans and their allies—civilians and military—is an individual duty

for every Muslim who can do it in any country in which it is possible to do it, in order to liberate the al-Aqsa Mosque and the holy mosque [Mecca] from their grip, and in order for their armies to move out of all the lands of Islam, defeated and unable to threaten any Muslim" (Osama bin Laden, in a translation of a statement he claimed to be a fatwa published in the Arabic language newspaper *al-Quds al-Arabi*, 23 February 1998).

When George W. Bush (above) took office in January 2001, it is doubtful that he understood the depth of bin Laden's hatred of America. Just eight short months later came the devastating September 11th attacks. Bush's reaction was swift and decisive. When it became clear that bin Laden was the probable instigator of the attacks, Bush delivered an ultimatum to the Taliban to turn over bin Laden or face the might of the U.S. military. The Taliban again refused and Bush ordered the invasion of Afghanistan on October 7, 2001, phase one of his War on Terrorism.

Every U.S. president must produce a National Security Strategy document. President George W. Bush's policy has been called the "Bush Doctrine."

The Bush Doctrine contained six principles:

1. The fight against terrorism must continue until it is won.

2. Major responsibility for combating terrorism rests with those countries where terrorist organizations actually operate.

3. When intervention is required, the Bush Doctrine emphasizes action by coalitions of the willing and able.

4. It reaffirms the importance of deterrence as the best way to guarantee peace and respect for international rules of good behavior.

5. Military intervention is not the first choice for dissuading countries from backing terrorism with weapons of mass destruction, including chemical, biological, and nuclear weapons.

6. As a last resort, the Bush Doctrine reserves a first strike option.

The Bush administration had also created the Homeland Security Department, intensified security at U.S. borders

Former President of Iraq, Saddam Hussein, makes a point during his initial interview by a special tribunal, where he is informed of his alleged crimes and his legal rights. This image is a work of a U.S. military or Department of Defense employee, (CC BY-SA 3.0), 2004.

and ports of entry, and hired and deployed more than 50,000 federal screeners in airports. New initiatives included improving intelligence through the Terrorist Threat Integration Center and disarming Saddam Hussein.

In 2003 the U.S. Invaded Iraq, and appeared to have defeated the Taliban by 2009. President Obama continued the war in Iraq and Afghanistan.

Assignment

Summarize President Bush's six principles.

THE KORAN

At the heart of much terrorism is militant Islam. At the heart of militant Islam is the Koran, the sacred book of Muslims, by whom it is regarded as the revelation of God. Supplemented by the so-called Hadith, or traditions, it is the foundation of Islam and the final authority in belief, worship, ethics, and social conduct. The name Koran, or better Qur'an, from the Arabic stem Qara'a, "to read," "to recite," means the "Reading," the "Recitation," i.e. the "Book," par excellence. It is also called—to select a few of many titles—"Alkitab" (The Book), "Furquan" (liberation, deliverance, of the revelation), "Kitab-ul-lah" (Book of God), "Al-tanzil" (The Revelation). It consists of 114 suras or chapters, some being almost as long as the Book of Genesis, others consisting of but two or three sentences. It is smaller than the New Testament, and in its present form has no chronological order or logical sequence (from *Catholic Encyclopedia*). It is like reading *Meditations* by Marcus Aurelius or *Sayings* by Confucius. There is virtually no history (cf. to the Book of Kings).

Selections from the Koran:

In the name of the merciful and compassionate God.
Read, in the name of thy Lord!
Who created man from congealed blood!
Read, for thy Lord is most generous!
Who taught the pen!
Taught man what he did not know!
Nay, verily, man is indeed outrageous at seeing himself get rich!
Verily, unto thy Lord is the return!
Hast thou considered him who forbids a servant when he prays ?
Hast thou considered if he were in guidance or bade piety?
Hast thou considered if he said it was a lie, and turned his back?
Did he not know that God can see?
Nay, surely, if he do not desist we will drag him by the forelock!—the lying sinful forelock! So let him call his counsel: we will call the guards of hell!
Nay, obey him not, but adore and draw nigh!

Assignment

Contrast the passage in the Koran with the passage from the Bible.

Psalm 23

A psalm of David.

The Lord is my shepherd; there is nothing I lack.
He lets me lie down in green pastures;
He leads me beside quiet waters.
He renews my life;
He leads me along the right paths
for His name's sake.
Even when I go
through the darkest valley,
I fear no danger,
for You are with me;
Your rod and Your staff—
they comfort me.
You prepare a table before me
in the presence of my enemies;
You anoint my head with oil;
my cup overflows.
Only goodness and faithful love will pursue me
all the days of my life,
and I will dwell in house of the Lord
as long as I live.

A TWILIGHT STRUGGLE

U.S. President Barack Obama and Vice President Joe Biden, along with members of the national security team, receive an update on Operation Neptune's Spear, a mission against Osama bin Laden, in one of the conference rooms of the Situation Room of the White House, White House photographer, 2011.

trillion dollars, the Stock Market was unstable, abortion had increased four-fold, and gay Americans were being openly recruited for the military. America, at the end of the first decade of the New Millinium, appeared to be in trouble.

Assignment

In what new direction did President Obama take the terrorist policy of the Bush administration?

SEAL trainees scan the room for possible threats as part of a SEAL qualification training exercise. U.S. Navy photo by Mass Communication Specialist 2nd Class Christopher Menzie, (CC BY-SA 3.0), 2007.

President Obama was inaugurated as president on January 20, 2009, and from the beginning of his administration he has downplayed the danger of terrorism. The images burned into the American heart hours after the attacks of September 11, 2001, are fading away, slowly if not deliberately being replaced by a new administration bent on repairing the U.S. image among Muslim nations. In fact, during the tenth-year anniversary, the word "terrorism" was assiduously avoided by President Obama and his aides.

Nonetheless, he has pledged to "go after" extremists and "win this fight." There even was a tangential reference to a "twilight struggle" as the U.S. relentlessly pursues those who threaten the country. In fact, President Obama's administration, piggybacking on President Bush's military successes in the Middle East, has brought the war in Iraq to some sort of resolution. In 2011, Osama bin Ladin was apprehended and killed by U.S. Navy SEALS. The war in Afghanistan, however, continues and resists any satisfactory resolution.

On the domestic front, President Obama continued to battle double digit-unemployment. In the middle of the Obama Administration the national debt soared over 14

HISTORICAL ESSAY

Marvin Olasky, editor, *World* magazine:

In our war against terrorism, it's a good thing that the grown-ups are in charge. My 11-year-old and I last week made a long-scheduled stop at Disneyland during a California speaking trip. We enjoyed Tomorrowland and the yester-days represented by Frontierland and Adventureland. We saw that the park has nothing resembling a Todayland. That is intentional. Walt Disney (left) built his vision in the 1950s and early 1960s when the Cold War was at its height and the likelihood of nuclear disaster seemed high. He wanted Disneyland to be not just a theme park but a portal to a better time and a different world. Meanwhile, in Washington last week, Rep. Peter DeFazio, D-Ore., was one of the congressmen fretting about tough anti-terrorist legislation. "This could be the Gulf of Tonkin resolution for civil liberties instead of a measure meant to fight terrorism," he complained, referring to congressional action in 1964 that led to the expansion of the Vietnam War. What kind of Fantasyland is Mr. DeFazio visiting? The news in 1964 was of two U.S. destroyers harassed off the coast of Vietnam. In 2001, we're talking about 6,000 civilians dying in televised destruction, and 60,000 or 600,000 more murders to come, if the terrorists succeed. Do the defenders of ideal civil liberty understand what a war against potential plague-distributors and well-prisoners requires? Civil libertarians at both extremes, right and left, should come out of their fantasies and focus on two questions: How low will the terrorists go, and how can we stop them? Radical Muslims have step-by-step violated the Islamic tradition of not attacking civilians or innocent bystanders. First, some Palestinian groups declared war on every Israeli, conveniently claiming that most receive some military training so they are not really civilians. Then, terrorists claimed that civilians at the World Trade Center are enemies because capitalists purportedly control the world. Osama bin Laden has taken a third step, claiming that all Americans who pay taxes are enemies. Judging by reports of terrorists scouting out Disneyland and other kid-friendly sites, a fourth step—targeting children—is likely. It would be great if we could rely on the basic human decency of our opponents—but they are showing a chilling willingness to go where no man has gone before. Given the severity of the threat, enormously tightened homeland security is clearly essential. Of course federal officials should be able to get an anti-terrorism wiretapping order that would follow a suspect to any phone the person uses. Of course federal officials should be able to get nationwide search warrants for terrorism investigations. One reason some Americans have difficulty with such proposals is that a generation of school kids has grown up not knowing much about history, except for how Japanese-Americans were forced into internment camps during World War II and how spy-hunters were supposedly hysterical during the following decade. We need to re-evaluate that history. Internment of citizens clearly was wrong, but some ethnic profiling is needed in wartime when terrorists are coming from a particular ethnic group. In our current crisis, aliens from bin Laden's recruitment countries should at the least be required to notify the FBI of all their travels. Such individuals should require FBI approval to receive pilot's licenses or commercial driver's licenses. Bin Laden has declared war on the United States, and those who support him should have no more rights than Nazi cells had in the United States during World War II. The battle against Communist spies that followed was generally necessary, even though it was given a bad name by Joe McCarthy during the 1950s. We can learn from the past if we do not consider ourselves superior to it. My son and I enjoyed Disneyland rides like "Pirates of the Caribbean," but "Pirates of Afghanistan" is another matter.

Assignment

Summarize Olasky's primary argument(s).

Chapter 33

CONTEMPORARY ISSUES: PART ONE

First Thoughts . . .

Ideological world views more than politics will determine the future of America. To that end, the next two chapters will explore several important social issues facing America in the next 50 years.

Chapter Learning Objectives . . .

In chapter 33 we will examine two conflicting opinions about abortion and form our own opinions. Next, we will look at the knotty issue of racial reconciliation. In spite of the fact that an African-American president was elected in 2008, there is still much work to be done. We will read and evaluate an essay about the future of homeschooling, a social movement whose impact far transcends its numbers. Finally, we will look at the music industry, specifically hip hop, and decide whether we think Christians should listen to this controversial music medium.

As a result of this chapter you should be able to:

1. Analyze both pro-choice and pro-life arguments about abortion.
2. Create your own arguments about abortion.
3. Summarize several ways that racial reconciliation may occur in the United States.
4. Speculate on the future of homeschooling.
5. Evaluate the appropriateness of hip-hop music for Christians listeners.

ABORTION

Pro-Choice Arguments:

1. Nearly all abortions take place in the first trimester [of pregnancy], when a fetus cannot exist independent of the mother. As it is attached by the placenta and umbilical cord, its health is dependent on her health, and cannot be regarded as a separate entity as it cannot exist outside her womb.

2. The concept of personhood is different from the concept of human life. Human life occurs at conception, but fertilized eggs used for in vitro fertilization are also human lives and those not implanted are routinely thrown away. Is this murder, and if not, then how is abortion murder?

3. Adoption is not an alternative to abortion, because it remains the woman's choice whether or not to give her child up for adoption. Statistics show that very few women who give birth choose to give up their babies—less than 3 percent of white unmarried women and less than 2 percent of black unmarried women.

4. Abortion is a safe medical procedure. The vast majority of women–88%–who have an abortion do so in their first trimester. Medical abortions have less than 0.5 percent risk of serious complications and do not affect a woman's health or future ability to become pregnant or give birth.

5. In the case of rape or incest, forcing a woman made pregnant by this violent act would cause further psychological harm to the victim. Often a woman is too afraid to speak up or is unaware she is pregnant, thus the morning-after pill is ineffective in these situations.

6. Abortion is not used as a form of contraception. Pregnancy can occur even with responsible contraceptive use. Only 8 percent of women who

In 2004 the March For Women's Lives took place in Washington DC. The streets were filled with men and women, young and old. Photograph by Patty Mooney (CC BY-SA 3.0).

have abortions do not use any form of birth control, and that is due more to individual carelessness than to the availability of abortion.

7. The ability of a woman to have control of her body is critical to civil rights. Take away her reproductive choice and you step onto a slippery slope. If the government can force a woman to continue a pregnancy, what about forcing a woman to use contraception or undergo sterilization?

8. Taxpayer dollars are used to enable poor women to access the same medical services as rich women, and abortion is one of these services. Funding abortion is no different from funding a war in the Mideast. For those who are opposed, the place to express outrage is in the voting booth.

9. Teenagers who become mothers have grim prospects for the future. They are much more likely to leave school; receive inadequate prenatal care; rely on public assistance to raise a child; develop health problems; or end up divorced.

10. Like any other difficult situation, abortion creates stress. Yet the American Psychological Association found that stress was greatest prior to an abortion, and that there was no evidence of post-abortion syndrome (Minnesota Family Council).

Pro-Life Arguments:

1. Since life begins at conception, abortion is akin to murder as it is the act of taking human life. Abortion is in direct defiance of the commonly accepted idea of the sanctity of human life.

2. No civilized society permits one human to intentionally harm or take the life of another human without punishment, and abortion is no different.

3. Adoption is a viable alternative to abortion and accomplishes the same result. And with 1.5 million American families wanting to adopt a child, there is no such thing as an unwanted child.

4. An abortion can result in medical complications later in life; the risk of ectopic pregnancies doubles, and the chance of a miscarriage and pelvic inflammatory diseases also increases.

5. In the instance of rape and incest, proper medical care can ensure that a woman will not get pregnant. Abortion punishes the unborn child who committed no crime; instead, it is the perpetrator who should be punished.

6. Abortion should not be used as another form of contraception.

7. For women who demand complete control of their body, control should include preventing the risk of unwanted pregnancy through the responsible use of contraception or, if that is not possible, through abstinence.

8. Many Americans who pay taxes are opposed to abortion, therefore it's morally wrong to use tax dollars to fund abortion.

9. Those who choose abortions are often minors or young women with insufficient life experience to understand fully what they are doing. Many have lifelong regrets afterwards.

10. Abortion frequently causes intense psychological pain and stress (Minnesota Family Counsel).

Pro-Life, March For Life 2008 US Capitol, US Supreme Court, Washington, D.C., Constitution Avenue by Eric Martin (CC BY-SA 3.0).

Assignment

A. What are the main arguments that pro-choice proponents employ?

B. What are the main arguments that pro-life proponents employ?

C. Which arguments do you find most persuasive? Why?

RACIAL RECONCILIATION

Introduction

America's love affair with racial divisiveness will not change until human hearts change—beginning with Christians' hearts. Critical to genuine reconciliation is an admission of past sins by whites and a commitment to personal engagement among the races. Blending races, intentionally or unintentionally, through transracial adoption or interracial marriage, while it is certainly theologically acceptable, will not really matter until white American hearts are changed. It is much more. "Becoming friends" will not remove 300 years of injustice and anger. Reconciliation is more than a relationship problem; it is a matter of justice. Or as John Perkins so directly states, "Black folks just don't trust white folks." Former Christian and Missionary Alliance president David Rambo said that blacks "are properly skeptical that evangelical commitment will not get us beyond affectionate embraces and politically correct jargon." It is necessary for white Americans to disown white privilege and intentionally set out to live lives of justice. This is one way systemic racism can be overcome.

In spite of past white Christian mistakes, however, some African-American Christians feel that Christianity is the key to racial reconciliation. They, in fact, claim that there is a natural marriage between Christianity and African-American heritage.

Nonetheless, for the last 30 years, there was little evidence that white Evangelicalism participated in discerning racial relations social analysis. An editorial appeared in *Christianity Today* magazine during the urban riots of the late '60s that blamed blacks for their own problems. In its April 26, 1968, issue, the magazine blamed the black community for King's assassination! This viewpoint did not endear white Evangelicalism to the African-American community.

Thankfully that situation is changing rapidly. In fact, the white Evangelical community—through Promise Keepers and other conservative groups—has taken the leadership in racial reconciliation. More than 1,000 Minnesota churches representing 60 denominations and including strong African-American leadership spent a year preparing for the June 1996 Billy Graham Crusade. This well-attended racially mixed crusade called the church to unity. It did much to advance racial reconciliation.

Step 1: Repentance

Most Americans agree on one thing: racial reconciliation is a laudable goal. What is new and exciting is the fact that the Church is finally taking the leadership in this movement. Industry and education are discussing "quotas" and "reparations." But only the Church of Jesus Christ—in its myriad representations—is seriously undertaking the arduous task of bringing about national racial reconciliation.

Racial reconciliation will not come without God's miraculous intervention. No social program, no good intention, no human activity for that matter will bring reconciliation among America's angry races. It will take a miracle. We need, from the very beginning, to admit humbly that reconciliation will occur only as we respond to God's mercy and grace so amply presented in Jesus Christ (John 3:16). He will be the author of reconciliation or it simply will not occur.

Most Christians acknowledge that it has never been the Lord's intention for His people to be divided along racial lines. Racial identification and racial anger happen automatically in the United States because race has such a ubiquitous presence. Racial reconciliation, on the other hand, will not occur naturally. It will take a lot of hard work. Racial reconciliation will not become a reality through human effort. Reconciliation must be part of a divine agenda. By dying on the cross, Jesus paid the price for reconciliation with God. Our reconciliation with Him is the only way that humankind can be empowered to seek reconciliation with other persons. Reconciliation is a work of the Holy Spirit.

The road to the cross begins with repentance. The first, and perhaps most formidable, task before white American

Christianity is a profound and sincere repentance for the horrific choices, concerning race relations, we have made both as a white Christian nation and a white Christian church in the last 300 years. We need to own the problem before we will know a solution. It is a personal issue before it is a community one.

The problem is sin. The doctrine of sin is the most empirically arguable doctrine of Christianity. It is everywhere present in American race relations. Raleigh Washington, a black pastor in Chicago, writes: "I tell people that the problem is not skin; the problem is sin. . . . My challenge to my black brothers and sisters is to speak the truth in what we see so that we can bring the power of the gospel to deal with it. Only as we acknowledge our need for spiritual renewal—spiritual solutions to spiritual problems—can we bring God's redeeming power to resolve the problems facing us as a people. Only as we acknowledge our need for spiritual renewal, only when we see racial anger as a spiritual problem, will we bring God's redeeming power to resolve the problems we face as a people."

Ted Peters, professor of systematic theology at Pacific Lutheran Seminary, argues that there are seven aspects of sin. First is anxiety, which denies our mortality through self-deception. Anxiety joined with unfaithfulness (the second aspect) overwhelms us with the need to find security at all costs. This leads to the third aspect—pride—which theologian Paul Tillich states is the root of all human sin. This pride blocks any semblance of empathy from manifesting itself in our lives. Fourth, there emerges a desire to possess and to master. Peters, like Augustine, argues that this concupiscence eventually drives us to ever-increasing and self-destructive consumption. Ergo, racism and other sins emerge.

Peters' final three aspects are truly hellish. Concupiscence leads to a self-deceiving cloak of rightness. Next, cruelty and oppression results. Finally, there is blasphemy, the rejection of grace. At this moment we are most like Satan. It is at this place that the white American nation remained stuck at the end of the 20th century.

A repentant white church must lead our country to repentant prayer. This is infinitely more valuable for America than all the reparations we would ever pay, all the social welfare programs we design. Many white Christian groups are doing just that.

Step 2: Forgiveness among All Races

At the same time, I ask the African-American community to forgive white America. Rev. Roland Gordon, an African-American pastor, wrote, "I saw that I had not truly come to terms with my obligation as a follower of Jesus Christ to forgive and genuinely to love, as Christ commands." Rev. Gordon forgave his white tormentors and found racial reconciliation.

African-American leader John Perkins offered the following recipe for racial reconciliation: "White people must allow the gospel to penetrate their culture. Whites must allow the gospel to speak deeply to their deep broken, exploitative, superior, and unjust lifestyles and attitudes. White Christians who claim Christ as Savior must also make him Lord over such areas as spending, racial attitudes, and business dealings. Whites must see that the oppression of black people in this country runs deep throughout both our cultures. And anything short of a fundamental change of values—which I believe possible only through a relationship with Jesus Christ—will result in no longer viewing the problem as "the black problem" and offering solutions like charity and welfare which have within them the same seeds of destructive exploitation and dehumanizing greed that oppress the poor in the first place. . . . Black people must allow the gospel to penetrate their culture. Integration, equal opportunity, welfare, charity, and all these programs fail to deal with the deep-seated values that cause the bankruptcy in our black communities. These programs only serve to conform people to this world. Only the gospel can transform people by the renewing of their minds (Romans 12:2)."

These are the words of John Perkins, who was beaten almost to death by whites, and this admonition was written in 1976! His son continued that crusade until his death a few years ago.

Perkins knew that it was impossible to overestimate the power of forgiveness. Jesus challenges all believers to forgive others who have wronged them (Matthew 6:14–15; 18:21–25). Forgiveness can release us all (James 5:19–20). Forgiveness is powerful and necessary medicine for America. It is, perhaps, the most important and unique contribution that African-American Christianity can offer to the American racial story. Forgiveness is not about right or wrong, it is about atonement, doing what God commands us to do. An African-American church leader recently reflected, "I can either be right or reconciled."

African-Americans have been wronged. From a human standpoint, they have every right to be unforgiving, but unforgiveness is destructive. From Jesus' standpoint, forgiveness is necessary.

To speak of forgiveness in race relations may seem to be an oxymoron. Nevertheless, I ask the African-American community to forgive. Forgive and remember—not forgive and forget. Some will say that because I am white I have no right to ask. I admit that I have no right, but I ask anyway.

We have learned in the 20th century through Proust that memory contains more than we at first are conscious of having received—it is involuntarily. Memory is also voluntary. Freud showed us that we remember only what we want to remember, in the way we want to remember it. Without memory, forgiveness is cheap and destructive. If the African-American community forgets the wrongs, in the sense of pretending that they did not occur, then they risk having the problems arise again. I ask my African-American brothers and sisters to remember and to forgive.

Step 3: A Christian Solution

Forgiveness entails four elements. It begins with a remembering and moral judgment. Second, although the move toward forgiveness demands the renunciation of vengeance, it does not mean that the African-American community abandons justice. Nor does it mean that African-Americans forget the injustice. No, on the contrary, I ask the African-American community to remember and to forgive anyway. Some of my African-American friends are right to suggest that that is easy for this white Southerner to ask, but I ask it anyway. Isaiah 65:17 reminds us, "Behold, I create new heavens and a new earth." Forgiveness brings this Scripture into action.

Repentance and forgiveness are only the beginning points. The gospel's central message is to reconcile alienated people to God and to each other, across racial, cultural, and social barriers. A solution that is not Christ-centered and people-centered is no solution at all. It must be a solution that deals with the roots of racism: sin.

The late Spencer Perkins and Chris Rice offer the following prescription for racial reconciliation: admit, submit, and commit. Everyone, first, must admit that there is a problem. Then, everyone submits to God and commits to a plan of reconciliation. Again, though, the Holy Spirit convicts and empowers. So, reconciliation is quintessentially a Christian event.

For many Christian thinkers, good intentions will not be enough. They claim that relationships need to be established between the races. Rice writes, "The gulf between black and white can be crossed only on a bridge built by the hands of God."

Concluding Reflections:

Harvard University's Dr. Robert Cole in his book *The Spiritual Life of Children* describes a 1962 interview he had with a small African-American child named Ruby Bridges. This child was being accosted by angry segregationists as she walked to school. Cole wanted to know why, in the face of so much hatred, she was smiling.

"I was all alone," she began, "and those people were screaming, and suddenly I saw God smiling, and I smiled."

Then she continued with these astonishing words: "A woman was standing there [near the school door], and she shouted at me, 'Hey, you little nigger, what you smiling at?'"

"I looked right at her face, and I said, 'at God.'"

"Then she looked up at the sky, and then she looked at me, and she didn't call me any more names."

In order for reconciliation to occur between races, there must be a profound and sincere acceptance of responsibility for our bad choices. For white Christians, in particular, we are challenged to own our responsibility. How blind and judgmental we can be, we religious people! At the same time, like Ruby Bridges, we must continue to believe racial reconciliation is possible, to remain hopeful in the face of hopelessness.

Jesus Christ is the Way and the Truth and the Life. And He loves all children, red and yellow, black and white. Period. I know that this seems simplistic and somewhat chauvinistic. There is no other way to eternal life or present happiness. And I suppose that is the bottom line in my discussion of racism. As early as 1976 John Perkins was saying the same thing—only the gospel can transform people (Romans 12:1). The goal was voiced by Martin Luther King: "The sons of former slaves and the sons of former slave-owners will sit down at the table of brotherhood together." This Christian ideal lost its spiritual moorings and the integration cure began to choke the life out of the very ideal of racial harmony it was intended to save. I believe that the time has come for white and black Christians to integrate with one another, but to do so in the name of Jesus Christ and bibical veracity.

Integration was a clear goal for the early Church. After all, the example of the cross drew all persons into hopeful relationship. Paul had no trouble defining the gospel and his life as 'the message of the cross.' On the contrary, he boldly declared that, though the cross seemed either foolishness or a stumbling block to the self-confident (i.e., modern humankind!), it is in fact the very essence of God's wisdom and power (1 Cor. 1:18–25). The cross will be a stumbling block to the white supremist and the black nationalist. But it will be the Christian's hope of glory. The world does not need a new religion, it needs Jesus Christ, crucified and resurrected. And, at risk of sounding simplistic and redundant, as we make Jesus Christ Lord of our lives, we will see our racial attitudes change.

Don't get me wrong. What I am suggesting is truly revolutionary, or, as Walter Brueggemann suggests, "subversive." The church, including my church, must be called to a higher commitment. A radical commitment. The choice for Christ occupies first place, above parents, children, jobs, and, if necessary, life itself. The gate leading to health and wholeness in our world is not regulation size. It is narrow. In that sense, I am calling us all to a radical faith, a prophetic faith. We are called to a major reclamation project of our views of atonement so completely presented in Scripture and in our confessions. And racism, after all, is a direct threat to the atonement.

The challenge for the Church is to be different in a meaningful way. To be in the world but not of it. To lead America away from the self-destructive cliff to which racism has brought us. The call to us all is to find our identity in Christ alone—not in color, creed, ethnicity, or any other category. I see many hopeful signs. In what is being called "The Memphis Miracle," black and white leaders shed tears, confessed failures, washed each other's feet, and agreed to dissolve their separate organizations to form a new one, free of barriers. They have created a new vision—or resurrected an old one—that holds great promise for our country. Almost every Christian organization in America is striving for racial reconciliation. I believe that the Christian community may yet fulfill God's purpose for the American nation: racial reconciliation.

Again, though, I am convinced that racial reconciliation is coming for one very important reason: men and women and the organizations that they represent are falling down on their knees and asking God to give them strength to change. Faith in the Lordship of Jesus Christ, more than any other single factor, will bring peace. This outspoken subservience to the Lordship of Christ, the open admission that peace will not come in any other way, makes the present moves toward reconciliation more hopeful. Nothing quite like this happened in earlier reconciliation attempts.

Whole denominations that were formerly almost completely white are gratefully becoming multiracial. For example, the almost completely white Mennonite Church is quickly becoming racially mixed. Total Mennonite Church membership grew from 99,719 members in 980 congregations in 1985 to 111,672 members in 1,099 congregations at the end of 1995. The even better news for the Mennonite Church is that 69 percent of new Mennonite Church congregations started in urban areas. Most of these new congregations are interracial and multicultural. This reflects the demographic trends in America where 47 percent of the U.S. population will be "minority" groups by 2050. The largest church in the Virginia Conference of the Mennonite Church is Calvary Community Church—an interracial church in Hampton Roads, Virginia. In 1997 the Mennonite Church elected an interracially married moderator for the first time in its history! Among the non-Pentecostal churches, the Mennonite Church is making the most progress toward racial integration, but other denominations—particularly Evangelical ones—are sure to follow.

In William Faulkner's *The Unvanquished*, a white boy named Bayard is reflecting about his black friend Ringo: "Ringo and I has been born in the same month and has both fed at the same breast and has slept together and eaten together for so long that Ringo called Granny 'Granny' just like I do, until maybe he isn't a nigger anymore or maybe I isn't a white boy anymore, the two of us neither, not even people any more: the two supreme undefeated like two moths, two feathers riding above a hurricane."

The Church is called to somehow ride above a hurricane. To be that peculiar people about whom we read in Scripture. To find a unity that transcends the substantial barrier race represents. This is no small feat, but one that the Church must undertake. And soon. By showing American society—especially the urban society—the way out of racism, the Church of Jesus Christ has a unique opportunity to reclaim Dietrich Bonhoeffer's "center of the city." Using Augustine's *City of God* as a standard, the Church is called to be an efficacious model of reconciliation to a fragmented and broken community. We are all—white, black, yellow, and red—on a journey.

Christians are called by God to serve our culture even though our ultimate loyalty and hope is in the city of God. I believe with all my heart that the road to Christian revival must pass through the school of racial reconciliation. There are several examples of racial reconciliation in our country today and I am truly encouraged. But there is much work that remains. As I have intimated before, until the Church finds a way to bring racial reconciliation in a widespread way into its own camp, American society at large has no hope of doing the same. As we begin the 21st century, this reclamation project will be America's most valuable gift to the world.

The whole world waits with bated breath. . . .

Assignment

Paraphrase the author's suggestions for racial reconciliation.

LESSON 3

LESSON 3

THE FUTURE OF HOMESCHOOLING AND CHRISTIAN EDUCATION

In 49 BC, the crossing of a small stream in northern Italy by ambitious Roman general Julius Caesar became one of the pivotal events in world history. From it sprang the Roman Empire and the genesis of modern Europe.

An ancient Roman law forbade any general to cross the Rubicon River and enter Italy proper with a standing army. To do so was treason. Caesar was well aware of this. Coming up with his troops on the banks of the Rubicon, he halted for a while, and revolving in his mind the importance of the step he considered, he spoke to his soldiers, "Still we can retreat! But once let us pass this little bridge, and nothing is left but to fight it out with arms!" He crossed the river and we all know the rest (Suetonius).

After raising four homeschooled children, attending 300-plus homeschool and Christian school conventions, participating in an HSLDA court case victory (Stobaugh vs. Pittsburgh Board of Edu-cation), and attending 15 or 16 field trips a year, it is time for the Stobaughs to cross the Rubicon.

America today is different from the America in which Karen and I began homeschooling in 1985. Really different. Our president wonders why we evangelicals cannot be "civil" in our discussions about things like abortion. Civil? Abortion is murder, Mr. President. Murder. I could be civil discussing tax increases or even troop surges overseas, but there are some things I just can't be civil about.

In 1 Kings 18–19, the famous Mt. Carmel challenge chapters, choleric Elijah is coming home—and no one wants him to come home. After a long time, in the third year, the word of the Lord comes to Elijah: "Go and present yourself to Ahab, and I will send rain on the land" (1 Kings 18:1). King Ahab and Queen Jezebel, of course, hate him. But even Obadiah—a faithful follower of God and trusted advisor to the king and queen, who has learned so well to survive in this hostile land, who has done so much good for God's people—is not too thrilled to see

him either. In fact, no one welcomes Elijah—not the hostile king and queen nor the pious evangelical Obadiah.

Even though Elijah brings good news—it is finally going to rain—no one welcomes him. Elijah's fish-or-cut-bait prophetic messages are irritating the life out of the status quo. That is bad enough. But what really scares the dickens out of everyone is the fact that Elijah has come home to Zion, to the City of God, to challenge the gods of society to a duel.

I don't know, when we crossed the Rubicon with our family's education. Perhaps it was when we turned off the television or refused to buy the latest entertainment center. Maybe it was when we drove our old cars another year so we could buy the best curricula for our kids. Or was it when we decided to read classics together in our home? Somewhere, sometime, we crossed the Rubicon and there is no going back.

To push my metaphor further, we were first "Obadiahs." Obadiah, like Daniel, was quite influential in an extremely evil regime. Ahab and Jezebel were very capable, successful monarchs. From their perspective, they were the sanctioned leaders. Elijah and the prophets were radical, unreasonable, uncompromising troublers of Israel. No doubt Ahab and Jezebel could not understand why Elijah would not carry on a civil discussion about what they saw as tangential, civil issues.

This generation is the Elijah generation. To Elijah, the behavior of Ahab and Jezebel was absolutely appalling. While claiming to worship the Hebrew God they also filled the land with syncretism, with apostate worship of the Baals. The crowning blow, to Elijah, was when these scoundrels placed the Asherah poles (places where believers could have sexual relations with temple prostitutes) on the hill next to the Temple. Enough was enough and Elijah was ordered home to confront these evil powers on Mt. Carmel.

And Elijah was not accommodating nor was he running away (don't you just wish, Ahab and Jezebel!); he was coming home to challenge the gods of this age.

Ahab and Jezebel were postmodernists. They celebrated the subjective. They were committed to compromise—it was their religion. Live and let live! What is the big deal?

Well, you see, Elijah could not compromise with the stuff they were doing. There was no wriggle room in Judah and there is getting to be precious little wriggle room in the U.S.A. too.

The world of the Baals, is falling apart, and quickly. As sociologist Peter Berger explains, "American mainline culture can no longer offer plausibility structures for the

common man. It no longer sustains Americans." Or, as my old friend Professor Harvey Cox at Harvard coyly observed, "Once Americans had dreams and no technology to fulfill those dreams. Now Americans have tons of technology, but they have no dreams left."

In short order the Ahabs and Jezebels are going to find out that Elijah is not in a compromising mood either. These are some things one cannot compromise. Ahab and Jezebel are going to meet a man of God who speaks with concrete clarity, who carries the weight of truth.

Elijah is coming this year. The days of Obadiah are over. Elijah is coming to town.

Are you ready? Can you give up your anonymity? Will you risk everything this year to do what God tells you to do? Will you go the extra mile for those of this generation to make sure that they will stand on Mt. Carmel and proclaim the sovereignty and goodness of our God so they can bring the Kingdom on this earth as it is in heaven? The stakes are high; the potential rewards astounding. We have a chance, perhaps in our lifetime, to experience an unprecedented revival. This is the generation of Elijah. The generation that

will have to walk the long, arduous walk up Mt. Carmel, and they will challenge the gods of this age. Bring it on! We are ready! Every knee shall bow, every tongue shall profess, that Jesus Christ is Lord. Bring on the fire of Elijah, again, on this nation! God is calling forth our children—Elijahs who will go to the high places of our nation to challenge the prophets of Baal—in the courts, in the universities, in the shops, in the homes, in the churches.

Elijah brought good news but not welcome news. Good news that we gave them in our modest homes. Year after year, one music lesson after another, one co-op meeting after another, one student after another, we raised this generation. And today they are on the threshold of changing their world. They are housewives. They own small businesses. They are writing scripts in Hollywood. Writing speeches for presidents. Lobbying for godly causes in Congress.

Do we have a vision of what lies ahead? Will we seek the Lord's face to cooperate in His equipping, enabling, and empowering process? Will we trust God? Elijahs are wild and crazy! They will move beyond our traditions and our comfort zones. Elijahs always do.

So Obadiah went to meet Ahab and told him the bad news, and Ahab went to meet Elijah. When he saw Elijah, he said to him, "Is that you, you troubler of Israel?" Elijah replied, "I have not made trouble for Israel, but you and your father's family have. You have abandoned the Lord's commands and have followed the Baals."

Challenge the gods of this age, homeschoolers and Christian school students!

After coming so far, after working so hard, will we Christian Educated students forget why we came? Are we at the place where we can get the solution to our problem, only to find we've forgotten why we came? The challenge for us in this 21st century is to sit down together and talk. Look around at all that God has done, and give thanks. And then go forth, Elijahs, and challenge the gods of this age—at Harvard, at the Supreme Court, in Hollywood. Give no quarter and ask for none. The God we serve deserves nothing less, accepts nothing less!

Assignment

Summarize the author's challenges for homeschoolers and private Christian school students.

CHRISTIANITY AND HIP HOP?

Christian hip hop faces opposition from church by Olivia Sanders:

The Ambassador, real name William Branch, recently released his third album, *The Thesis*, which continues his work in the musical field of Christian hip hop. The controversial style of music has raised concerns with certain churches across the country.

Philadelphia rapper The Ambassador performed earlier this month for a hip hop forum. The forum sought to gather students to discuss the spiritual, racial and social aspects of hip-hop. Some students came from as far away as Baylor University to attend the forum, all because of The Ambassador. If you don't know his name, it may be because he is a Christian hip hop artist.

But just what exactly is Christian hip hop? Can Christianity and hip-hop even coexist?

The Daily sat down with The Ambassador, also known as William Branch, while he was at NT. He addressed his success as a Christian rap artist and the negativity that Christian rap artists face from fellow Christians.

With the release of his album, *The Thesis*, Branch made history, debuting at no. 5 on the Billboard Gospel Charts, a noteworthy feat for a genre that is still an underground movement.

According to Branch, Christian hip-hop is a combination of the two worlds. It is Christian in that's its governed by the desires and the plan of Jesus Christ. And it is hip-hop because it shares a mutual enjoyment of, and connection to, the inner-city movement. More and more Christian hip-hop is making a name for itself as an increasing number of mainstream Christian artists gain popularity, artists such as GRITS, T-Bone, Gospel Gangstaz, and The Cross Movement, of which Branch is a member. According to his website, Branch has been ministering the gospel through rap and preaching for nearly 15 years, seeking to be a model and a messenger of the gospel's transforming power, especially

The Christian music rap/hip hop group GRITS by Johnathon Powell, (CC BY-SA 3.0), 2005.

(but not exclusively) among the hip-hop generations. The Ambassador thinks of himself as a missionary to the hip-hop community.

"The hip-hop community is one the neediest, yet one of the most neglected by the community of faith (the church)," Branch said.

It is this alienation that fuels the mission of The Ambassador and Christian rappers out there. In the face of adversity, Christian hip-hop is trying to hold its own against those who oppose its views. Wikipedia uses the following description for the musical style on its website: "Christian hip-hop has a history of being dismissed by churches worldwide as sacrilegious, or 'devil music.'"

That definition seems to perfectly fit the opinions of Elder G. Craige Lewis, a Fort Worth minister who feels, because of the genre's origin, and what it originally represented in its earlier stages, hip-hop cannot be embraced by Christians. Lewis and his ministry have set up a website at www.exministries.com, on which he presents his ministry's objective in educating Christians about hip-hop music and its origin.

According to Elder Lewis's website, "Lewis travels the country, spreading the message of the enemy's deception, and thousands are healed, delivered, and set free from the powerful message that he carries." Lewis and Ex Ministries feel that hip-hop has an entire culture backing it. According to their website, "It's not just music. It's a way of life for the black community as well as white America. It has influenced our youth in a way that no other tool of the enemy could have."

According to www.reference.com, "The sometimes rebellious, egotistical, and degenerate attitudes often portrayed in the lyrics and videos of certain hip-hop artists have shown negative effects on some of their idolizing fans." It is these effects that people like Lewis and Ex Ministries are trying to combat by revealing what they feel is the truth about hip-hop culture. Ex Ministries does state that: "We do have very powerful Christian rap groups that preach the Word of God through rap, but we must not get confused and call what they are doing hip-hop. You have to understand that God does not embrace anything that has a corrupt origin."

Branch has a different take on the situation.

"Placing an adjective on it has altered this hip-hop," he said. "We have termed it Christian hip-hop or holy hip-hop. That's our way of changing it. So, we don't change hip-hop. That's just another earthly topic. We've modified it."

"Someone has to uphold the standard that God has given us in His Word," a quote on the site of Ex Ministries states. "We must be separate from the world in order to reach the world. We must be examples of true Christians in order to win the lost. We cannot appear to be lost or conform to the world's standards because we want to appeal to them."

The Ambassador doesn't find the description particularly fitting. "If we 'look' hip-hop, we are failing to do this," he said. "This is a true statement, but its application takes skill. If I have a doo-rag on, have I violated this principle? If my fitted cap is cocked to the side, have I violated this principle? If my white tee is 5X, have I ceased to be separate from the world in the sense that Jesus intended it? Lewis would say yes, but the Scriptures would disagree."

Assignment

Should Christians be involved with hip-hop music? Why? Why not? How do Christians discern and navigate through these cultural issues?

Graffiti "Hip Hop" in Eugene, Oregon by Shad Bolling (CC BY-SA 3.0), 2006.

Chapter 34

CONTEMPORARY ISSUES: PART TWO

First Thoughts . . .

James Davison Hunter's 1991 *Culture Wars: The Struggle to Define America* describes what he saw as a dramatic realignment and polarization that had transformed American politics and culture. He argues that the future of America will be determined by who wins the "culture war" of a few defining issues.

Chapter Learning Objectives . . .

In chapter 34 we will examine affirmative and negative opinions about euthanasia, global warming, health care, and population growth. We will discuss these conflicting opinions and form our own opinions about these subjects.

As a result of this chapter you should be able to:

1. Analyze different positions concerning euthanasia and form your own opinion.
2. Evaluate the veracity of arguments surrounding global warming.
3. Summarize an article on health insurance and form your own opinion on this subject.
4. Decide if there is a population explosion/crisis or not.

EUTHANASIA

Right to Die

Euthanasia or Physician-Assisted Suicide: Affirmative

The right of a competent, terminally ill person to avoid excruciating pain and embrace a timely and dignified death bears the sanction of history and is implicit in the concept of ordered liberty. The exercise of this right is as central to personal autonomy and bodily integrity as rights safeguarded by this Court's decisions relating to marriage, family relationships, procreation, contraception, child rearing and the refusal or termination of life-saving medical treatment. In particular, this Court's recent decisions concerning the right to refuse medical treatment and the right to abortion instruct that a mentally competent, terminally ill person has a protected liberty interest in choosing to end intolerable suffering by bringing about his or her own death.

A state's categorical ban on physician assistance to suicide—as applied to competent, terminally ill patients who wish to avoid unendurable pain and hasten inevitable death—substantially interferes with this protected liberty interest and cannot be sustained.

—American Civil Liberties Union
Amicus Brief, *Vacco v. Quill* 1996

Euthanasia or Physician-Assisted Suicide: Negative

The history of the law's treatment of assisted suicide in this country has been and continues to be one of the rejection of nearly all efforts to permit it. That being the case, our decisions lead us to conclude that the asserted "right" to assistance in committing suicide is not a fundamental liberty interest protected by the Due Process Clause.

—*Washington v. Glucksberg*
U.S. Supreme Court Majority Opinion 1997

End-of-Life Suffering

Affirmative:

At the Hemlock Society we get calls daily from desperate people who are looking for someone like Jack Kevorkian to end their lives which have lost all quality. . . . Americans should enjoy a right guaranteed in the European Declaration of Human Rights—the right not to be forced to suffer. It should be considered as much of a crime to make someone live who with justification does not wish to continue as it is to take life without consent.

—Faye Girsh, Ed.D.
Senior Adviser, Final Exit Network
"How Shall We Die," *Free Inquiry*, Winter 2001

Negative:

Activists often claim that laws against euthanasia and assisted suicide are government mandated suffering. But this claim would be similar to saying that laws against selling contaminated food are government mandated starvation.

Laws against euthanasia and assisted suicide are in place to prevent abuse and to protect people from unscrupulous doctors and others. They are not, and never have been, intended to make anyone suffer.

> —International Task Force on Euthanasia and Assisted Suicide
> "Euthanasia and Assisted Suicide: Frequently Asked Questions"
> www.internationaltaskforce.org Aug. 9, 2006

Legalized Murder

Affirmative:

Especially with regard to taking life, slippery slope arguments have long been a feature of the ethical landscape, used to question the moral permissibility of all kinds of acts. . . . The situation is not unlike that of a doomsday cult that predicts time and again the end of the world, only for followers to discover the next day that things are pretty much as they were. . . . We not only can distinguish between [voluntary and nonvoluntary] cases [of euthanasia] but do. . . . We need the evidence that shows that horrible slope consequences are likely to occur. The mere possibility that such consequences might occur, as noted earlier, does not constitute such evidence.

> —R. G. Frey, D.Phil.
> Professor of Philosophy, Bowling Green State University
> "The Fear of a Slippery Slope," Euthanasia and Physician-Assisted Suicide: For and Against 1998

Negative:

In debates with those bioethicists and physicians who believe that euthanasia is both deeply compassionate and also a logical way to cut health care costs, I am invariably scorned when I mention "the slippery slope." When the states legalize the deliberate ending of certain lives—I try to tell them—it will eventually broaden the categories of those who can be put to death with impunity. I am told that this is nonsense in our age of highly advanced medical ethics. And American advocates of euthanasia often point to the Netherlands as a model—a place where euthanasia is quasi-legal for patients who request it. . . .

Yet the September 1991 official government Remmelink Report on euthanasia in the Netherlands revealed that at least 1,040 people die every year from involuntary euthanasia. Their physicians were so consumed with compassion that they decided not to disturb the patients by asking their opinion on the matter.

> —Nat Hentoff
> Columnist, The Village Voice
> "The Slippery Slope of Euthanasia," *The Washington Post*
> Oct. 3, 1992

Assignment

Which arguments do you find most persuasive? Why?

GLOBAL WARMING

Global warming a serious problem?

There are some disadvantages to global warming and there are some advantages. Unfortunately, the disadvantages will have a more severe impact on people.

Disadvantages:

1. Global temperatures will rise (by 5°F by the year 2100)
2. Sea levels will flood coastal cities
3. More frequent extreme weather (e.g., floods, hurricanes, droughts)
4. Compromised food supplies
5. Disruption (or extinction) of some plant and animal species

Advantages:

1. Less severe winters in some regions
2. More rain in some dry regions, less rain in some wet regions
3. Increased food production in some regions
4. Extended population ranges for some species of plants and animals

Affirmative

- In 1997, 2,500 scientists signed a statement saying we should act now to reduce the impact of severe climate change.
- Also in 1997, 2,700 economists—including eight Nobel Prize winners—agreed that "preventive steps are necessary" to prevent the economic problems that will result from severe climate change.

- In 1998, the leaders of the world's 1,000 largest corporations agreed that climate change is the most critical problem facing humanity.

Our planet has been slowly warming since last emerging from the "Little Ice Age" of the 17th century, often associated with the Maunder Minimum. Before that came the "Medieval Warm Period," in which temperatures were about the same as they are today. Both of these climate phenomena are known to have occurred in the Northern Hemisphere, but several hundred years prior to the present, the majority of the Southern Hemisphere was primarily populated by indigenous peoples, where science and scientific observation was limited to nonexistent. Thus we cannot say that these periods were necessarily "global" (Greg Pryor).

Negative

Sorry, folks, but we're not exactly buying into the Global Hysteria just yet. We know a great deal about atmospheric physics (bio), and from the onset, many of the claims were just plain fishy. The extreme haste with which the entire world seemingly, immediately accepted the idea of Anthropogenic (man-made) Global Warming made us more than a little bit suspicious that no one had really taken a close look at the science. We also knew that the catch-all activity today known as "Climate Science" was in its infancy, and that atmospheric modeling did not and still does not exist which can predict changes in the weather or climate more than about a day or two in advance.

So the endless stream of dire predictions of what was going to happen years or decades from now if we did not drastically reduce our CO_2 production by virtually shutting down the economies of the world appeared to be more the product of radical political and environmental activism rather than science. Thus, we embarked on a personal quest for more information, armed with a strong academic background in postgraduate physics and a good understanding of the advanced mathematics necessary in such a pursuit.

This fundamental knowledge of the core principles of matter and its many exceptionally complex interactions allowed us to research and understand the foundations of many other sciences. In short, we read complex scientific articles in many other scientific disciplines with relative ease and good understanding—like most folks read comic books.

As our own knowledge of "climate science" grew, so grew our doubts over the "settled science." What we found was the science was far from "settled". . . in fact it was barely underway.

It was for a while a somewhat lonely quest, what with "all the world's scientists" apparently having no doubt. Finally, in December 2007 we submitted an article to one of our local newspapers, the *Addison Independent*, thinking they would be delighted in having at minimum an alternative view of the issue. Alas, they chose not to publish it, but two weeks after our submission (by the strangest coincidence), published yet another "pro-global-warming" feature written by an individual who, to the best we could determine, had no advanced training in any science at all, beyond self-taught it would appear. Still, the individual had published a number of popular books on popular environmental issues, was well-loved by those of similar political bent, and was held in high esteem among his peers. We had learned a valuable lesson: Popular journalists trump coupled sets of second-order partial differential equations every time. Serious science doesn't matter if you have the press in your pocket.

In fairness to the *Addison Independent* and its editors, our article was somewhat lengthy and technical, and presumably the average reader most likely could not follow or even be interested in an alternative viewpoint, since everyone knew by now that the global warming issue was "settled science." And we confess that we like the paper, subscribe to it, and know a number of folks who work there personally. They're all good folks, and they have every right to choose what does or doesn't go in their publication. They also have a right to spin the news any direction they choose, because that's what freedom of the press is all about. Seems everyone, both left and right, does it—and it's almost certain we will be accused of doing the same here. And we just may be, as hard as we may try to avoid it. We humans aren't all shaped by the same cookie cutter, and that's a blessing that has taken us as a species to the top of the food chain.

But by then we had been sharing our own independent research of the literature with others via e-mail, and receiving a surprising amount of agreement back in return. One local friend, in particular, kept pressing us to publish, and even offered to set up a "debate" with the popular journalist who had usurped our original article. This we politely declined, arguing that "debate" cannot prove or disprove science . . . science must stand on its own.

But then something unusual happened. On December 13, 2007, 100 scientists jointly signed an Open Letter to Ban Ki-Moon, Secretary-General of the United Nations, requesting they cease the man-made global warming hysteria and settle down to helping mankind better prepare for natural disasters. The final signature was from the president of the World Federation of Scientists. At last, we were not alone (James P. Eden).

Assignment

Is the earth experiencing global warming? Why or why not?

HEALTH CARE

"What the Health-Care Debate Is Really All About" by James C. Capretta:

The choice the country faces in health-care reform is a stark one with profound ramifications: What process will best deliver affordable quality health-care to all Americans, a government-driven or market-driven one?

It's not unusual for political and legislative battles in the nation's capital to be sharply partisan. But even by Washington standards, the health-care debate has been exceptionally contentious and polarizing. The bills that have passed in the House and the Senate are supported almost exclusively by Democrats, and Congressional Republicans are nearly unanimous in the view that these bills merit their total and unyielding opposition (so far, only one House Republican has voted for the Democratic proposals). Both sides are waging the fight with such an extreme take-no-prisoners attitude that even long-time Washington observers have been taken aback by the intensity of the struggle.

All of this political fighting can be disconcerting to average citizens. Why, on an issue that is plainly so important, can't our nation's elected leaders check their politics at the door and work out an agreement that elicits broad-based support instead of war-room-like campaigns to prevail over their opponents?

The answer is that the disagreement over what must be done to improve American health-care is profound and largely irreconcilable. This isn't your usual, run-of-the-mill political fight. The two sides hold diametrically opposed views that simply do not easily allow for compromise. Moreover, the outcome of the battle will be highly consequential, not just for our system of financing and delivering health-care, but also for our economy and democratic processes. In short, the stakes are very, very high, and both sides know it.

Many people suppose that the heart of the disagreement is over whether or not to expand coverage to more

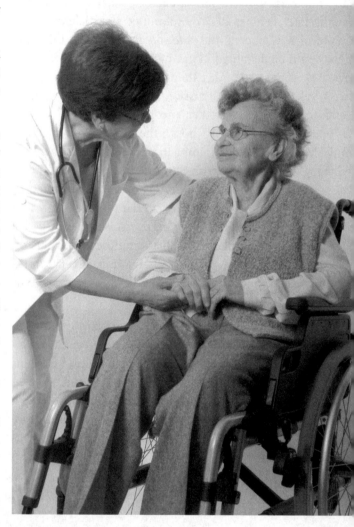

people. It is, of course, a primary objective of the Democratic sponsors of the current initiative to ensure that every American, or nearly so, is enrolled in some kind of health insurance plan on a continuous basis.

But Republicans are not opposed to expanding coverage to the uninsured. In 2008, presidential candidate John McCain proposed a plan which would have provided to every American household a tax credit which could only be used to purchase a health insurance policy. It was, in a very real sense, a "universal coverage" plan in that it sought to ensure that every American would have the financial wherewithal, provided by the federal government, to acquire some level of health insurance protection. The issue, then, is not over expanding coverage to all.

No, the real sticking point between the two sides is over how to allocate resources in the health-care sector. Both sides agree that the status quo is unsustainable, largely because costs are rising much more rapidly than wages or governmental revenues. The crucial question is what to do about the problem. Put differently, the question health-care reform advocates must answer is this: what process will be put in place to bring about continual improvement in the productivity and quality of patient care? That might strike some as more of a technical question than one of fundamental importance. But, in reality, it's just another way of saying that resources are scarce and must be allocated in some fashion. The only way to slow rising costs without lowering the quality of care provided is to improve the efficiency of the interactions between doctors and hospitals and those they care for. The question before policymakers is what reforms are most likely to lead to better care at less cost.

The Obama administration believes a governmental process is the answer. There are a series of provisions in the House and Senate bills which try to use the leverage of Medicare payment policy to force doctors and hospitals to change how they practice medicine. For instance, there are penalties for hospitals that have too many of their patients readmitted for care, and for physicians who are outliers in terms of how many services they render for certain diagnoses.

Other reforms are introduced as pilot programs that might be expanded later. In addition, the Senate bill picks up on the idea pushed by the administration to set up an independent Medicare commission which would make ongoing recommendations for cost-cutting in the program through provider-payment reforms. Congress could not reject the commission's proposals without substituting ideas that achieve similar levels of savings, but the commission couldn't make any recommendations that alter any aspect of the program other than payment policies for providers of services.

Some of these reforms might actually work and marginally improve matters from the status quo. But would they fundamentally change Medicare, much less the rest of American health care? No, they wouldn't.

The Congressional Budget Office (CBO) projects that relatively small savings will result from the Medicare commission idea, and even smaller amounts will be saved by the other reforms touted by the administration. In ten years'

time, even if all of the ideas were fully implemented, Medicare and the rest of American health-care would look and operate largely as it does today, which is to say as a fee-for-service insurance model that rewards volume and fragmentation, not integration and efficiency. Adding tens of millions of people to an unreformed system will only exacerbate rising costs, putting even more pressure on the federal budget as well as household incomes.

Proponents of a governmental process have an unbounded confidence in the ability of the federal government to centrally plan and control an extremely complex sector of the American economy. But there is nearly a half century of experience with the Medicare program indicating that this confidence is entirely misplaced.

There have been countless efforts over the years to measure quality and set payments in the Medicare program accordingly to encourage patients to see the doctors and go to the hospitals that are the most efficient and provide the best care. Most of the ideas have been tested in demonstration programs, or floated as legislative initiatives. But virtually none of them have gone anywhere.

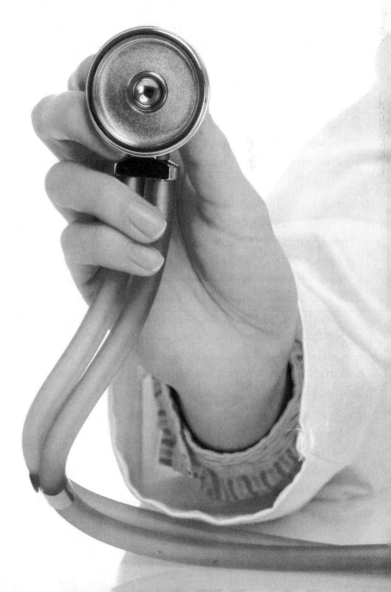

Why? The answer is simple: Politicians are incapable of building what amounts to a government-administered "preferred provider network." They simply can't pick one hospital over another, or one physician practice over another, because that implies that some physicians or hospitals in their districts are inferior. And that's just not something an elected official ever wants to do.

So, instead, they prefer to hit spending targets with across-the-board payment-rate reductions which treat all licensed providers equally. Every hospital, doctor, and other service provider gets cut the same, without regard to any measure of how well or badly they treat patients. That's been the history of the Medicare program, and, in fact, that's how the current Congress plans to achieve most of the $500 billion in Medicare savings in the health-care bills.

But these kinds of arbitrary price controls are also very dangerous for the quality of American medicine. They drive out willing suppliers of services, after which the only way to balance supply and demand is with waiting lists and rationing of care. That's why so many other countries have months-long waits for expensive care. They control costs by artificially holding down prices with government regulation. And they pay the price "off-budget" by making their citizens wait for care they would rather access much more quickly.

That's the big danger of the health-care bills being drafted in Congress. They would put the federal government in the cost-control driver's seat, and all experience indicates that will lead, in time, to arbitrary price setting and rationing.

There is an alternative to this kind of governmental process. It involves building a real marketplace, one where cost-conscious consumers choose between competing insurers and delivery systems based on price and quality. The government can and should play an important oversight role in such a reformed system. But the difficult organizational changes and innovations necessary to provide better care at lower cost would come from those delivering the services, not Congress, or the Department of Health and Human Services, or even an independent commission.

The new Medicare prescription drug benefit was constructed just this way when it was enacted in 2003. Beneficiaries get a fixed dollar entitlement that they can use to buy coverage from a number of different competing plans. The insurers understand that they have to keep costs down to attract price-sensitive enrollees. And the government has no role in setting premiums or drug prices.

And how is it working? Costs have come in 40 percent below original expectations.

Opponents of a market-based reform argue that it is impossible to reconcile price-based allocation of health services with equity. But that is not true. In the Medicare drug program, low-income seniors get additional help to pay for their prescriptions through a special funding stream. And all indications are that poor seniors are getting what they need from the program.

The country faces a choice here. We can choose to rely entirely on the federal government to allocate resources in the health-care sector, or we can choose to let consumers and suppliers make decisions in a decentralized marketplace with the government providing oversight and enforcing consumer protections. There is an irreversible aspect to this decision, whenever it is made, which perhaps explains why it has been delayed so long in our political processes. Once we finally decide, definitively, to head down one of these paths, it will be very difficult to change course later and go the other way. Which is why all concerned are bringing to the current fight in Congress every resource they can muster to prevail.

Assignment

Are you in favor of national health insurance? Why? Why not?

POPULATION EXPLOSION

One argument is the "Population Explosion Myth."

Dr. Dennis Cuddy, Ph.D., states, "Today we constantly hear about the suffering people of an overly crowded India. While there is little doubt that many people in India do suffer from a lack of food, this is not necessarily because of the number of people inhabiting that vast land. India had less people per square mile than England, West Germany, or Taiwan. . . . There is actually not a 'population problem' as such today, as all the people of the world could fit side-by-side into Greater Jacksonville, Florida. What we do have is a problem of food distribution and the availability of natural resources."

Nick Eberstadt of Harvard's Center for Population Studies found that "the world's population growth peaked at 1.9 percent around 1970 and is now down to 1.7 percent. In Western Europe the growth rate has dropped 50 percent in North America 30 percent in China 30 percent and in India 10 percent Interestingly, demographer Donald Bogue in a Population Reference Bureau paper estimated that only 4.7 percent of the decline in the world fertility rate could be attributed to family planning efforts. Currently, the U.S. fertility rate is 1.7 (a rate of 2.1 is necessary merely to maintain a population replacement level). And the decline in fertility in this country is most pronounced among blacks, American Indians, and Mexican-Americans (25 percent of native American women have been sterilized with monies earmarked by treaty agreements for medical needs, and 35 percent of all Puerto Rican women have been sterilized).

"What this dramatic decline in the fertility rate means is that in the not too distant future, there will be a disproportionate number of elderly compared to the number of youth. Because this will place a tremendous economic burden upon the nonelderly to care for our older citizens, there will be a growing advocacy for euthanasia" (Glen Stocker).

Another argument is that rapid human population growth has a variety of consequences. Population grows fastest in the world's poorest countries. High fertility rates have historically been strongly correlated with poverty, and high childhood mortality rates. Falling fertility rates are generally associated with improved standards of living, increased life expectancy, and lowered infant mortality. Overpopulation and poverty have long been associated with increased death and disease. People tightly packed into unsanitary housing are inordinately vulnerable to natural

disasters and health problems.

However, most of the world's 1.2 billion desperately poor people live in less developed countries (LDCs). Poverty exists even in MDCs. One in five Soviet citizens reportedly lives below the country's official poverty line. In the United States, 33 million people—one in eight Americans—are below the official poverty line. The rapid expansion of population size observed since the end of World War II in the world's poorest nations has been a cause of their poverty.

Poverty is a condition of chronic deprivation and need at the family level. Poverty is a major concern of humankind, because poverty everywhere reduces human beings to a low level of existence. Poor people lack access to enough land and income to meet basic needs. A lack of basic needs results in physical weakness and poor health. Poor health decreases the ability of the poor to work and put them deeper into poverty.

Instead of allowing poverty to persist, it is important to limit our number because in dense populations too many lack adequate food, water, shelter, education, and employment. High fertility, which has been traditionally associated with prosperity, prestige, and security for the future, now jeopardizes chances for many to achieve health and security.

Rich and poor countries alike are affected by population growth, though the populations of industrial countries are growing more slowly than those of developing ones. At the present growth rates, the population of economically developed countries would double in 120 years. The Third World, with over three-quarters of the world's people, would double its numbers in about 33 years. This rapid doubling time reflects the fact that 37 percent of the developing world's population is under the age of 15 and entering their most productive childbearing years. In the Third World countries (excluding China), 40 percent of the people are under 15; in some African countries, nearly half are in this age group.

The world's current and projected population growth calls for an increase in efforts to meet the needs for food, water, health care, technology, and education. In the poorest countries, massive efforts are needed to keep social and economic conditions from deteriorating further; any real advances in well-being and the quality of life are negated by further population growth. Many countries lack adequate supplies of basic materials needed to support their current population. Rapid population growth can affect both the overall quality of life and the degree of human suffering on earth (Carolyn Kinder).

Assignment

Which argument do you find most persuasive? Why?

GLOSSARY

Adams, Abigail – Wife of the first vice president (who became the second president) of the United States and had great influence on many people of the nation, being outspoken for laws to allow equal rights for women, and also strongly opposed to slavery.

Absurdism – One of seven world views, this one proposing that anarchy rules, and there is neither a god nor any reason to have one.

Age of Enlightenment – A term used to describe a time in Western philosophy centered upon the 18th century, in which rationalism was advocated as the primary legitimacy for authority.

Algonquian – A now-extinct language that was common to many native peoples from present-day New York south to Florida.

Alien and Sedition Acts – A series of acts created by Congress to dampen opposition.

Anarchist Movement – Argued that no government, even good governments, should exist because they limit human potential.

Appomattox Courthouse – The scene of the final surrender of Confederate forces in the East to Union forces.

Aristotle – He argues that the empirical world is primary.

Articles of Confederation – The government adopted by the 13 colonies during the American Revolution.

Auburn Prison – A prison founded as a model for the contemporary ideas about treating prisoners, known now as the Auburn System. This was one of the earliest attempts to reform prisoners.

Awakening – A revival period that is of significant duration and effect.

Aztec Pyramid – Built in order to worship their various deities. Human sacrifices were made to appease the gods.

Battle of New Orleans – A lopsided victory that propelled Andrew Jackson to prominence.

Bill of Rights – First ten amendments that assured certain natural rights.

Bradford, William – The first governor of Plimouth Plantation.

Caravel – A Portuguese ship, with technological advances increasing speed and dependability, making the Orient more accessible.

Chattel slavery – A form of slavery where there was no intention of release, as opposed to indentured servitude where a person was released after working for seven years.

Citizen Genet – An ambassador sent to our government by the French Republic in April 1793. Washington was not in favor of offering aid to the French (at war with England).

Clovis People Group – Identified by the distinctive Clovis point, what we call "Indian head shafts."

Colonial women – Mothers often provided the family's religious leadership in New England, bringing up the children to be good Christians and homeschooling them so they could read and study the Bible.

Colony – A body of people living in a new territory but retaining ties with the parent state.

Columbus, Christopher – The most famous European to explore North America. Born in Italy in 1451, he saw the end of the Middle Ages and beginning of the Age of Exploration.

Common Sense – Written by Thomas Paine, this tract energized the American colonies in the darkest days of 1776 and helped keep America on its road to independence.

Conwell, Russell – "Acres of Diamonds" originated as a speech that Russell Conwell delivered more than 6,000 times around the world, and first published in 1890. The central idea is that one need not look elsewhere for opportunity, achievement, or fortune—the resources to achieve all good things are present in one's own community.

Cortez, Hernando – Spanish explorer, dismantled the Aztec monarchy and gained control of all Tenochtitlan in just two years.

Culture Creators – A term that refers to the 10 percent to 15 percent of the members of a society who create most new culture—that is, write new books, produce new art, and invent new products.

Danish Vikings – A warlike people with strong families and well-developed culture were the first Europeans to settle in North America.

Davis, Jefferson – Became the president of the Confederate States of America.

Dawes Act of 1887 – Ended reservations and gave land to individual tribal members.

De Balboa, Vasco Núñez – A Spanish conquistador, he was the first European to see the eastern part of the Pacific Ocean in 1513.

Deism – One of seven world views, this one proposing that God was present, but is present no longer.

Delaware Tribe – Among the first Indians to come in contact with the Europeans.

De Leon, Ponce – Organized an expedition to find the "Fountain of Youth" in 1513. Instead, he landed in North America.

De Loyola, Ignatius – A Roman Catholic who established a great following in Spain and France, known as the Ignatius' order.

Democratic Republicans – The Democratic Republican party was also called the Republican Party. It was the party that supported a small federal government, low tariffs, and generally was prejudiced toward France.

Descartes, Rene – The founding father of modern philosophy.

Dix, Dorothea – A Boston teacher who devoted herself to a ministry to the mentally challenged throughout the United States.

Eastern State Model – A prison model that attempted to reform prisoners by keeping them isolated from other prisoners.

Electoral College – Really elects the president; the popular vote merely informs their decision.

Eliot, John – One of America's earliest missionaries.

Emancipation Proclamation – Freed all slaves in Confederate-occupied territories.

Emigration – Refers to moving from a nation permanently to another nation.

Encomienda – The encomienda was a labor system—formed of servitude slavery—Spanish officials employed during the colonization of the Americas.

Euthanasia – The word means "good death," and refers to assisting to relieve the pain and suffering of an individual by ending his or her life.

Existentialism – One of seven world views, this one proposing that truth is open to debate and everything is relative.

Federalist Papers, The – A series of position papers advocating ratification of the Constitution.

Federal Writers' Project – Over 2,000 ex-slaves' interviews were compiled and analyzed by George P. Rawick.

First Great Awakening – The first main revival in American history.

First Indian Treaty – A treaty with the Delaware people and the newly formed United States government on September 17, 1778.

Fort Sumter – In Charleston Harbor, South Carolina. It was a Union fort that the North refused to surrender to the South. Its attack precipitated the American Civil War.

French and Indian War, The – Also known as the Seven Years' War, this was a major North American conflict between Great Britain and France from 1754 to 1763.

Geronimo – An Apache who fought against resettlement; perhaps the most famous Native war chief.

Ghettoization – Describes the systematic accumulation of poor Americans in poor urban areas.

Great Depression, The – An economic calamity that had its start in the stock market crash of 1929 and lasted until 1941, where unemployment in America rose above 25 percent.

Great Society – President Johnson's legislative attempt to bring equality among races, justice to the poor.

Half-way Covenant– A way for young people to join the church without a profession of faith.

Hamilton, Alexander – Patriot and famous federalist, was central to the creation and ratification of the U. S. Constitution.

Hessians – German mercenaries hired by Great Britain to quell the American revolt.

Hudson, Henry - An English sea-captain who discovered the river now called by his name.

Hobbs, Thomas – Suggested to the world that the primary, perhaps only purpose of governments was to protect people.

Holocaust, The – Meaning "a whole burning" or "consumed by fire," this event was a systematic murder of millions of Jews and others by Nazi-controlled Germany.

Human sacrifice – The Aztecs believed it was necessary to appease the gods.

Hume, David – A Scottish philosopher who encouraged the advent of modernism, that questioned the truth of traditional values.

Immigration – The act or process of moving into another nation with the intention of living there permanently.

Incan architecture – Highly developed irrigation systems, palaces, temples, fortifications, and a vast network of roads, can still be seen throughout the Andes.

Incan sculpture – The Incans developed unique abstract traditions of sculpture.

Indentured servitude – Immigrants would gain means of passage in return for their promise to work for a term to repay their debt.

Intolerable Acts – Taxes imposed only on Boston to pay for the destroyed tea.

Iroquois Confederation – One of the most influential Native American tribes.

Islamic symbol – The star and crescent is the best-known symbol used to represent Islam.

Jamestown Settlement – The first English settlement on the mainland of North America, in 1607.

Jim Crow Laws – Laws enacted to control African-Americans.

Kierkegaard, Søren – Focused on the priority of concrete human reality over abstract thinking, highlighting the importance of personal choice and commitment.

La Salle, Robert – Sent by King Louis XIV, he was the first European to travel the Mississippi River to establish fur-trade routes.

Lewis and Clark Expedition – Surveyed the Louisiana Purchase.

Liberator, The – An anti-slavery magazine published by William Lloyd Garrison.

Locke, John – Argued there were inalienable rights that no government could give or take away.

Lockian Basic Rights – John Locke championed the notion that people have certain basic rights.

Louisiana Purchase – The largest land purchase in history. It made the U.S. a continental country.

Machu Picchu – Referred to as "the Lost City of the Incas," Machu Picchu is one of the most familiar symbols of the Inca Empire.

Madison, James – Author of the U.S. Bill of Rights, which includes the Second Amendment.

Manifest Destiny – A theory popular among antebellum Americans that argued that America's destiny was to control the entire North American continent.

Marbury v. Madison – The Supreme Court, for the first time, practiced judicial review—determining whether enacted laws were constitutional.

Maryland – The first settlement in America in which all people had entire liberty to worship God in whatever way they thought right.

Mayas – Developed as a series of largely autonomous city-states. Created an advanced writing system, the mathematical concept of zero, and discovered a 365-day solar year.

Mayflower Compact – One of the first democratic documents in the Western Hemisphere.

McCulloch v. Maryland & Gibbons v. Ogden – Both increased federal powers to tax and to claim eminent domain.

Mercantilism – A theory stating that in order for a nation to be great, it must have colonies to provide natural resources and markets for the home industries.

Metaphysics – Philosophical speculation about the nature, substance, and structure of reality.

Middle Passage – A trade route across the South Atlantic to primarily Brazil and the Caribbean, where traders would transport cargo. The fatality rate of slaves being transported on the route was extremely high.

Miller, Perry – One of the foremost 20th century Puritan historians.

Missouri Compromise – Postponed, but did not solve, the problem of slavery.

Monroe Doctrine – Stated that America would not involve itself in European affairs and that Europe should not involve itself in Western Hemisphere affairs.

Moody, D. L. – An American evangelist who founded the Northfield Schools in Massachusetts, Moody Church and Moody Bible Institute in Chicago, and the Colportage Association.

Mormonism – The first indigenous American religion. While it purports to be "the Church of Jesus Christ of the Latter Day Saints" it in no way fits into orthodox Christianity and, in fact, most Biblically literate Americans do not consider this religion to be Christian at all.

National Draft – The first national draft occurred during the Civil War.

Nationalism – A political policy that emphasized "home nation first."

National Road – Efficient transportation naturally had a positive effect on industrialization.

Nativism – An anti-immigration, anti-Catholic movement.

Naturalism – One of seven world views, this one proposing that all reality is reducible to impersonal processes and energy events.

Navigation Acts – Gave a monopoly of colonial commerce to British ships.

New Jersey Plan – Advocated strong state governments.

Nova Scotia – Means "New Scotland." The permanent colony of New France, created in 1604.

Olmec Culture – Influence behind the Maya, Aztec, and other societies. Remembered for constructing massive earthen mounds, sculpting giant basalt heads, and building large and prosperous cities that existed for hundreds of years.

Ordinance of Nullification – A political theory that argued that states had the right to "nullify" or "to ignore" certain laws.

O'Sullivan, John – Coined the phrase "Manifest Destiny."

Parris, Samuel – Pastor at Salem, Massachusetts, during the Witch Trials.

Penn, William – A Quaker, he purchased and settled what is now Pennsylvania.

Pizarro, Francisco – In 1527, he, with 175 armed men, conquered the entire Incan Empire.

Plato – He argues that the unseen world is primary.

Pocahontas – Powhatan's favorite daughter married a settler, John Rolfe, in 1614, ensuring a few peaceful years between the Powhatans and the English.

Polo, Marco – Explored China and the East Indies, bringing exotic spices and teas to Europe. He set up a trade route to China.

Proclamation of 1763 – Mandated that no further settlements would occur over the Appalachian Mountains.

Progressive Movement – A period, in America, of reform that lasted from the 1880s to the 1920s. Responding to the changes brought about by industrialization, the Progressives advocated a wide range of economic, political, social, and moral reforms.

Puritans – Wanted the Church of England to embrace Calvinism. They sought to reform the Church of England.

Queen Isabella and King Ferdinand – Supported Columbus in 1492, in search of a water-route to the lucrative East Indies, after he had been rejected by King John II.

Realism - One of seven world views, this one proposing that reality is a world with no purpose, no meaning, and no order.

Reconstruction – The adjustment period of 1865 to 1877, just after the Civil War.

Revivalism – A means by which American churches gain converts and change lives.

Romanticism (Transcendentalism) - One of seven world views, this one proposing that God was nature and "it" was good.

Rousseau, Jean-Jacques – Argued that government existed only with the consent of the governed.

Samoset and Squanto – Native Americans who helped the Pilgrims.

Second Great Awakening – A powerful revival that broke out all over America in the 1830s.

Separatism – Intentional separation from white American-dominated culture and retreat into pan–African-American nationalistic culture.

Separatist Pilgrims – Sought to separate from the Church of England.

Shays Rebellion – The post-Revolutionary clash between New England farmers and merchants that tested the precarious institutions of the new republic.

Smallpox – One of the devastating diseases that drastically diminished the Native American population.

Socrates – One of the most influential figures in Western Philosophy, who wrote nothing but profoundly influenced Plato and Aristotle.

Spoils System – A political system that used political favors to reward friends.

Tariff – Taxes placed on imported manufactured products to protect early American industries.

Temperance – A social movement against the use of alcoholic beverages.

Theism – One of seven world views, this one proposing that God is personally involved with humankind.

Tories – American citizens who were loyal to England.

Townshend Duties – A series of taxes placed on imported products.

Trail of Tears – The Indian Removal Act of 1830, signed by President Andrew Jackson, forced the removal of Cherokee natives from Georgia some 800 miles west, with about 4,000 perishing along the way.

Transcendentalism – The American version of Romanticism, an artistic movement that celebrated nature as the highest power in the universe.

Treaty of Ghent – Ended the War of 1812.

Trust – A legal entity that allows individuals to control large corporations without being employees or even owners of the corporation

Tubman, Harriet – An African-American who fled slavery and then guided runaway slaves to freedom in the North.

Utopia – A term coined by 17th-century statesmen-philosopher Sir Thomas More, who created a perfect, imaginary society called "utopia."

Vietnamization – A description of American attempts to turn the Vietnam War over to South Vietnamese leadership.

Virginia or London Company – A stock-option company set up to raise funds for new colonizing enterprises.

Virginia Plan – Advocated a strong central government.

Voltaire – Philosopher who, along with Rousseau, was the father of both the Enlightenment and the French Revolution.

Wahunsonacock – The undisputed ruler of 1600 Tidewater Virginia.

Washington, Booker T. – A former slave who became the foremost African-American educator of the late 19th and early 20th centuries.

Washington, George – Grew up in the rugged New World, and became the chosen leader of the armies of the Revolution and the first president of the United States.

Whitefield, George – Famous for saying, "I believe like a Presbyterian but I preach like a Baptist."

Williams, Roger – A Puritan who was driven from his home because of his faith.

Worldview – The way a person understands, relates to, and responds from a philosophical position that he embraces as his own.

BIBLIOGRAPHY

Alvarez, Julia. *How the Garcia Girls Lost Their Accent* (New York: Plume Books, 1992).

Ambrose, Stephen E. *Eisenhower: Soldier and President.* New York: Simon & Schuster, 1990.

Arac, Jonathan. *Postmodernism and politics.* Minneapolis: U of Minnesota P, 1986.

Axtell, James. *The Invasion from Within: The Contest of Cultures in Colonial North America.* (1986).

Bailyn, Bernard et al *The Great Republic* (3rd ed. Lexington, Mass., 1985).

Bailyn, Bernard et al. *The Origins of American Politics.* (1968).

Barolini, Helen. *Umbertina: A Novel* (New York: Feminist Press, 1999).

Bell, Thomas. *Out of this Furnace* (Pittsburgh: University of Pittsburgh Press, 1976).

Berlin, Ira. *Slaves without Masters* (New York, 1972).

Blassingame, John W. *The Slave Community: Plantation Life in the Ante-bellum South* (New York, 1972).

Boyer, Paul and Stephen Nissembaum, *Salem Possessed: The Social Origins of Witchcraft.* (1974).

Boyesen, Hjalmar Horth. *Falconberg* (New York: Charles Scribner's Sons, 1899).

Commoner, Barry. *The Closing Circle: Nature, Man, and Technology.* (New York: Knopf, 1971).

Cronon, William. *Nature's Metropolis: Chicago and the Great West.* (New York: Norton, 1991).

Curti, Merle. *The Making of An American Community* (Madison, WI., 1959).

Curtis, James C. *Andrew Jackson and the Search for Vindication.* (1976).

David, Paul. *Reckoning with Slavery* (New York, 1976).

Davidson, J.W. & M. Lytle, *After the Fact* (New York, 1982).

Degler, Carl. *Out of Our Past* (New York, 3rd ed., 1985).

Demos, John. *A Little Commonwealth: Family Life in Plymouth Colony.* (1970).

Dublin, Thomas. *Women at Work: The Transformation of Work and Community in Lowell, Massachusetts, 1826-1860.* (1979).

Farragher, John M. *Daniel Boone, The Life and Legend of an American Pioneer.* (1992).

Faragher, John Mack. *Women and Men on the Overland Trail* (New Haven, 1979).

Fischer, David Hackett. *Paul Revere's Ride.* (1994).

Fogel, Robert W. and S. Engerman. *Time on the Cross, vol. 1* (Boston, 1974).

Fogel, Robert W. *Without Consent or Contract* (New York, 1989).

Foner, Eric. *Free Soil, Free Labor, Free Men: The Ideology of the Republican Party Before the Civil War* (1970).

Foner, Eric. *Nothing But Freedom* (Baton Rouge, 1983).

Foner, Eric. *Reconstruction: America's Unfinished Revolution* (New York, 1988).

Genovese, Eugene. *Roll, Jordan, Roll: The World the Slaves Made* (New York, 1974).

Ginzberg, Lori. *Women and the Work of Benevolence* (New Haven, 1990).

Griffith, Elizabeth. *In Her Own Right* (New York, 1984).

Gutman, Herbert. *The Black Family in Slavery and Freedom* (New York, 1975).

Gutman, Herbert. *Slavery and the Numbers Game* (Urbana, Ill., 1975).

Johnson, Curtis. *Islands of Holiness* (Ithaca, N.Y., 1989).

Jones, Jacqueline. *Labor of Love, Labor of Sorrow* (New York, 1985).

Jordan, Winthrop. *The White Man's Burden: Historical Origins of Racism in the United States* (1974).

McElvaine, Robert S. *The Great Depression: America, 1929-1941.* New York: Times Books, 1993.

McPherson, James M. *Battle Cry of Freedom: The Civil War Era.* (1988).

Nash, G. et al. ,*The American People, 5th ed.*(New York, 2001).

Pessen, Edward. *Jacksonian America: Society, Personality, and Politics* (Homewood, Ill., 1969).

Pessen, Edward. *Riches, Class, and Power in America before the Civil War* (Lexington, Mass., 1973).

Potter, David M. *The Impending Crisis, 1848-1861.* (1976).

Potter, David M. *People of Plenty: Economic Abundance and the American Character.* Chicago: Chicago UP, 1954.

Preston, Richard A. et al. *Men in Arms: A History of Warfare and Its Interrelationships With Western Society.* 5th ed. Fort Worth: Harcourt Brace Javanovich College Publishers, 1991.

Remini, Robert. *Andrew Jackson and the Course of American Freedom, 1822-1832* (New York, 1981).

Reynolds, Henry. *The Other Side of the Frontier rev. ed.,* (Ringwood, Vic., 1990).

Rogin, Michael. *Fathers and Children: Andrew Jackson and the Subjugation of the American Indian* (New York, 1975).

Rothman, David. *The Discovery of the Asylum: Social Order and Disorder in the New Republic.* (1971).

Sellers, Charles. *The Market Revolution* (New York, 1992).

Stampp, Kenneth. *The Era of Reconstruction* (New York, 1965).

Susman, Warren I. *Culture as History: The Transformation of American Society in the Twentieth Century.* New York: Pantheon Books, 1973.

Taylor, George R. *The Transportation Revolution* (New York, 1951).

Thernstrom, Stephan. *Poverty and Progress: Social Mobility in a Nineteenth Century City* (Cambridge, Mass., 1964).

Ulrich, Laurel Thatcher. *A Midwife's Tale: The Life of Martha Ballard, Based on Her Diary, 1785-1812* (1982).

Watson, Steven. *The Birth of the Beat Generation: Visionaries, Rebels, and Hipsters, 1944-1960.* New York: Pantheon, 1995.

Wilde, Alan. *Horizons of assent: modernism, postmodernism, and the ironic imagination.* Baltimore: Johns Hopkins U P, 1981.

Wilentz, Sean. *Chants Democratic* (New York, 1985).

Aerial view of the World Trade Center site. Image taken by NOAA's Cessna Citation Jet on Sept. 23, 2001 from an altitude of 3,300 feet (PD-US).

APPENDIX: TIMELINE

A Timeline of Reconstruction

1865

- Thirteenth Amendment approved in January. Ratified in December. Abolished slavery in the United States.
- Congress establishes the Freeman's Bureau in March to provide assistance to the emancipated slaves.
- End of the Civil War (April 9, 1965). Lee surrenders to Grant.
- Assassination of President Lincoln, April 15. Vice President Andrew Johnson becomes president.
- President Johnson presents plans for Reconstruction.
- Benjamin Butler, a notorious Union general in the Civil War and advocate of rights for African-Americans, elected to Congress as a radical member of the Republican party.
- Mississippi enacts the Black Code (laws promulgated to control African-Americans).
- Joint Committee of Fifteen on Reconstruction created.
- Ku Klux Klan was created in Tennessee.

1866

- Thirteenth Amendment approved in January. Ratified in December. Abolished slavery in the United States.
- Civil Rights Act passed despite Johnson's earlier veto.
- The 14th Amendment approved by Congress, guaranteeing equal citizenship for all Americans.
- Memphis race riot/Massacre (May 1).
- Freedom Bureau's responsibilities and powers expanded by Congress. Legislation is vetoed by Johnson but Congress overrides his veto.

1867

- First Reconstruction Act passed over Johnson's veto.
- Second Reconstruction Act passed over Johnson's veto.
- Third Reconstruction Act passed over Johnson's veto.
- Republican convention in New Orleans. Party platform includes equality for African-Americans.

1868

- Former slave Oscar J. Dunn elected lieutenant governor of Louisiana.
- Fourth Reconstruction Act passed.
- Thaddeus Stevens, radical republican and supporter of land for Freedmen, dies.
- John W. Menard of Louisiana elected to the United States Congress.
- Menard is barred from his seat by white members of Congress. When Menard pleaded his case to be seated, he became the first black representative to speak on the floor of the House.
- James J. Harris and P. B. S. Pinchback are the first African-American delegates to a Republican convention. They support the nomination of Ulysses S. Grant for president.

1869

- Former Union General U. S. Grant becomes president. Although allied with the Radical Republicans in Congress he does not provide strong leadership for Reconstruction.

1870

- Hiram Revels elected to U.S. Senate as the first black senator.
- Jasper J. Wright elected to South Carolina supreme court.
- Fifteenth Amendment ratified. The 15th Amendment to the U.S. Constitution gave the vote to all male citizens regardless of color or previous condition of servitude.
- Joseph H. Rainey, first black member sworn in as member of U.S. House of Representatives, December 12, 1870.
- Forty-first Congress. Two black members in the House of Representatives, including Robert Brown Elliot from the 3rd District in South Carolina.

1871

- Forty-second Congress. Five black members in the House of Representatives: Benjamin S. Turner of Alabama; Josiah T. Walls of Florida; and Robert Brown Elliot, Joseph H. Rainey, and Robert Carlos DeLarge of South Carolina.
- Act to Enforce 14th Amendment (Ku Klux Klan Act).

1872

- Freedman's Bureau abolished.

1873/1874

- P. B. S. Pinchback, acting governor of Louisiana from December 9, 1872, to January 13, 1873. Pinchback, a black politician, was the first black to serve as a state governor, although due to white resistance, his tenure is extremely short.

- Blanche K. Bruce elected to U.S. Senate.
- Robert Smalls, black hero of the Civil War, elected to Congress as representative of South Carolina.
- Forty-third Congress. Six black members in the House of Representatives.
- Forty-fourth Congress. Six black members in the House of Representatives.

1875

- Civil Rights Act enacted by Congress. It provides blacks with the right to equal treatment in public places and transportation. The Supreme Court later declared this Act unconstitutional.
- Blanche Kelso elected as senator of Mississippi. He is the first African-American senator to serve a complete six-year term.

1876

- U.S. Senate votes not to seat P. B. S. Pinchback.
- Wade Hamilton inaugurated as governor of South Carolina. The election of Hampton, a leader in the Confederacy, confirms fears that the South is not committed to Reconstruction.

1877

- Rutherford B. Hayes inaugurated president of the United States.
- Forty-fifth Congress. Four black members in House.
- Last federal troops leave South Carolina, effectively ending the federal government's presence in the South.
- Essentially, Reconstruction ends.

Important Dates and Events of World War II:

1941

- Dec. 7 - Japanese attack naval base at Pearl Harbor.
- Dec. 8 - Roosevelt gives "Day of Infamy" speech; United States and Britain declare war on Japan.
- Dec. 11 - Germany declares war on the United States.

- Dec. 16 - Rommel's Afrika Korps forced to retreat in North Africa.
- Dec. 19 - Hitler assumes post of commander-in-chief of German Army.

1942

- Jan. 1 - Mass gassing of Jews begins at Auschwitz, and Allies forge Declaration of the United Nations.
- Jan. 13 - German U-boats begin sinking ships off American coast in Operation Drumbeat.
- Jan. 20 - Nazis coordinate "Final Solution" efforts at Wannsee Conference.
- Jan. 21 - Rommel counterattacks in North Africa.
- May 8 - Germans launch summer offensive in the Crimea.
- May 30 - Royal Air Force launches first 1,000 bomber raid on Cologne, Germany.
- June 4 - Japanese navy resoundingly defeated at Battle of Midway.
- June 5 - German siege of Sevastopol begins.
- June 10 - Nazis annihilate Czech town of Lidice in retaliation for Heydrich's assassination.
- June 21 - German Afrika Korps recaptures Tobruk.
- July 3 - Sevastopol falls to German Army.
- July 5 - Nazi conquest of Crimea achieved.
- July 9 - German Army begins push towards Stalingrad.
- Aug. 7 - General Bernard Montgomery assumes command of British Eighth Army in North Africa.
- Sept. 13 - German attack on Stalingrad begins.
- Oct. 23–Nov. 3 - Afrika Korps decisively defeated by British at El Alamein.
- Nov. 8 - Allied invasion of North Africa begins in Operation Torch.
- Nov. 11 - Axis forces occupy Vichy, France.
- Nov. 19 - Soviet forces encircle German Sixth Army at Stalingrad.

- Dec. 31 - German and British ships engage in the Battle of the Barents Sea.

1943

- Jan. 2–3 - German Army retreats from Caucasus.
- Jan. 10 - Red Army begins siege of German-occupied Stalingrad.
- Jan. 14-23 - Roosevelt and Churchill meet at Casablanca, issue unconditional surrender demand.
- Jan. 23 - British forces take Tripoli.
- Jan. 27 - U.S. Air Force opens daylight bombing campaign with attack on Wilhelmshaven, Germany.
- Feb. 2 - German Sixth Army at Stalingrad surrenders to the Russians; war in Europe reaches its turning point.
- Feb. 8 - Red Army takes Kursk.
- Feb. 14-25 - Battle of Kasserine Pass fought in North Africa between German and U.S. forces.
- Feb. 16 - Red Army retakes Kharkov.
- Mar. 2 - Afrika Korps withdraws from Tunisia.
- Mar. 15 - German Army recaptures Kharkov.
- Mar. 16–20 - German submarines achieve their largest tonnage total of the war.
- Apr. 19 - S.S. begins "liquidation" of the Warsaw ghetto.
- May 7 - Allies capture Tunisia.
- May 13 - Remaining Axis troops in North Africa surrender to Allies.
- May 16-17 - RAF targets German industry in the Ruhr.
- May 22 - U-boat operations suspended in the North Atlantic due to steep losses.
- June 11 - Nazis order destruction of Polish ghettos.
- July 5 - Largest tank battle in history begins at Kursk.
- July 9–10 - Allied forces land at Sicily.
- July 22 - American forces take Palermo, Sicily.
- July 25-26 - Mussolini and the Fascists overthrown.

- July 27-28 - Allied bombing raid creates firestorm in Hamburg, Germany.
- Aug. 12-17 - Axis forces withdraw from Sicily.
- Aug. 17 - USAF suffers steep losses in bombing run on ball-bearing plants at Regensburg and Schweinfurt, Germany.
- Aug. 23 - Red Army retakes Karkhov.
- Sept. 8 - New Italian government announces Italy's surrender.
- Sept. 9 - Allied forces land in Salerno and Taranto.
- Sept. 11 - German Army occupies Italy.
- Sept. 12 - Nazi commandos rescue Mussolini.
- Sept. 23 - Fascist government re-established in Italy.
- Oct. 1 - Allies take Naples.
- Nov. 6 - Red Army recaptures Kiev.
- Nov. 28 - "Big Three" (Roosevelt, Stalin, and Churchill) meet at Tehran.
- Dec. 24-26 - Soviets begin large offensive in Ukraine.

1944

- Jan. 6 - Red Army advances into Poland.
- Jan. 22 - Allied forces land at Anzio, Italy.
- Jan. 27 - Red Army breaks 900-day siege of Leningrad.
- Jan. 31 - American forces invade Kwajalein.
- Feb. 16 - German 14th Army counterattacks at Anzio.
- Feb. 18-22 - American forces take Eniwetok.
- Apr. 8 - Red Army begins offensive in the Crimea.
- May 9 - Soviet troops recapture Sevastopol.
- May 12 - German forces in the Crimea surrender.
- June 5 - Allied forces enter Rome.
- June 6 - D-Day: invasion of Europe begins with Allied landings at Normandy.
- June 9 - Red Army advances into Finland.

- June 13 - Germans begin launching V-1 rockets against London.
- June 15 - American marines invade Saipan.
- June 19–20 - "Marianas Turkey Shoot" results in destruction of 200+ Japanese aircraft.
- June 22 - Red Army begins massive summer offensive.
- June 27 - American forces liberate Cherbourg.
- July 3 - Soviet forces recapture Minsk.
- July 9 - Allied troops liberate Caen.
- July 18 - American troops liberate St Lô.
- July 20 - Hitler survives assassination attempt.
- July 24 - Soviet forces liberate concentration camp at Majdanek.
- July 25–30 - Allied forces breakout of Normandy encirclement in Operation Cobra.
- July 28 - Red Army recaptures Brest-Litovsk.
- Aug. 1 - Polish Home Army begins revolt against Nazis in Warsaw.
- Aug. 15 - Allies invade Southern France.
- Aug. 19-20 - Soviet forces invade Romania.
- Aug. 23 - Romania capitulates to Soviets.
- Aug. 25 - Paris liberated.
- Aug. 31 - Red Army takes Bucharest.
- Sept. 3 - Brussels liberated.
- Sept. 4 - Antwerp liberated.
- Sept. 8 - Soviets and Finns sign peace treaty.
- Sept. 13 American troops reach the Siegfried Line in western Germany
- Sept. 26 - Red Army occupies Estonia.
- Oct. 2 - Nazis brutally crush revolt in Warsaw; Allies advance into Germany.
- Oct. 5 - British invade Greece.
- Oct. 14 - British liberate Athens.
- Oct. 14 - Rommel forced to commit suicide for alleged involvement in July assassination plot against Hitler.
- Oct. 20 - Belgrade, Yugoslavia, falls to Soviet forces.

- Oct. 23–26 - U.S. naval forces destroy remnants of Japanese Navy at the Battle of Leyte Gulf, the largest naval engagement in history.
- Dec. 3 - Civil war erupts in Greece; Japanese retreat in Burma.
- Dec. 15 - American forces invade Philippine island of Mindoro.
- Dec. 16 - German Army launches "Battle of the Bulge" offensive on the Western Front.
- Dec. 17 - Waffen SS executes 81 American prisoners of war in "Malmedy Massacre".

1945

- Jan. 9 - American forces invade Philippine island of Luzon.
- Jan. 16 - Battle of the Bulge ends in German defeat.
- Jan. 17 - Red Army liberates Warsaw.
- Jan. 19 - German lines on Eastern Front collapse; full retreat begins.
- Jan. 20 - Hungary signs armistice with Allies.
- Jan. 26 - Soviets liberate Auschwitz.
- Jan. 27 - Red Army occupies Lithuania.
- Feb. 4-11 - Roosevelt, Churchill and Stalin meet at Yalta Conference.
- Feb. 13-14 - Allied incendiary raid creates firestorm in Dresden.
- Feb. 19 - American forces land on Iwo Jima.
- Mar. 7 - Allies capture Cologne; Ludendorff; Rail Bridge on Rhine River captured intact at Remagen.
- Mar. 9 - Tokyo firebombed.
- Mar. 16 - Japanese resistance on Iwo Jima ends.
- Mar. 21 - Allies take Mandalay, Burma.
- Mar. 30 - Red Army liberates Danzig.
- Apr. 1 - American troops encircle German forces in the Ruhr.
- Apr. 12 - Franklin Delano Roosevelt dies of stroke; Harry Truman becomes president.
- Apr. 12 - Allies liberate Belsen and Buchenwald concentration camps.
- Apr. 16 - Red Army launches Berlin offensive; Allies take Nuremberg.

- Apr. 18 - German forces in the Ruhr capitulate.
- Apr. 28 - Mussolini hanged by Italian partisans; Venice falls to Allied forces.
- Apr. 29 - Dachau concentration camp liberated.
- Apr. 30 - Adolf Hitler and wife Eva Braun commit suicide in Chancellery bunker.
- May 2 - All German forces in Italy surrender.
- May 7 - Unconditional surrender of all German forces
- May 8 - Victory in Europe (VE) Day
- May 23 - SS Reichführer Heinrich Himmler commits suicide.
- June 5 - Allies divide Germany into occupation zones.
- June 26 - United Nations World Charter signed in San Francisco
- July 16 - First U.S. atomic bomb tested at Los Alamos, New Mexico; Potsdam Conference begins.
- July 26 - Clement Attlee becomes British Prime Minister.
- Aug. 6 - First atomic bomb dropped Hiroshima
- Aug. 8 - Soviet Union declares war on Japan; Soviet forces invade Manchuria.
- Aug. 9 - Second atomic bomb dropped on Nagasaki
- Aug. 14 - Unconditional surrender of Japanese forces
- Aug. 15 - Victory over Japan (VJ) Day
- Sept. 2 - Japanese delegation signs instrument of surrender aboard battleship Missouri in Tokyo Bay.
- Nov. 20 - Nuremberg War Crimes Tribunal begins.

1946

- Jan. 7 - United Nations meets for first time in London.
- Oct. 16 - Hermann Göring commits suicide; 11 other war criminals hanged.

Important Dates and Events in Black History:

1954

- *Brown v. Board of Education*: U.S. Supreme Court bans segregation in public schools.

1955

- Bus boycott launched in Montgomery, Ala., after an African-American woman, Rosa Parks, is arrested December 1 for refusing to give up her seat to a white person.

1956

- December 21. After more than a year of boycotting the buses and a legal fight, the Montgomery buses desegregate.

1957

- At previously all-white Central High in Little Rock, Ark., 1,000 paratroops are called by President Eisenhower to restore order and escort nine black students.

1960

- The sit-in protest movement begins in February at a Woolworth's lunch counter in Greensboro, N.C., and spreads across the nation.

1961

- Freedom rides begin from Washington, D.C.: Groups of black and white people ride buses through the South to challenge segregation.
- King makes his only visit to Seattle. He visits numerous places, including two morning assemblies at Garfield High School.

1962

- Two killed, many injured in riots as James Meredith is enrolled as the first black at the University of Mississippi.

1963

- Police arrest King and other ministers demonstrating in Birmingham, Ala., then turn fire hoses and police dogs on the marchers.
- Medgar Evers, NAACP leader, is murdered June 12 as he enters his home in Jackson, Miss.
- 250,000 people attend the March on Washington, D.C., urging support for pending civil-rights legislation. The event is highlighted by King's "I have a dream" speech.
- Four girls are killed Sept. 15 in bombing of the Sixteenth Street Baptist Church in Birmingham, Ala.

1964

- Three civil-rights workers are murdered in Mississippi.
- July 2 - President Johnson signs the Civil Rights Act of 1964.

1965

- Malcolm X is murdered Feb. 21, 1965. Three men are convicted of his murder
- August 6 - President Johnson signs the Voting Rights Act of 1965.
- August 11-16 - Watts riots leave 34 dead in Los Angeles.

1978

- U.S. Supreme Court outlaws racial quotas in a suit brought by Allan Bakke, a white man who had been turned down by the medical school at University of California, Davis.

1989

- Douglas Wilder of Virginia becomes the nation's first African-American to be elected state governor.

1992

- The first racially based riots in years erupt in Los Angeles and other cities after a jury acquits L.A. police officers in the videotaped beating of Rodney King, an African-American.

2008

- President Barack Obama is elected president of the United States.

Your High School History Curriculum

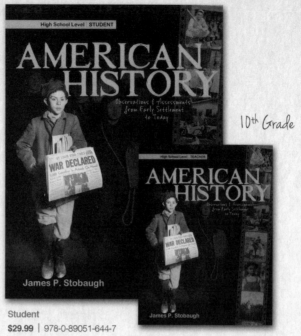

10th Grade

Student
$29.99 | 978-0-89051-644-7

Teacher
$14.99 | 978-0-89051-643-0

11th Grade

Student
$24.99 | 978-0-89051-646-1

Teacher
$14.99 | 978-0-89051-645-4

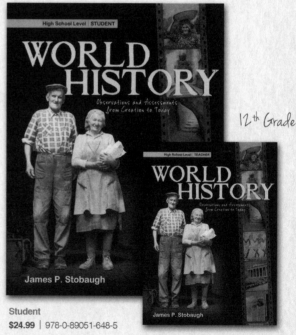

12th Grade

Student
$24.99 | 978-0-89051-648-5

Teacher
$14.99 | 978-0-89051-647-8

Available where fine books are sold or nlpg.com

follow the Author:

 facebook.com/**JPStobaugh**   **@JamesPStobaugh**   forsuchatimeasthis.com